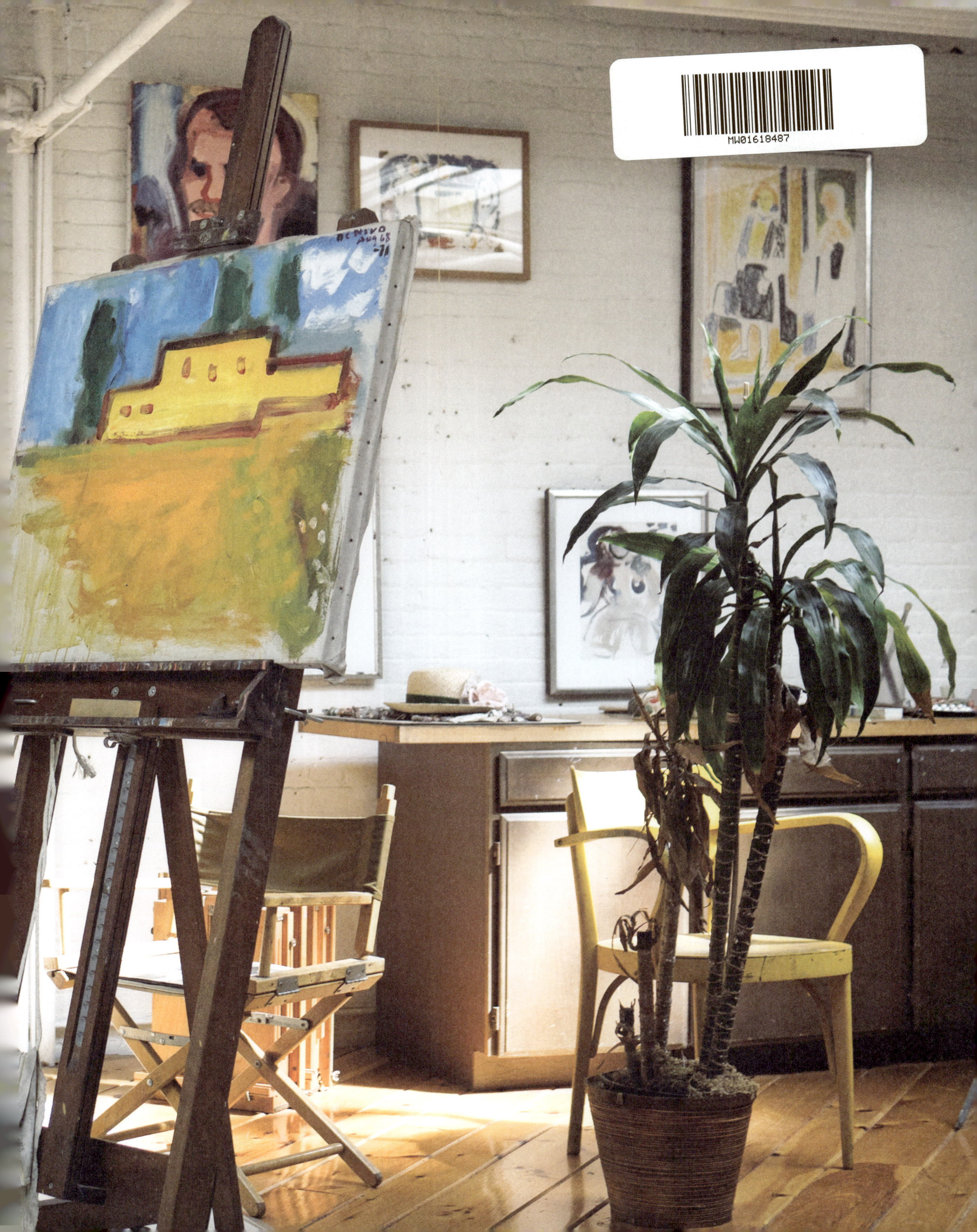

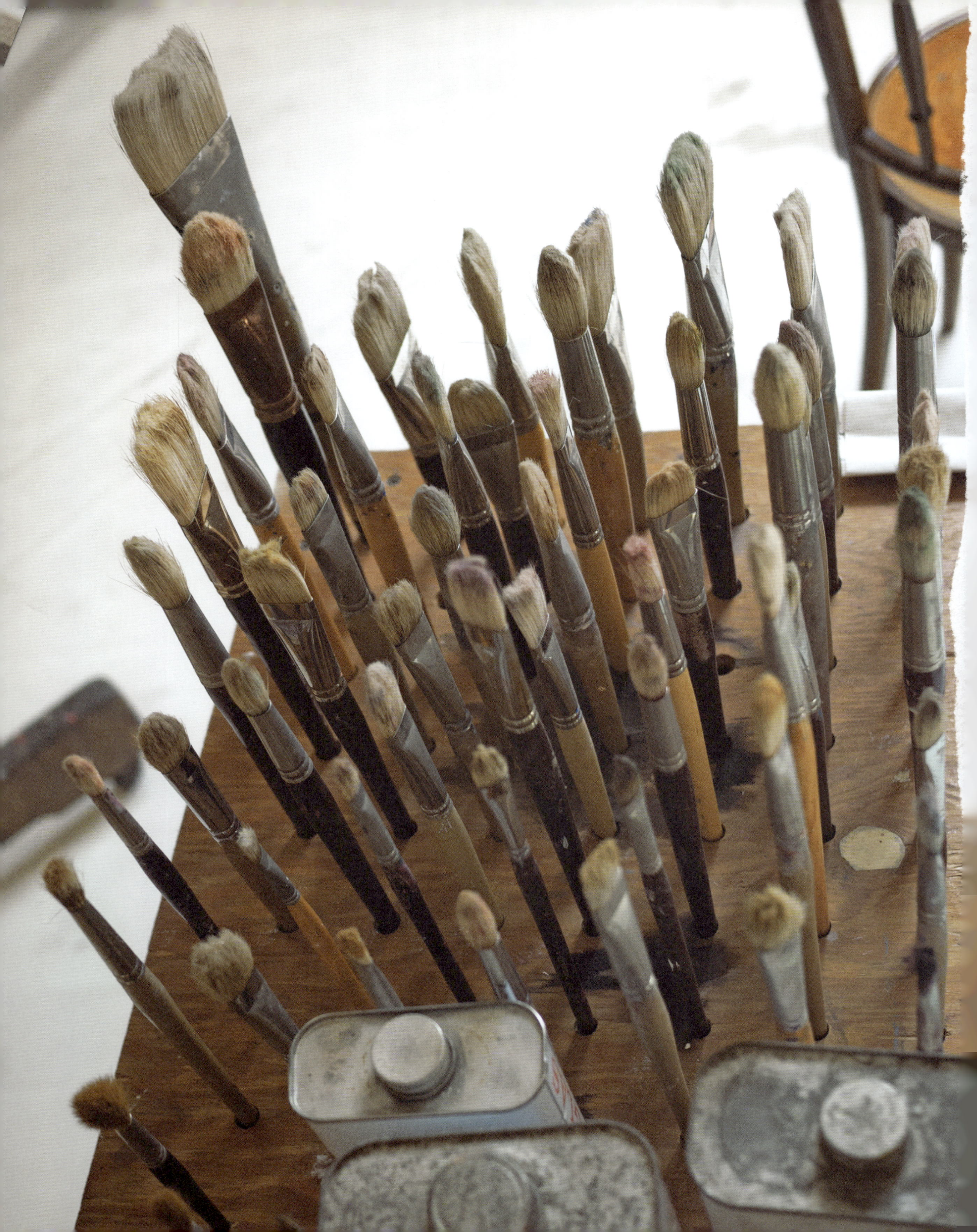

ROBERT DE NIRO, SR.

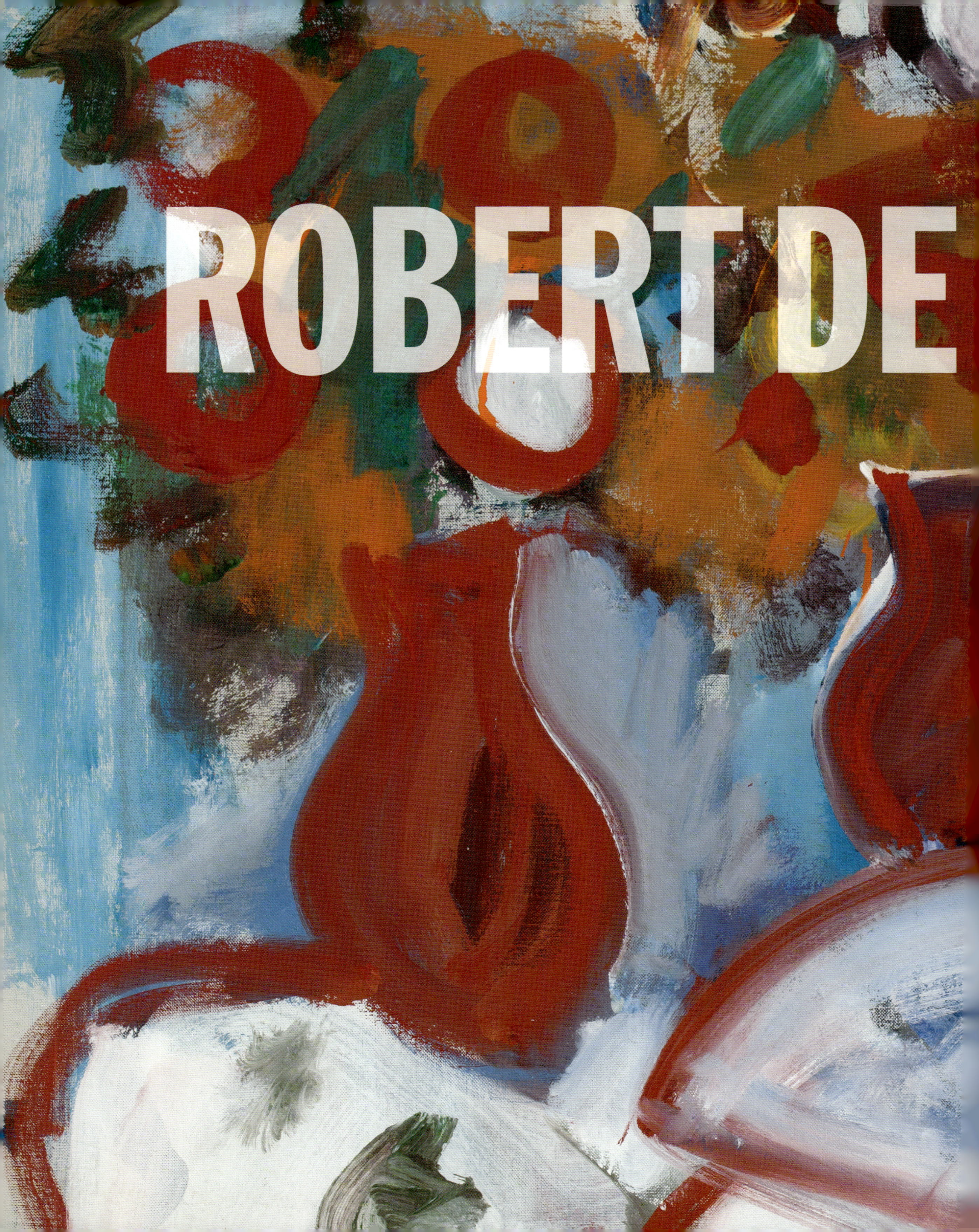
ROBERT DE

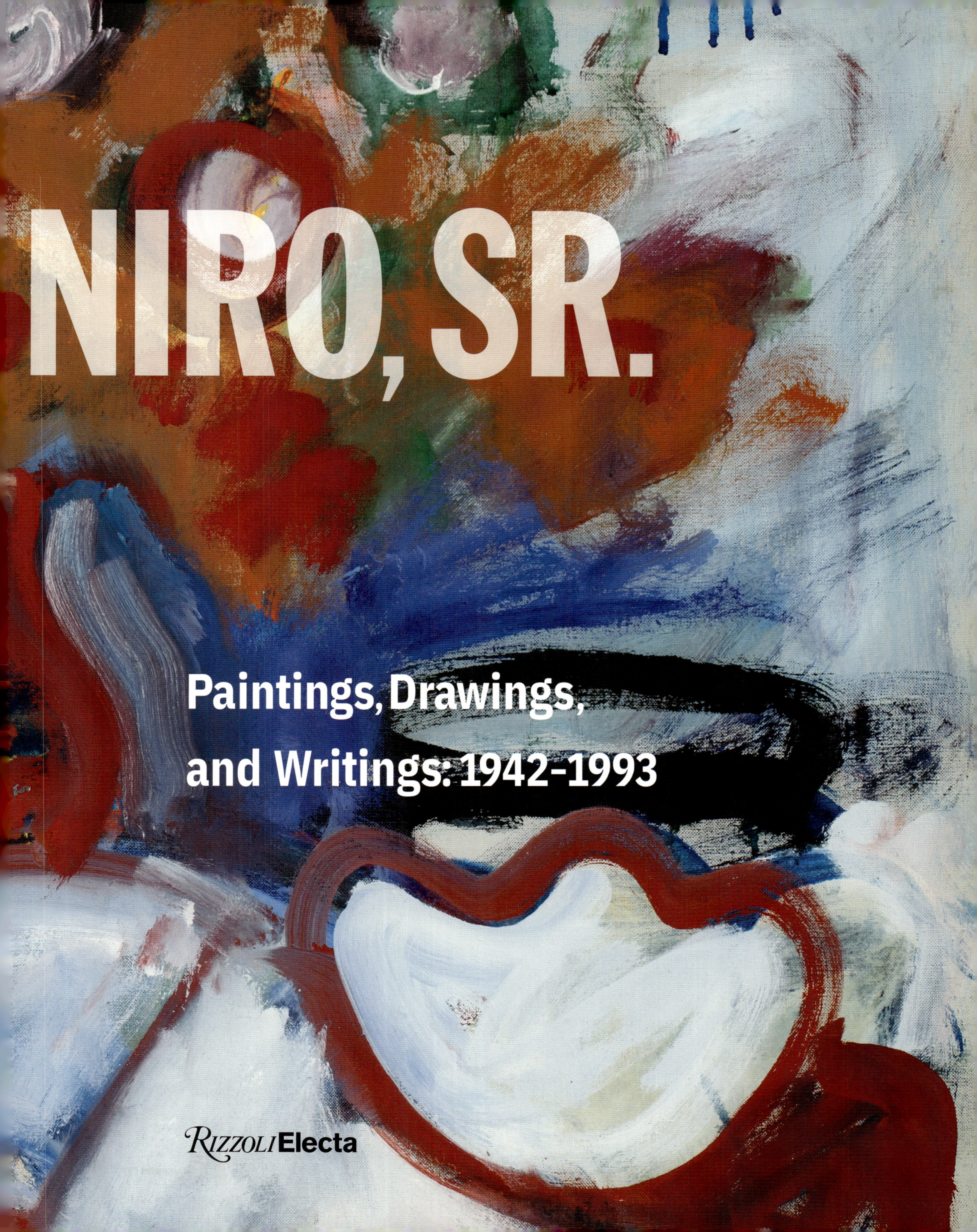

NIRO, SR.

Paintings, Drawings, and Writings: 1942–1993

Rizzoli Electa

First published in the United States of America in 2019 by
Rizzoli Electa
A Division of Rizzoli International Publications, Inc.
300 Park Avenue South
New York, New York 10010
www.rizzoliusa.com

Introduction: Robert De Niro
Texts: Susan Davidson, Robert Kushner,
Robert Storr, and Charles Stuckey

For SNAP Editions, New York
Editor: Sarah S. King
Associate Editors: Annikka Olsen and Nathan Jones
Design: Joseph Guglietti

For Rizzoli Electa
Publisher: Charles Miers
Associate Publisher: Margaret Chace
Editor: Ellen R. Cohen
Managing Editor: Lynn Scrabis
Production Manager: Colin Hough-Trapp

Printed in China

2019 2020 2021 2022 2023 / 10 9 8 7 6 5 4 3 2 1

ISBN: 978-0-8478-6288-7
Library of Congress Control Number: 2019905876

Visit us online:
Facebook.com/RizzoliNewYork
Twitter: @Rizzoli_Books
Instagram.com/RizzoliBooks
Pinterest.com/RizzoliBooks
Youtube.com/user/RizzoliNY
Issuu.com/Rizzoli

Endpaper: Robert De Niro, Sr.'s New York studio.
Photos by Brigitte Lacombe.

Preceding pages: *Table Still Life with Red Vases, Fan and Bowl*, 1968 (detail). Oil on canvas, 30 x 34 inches. Plate 75.

Overleaf: Robert De Niro, Sr., in his studio, ca. 1958.
Photo by Rudy Burckhardt.

Pages 10–11: *Moroccan Women*, 1979 (detail). Oil on linen, 64 x 53 inches. Plate 102.

CONTENTS

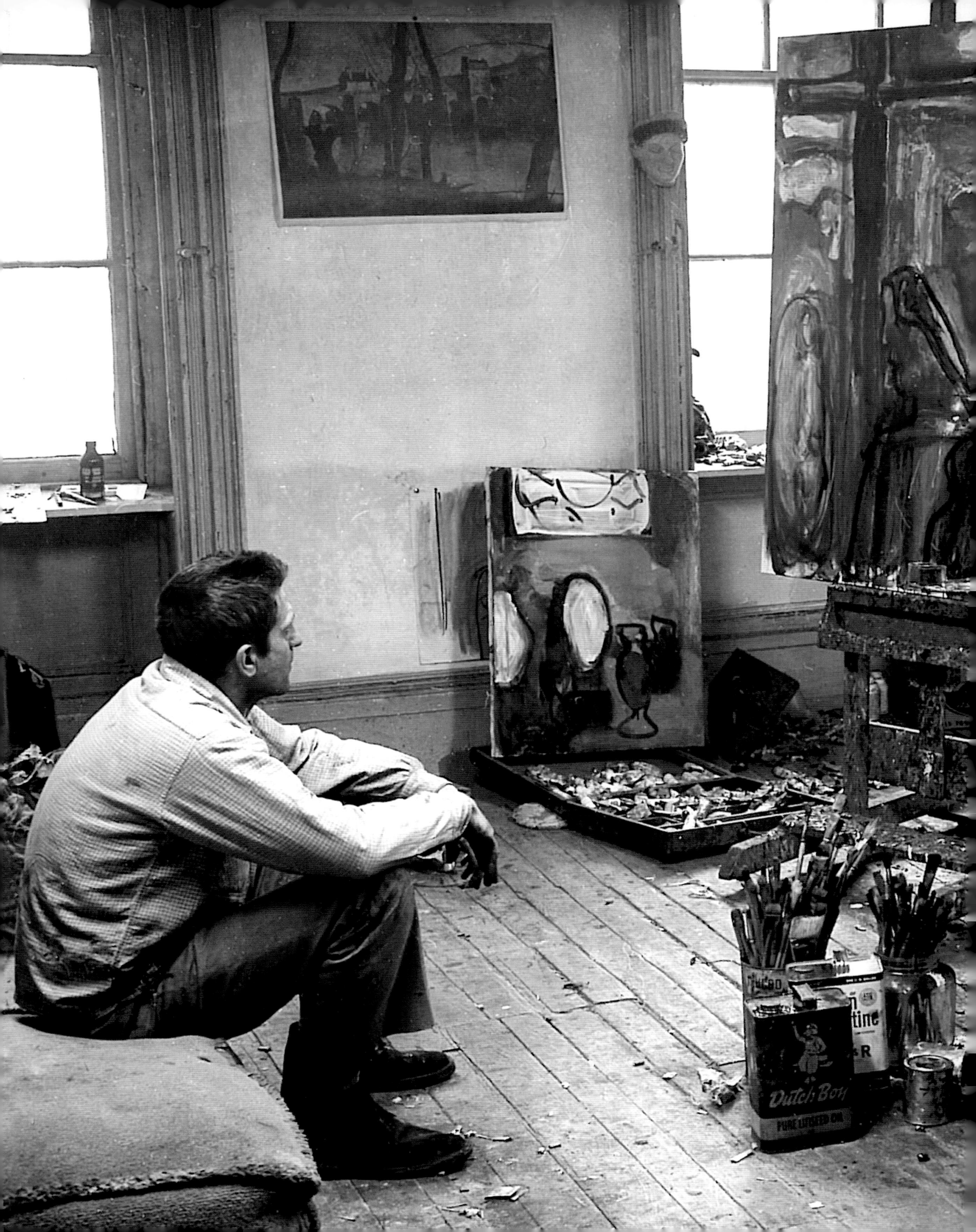
Dutch Boy

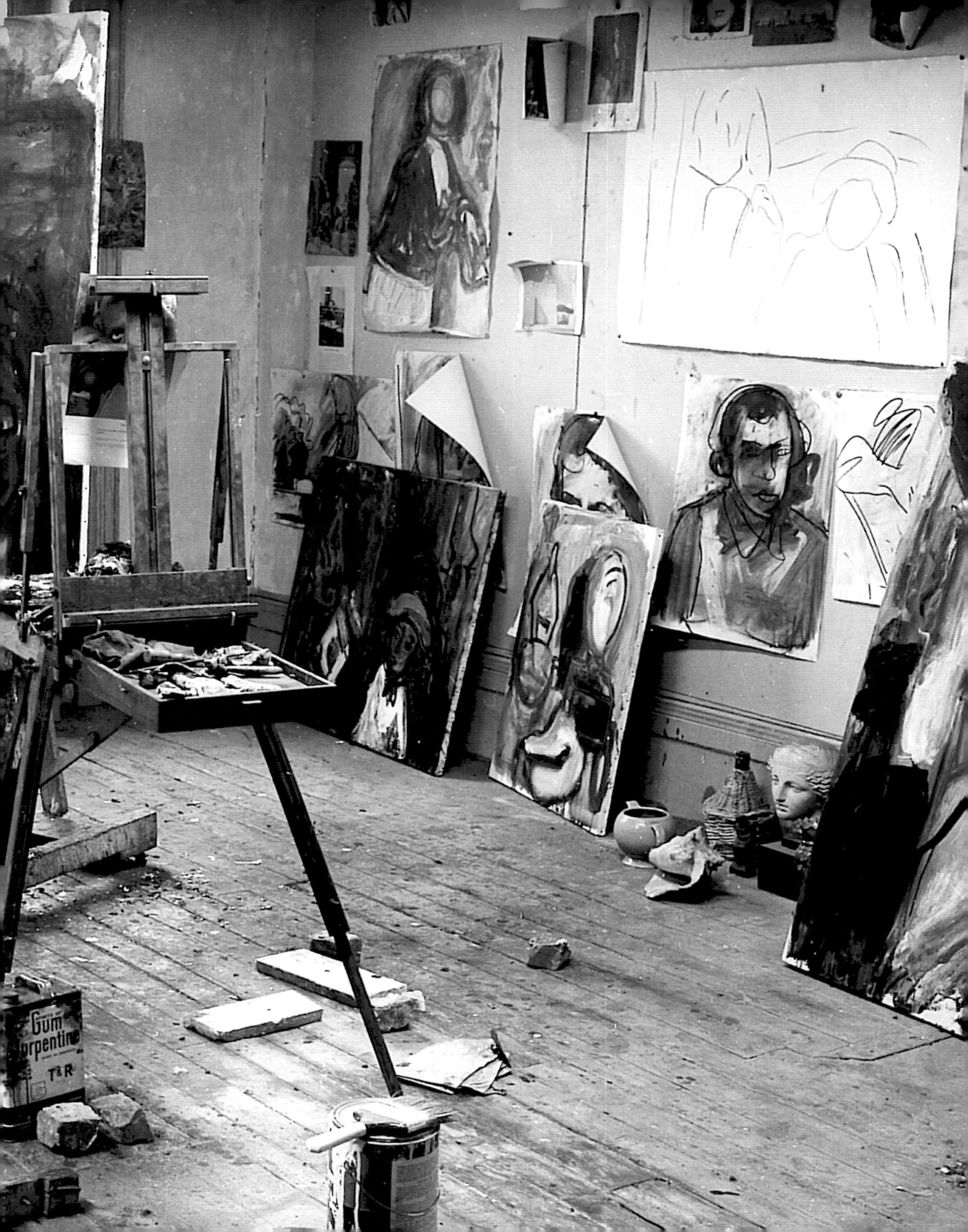
Gum
T&R

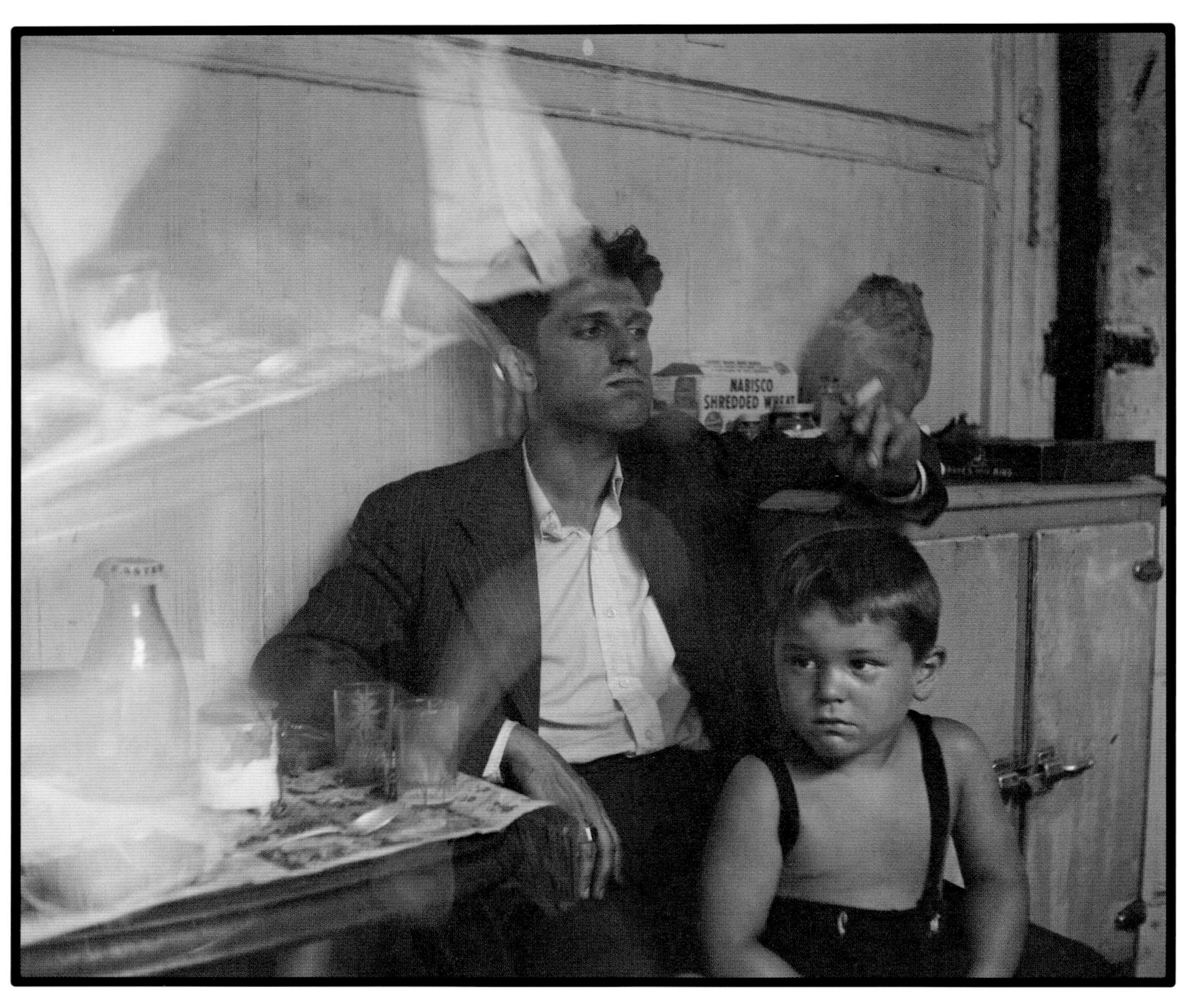

Robert De Niro with his father, Robert De Niro, Sr., ca. 1945

INTRODUCTION

Robert De Niro

IT HAS BEEN IMPORTANT TO ME to preserve my father's artistic legacy, to tell the story of his life and his art, and to make sure that they are known and understood by my family, my children and grandchildren. I have kept his studio as it was during his lifetime, so that they will have a sense of what this man—their grandfather, their great-grandfather—did there, and, ultimately, of who he was. What he accomplished in his art was uniquely his and will carry on, as far as I'm concerned, forever. I remember as a kid being in his studio and listening to him talk about dealers and artists, and the great works of art and literature he loved, and I understood, even at that young age, that my father was passionate about what he did.

In the years since his death, I have worked to find ways for his work to be seen—not only by his family and friends, but also by a wider, cross-generational audience—in exhibitions at museums; at his gallery, DC Moore; and at such other public venues as the Tribeca Grill and Greenwich Hotel in New York. Art is made to be seen and experienced. Throughout his life, my father believed that his work would outlast him, and that it would continue to find new and appreciative viewers in the years to come. This book is my way of helping make that happen.

I am not an art historian or a documentarian, and I know that I alone cannot be the curator of my father's legacy. I documented his life in the HBO film *Remembering the Artist: Robert De Niro, Sr.*, which memorializes his life and work in the way I know best. With this volume, I turn to art historians and curators Robert Storr, Charles Stuckey, and Susan Davidson, and the artist Robert Kushner to view my father's work through the lens of their expertise. Their essays each look at him from a different angle, and my hope is that they will help us to better understand Robert De Niro, Sr., the way I knew, felt, saw, and experienced him—as a committed and gifted artist.

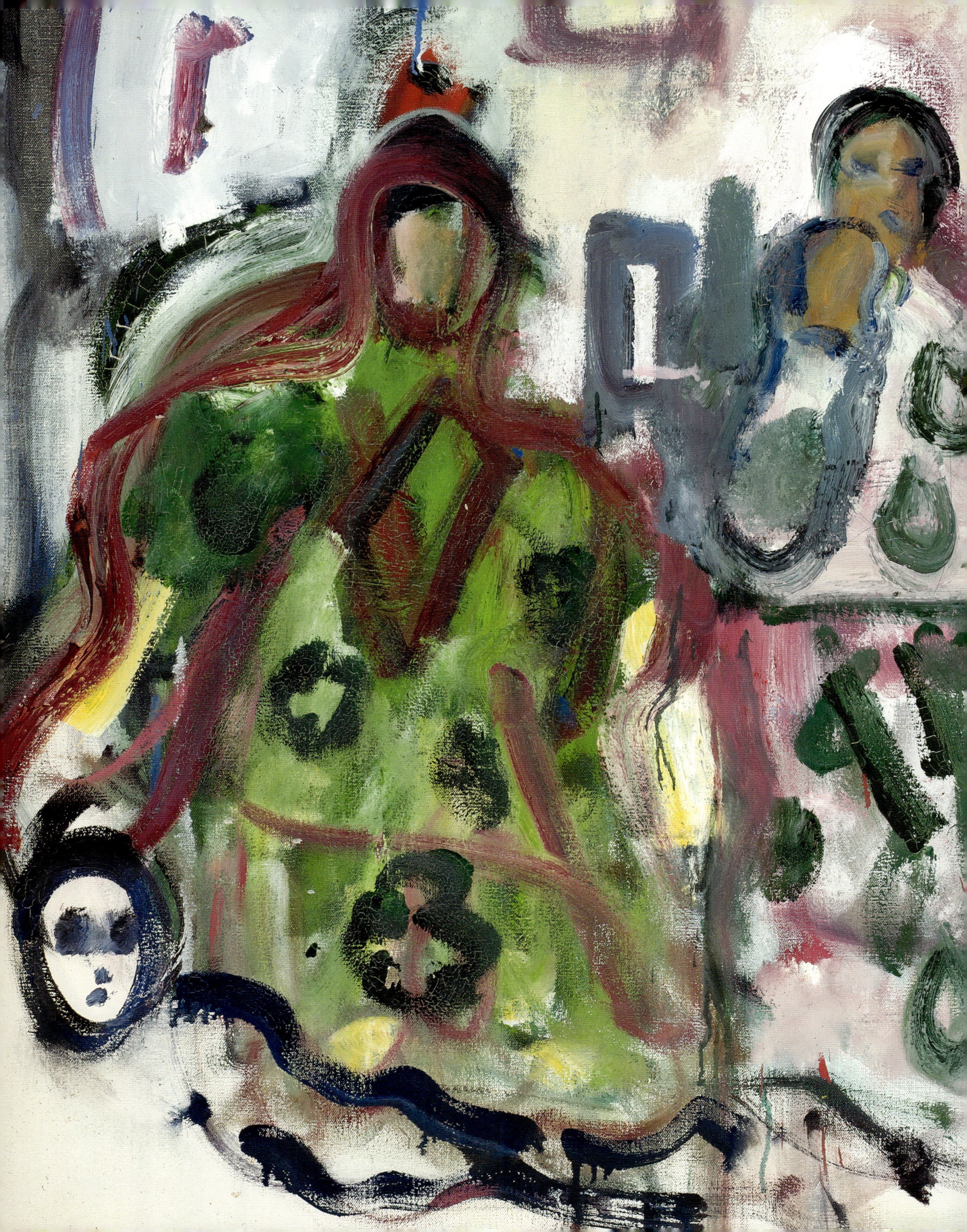

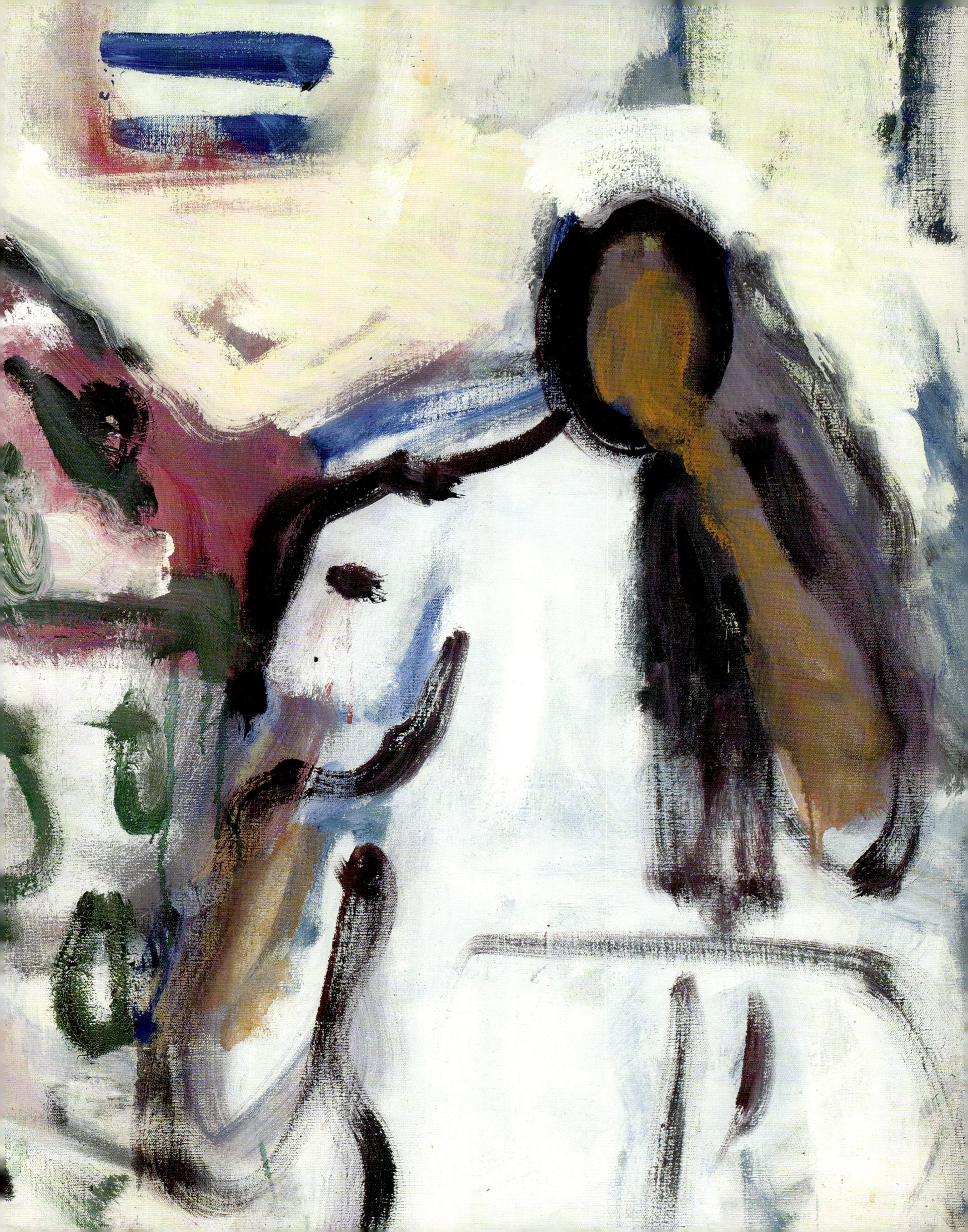

Robert Storr

LATE LAURELS FOR A PAINTER'S PAINTER

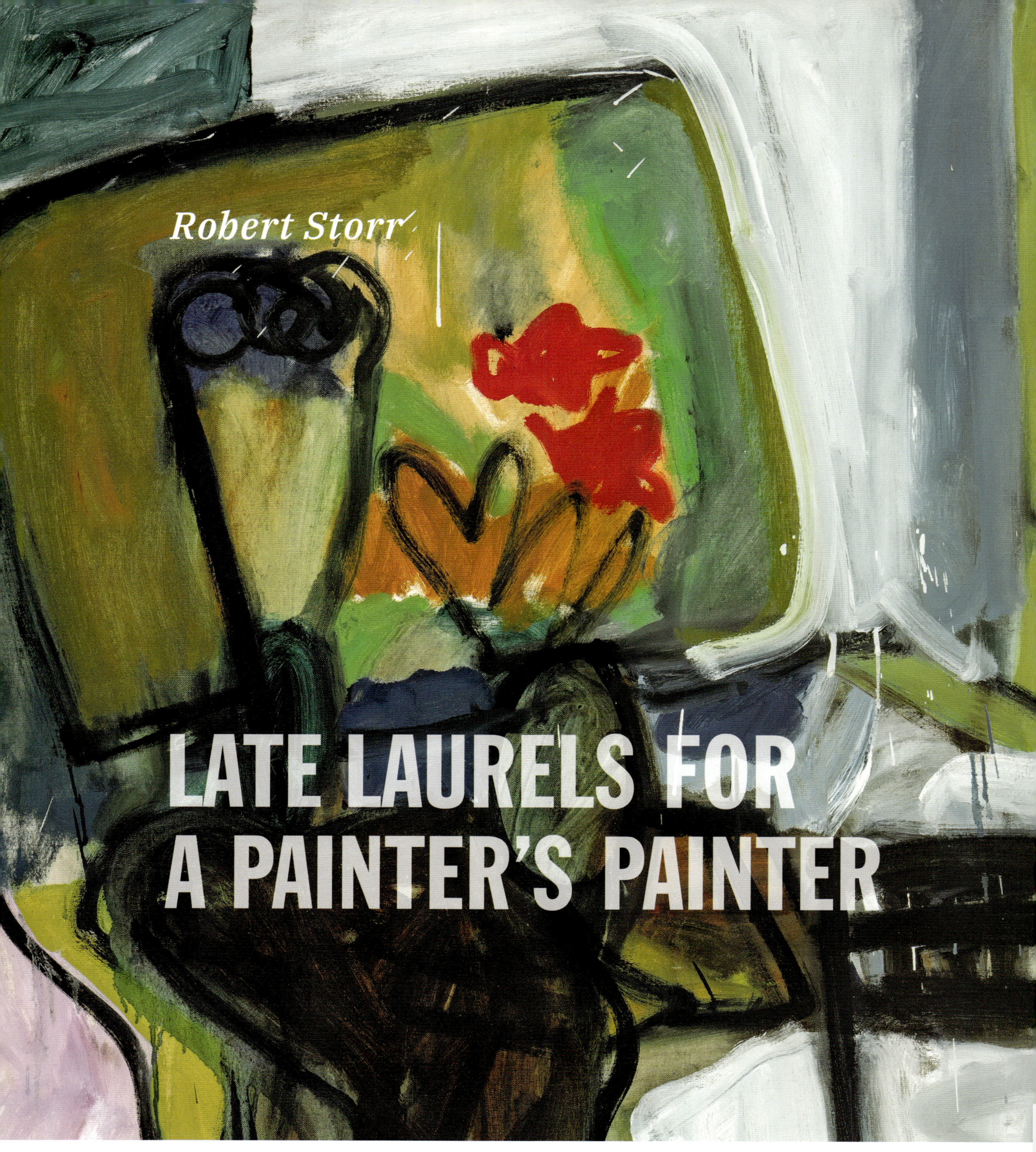

Still Life and Chair, 1959 (detail). Oil on canvas, 50 x 42 inches. Plate 39

I THINK CONTINUALLY of those who were truly great.

Who, from the womb, remembered the soul's history

Through corridors of light, where the hours are suns...[1]

WRITTEN IN 1933, these lines by Stephen Spender eloquently bespeak the sensibility of his generation—that of writers and artists who came of age between the two world wars. And, in so doing, they point toward Spender's own poetic predicament. As a man wholeheartedly and outspokenly devoted to the greatness of the great, he seems to have sublimated what literary critic Harold Bloom would later call "the anxiety of influence," in the process sparing himself the all-too-human emotions of envy, bitterness, and self-reproach by transforming that anxiety into a sonorous homage to his historical precursors. Indeed, Spender even appears to have sidestepped rivalry with immediate contemporaries and friends in whose company he morphed into one of his era's emblematic British versifiers and cultural bellwethers. Not least among that group was the looming, heavily wrinkled, ever-rumpled leftist-turned-Christian bard of calamitous modernity, W. H. Auden. Auden was seconded by Cecil Day-Lewis, a communist in his youth, like Spender, who in later years became the poet laureate of the United Kingdom, and father of the renowned contemporary actor Daniel Day-Lewis.

Robert De Niro, Sr., also the father of a well-known actor, faced similarly daunting odds. And if there is truth to the old adage, "Those whom the gods would destroy they first make mad," then a variation better suited to our celebrity-besotted times might go, "Those whom the gods would destroy they first make famous." De Niro, Sr., was sorely tested in that regard as well. That he was not destroyed by brief, early fame—as others of his milieu were—is a powerful testament to the depth and authenticity of his artistic calling. Another monitory proverb, this one from the New Testament, may well have echoed in the mind of the quietly religious De Niro: "Many are called but few are chosen." What does one say of those with a clear sense of vocation and manifest promise who are passed over in the final judgment? Or, to put it in more narrowly professional terms, what of those blessed with talent and drive who attract notice for those very qualities but are soon eclipsed by colleagues equally if not more talented and driven, peers who are chosen by a consensus of taste to represent their time? What becomes of those who are picked up, approvingly examined by public opinion, and then, for a host of elusive

1. Stephen Spender, "The Truly Great," *A Pocket Book of Modern Verse*, rev. ed., Oscar Williams, ed. (New York, NY: Washington Square Press, 1968), 505.

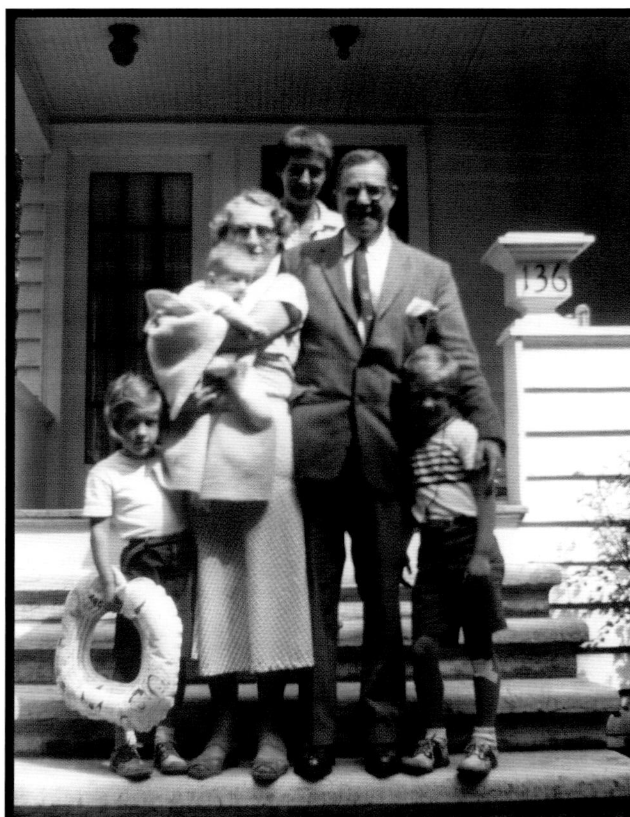

Robert De Niro, Sr., at middle in background, with his family at their home in Syracuse, New York, ca. 1932.

reasons, dropped and left to their own devices? How do they muster the courage and stamina to carry on despite the disappointment that inevitably results from being seduced and abandoned by fame in this manner?

I ask these questions because such was the plight of many charter members of the second wave of the New York School of the 1950s. The first wave had been men and women who began their careers during the Great Depression, and served their apprenticeships working for the New Deal WPA arts programs. Artists whose journeyman years coincided with World War II and its immediate aftermath include: Jackson Pollock, Lee Krasner, Arshile Gorky, Willem de Kooning, Philip Guston, Adolph Gottlieb, Barnett Newman, Mark Rothko, and Clyfford Still—artists who now compose the art-historical canon for this period.

Here is the rest of De Niro's basic backstory. Born in 1922 in Syracuse, New York, into an Irish-Italian household, Robert De Niro's trajectory was different from—and, to a degree, more direct than—those of his generally zigzagging New York School elders. In 1933, at eleven years of age, he started taking classes at the Syracuse Museum of Fine Arts. He rapidly excelled and continued to study there until he reached sixteen. His exceptional gifts made him a local prodigy, and for much of his time at the Museum he was granted a room of his own in which to work. In 1938, De Niro studied at the summer school of Ralph Pearson in Gloucester, Massachusetts, on Cape Ann, long a haven for artists from

Winslow Homer on through Edward Hopper, George Bellows, John Sloan, and Stuart Davis. During the summer of 1939, De Niro headed south to Cape Cod, where he enrolled in Hans Hofmann's school in Provincetown, Massachusetts. Eager to expand his artistic horizons still further, De Niro moved on to the experimental Black Mountain College in North Carolina, which he attended from 1939 to 1940. There, the former Bauhaus master Josef Albers taught many artists who would later rise to prominence. Among them were Robert Rauschenberg and Cy Twombly, leading lights of the Neo-Dada tendency, which by the end of the 1950s turned the tables on then-dominant Abstract Expressionism. In the process, this stylistic shift turned the world of more tradition-minded, mid-twentieth-century modernists like De Niro upside down.

By 1941, De Niro set himself up for the first time in New York City, where he resumed studying with Hofmann. In the same class was Virginia Admiral, an ambitious young artist from Berkeley, California. Hofmann acknowledged both as being among his favorite students. Sponsoring De Niro for a teaching post a decade later, Hofmann wrote: "The critic [unnamed] recognizes him as one of the most promising among the younger painters in America."[2] In 1942, De Niro and Admiral married, and, while their union lasted only briefly, a son, Robert, Jr., was born in August 1943. From journals De Niro kept later in life, it appears that the breakup was primarily due to his previously repressed homosexuality. Although De Niro stayed in close touch with Admiral until his death in her SoHo loft fifty years later, he suffered his entire life from being "different" and from the loneliness it imposed on him, conditions he conflated with his status as a painter.

To appreciate just how isolated one could be under the circumstances, it helps to be reminded of America's rampant homophobia during that period, both within De Niro's creative enclave and in American society at large. One of the features of McCarthy-era hysteria in the 1950s was the far right's portrayal of homosexuality as a "weakness" that could be exploited by agents of international communism, even though McCarthy's chief counsel, Roy Cohn, was gay, and McCarthy himself very well may have been. Closer to home was the heavy-drinking macho culture of the downtown art scene. Although a droll, party-loving man, De Niro avoided the Cedar Tavern and other places where boastful boozing redefined bohemianism as being "one of the boys," and professional pecking orders were established and contested. Meanwhile, in his solitary search for what Walt Whitman called "amativeness" and "adhesiveness"—pleasure and fellowship—he frequented the bars, restaurants, baths, and cruising grounds to which other gay men more or less secretly flocked.

2. Hans Hofmann, recommendation letter on behalf of Robert De Niro, Sr., ca. 1951, courtesy the Estate of Robert De Niro, Sr.

Meanwhile, Hofmann, affable and accessible in the context of his school, likewise stood apart from the burgeoning downtown scene. His education alongside Henri Matisse at the Parisian Académie Colarossi and the special insights into Fauvism that this association afforded him informed everything he did and all that he conveyed to those who came under his tutelage. Of particular consequence was the bold, high-key palette and space-creating chromatic dynamics Hofmann deployed in his own work and encouraged in that of his disciples. This lineage was important, because from the mid-1940s through the 1950s, the heyday of Abstract Expressionism, when push came to shove among artists vying for position within the New York avant-garde, those who sided with Picasso in his great rivalry with Matisse, like Pollock, Gorky, de Kooning, Robert Motherwell, and others, decidedly had the edge. As a follower of Hofmann, and so at one remove from his French *maître*, De Niro put himself at a relative disadvantage with respect to evolving critical consensus, though in every other regard his choice of Hofmann as a teacher was forward-looking. Connecting the dots from Gloucester to Provincetown to Greenwich Village, as if all were suburbs of Paris, De Niro demonstrated beyond all doubt that he was no provincial at a time when America-First chauvinism was still very much in style.

In fact, De Niro's attraction to Hofmann was shared by many of the best and brightest artists of his day, as well as of the generation before his. Among the latter must be counted Burgoyne Diller, Louise Nevelson, and Lee Krasner—Jackson Pollock's wife—as well as the future critic Clement Greenberg. Among De Niro's coevals numbered painters as disparate as Helen Frankenthaler, Alfred Jensen, and Myron Stout. Also of note, though younger, were Jane Freilicher, Larry Rivers, and Nell Blaine. These three constituted a special group, insofar as all applied Hofmann's lessons primarily to figurative rather than abstract work, though early in her career Blaine, who felt an affinity for artists like Piet Mondrian, Fernand Léger, and Jean Hélion, made paintings that were more abstract than not. Nevertheless, Blaine, Freilicher, and Rivers became the core of a cenacle that, with the addition of Fairfield Porter and Alex Katz, evolved during the 1950s into New York School painterly realists—a road not taken by De Niro, despite his links to those artists.

Distinguished by a lush painterly touch that usefully compares with Blaine's, De Niro's work of the early 1940s was devoted to more or less veiled and generalized still lifes and landscapes. By the end of World War II, De Niro and Blaine's fluency and verve brought each to the attention of the international patron Peggy Guggenheim, who exhibited their work at her eclectic gallery, Art of This Century. In 1945, Blaine made her debut there in a landmark group show called *The Women*. That same year De Niro was included in a salon show there, followed by a solo exhibition in 1946.

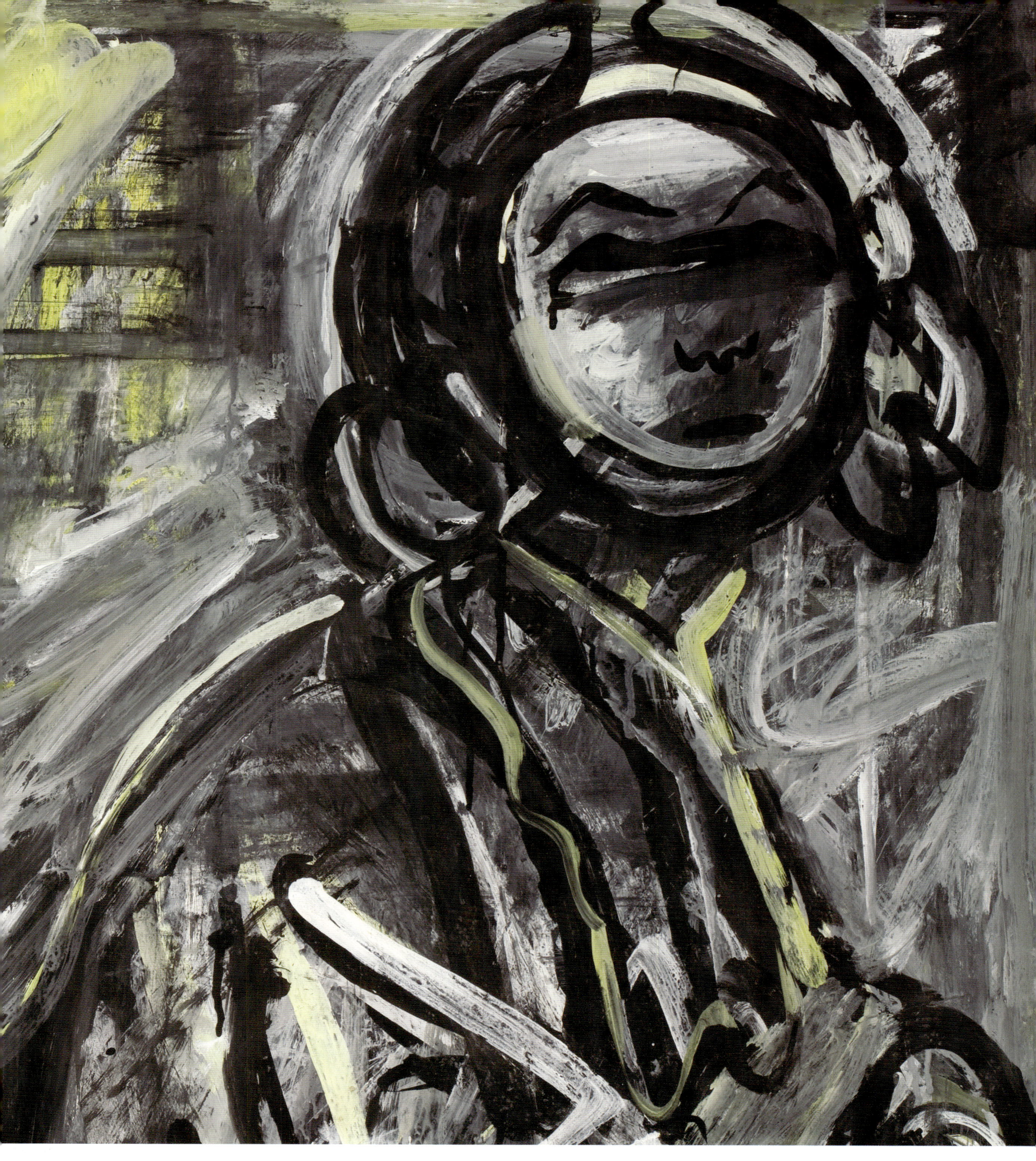

Lola Montez with Cigarette, 1958–59 (detail). Gouache and ink on paper, 36 x 24 inches. Plate 36

At this crucial moment, the dilettante dauber and fledgling arbiter of taste Greenberg gave De Niro the nod. His short review of De Niro's 1946 one-man show at Guggenheim's trend-setting space contained this assessment:

> Peggy Guggenheim has discovered another important young abstract painter at her Art of This Century Gallery—Robert De Niro, whose first show (through May 11) exhibits monumental effects rare in abstract art. In two of De Niro's ten pictures, "Ubu Roi" and "Fruits and Flowers," the originality and force of his temperament demonstrate themselves under an iron control of the plastic elements such as is rarely seen in our time outside the painting of the oldest surviving members of the school of Paris.[3]

The remainder of Greenberg's comments were mixed, in the classic manner of critics who enthuse first, to grab the reader's attention, and detract later, so as not to be caught too far out on a limb. Yet, even with Greenberg's strategic disclaimers, these were heady words. And combined with the fact that he was appearing at Art of This Century, whose regulars included everyone from Yves Tanguy and Alexander Calder to Mondrian and Joan Miró, meant that De Niro found himself not only in the fastest of transatlantic company, but also within the inner circle of their "advanced" American counterparts. Greenberg's endorsement was enough to put a chip on any young artist's shoulder.

In retrospect, though, De Niro's fleeting affiliation with the avant-garde may have been the cruelest misfortune possible for an emerging artist whose true sensibility had little to do with breaking away from the past. Quite the contrary, De Niro was the kind of artist—as numerous in the modern era as they were in any previous one—who feels utterly at ease in art history and wants nothing more than to pay lively and inventive homage to the work they love. Such artists differentiate themselves from academics in that they refrain from extrapolating "sure-fire" formulas for making "successful" art from precedents. Rather, they strive to assimilate those precedents until they become a kind of second nature. In fact, so thoroughly do they command these strategies that they can reinterpret and "perform" them like classical musicians composing a cadenza or jazzmen riffing on a familiar theme—on the spot and in real time.

In that connection, Harold Rosenberg, Greenberg's principal rival as postwar critical advocate for the "new," had it right when he wrote that the litmus test for "quality" in contemporary art is "freshness." And, one might add, its corollary in matters of execution is "immediacy." Thanks in large measure to Hofmann, what De Niro did have in common with the Abstract Expressionists, whose concerns differed in so many other ways from his, was the value he placed on direct mark-making. That capacity and the

3. Clement Greenberg, Exhibition Review, *The Nation*, May 18, 1946.

flair he added to it are most obviously on display in the palpable figurative armatures of virtually all his pictures, in both painting and drawing. When it came to the "Action Painters"—Rosenberg's alternative label for the Abstract Expressionists, one that emphasizes spontaneous in-the-moment creation—the two modes are at their most forceful when it becomes hardest to distinguish between them, with only the record of the hand's trace there to guide us.

Blessed with decisiveness and dexterity as both draftsman and painter, De Niro was singularly well equipped to take on the challenge of a style predicated on improvisational composition and realization. As films of him at work in the studio attest, he went "straight at it" without visible hesitation, sure in the knowledge that his first impulses were likely to result in a contour that accorded with his initial intention. If they did not, however, if the spontaneously inscribed shapes, gestures, and areas of color failed to hang together or did so too decoratively, he could just as easily undo what he had done, leaving himself loose ends and suggestive passages with which to restart the process, thereby articulating a fully charged, allover pictorial surface.

Whether on paper or canvas, his loosely delineated forms and spontaneous paint handling were coupled with an ability always to land squarely no matter how far he let himself go. These qualities would constitute the essence of De Niro's signature manner for the remainder of his career. From the early 1940s until the early 1990s, his paintings and drawings show no dramatic stylistic developments, but they retain a panache and aplomb that allow the viewer to concentrate fully on the nuances of the artist's virtuosity. The radiance of a specific yellow, pink, or orange set in contrast to one another or to cooler hues; the curve of a hip or the oval of a face; the wide sweep of a heavily loaded brush overlapping or erasing another broad stroke, even as together they highlight more controlled gestures or calligraphic squiggles—again and again he directs our attention to the particular. For De Niro, drawing with paint, charcoal, or ink was a kind of rhythmic stenography, a system of dots and dashes, bars and trailing serpentine lines whose varying width and density partly or wholly surround comparative areas of translucent or impasto scumbling, and are in turn set off by them. He could do it all day, every day, with unflagging flair—and he did. Therein lies the enduring vitality of his art.

The one significant exception to the consistency of his compositions after the early 1940s is the appearance of Crucifixions as a principal theme, starting in the early 1950s and continuing through the remainder of his life. Considering how deeply steeped he

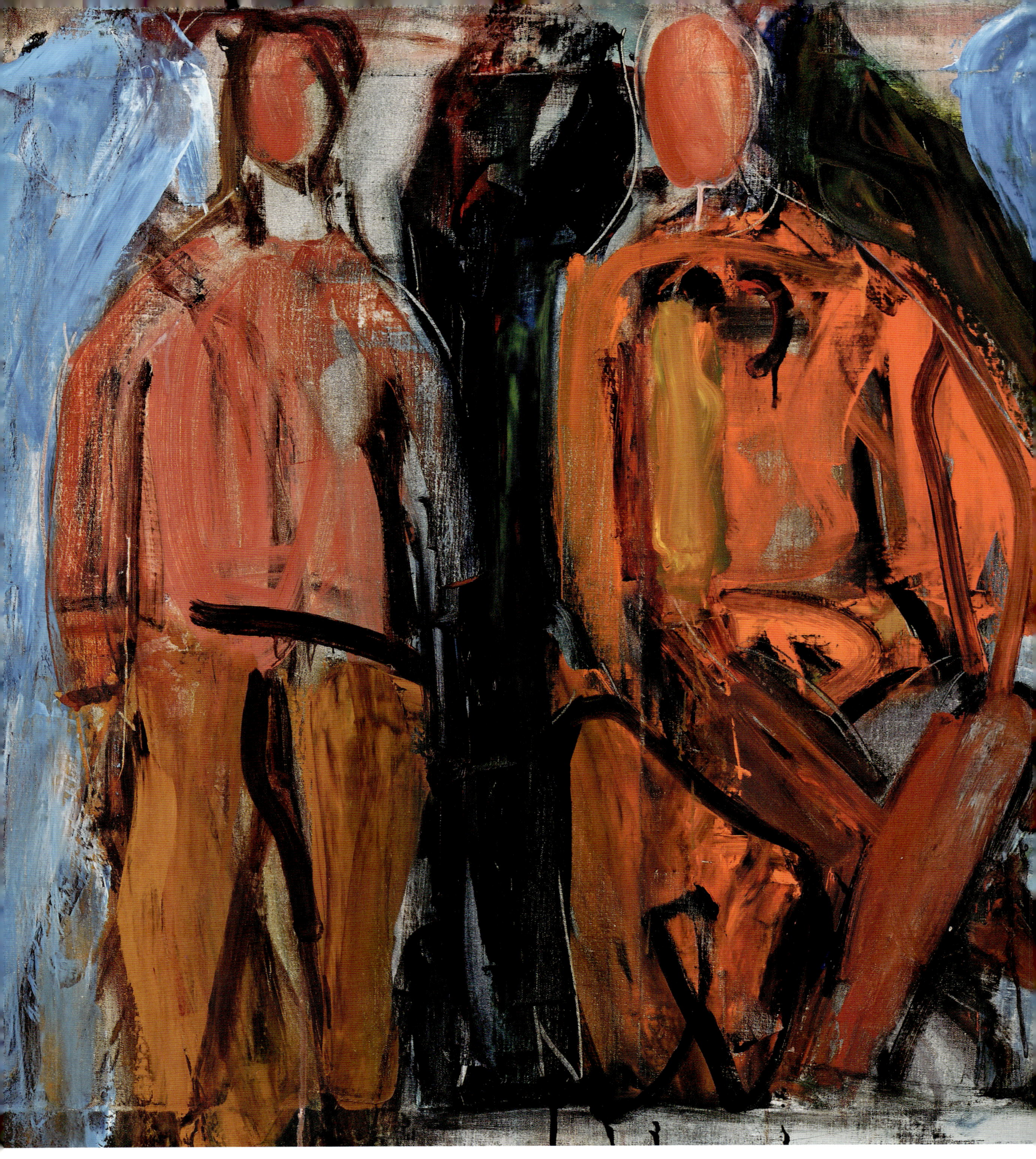

Bonjour Mr. De Niro, ca. 1955 (detail). Oil on canvas, 35¾ x 47¾ inches. Plate 30

was in the Old Masters, and how essential the Catholic Church was in commissioning work from them, it is unsurprising that De Niro should have gravitated to the cross as an image. Moreover, as a Modernist, he must have seen the three crosses on Calvary as an irresistible invitation to conjure with an iconic form. Although modern art is often mistakenly assumed to be secular, numerous others before De Niro had brought the cross into their art, including Kazimir Malevich and Matisse, whose Chapel of the Rosary at Vence opened in 1951. Certainly they too were cognizant of its religious meaning. Even Barnett Newman had painted a cycle of abstractions titled *The Stations of the Cross: Lema Sabachthani* (1958–66).

That the motif had sacred meaning for De Niro seems clear from his writings, for what else does a cross symbolize but the physical and psychological suffering of a man fated by his nature to be persecuted? Although De Niro's involvement with the subject started before Newman began working on his series, the possibility arises—given how freely news circulated from studio to studio in downtown Manhattan—that De Niro's subsequent variations on the theme were to some extent an oblique but intensely physical rejoinder to Newman's disembodied tableaux. But as a man who filled his diaries with references to hours of prayer, De Niro came to the subject for very different reasons than did the Jewish Newman or the agnostic Matisse.

De Niro brought to his spontaneous sessions at the easel not only a natural facility, honed by the disciplined rehearsal of particular painterly and graphic moves, but also a total immersion in what Al Held, another painter of De Niro's generation, called "painting culture." Few artists today have comparable command of it. Of those who do, most, whether they admit it or not, are truly academic. Which is to say, they are more fixated on what has been done than on what might yet be done, believing mistakenly that they do honor to the Old Masters by producing what amounts to inferior pastiches of their work.

De Niro was not of that stripe. His "painting culture" was encyclopedic. Using postcards and reproductions to transform his loft, studio to bedroom, into what André Malraux called an Imaginary Museum, he lived, breathed, and dreamed the glories of the past. Moreover, his study of "the greats" entailed not only frequent museum crawls, alone or in the company of friends and fellow artists, but also, since this was the golden age of art book publishing in the United States,[4] regular perusal of monographs devoted to his favorite painters. Accordingly, on the shelves in De Niro's studio (which his son has kept intact) can be found the majority of the uniform volumes then published by

Harry N. Abrams, specifically those on Tintoretto, Zurbarán, Poussin, Chardin, Ingres, Turner, Manet, Corot, Seurat, Braque, Vuillard, Bonnard, and Rouault. Other volumes near to hand include pocket-sized picture books published by Skira, and massive tomes issued by other imprints reproducing the complete works of Leonardo da Vinci, Michelangelo, and Raphael. There is much more besides—all evidence of De Niro's exceptional avidity and appetite for art.

Nevertheless, this deep art-historical grounding came at a cost, especially during a century in which Anti-Art in its various guises left in the lurch those who remained true to their artistic heroes. Artists wishing to avoid that fate had to find ways of temporarily banishing their historical role models from their studios. The first-generation Abstract Expressionist Philip Guston, who was at least as enamored of "the greats" as De Niro, used to tell a story—or rather a Zen parable—that he learned from the composer John Cage. "When you are working," Cage said, "everybody is in your studio—the past, your friends, the art world, and above all your own ideas—all are there. But as you continue painting, they start leaving, one by one, and you are left completely alone. Then, if you are lucky, even you leave."[5]

Perhaps the simplest way of distinguishing De Niro from New York School colleagues like Guston is to point out that he never felt crowded by the past, though he did feel terribly alone in so many other respects. An inherently prickly man made more so by setbacks and loneliness, De Niro was quick to alienate many of his friends and allies. By contrast, he regarded the company of his mentors and preferred masters—his imaginary art-historical playmates, one might say—as protectors in a hostile world. Or so it would seem from the evidence of his pictures and writings. De Niro's spirited version of Gustave Courbet's *Bonjour Monsieur Courbet* hung in his living quarters, and essays on Boucher, Bonnard, Degas, Manet, Munch, Rousseau, Soutine, Van Gogh, and others attest to his ever-thoughtful engagement with painting's Grand Tradition.

At the outset of this essay I asked a series of rhetorical questions about "failure" in our success-haunted world. The answers are provided by the late Irving Sandler, doyen of New York School critics and friend of most of the consequential artists of his era, as well as respectful colleague of many who simply showed up and did their best. With contagious enthusiasm, Sandler declared that De Niro painted for the Old Masters. For almost seventy years no one in this country who monitored the appearance of new talent or watched the rise and fall of reputations was more acutely conscious than Sandler of the spasmodic mechanisms of cultural reception, or of the high turnover of

5. Philip Pavia and Irving Sandler, eds., "The Philadephia Panel," *It Is*, Spring 1960, 37.

artists who from one day to the next are touted as the coming attractions and shortly thereafter dismissed with a shrug as "has-beens." Nor, since he knew "everyone," was anyone more conscious than he of the human cost of the art world's fickleness. Now that more college and university students than ever are declaring art as their major, and more galleries, magazines, museums, prizes, and residencies than ever are there to pick up—and drop—them, we do well to examine and fairly judge De Niro's life in art. For not only is his achievement of lasting worth, it tells a cautionary tale as well. In an ostensibly "postmodern age," when interest in the continuity of the modern tradition De Niro held dear has dwindled, his paintings and drawings vibrate with the conviction and complexity of the modernist faith at its height, when young artists cared more for making well-conceived and solidly constructed images than contriving casually ironic sendups of historical precedents. In just what ways is the umpteenth "critical" simulacrum of a famous work from the past more interesting than one intelligently conceived in admiration of it?

Leaving that question to hang in the air, I will end by giving Sandler the last word. He shared the long view that De Niro adopted, and he outlasted Greenberg and all his acolytes without ever losing his enthusiasm for the art of his time, which is to say, of the present. So, when it comes to the judgment of history, listen to a historian, and recapture the spirit of the era when De Niro burned bright. Interviewed for a film made by Robert De Niro, Jr., in homage to his father, Sandler, wisely but also with an undiminished ardor characteristic of his generation, said:

> About his need to paint in spite of lack of recognition, or whatever, he just had to paint. Sure, you go on painting—after all there's Michelangelo back there, Piero della Francesca, Velázquez, these are your gods. You're painting for the greater glory of art, not for anybody out there, really. You're painting for the big guys up there, and you're trying to emulate and if possible to beat them and hopefully to live for the ages like they do.

PAINTINGS & DRAWINGS 1942-1965

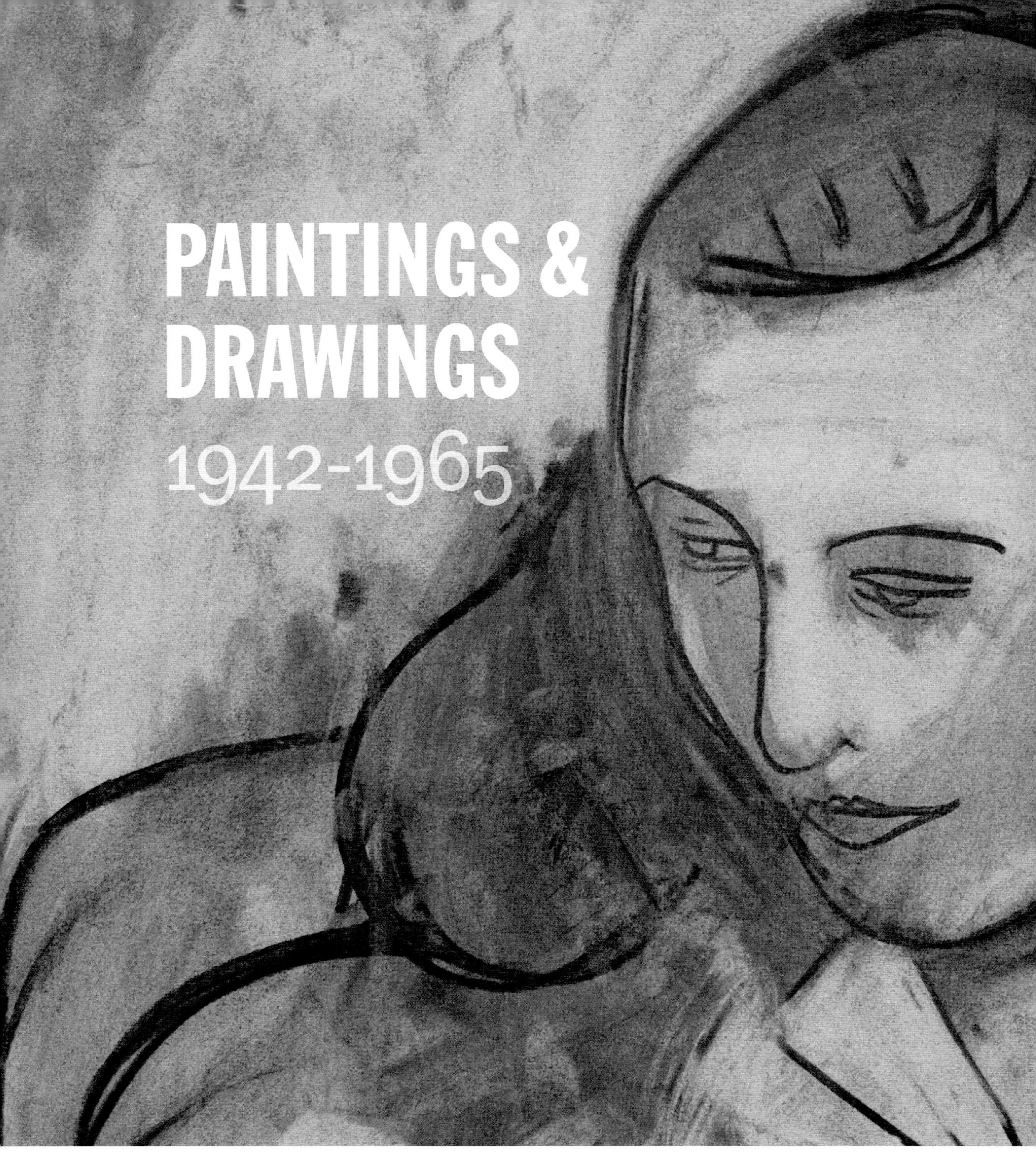

Portrait of a Young Woman, 1959 (detail). Charcoal on paper, 19½ x 25½ inches. Plate 43

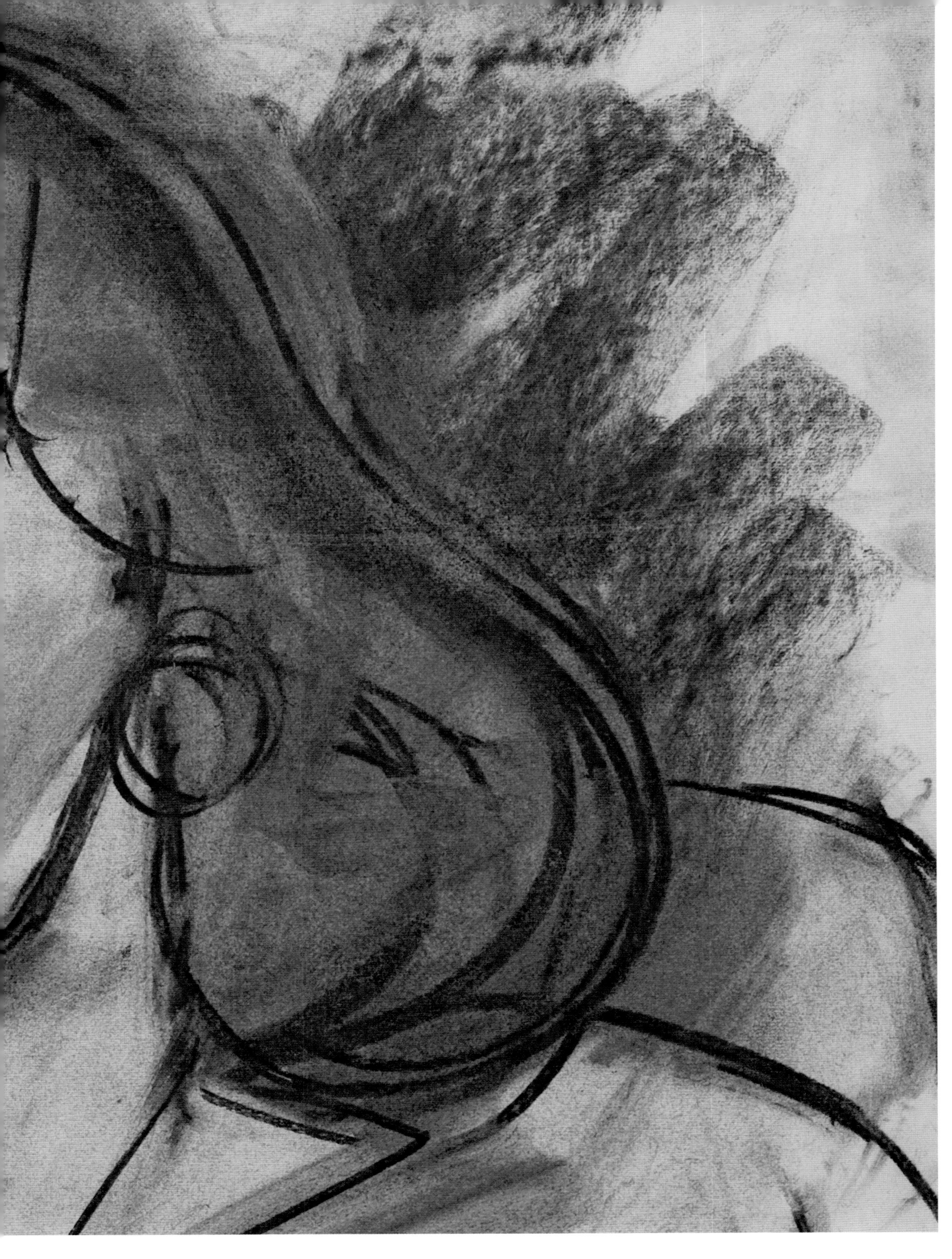

1. **Reclining Nude with Attendant**, 1942. Oil on linen, 22 x 26 inches

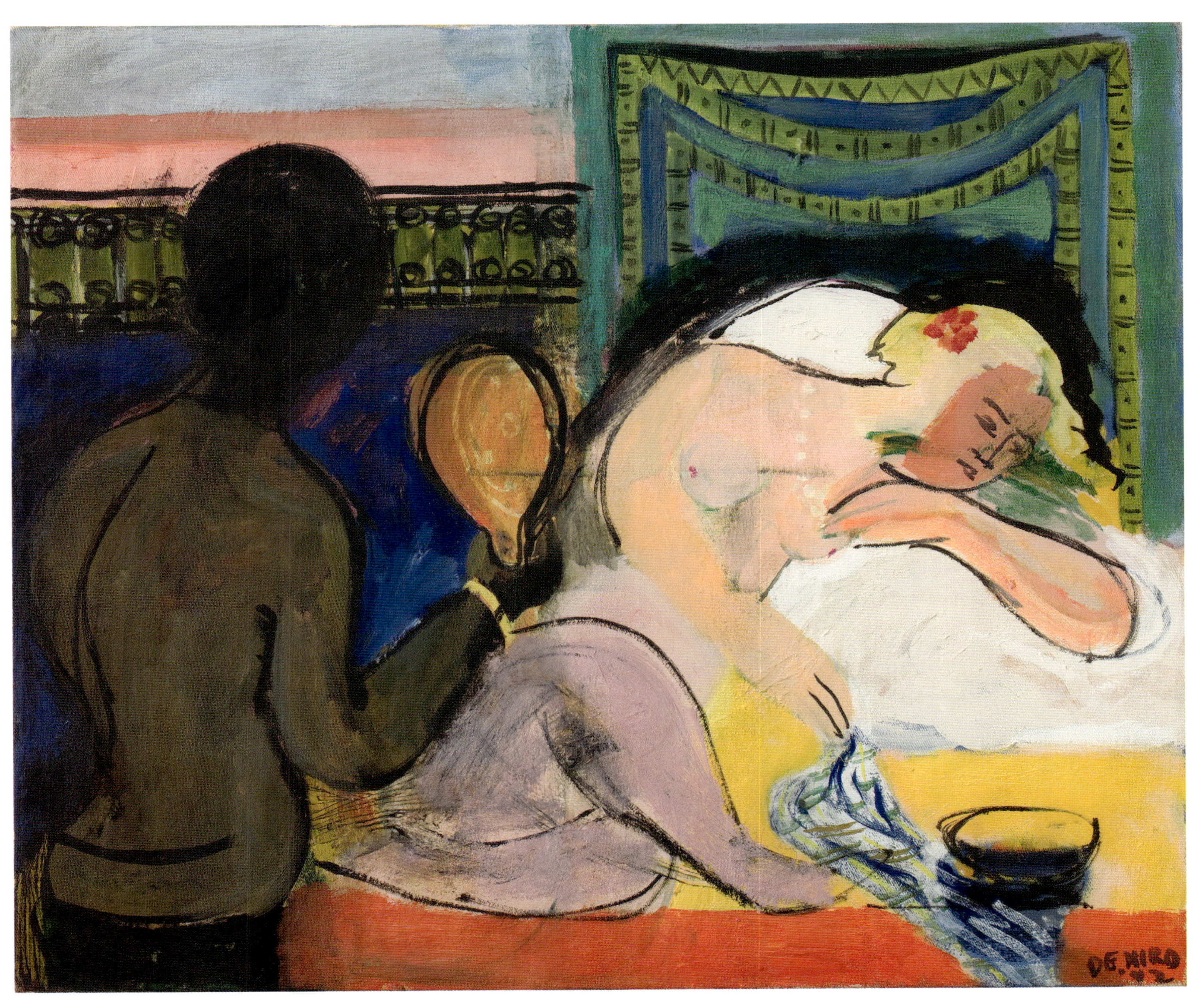
DE.NIRO

2. **Venice at Night Is a Negress in Love**, ca. 1942–43. Oil on canvas, 37 ½ x 43 ½ inches

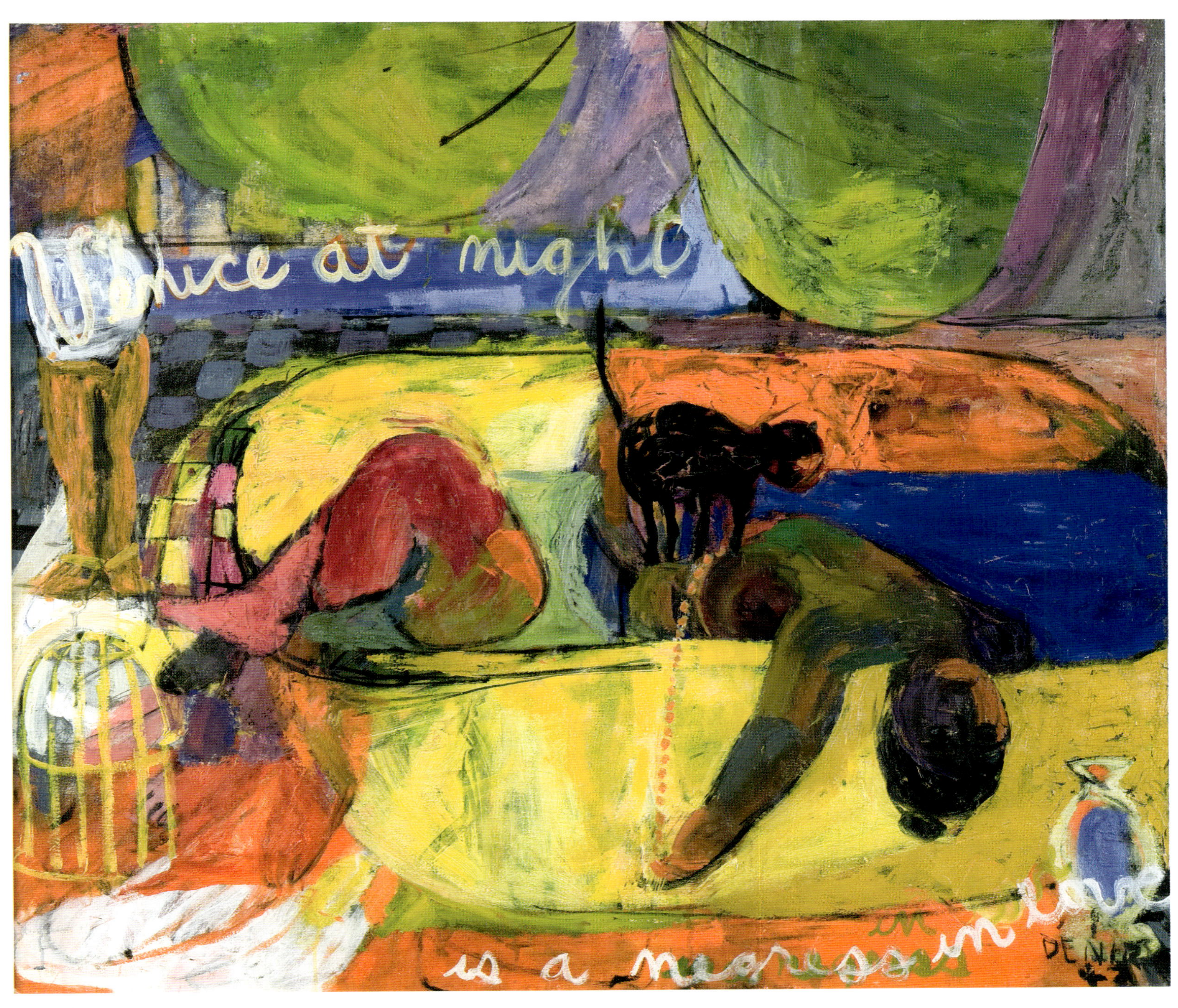
at night
is a

3. **Still Life**, ca. 1946. Oil on canvas, 36 x 33 ¼ inches

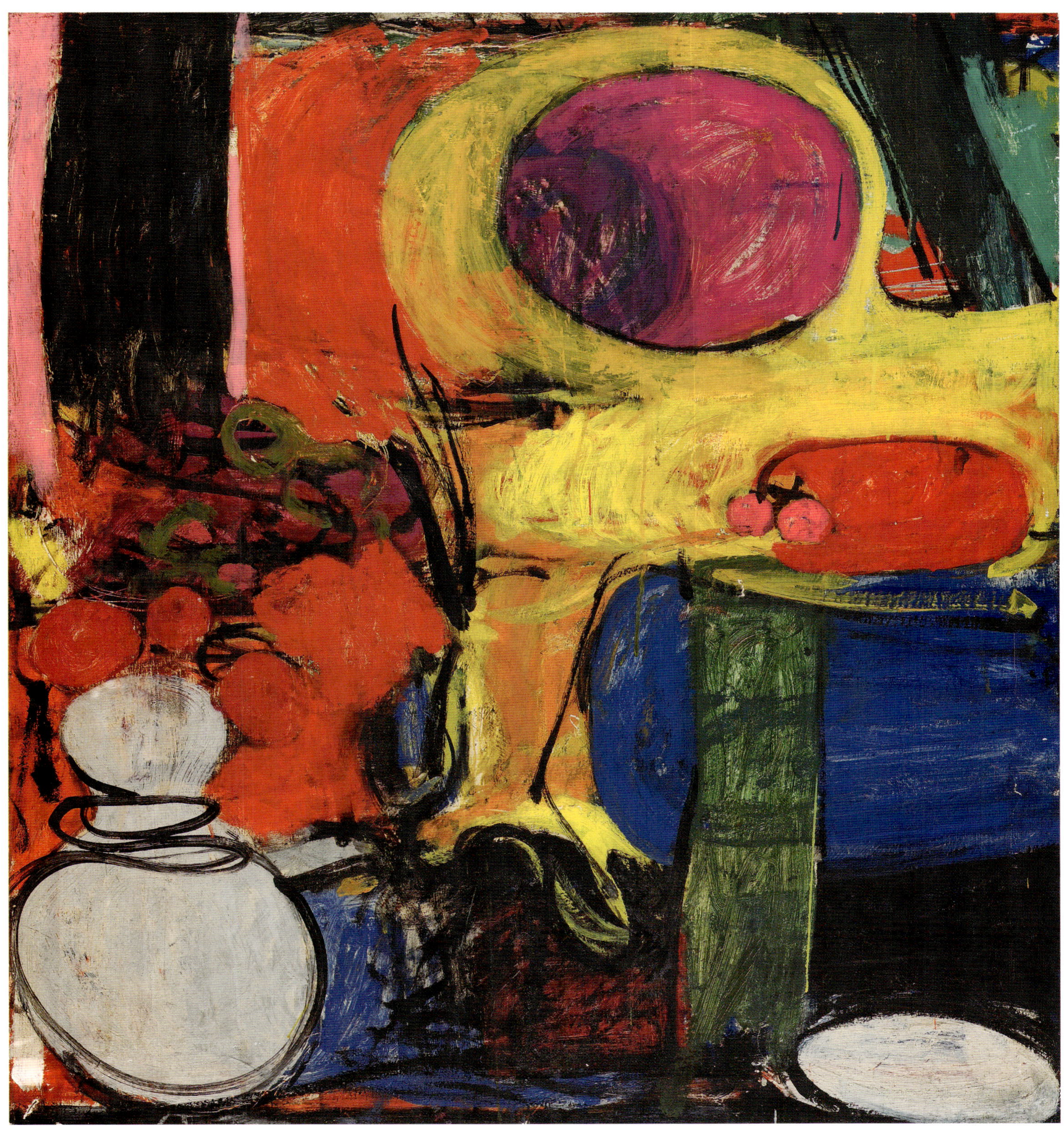

4. **Untitled**, 1946. Oil on canvas, 37 ¼ x 34 ¼ inches

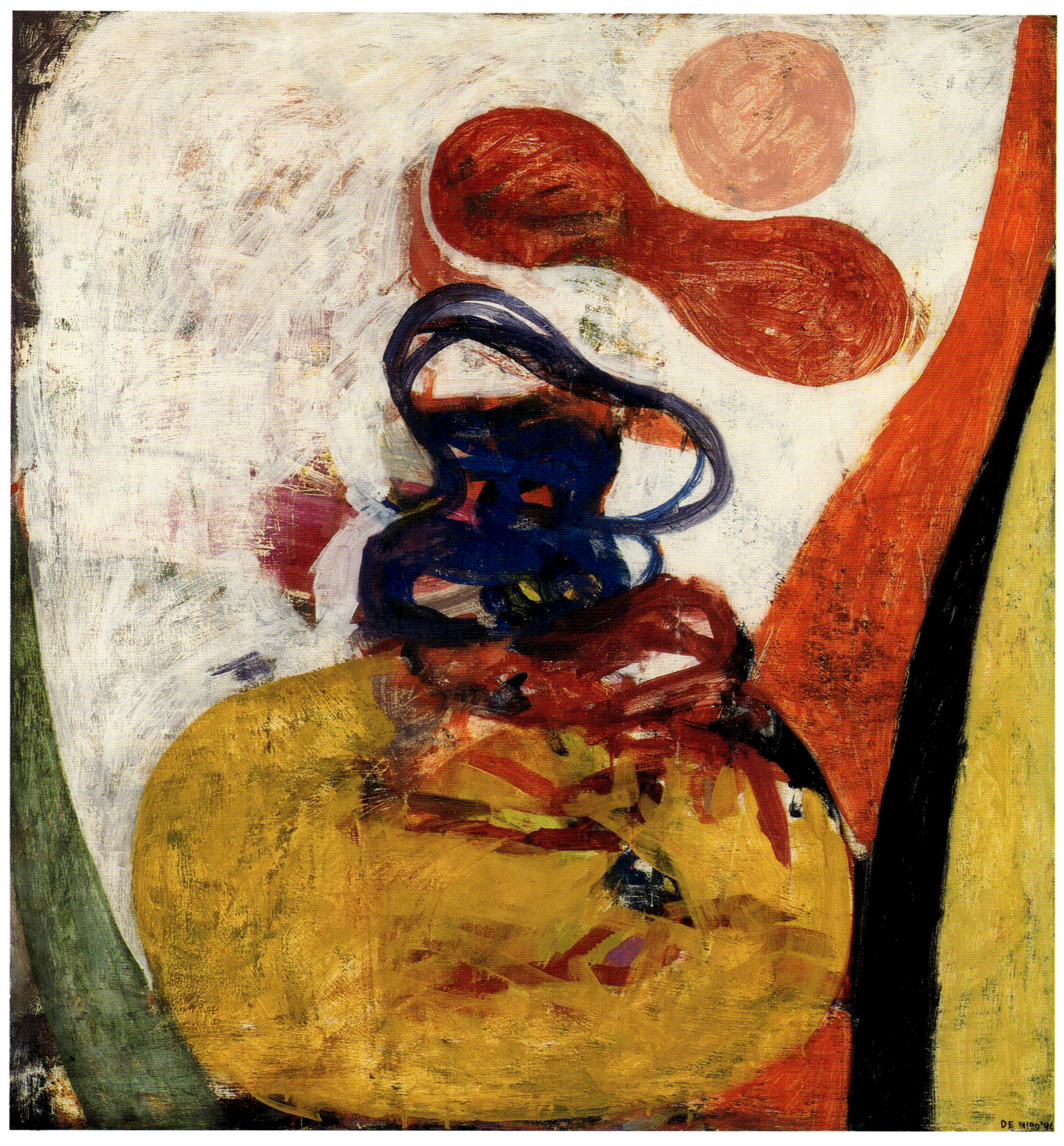

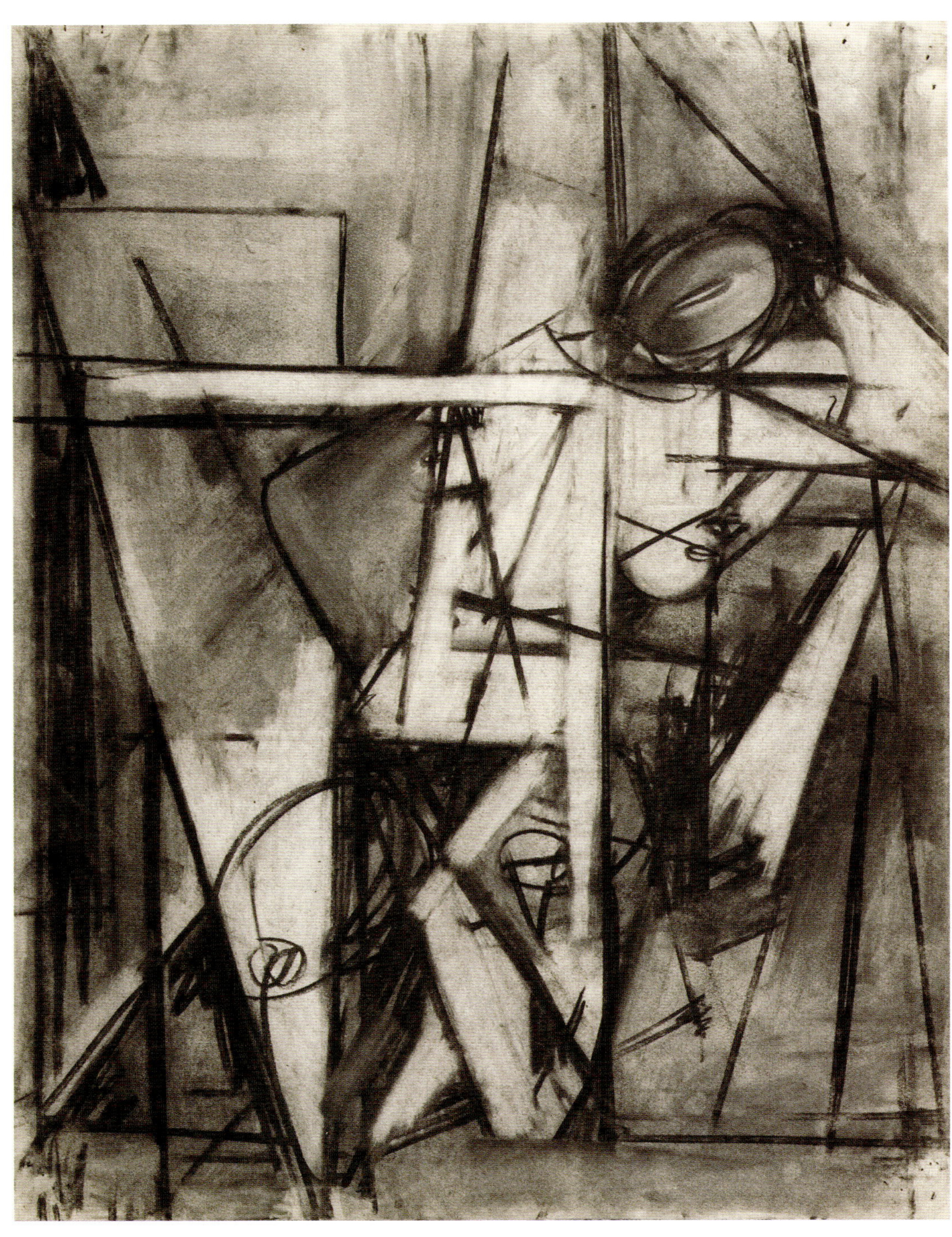

5. **Cubist Figure Study**, ca. 1940s. Charcoal on paper, 25½ x 19½ inches

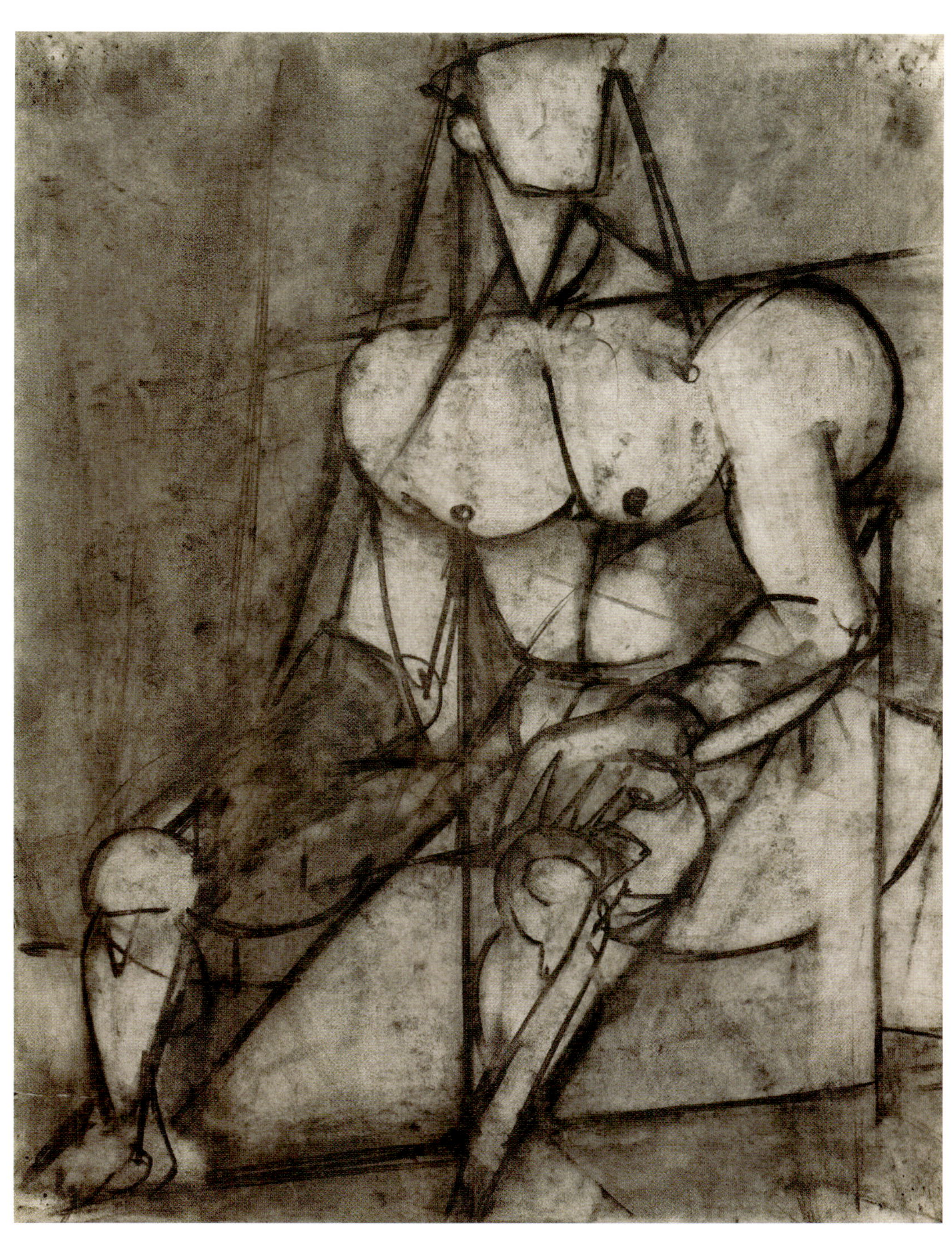

6. **Male Cubist Figure, Seated**, ca. 1940s. Charcoal on paper, 25 ½ x 19 ½ inches

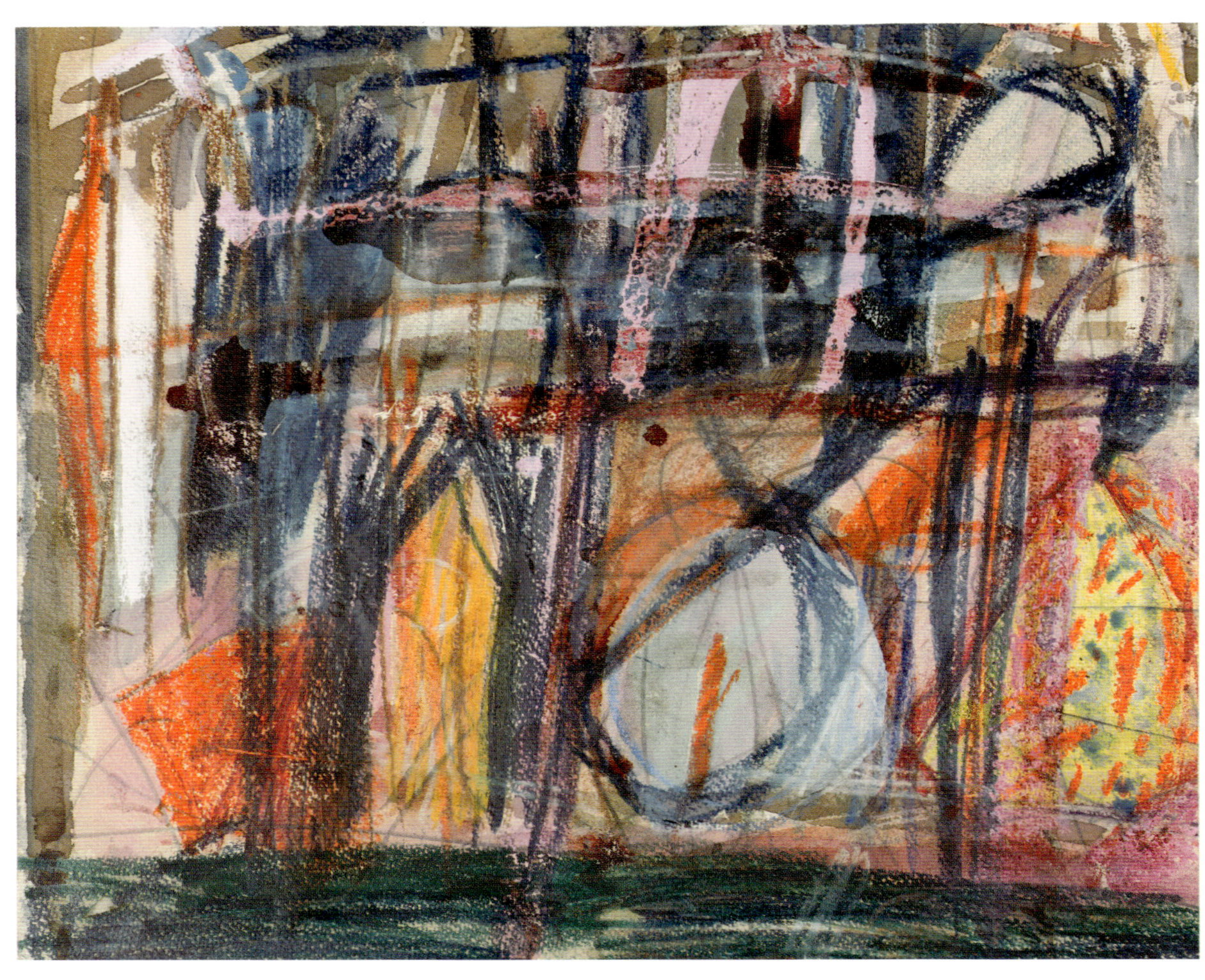

7. **Iglesia de Paz**, ca. 1950. Mixed media on paper, 13 x 16 inches

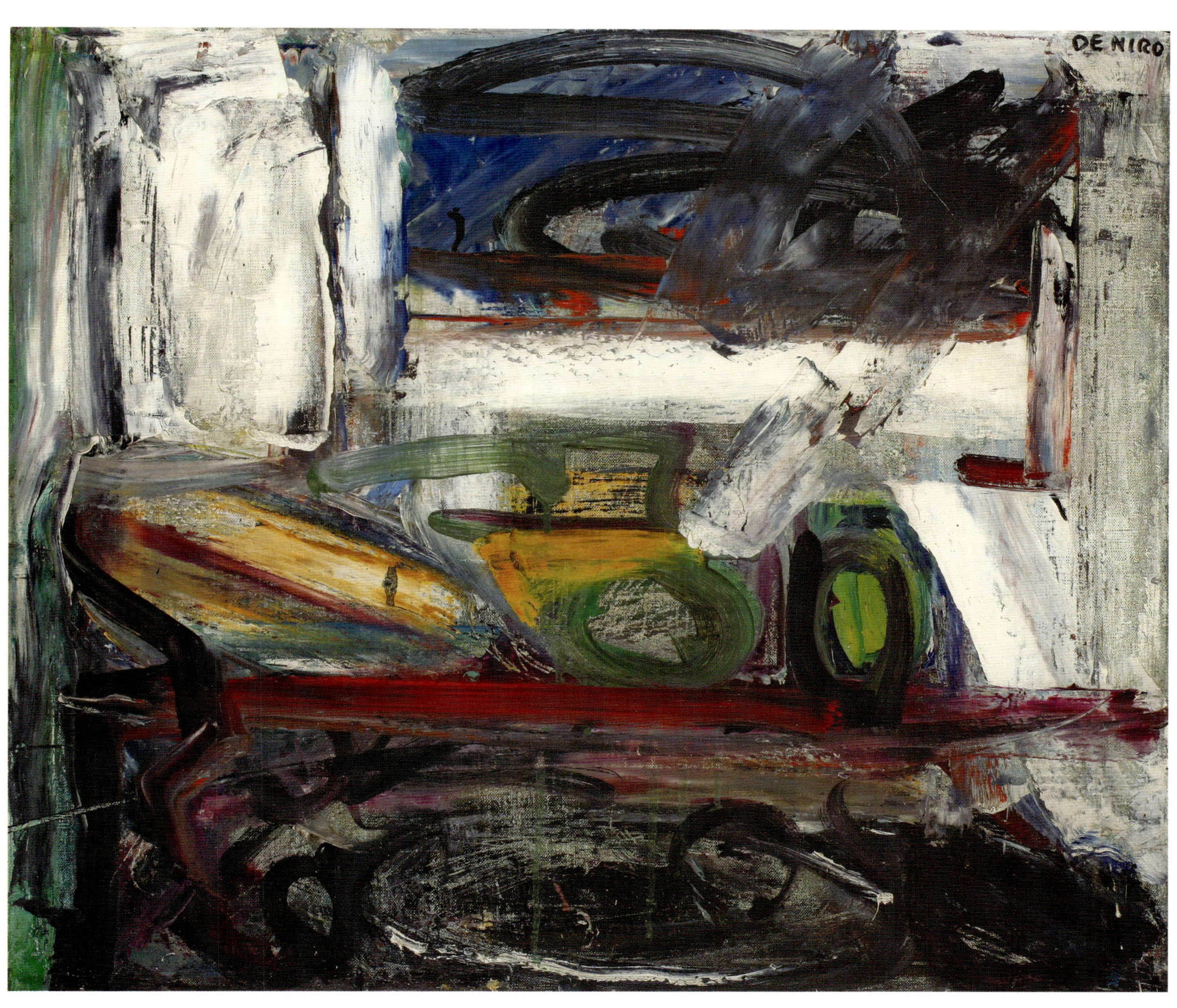

8. **Untitled Abstraction**, ca. 1947–48. Oil on linen, 22 x 26 inches

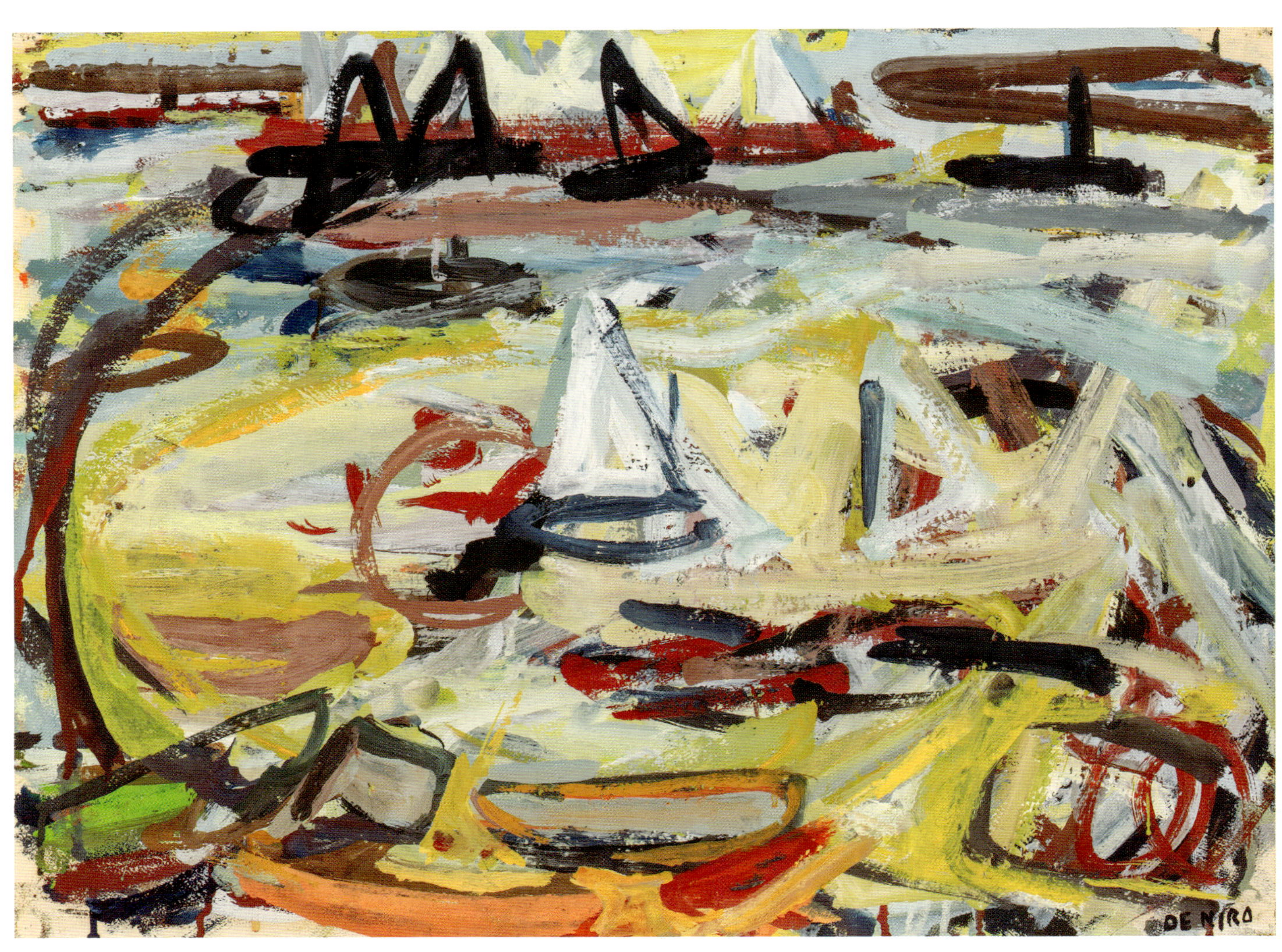

9. **P-Town**, ca. 1950. Gouache on paper, 17½ x 23½ inches

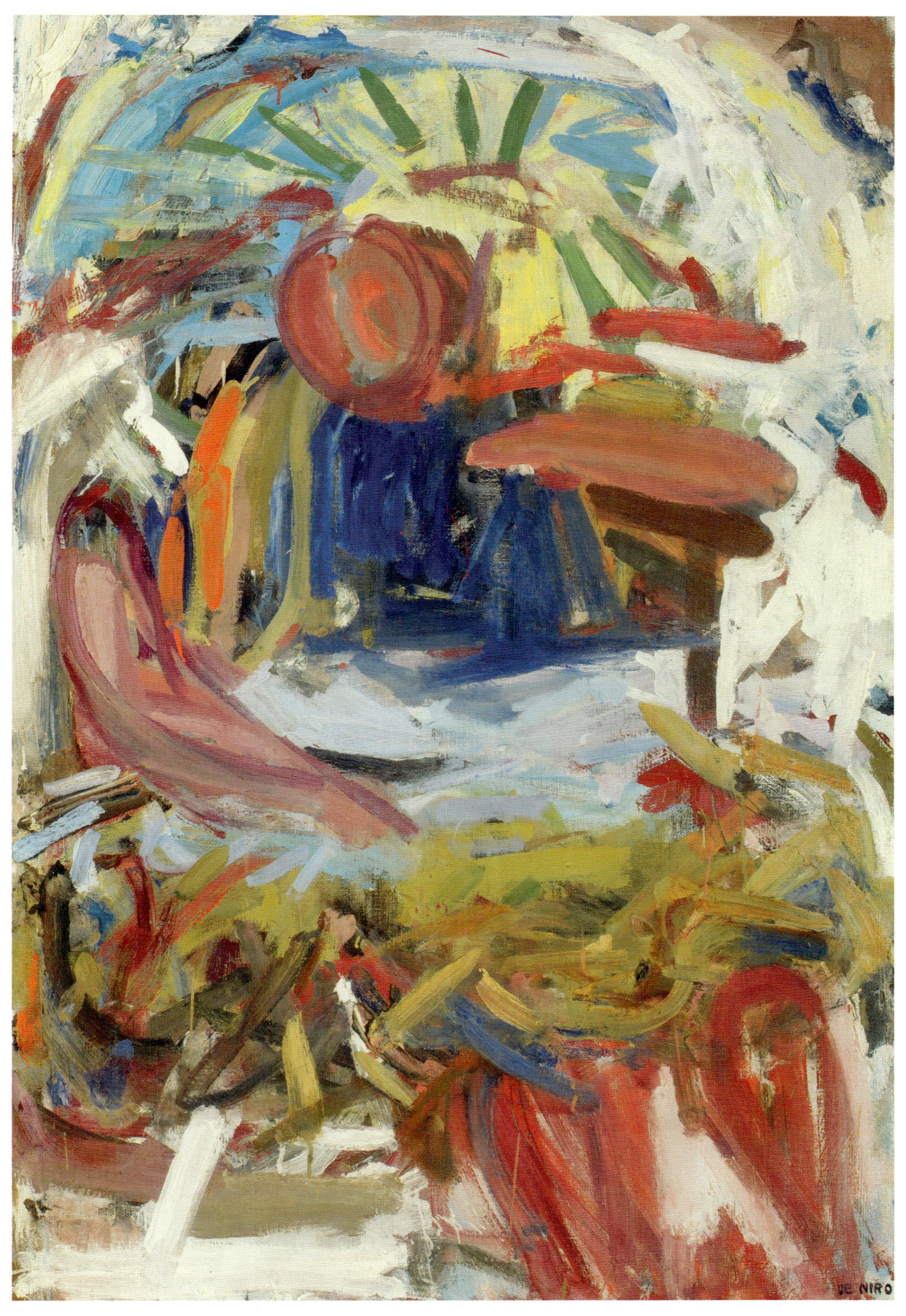

10. **Untitled**, ca. 1950. Oil on canvas, 50½ x 34 inches

11. **Still Life with Greek Head**, 1951. Oil on canvas, 30 x 24 inches

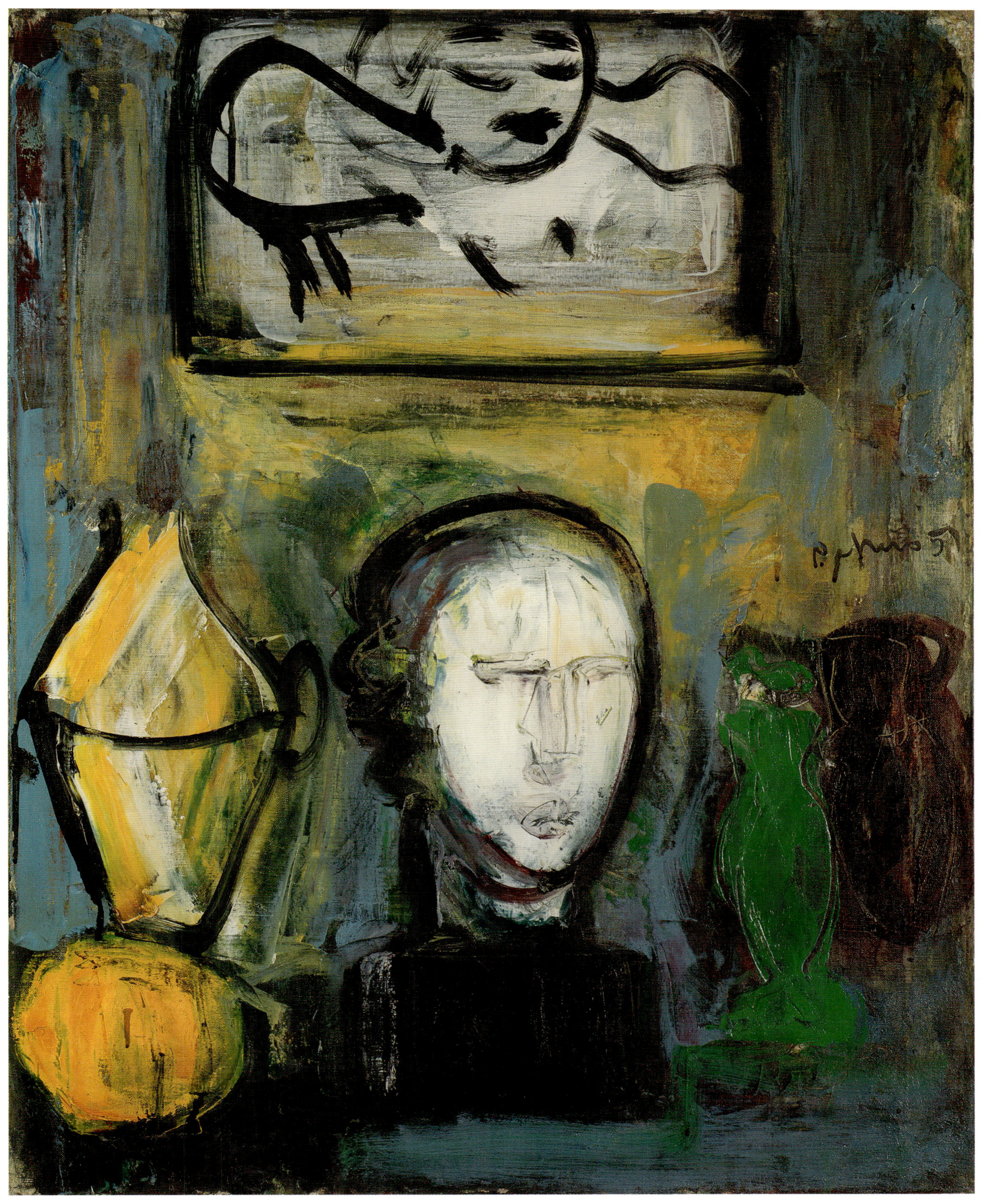

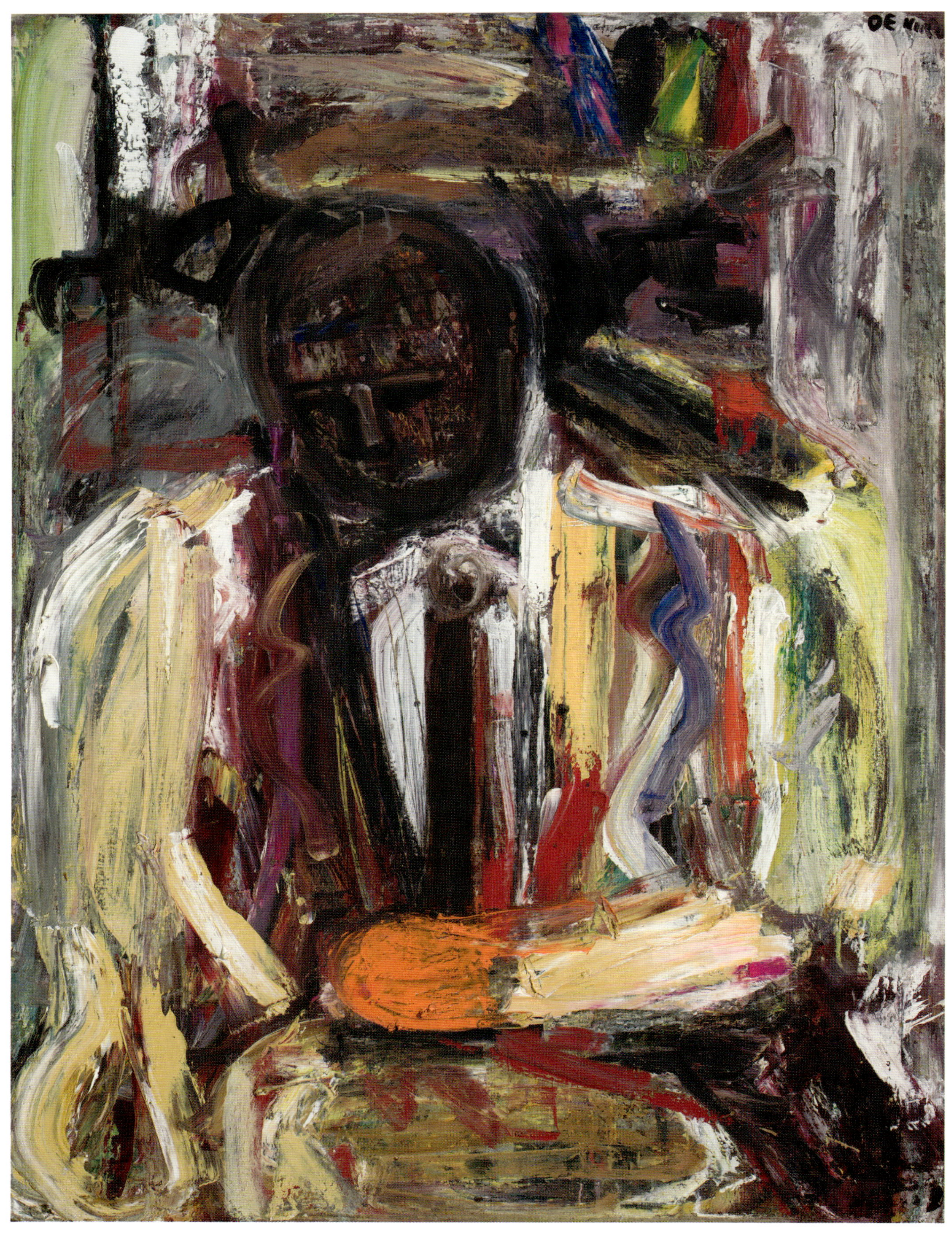

12. **Untitled (Seated Man)**, ca. 1950. Oil on canvas, 42½ x 30½ inches

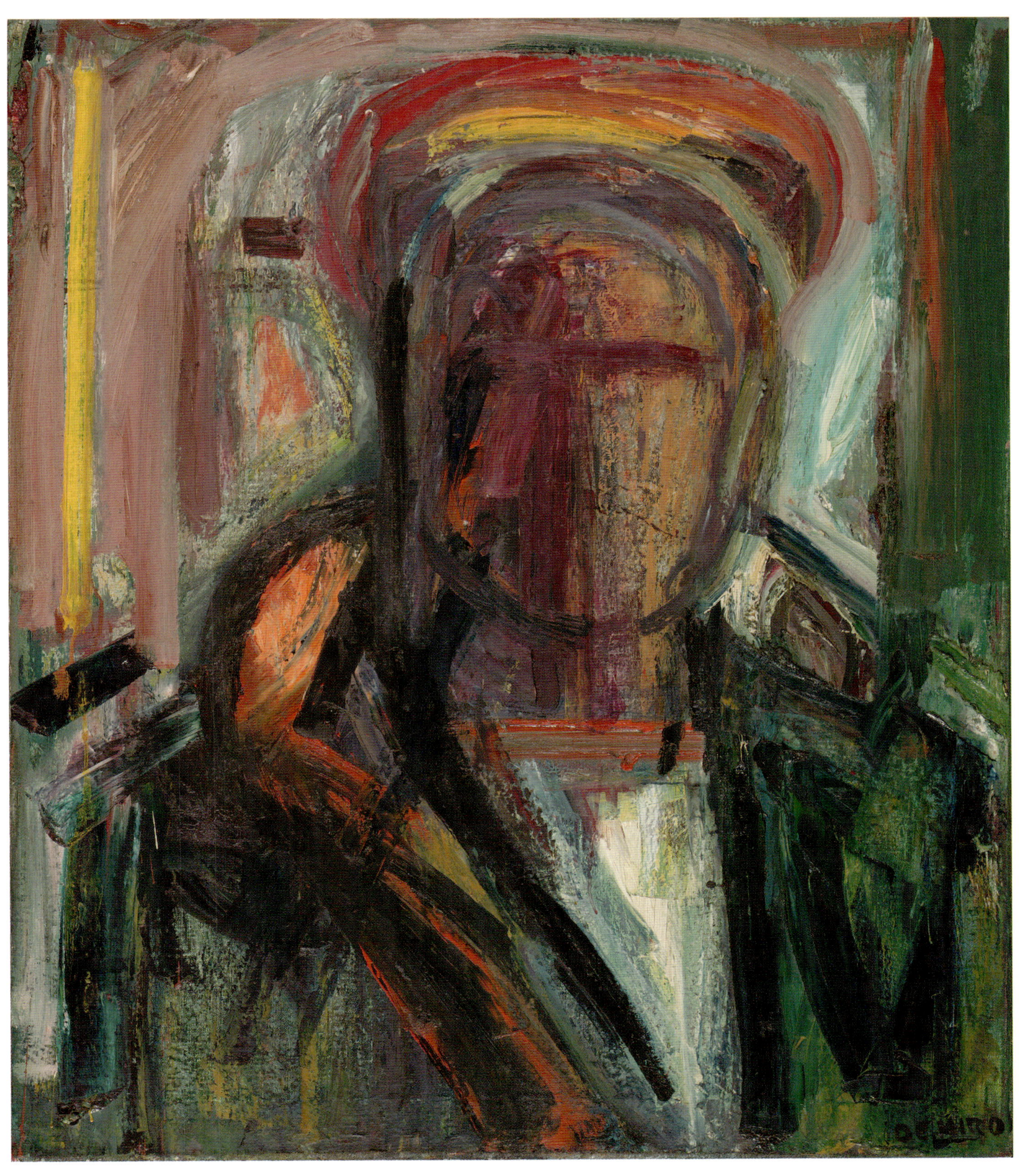

13. **Self-Portrait**, 1951. Oil on canvas, 35⅛ x 30 inches

14. **Moroccan Women**, ca. 1951. Oil on canvas, 58 x 42 inches

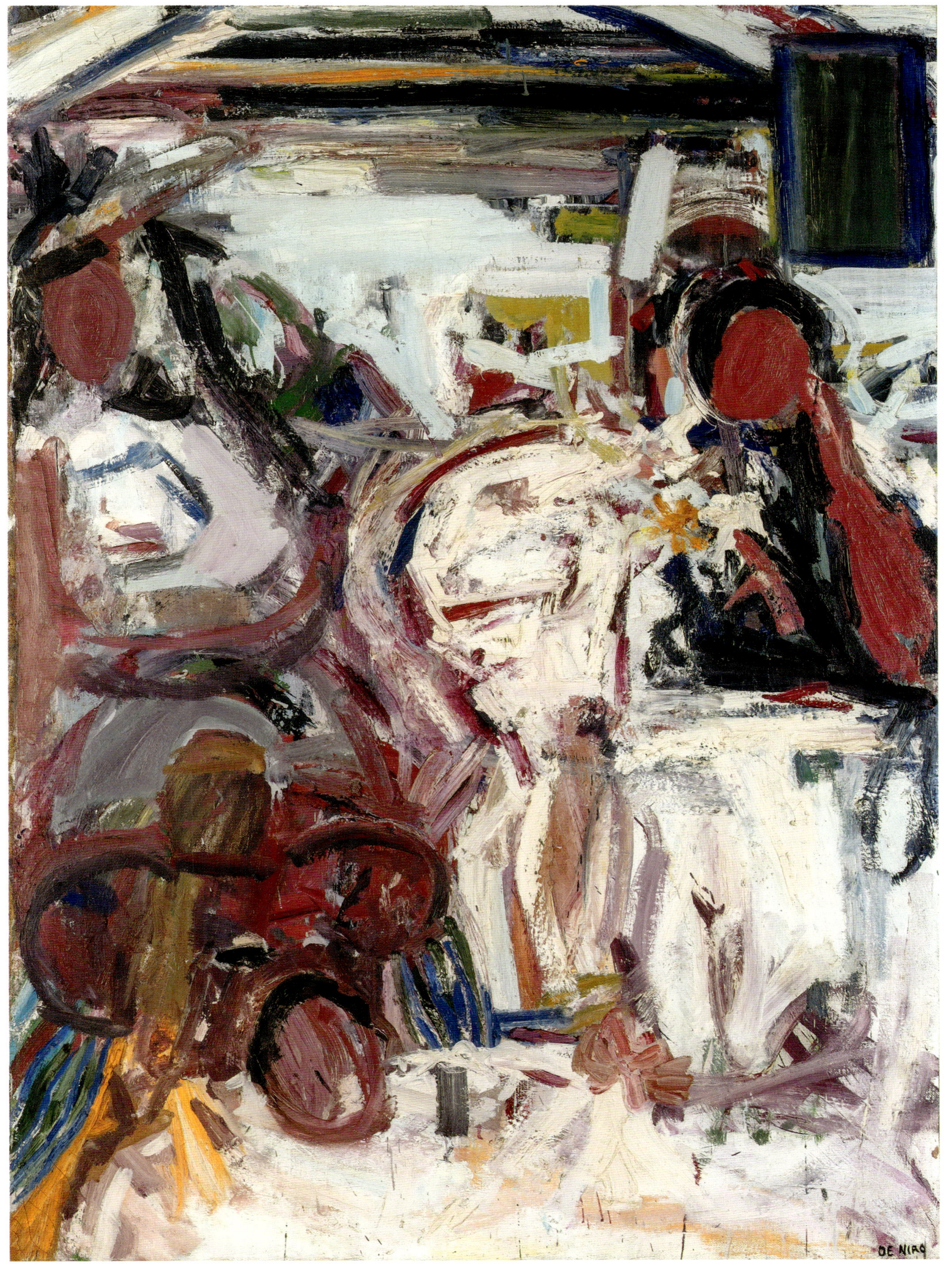
DE NIRO

15. **Portrait of Virginia (Portrait of the Artist's Wife)**, ca. 1950. Oil on canvas, 34 ½ x 33 ½ inches

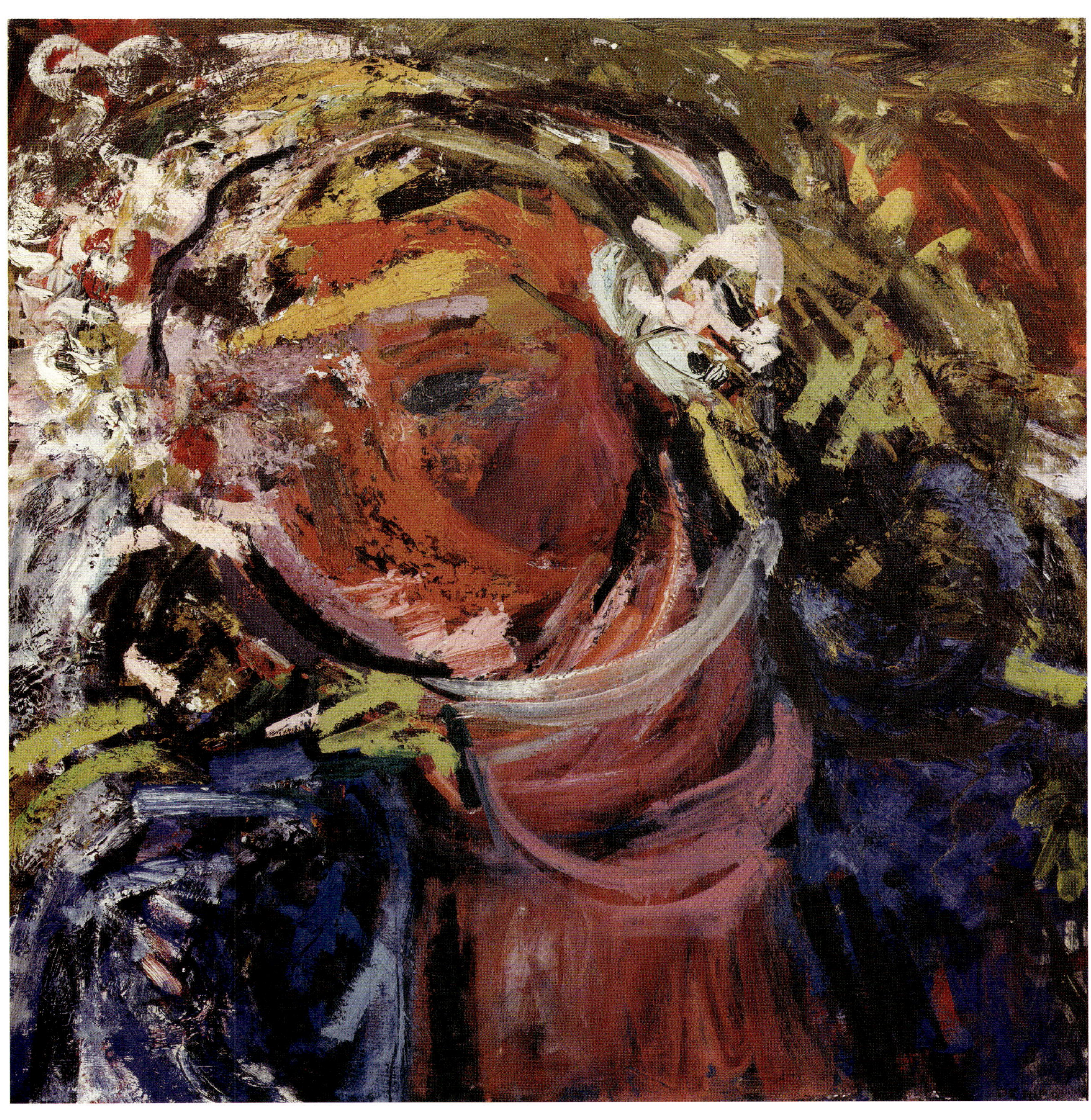

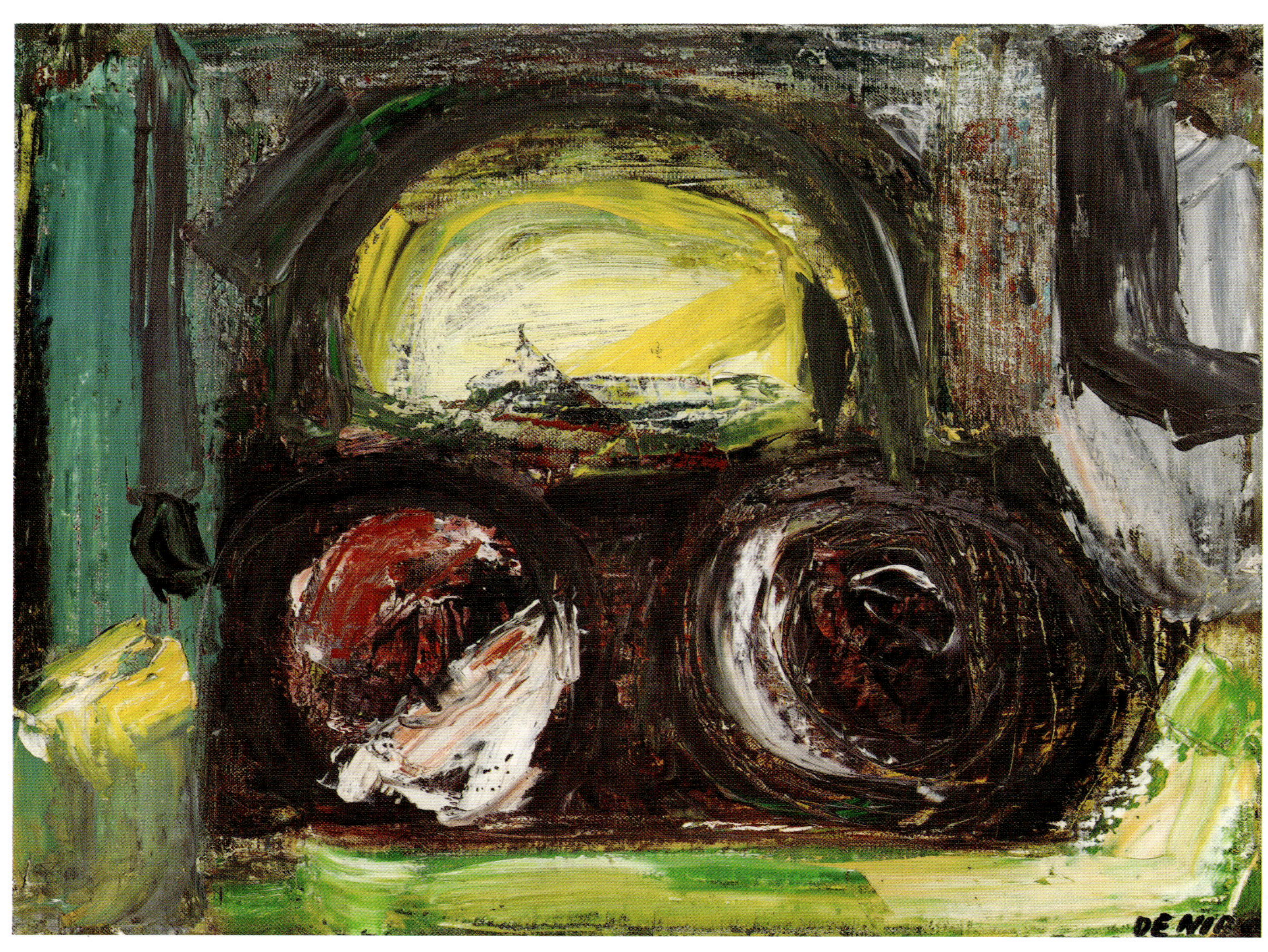

16. **Untitled (Still Life)**, ca. 1952–53. Oil on canvas, 15¼ x 20½ inches

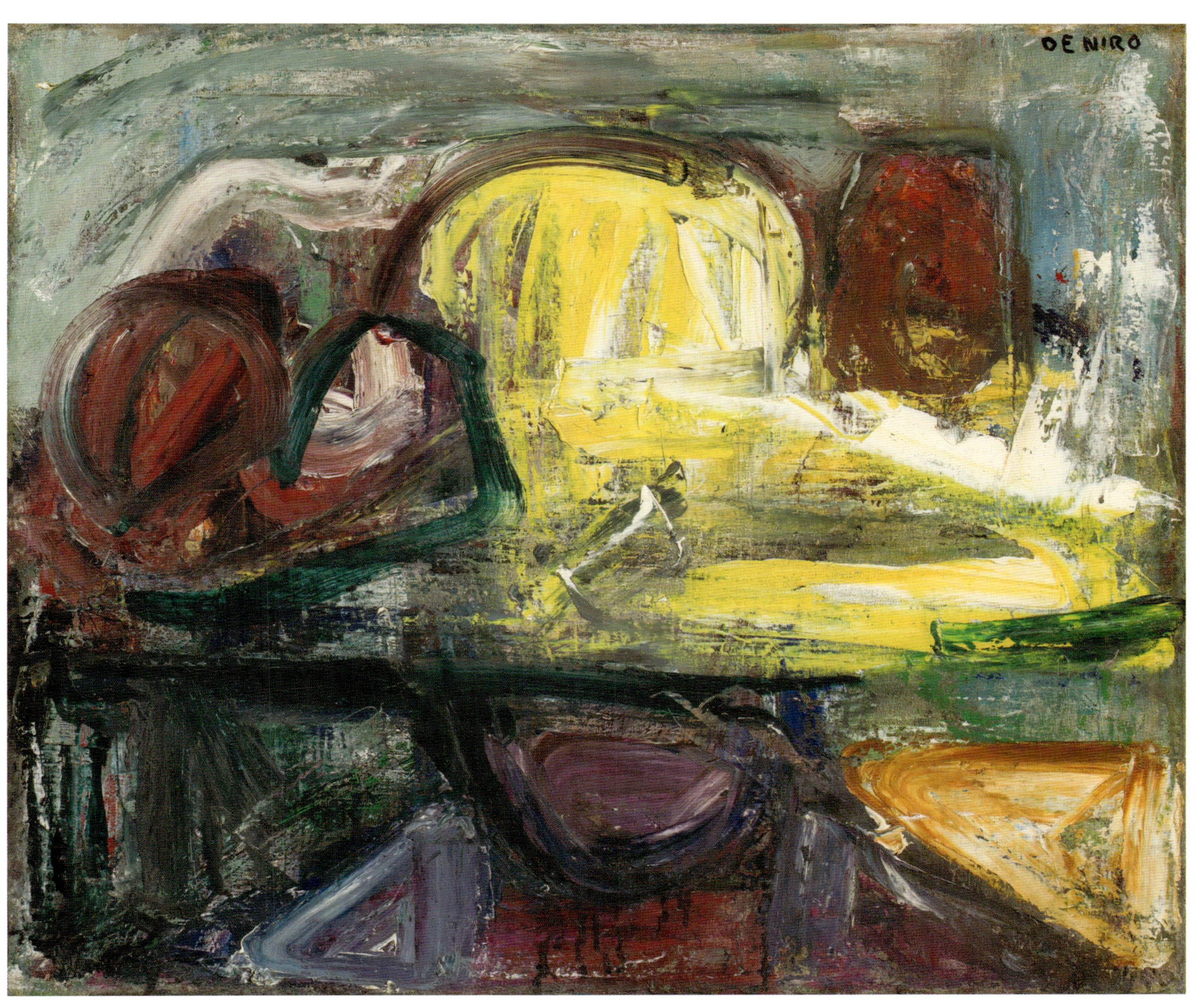

17. **Straw Hat with Flowers**, ca. 1952–53. Oil on canvas, 22½ x 26½ inches

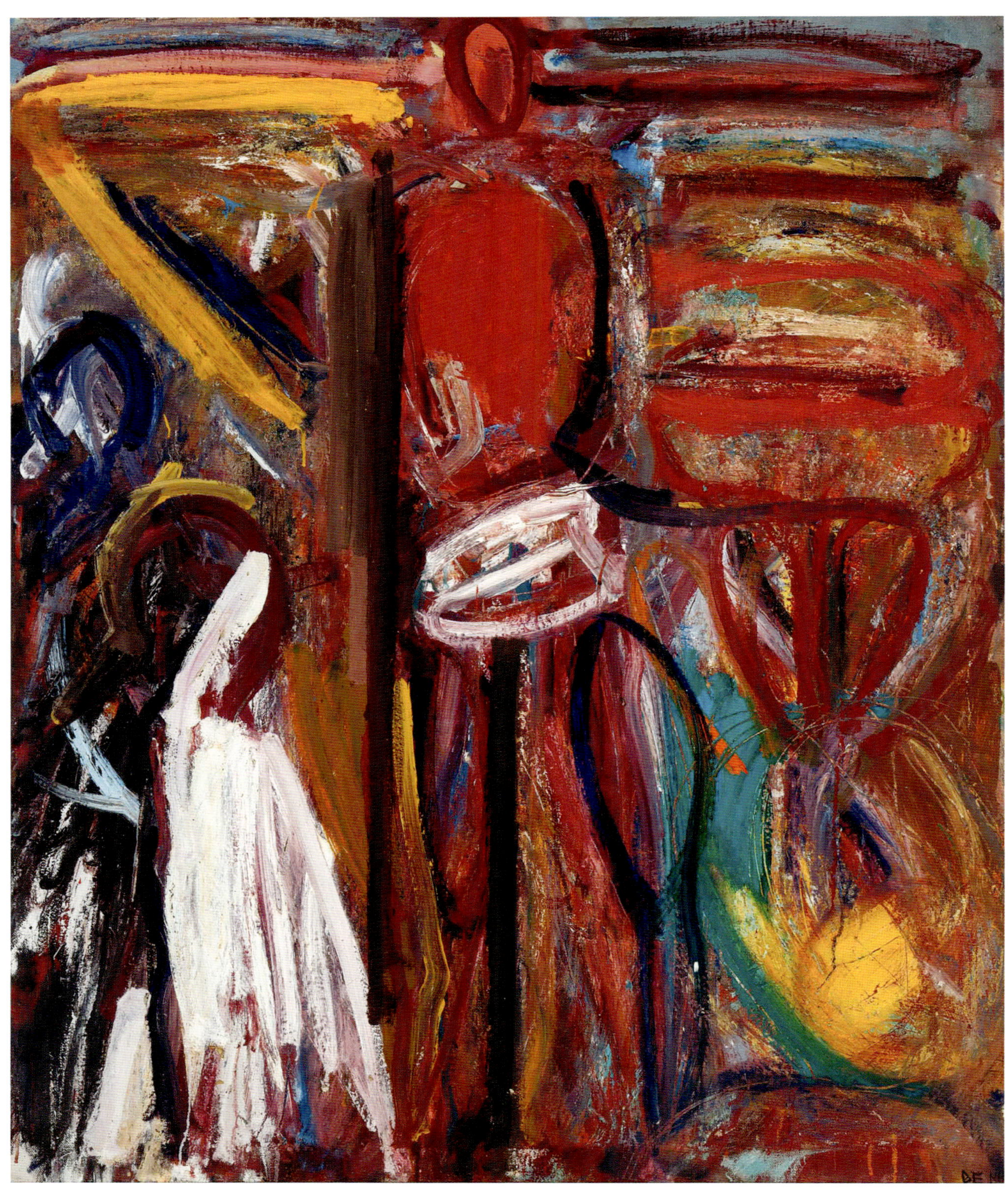

18. **Crucifixion**, 1952. Oil on canvas, 48 x 40 inches

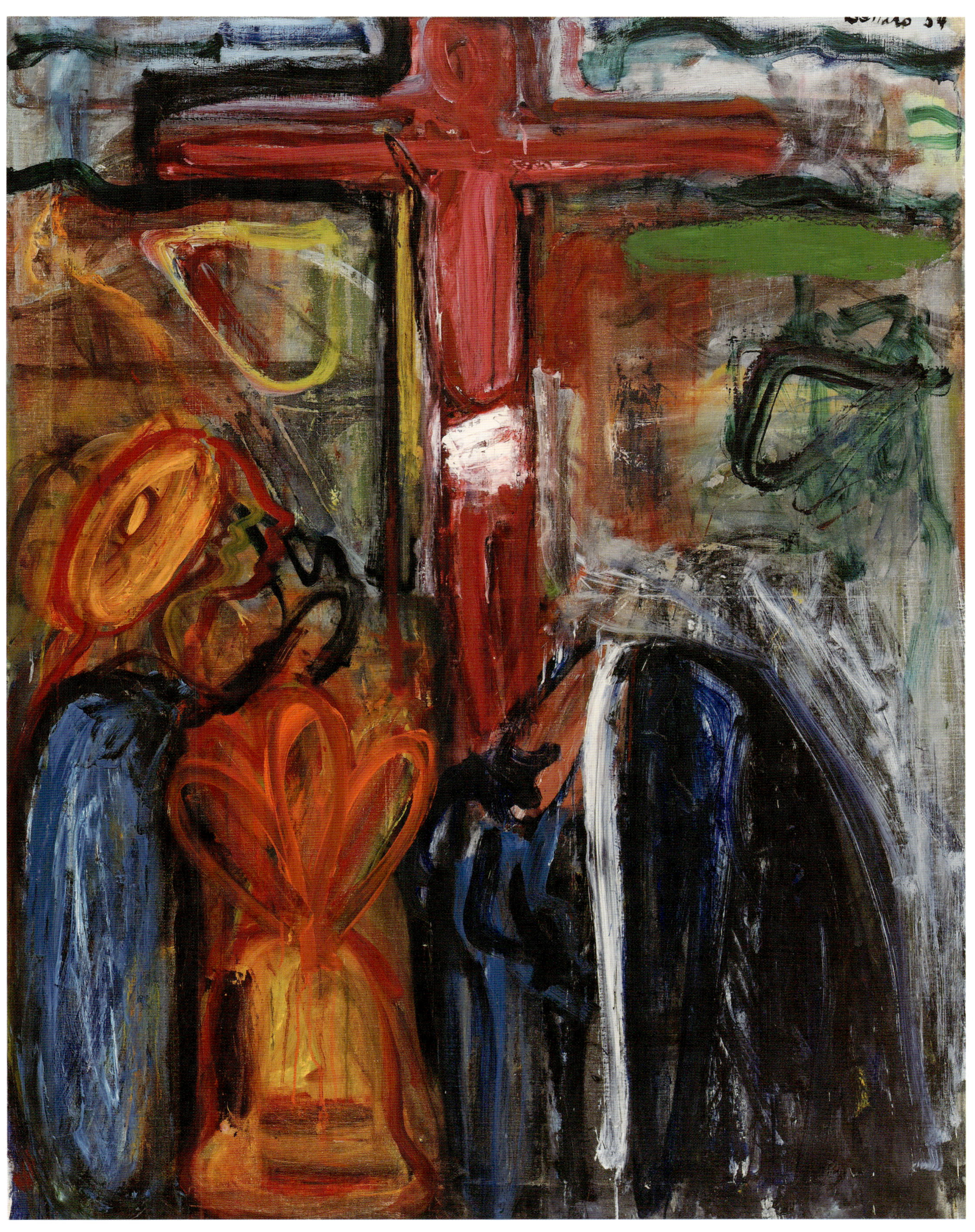

19. **Crucifixion**, 1954. Oil on canvas, 59 x 46 inches

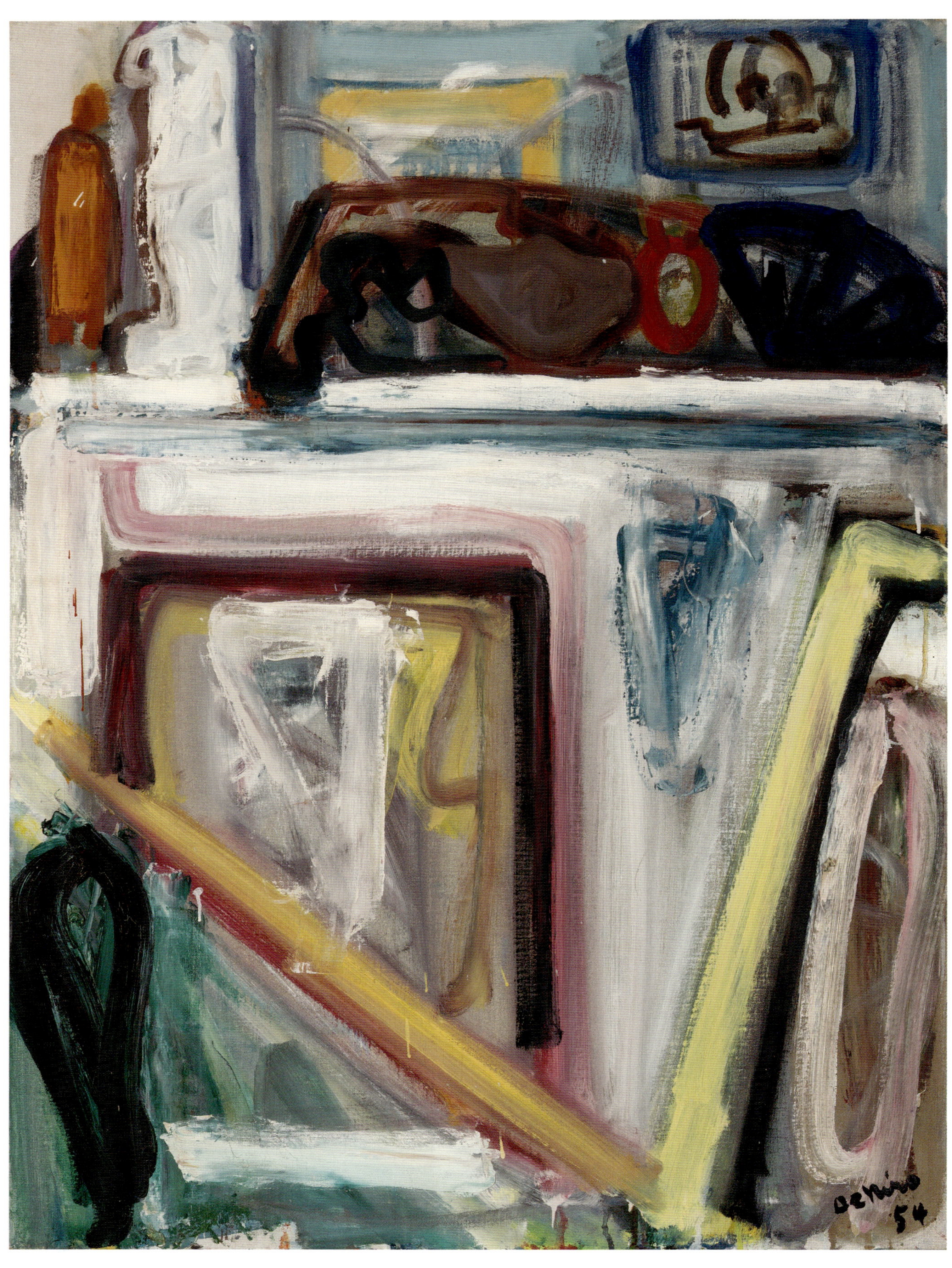

20. **Mantel with Black Fan and Plaster Cast no. 3**, 1954. Oil on canvas, 40 x 29½ inches

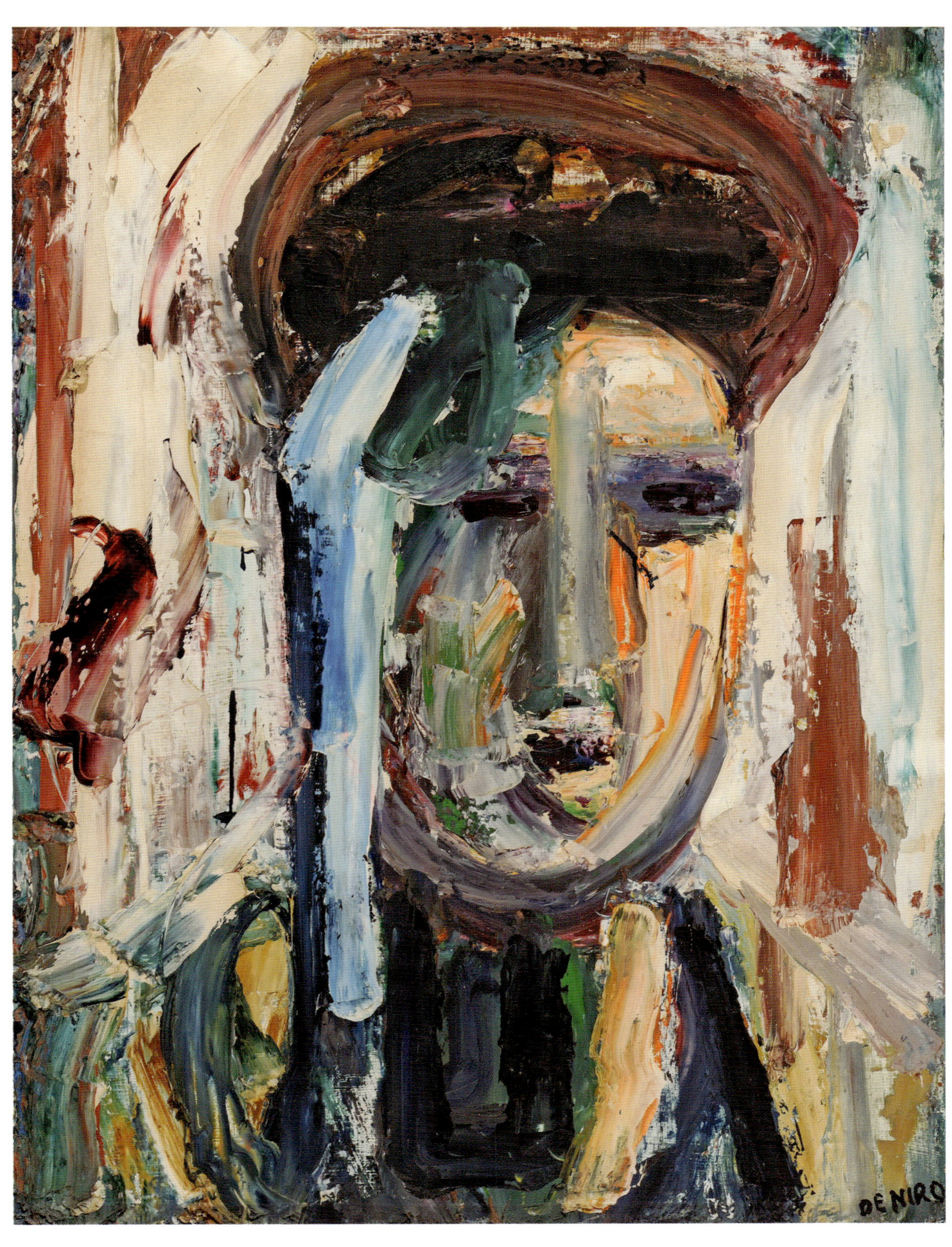

21. **Self-Portrait**, ca. 1954. Oil on Masonite, 25¾ x 19¾ inches

22. **Still Life with Plaster Cast**, 1954. Oil on canvas, 40¼ x 29¾ inches

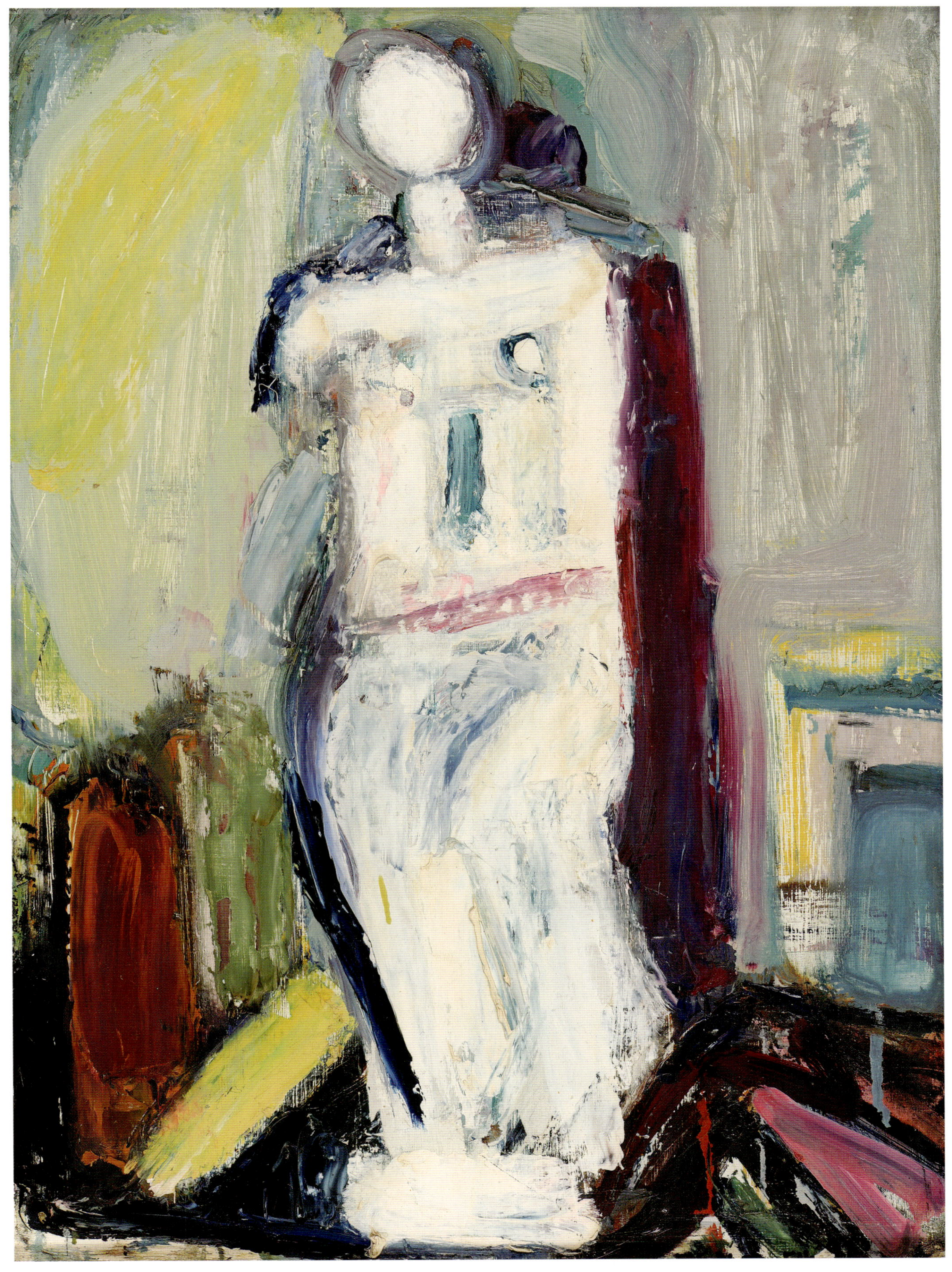

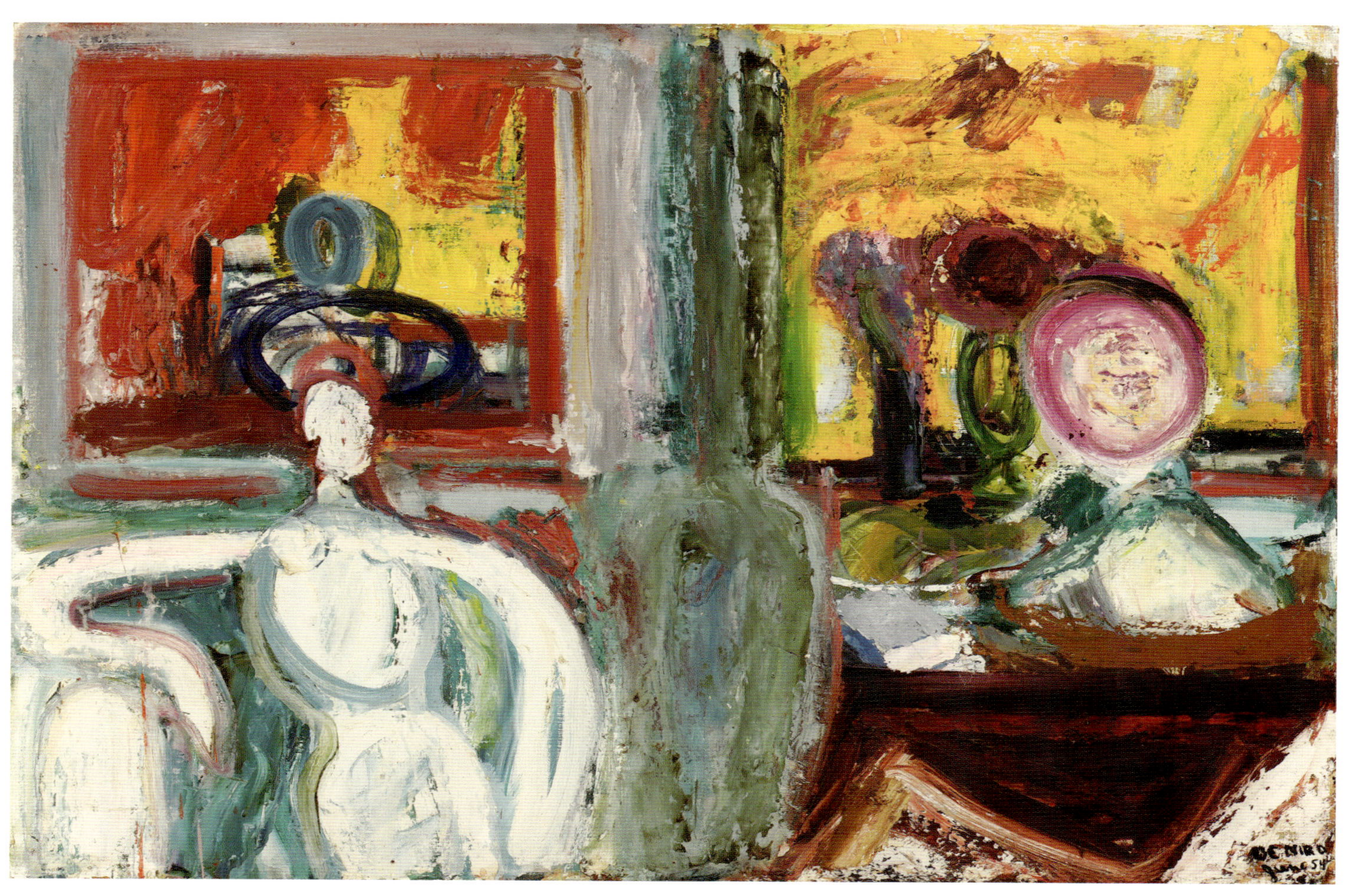

23. **Still Life with Plaster Statue**, 1954. Oil on canvas, 20⅜ x 31¾ inches

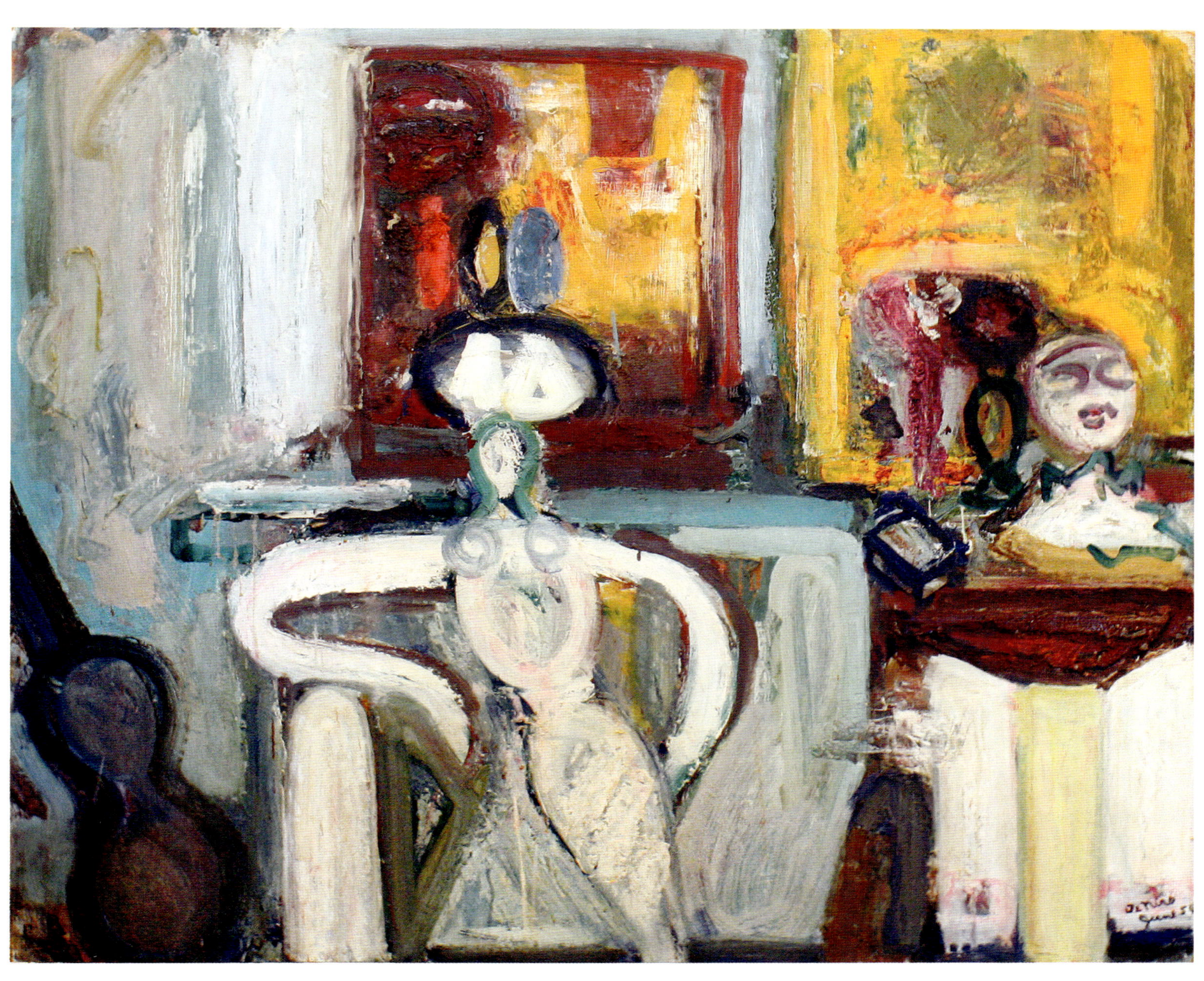

24. **Guitar, Plaster Statue**, 1954. Oil on board, 34 x 42 inches

25. **Seated Bathers**, 1954. Oil on canvas, 51 x 68 inches

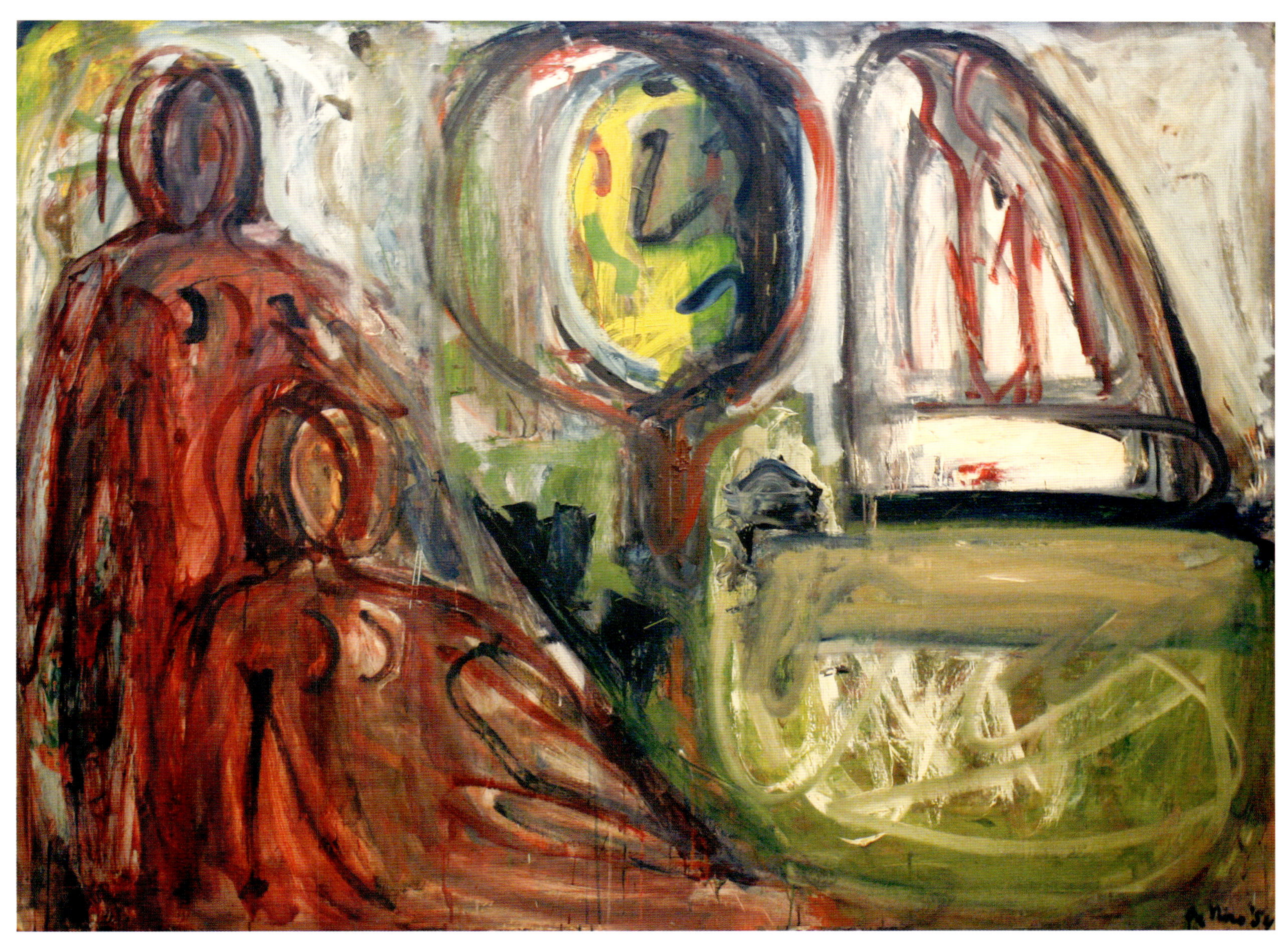

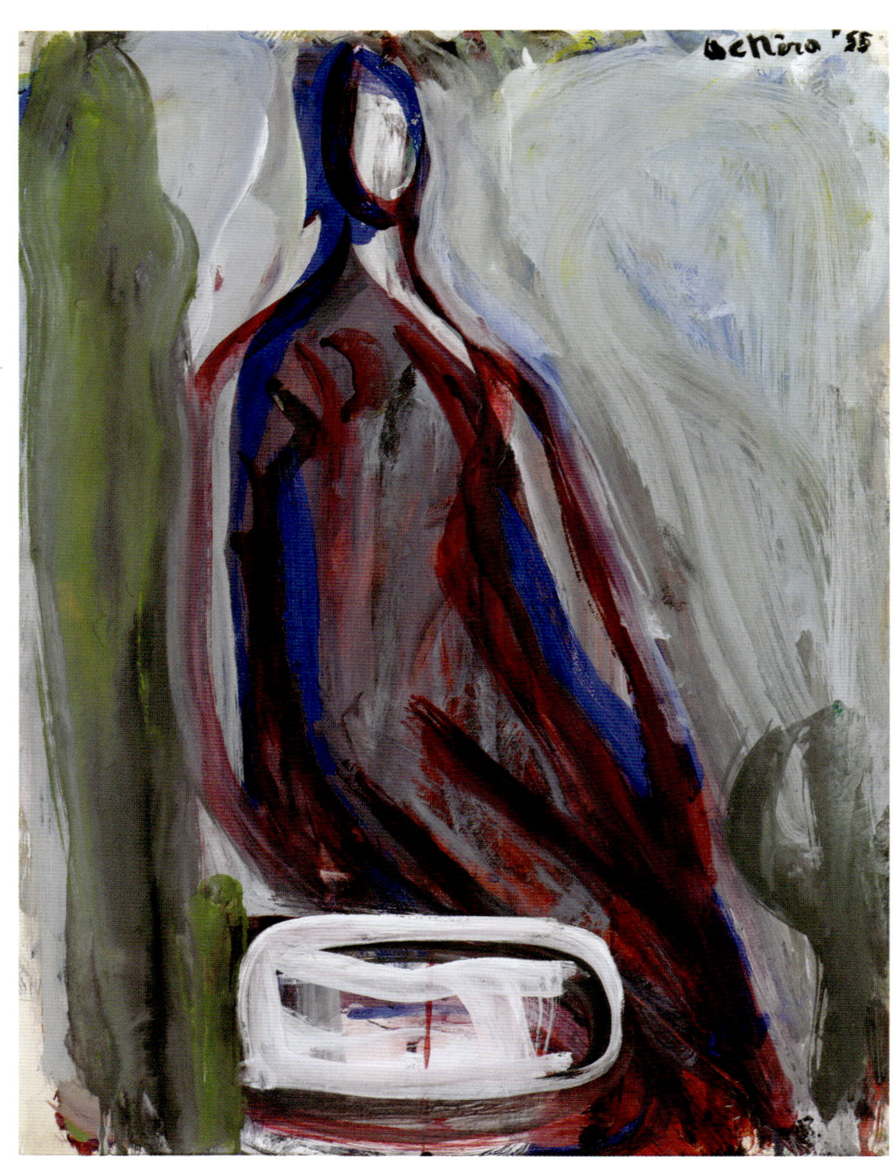

26. **Small Single Bather**, 1955. Tempera on paper, 20 x 15 inches

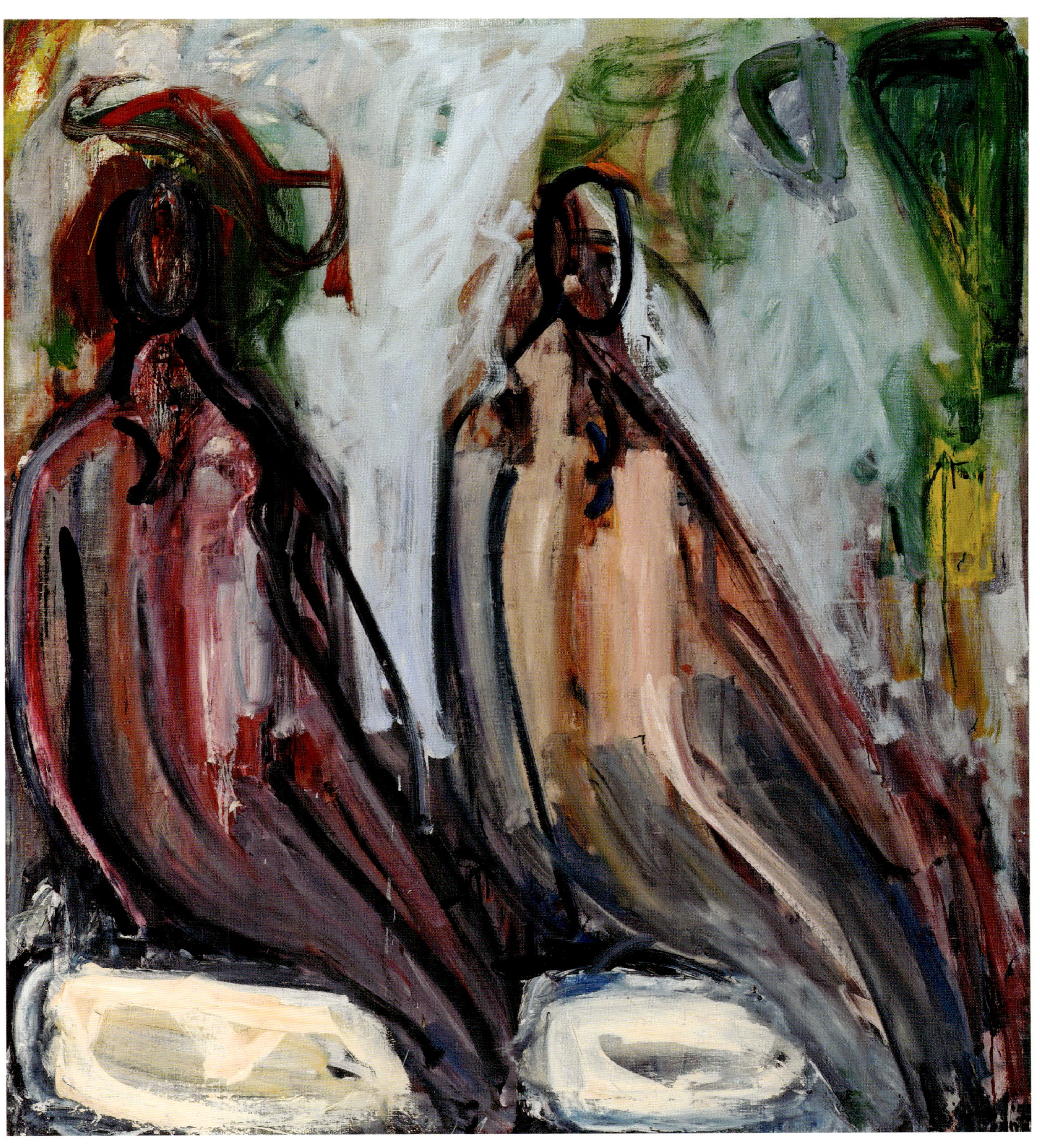

27. **Seated Bathers**, 1955. Oil on canvas, 56½ x 50½ inches

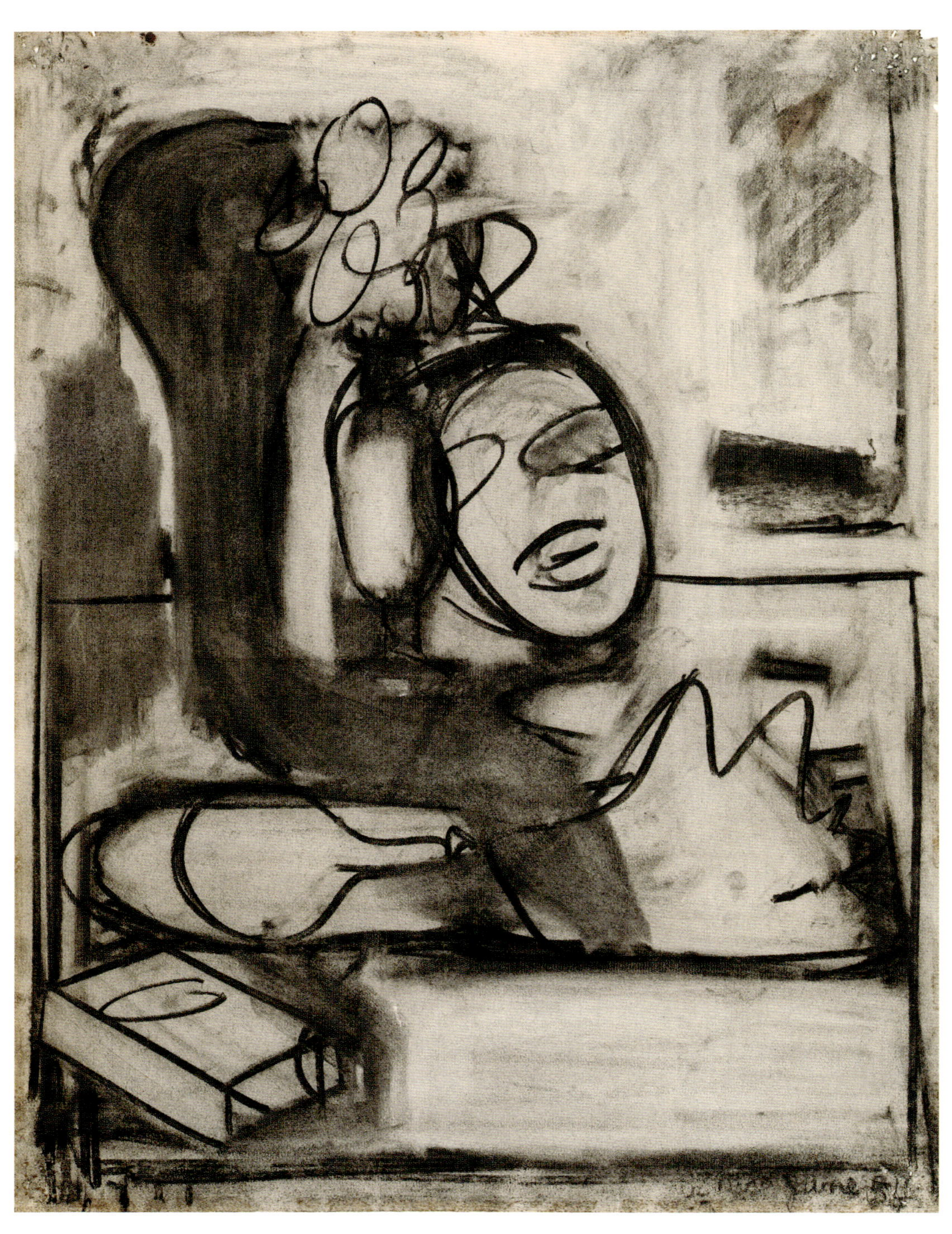

28. **Still Life – Flowers**, 1954. Charcoal and chalk on paper, 25 ½ x 19 ¾ inches

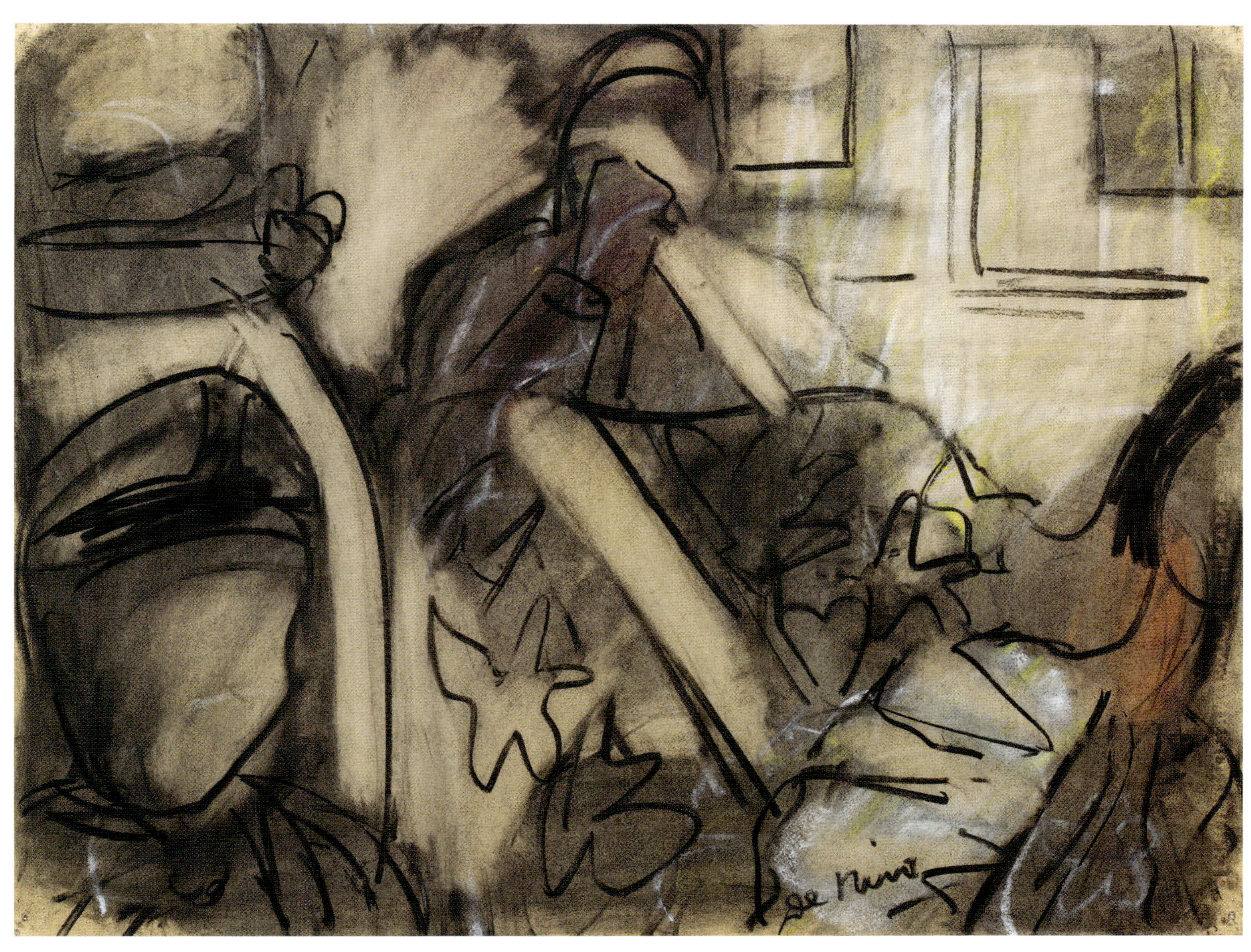

29. **Untitled (Figurative)**, 1955. Charcoal and pastel on paper, 19¾ x 25½ inches

30. **Bonjour Mr. De Niro**, ca. 1955. Oil on canvas, 35¾ x 47¾ inches

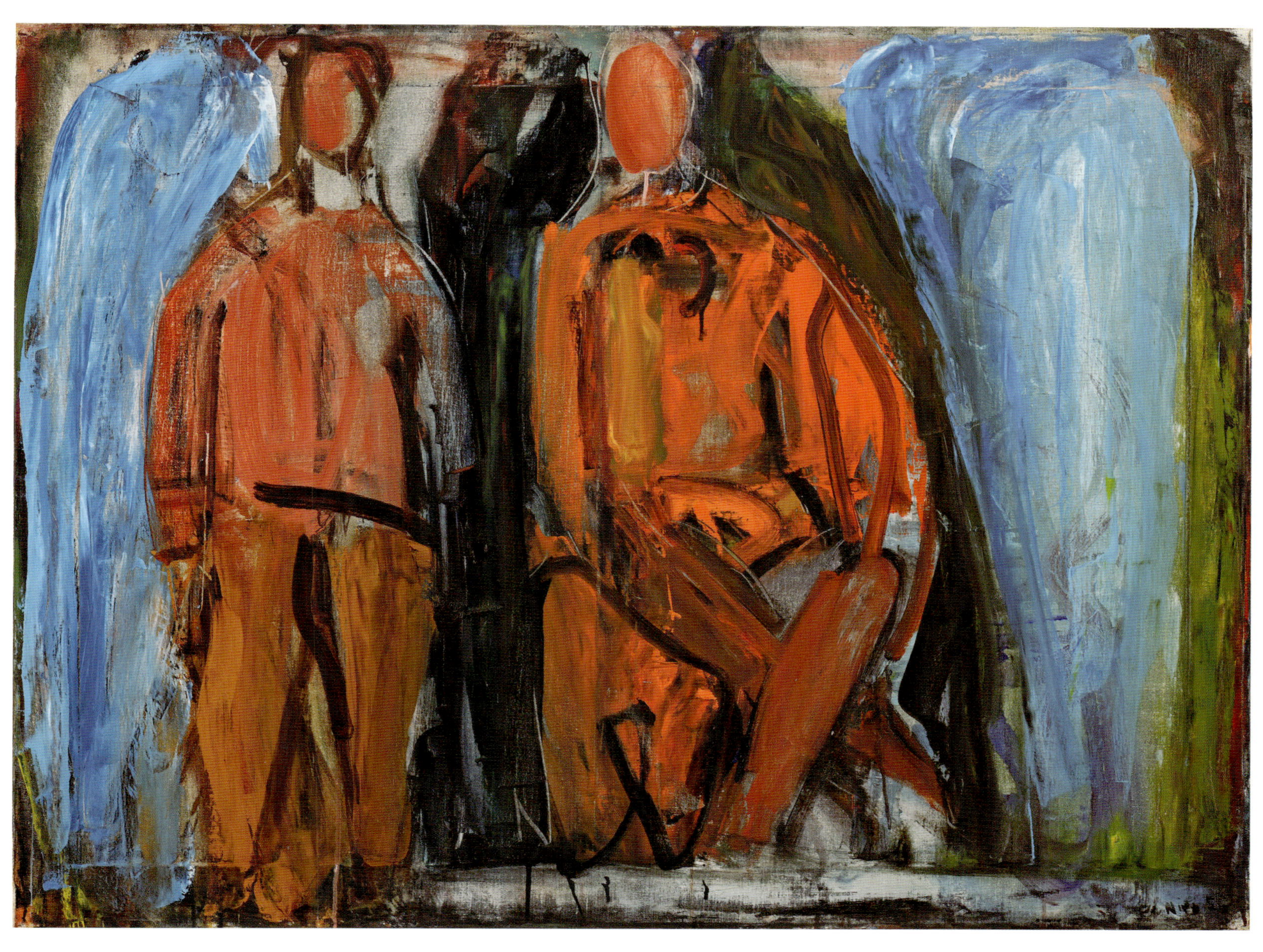

31. **River Bathers**, 1956. Oil on canvas, 60 x 72 inches

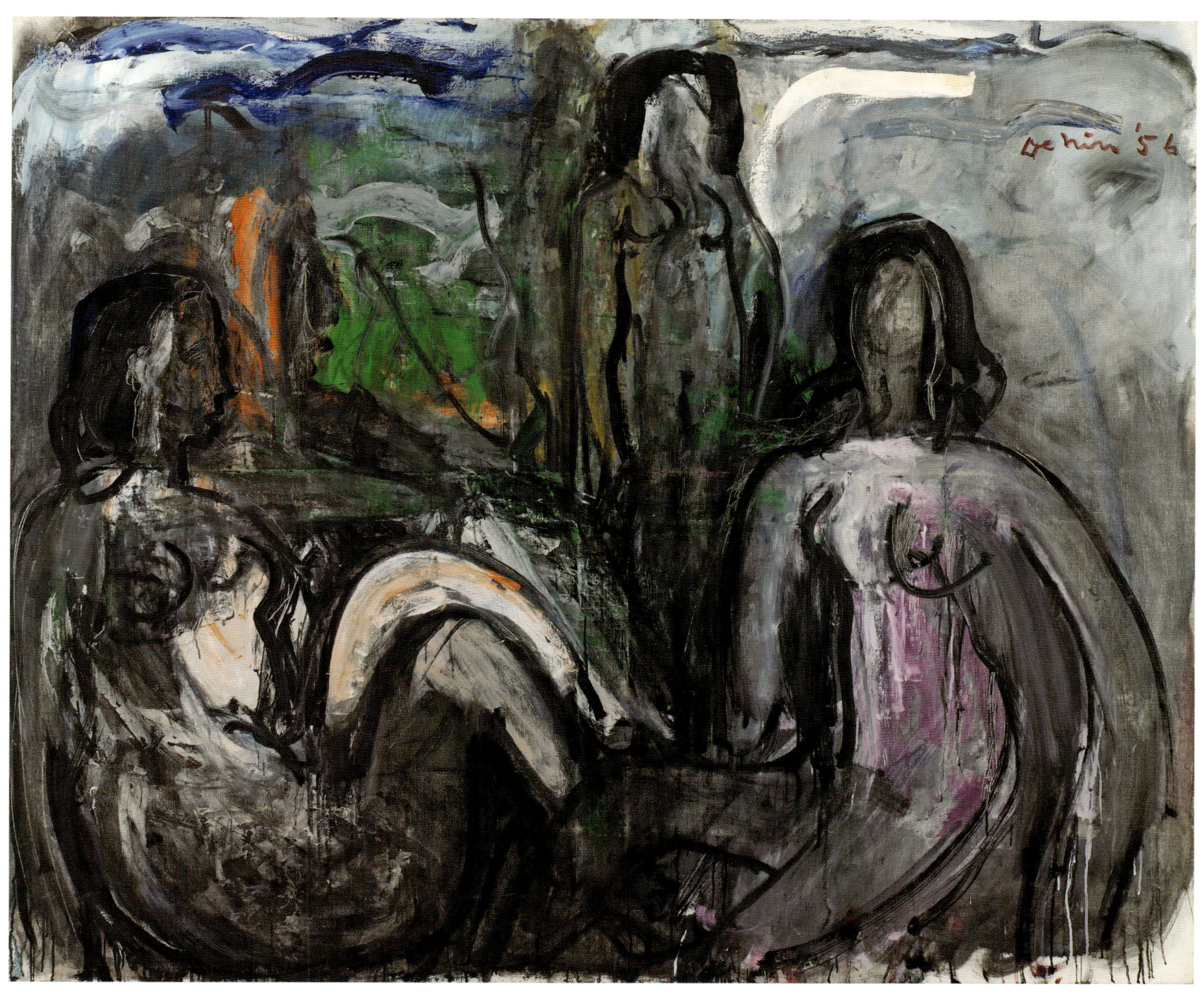

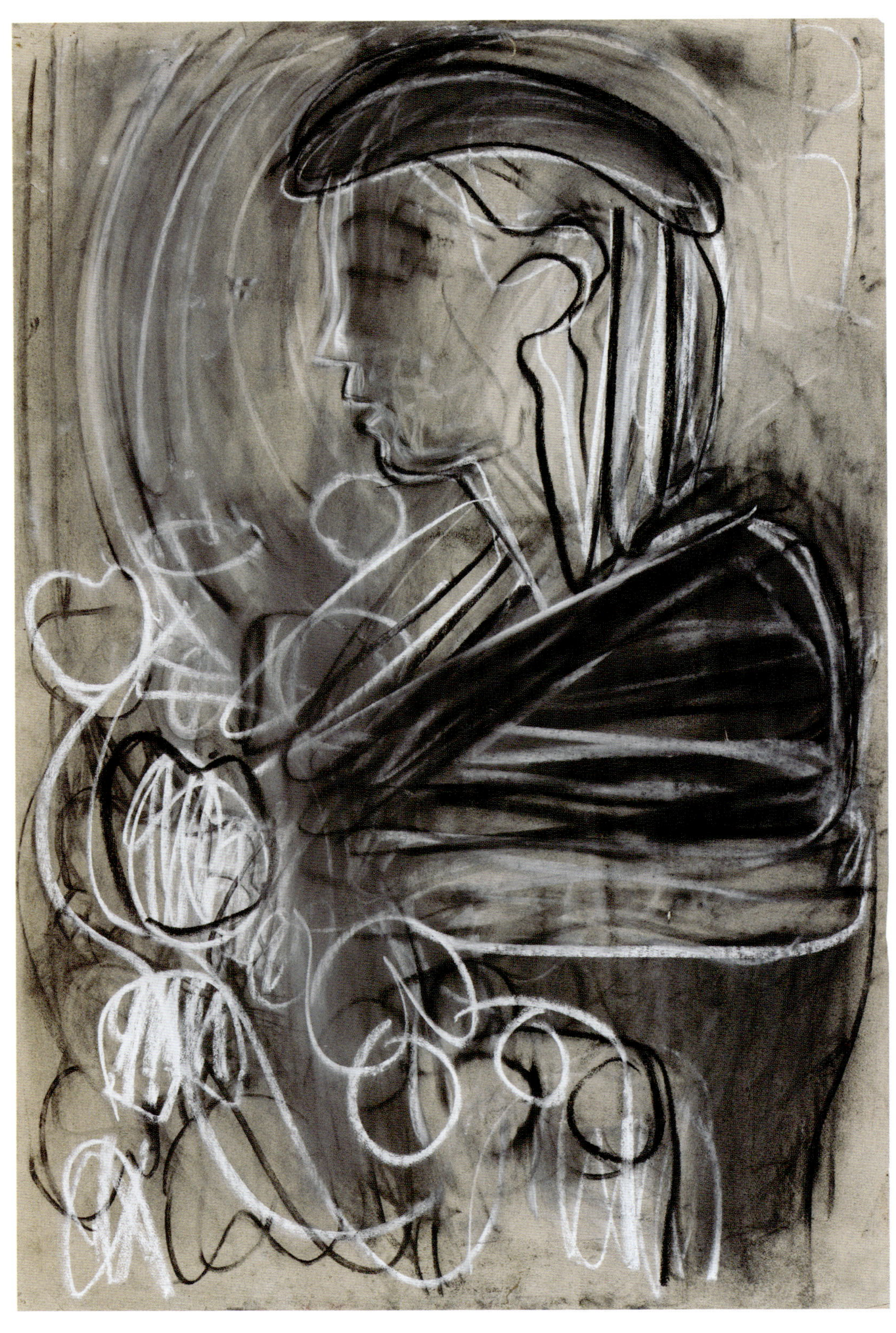

32. **Greta**, n.d. Charcoal and chalk on paper, 36 x 23 ¾ inches

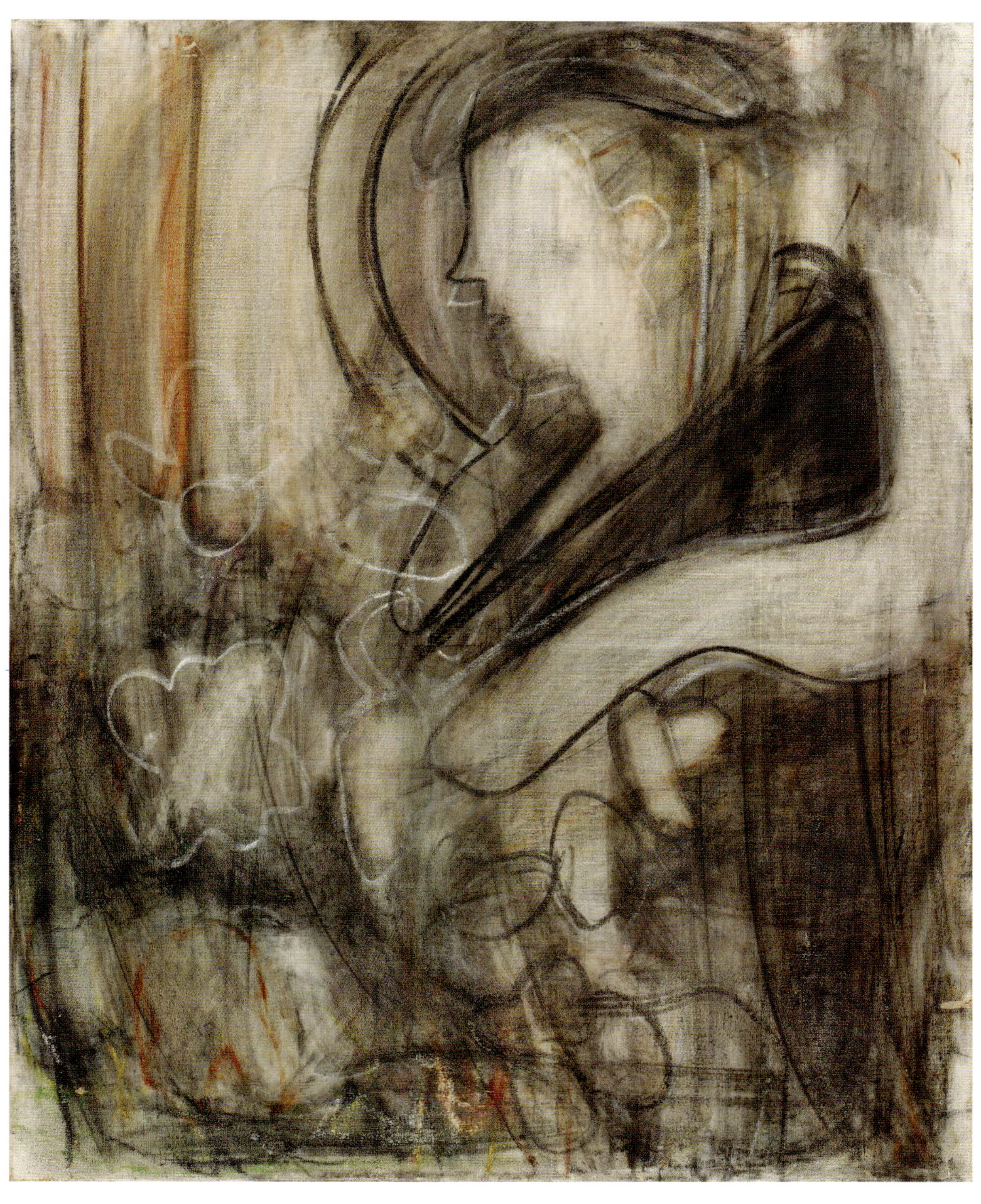

33. **Garbo**, n.d. Charcoal and chalk on paper, 30¼ x 24¼ inches

34. **Garbo as Anna Christie**, 1957. Oil on canvas, 31⅛ x 36¼ inches

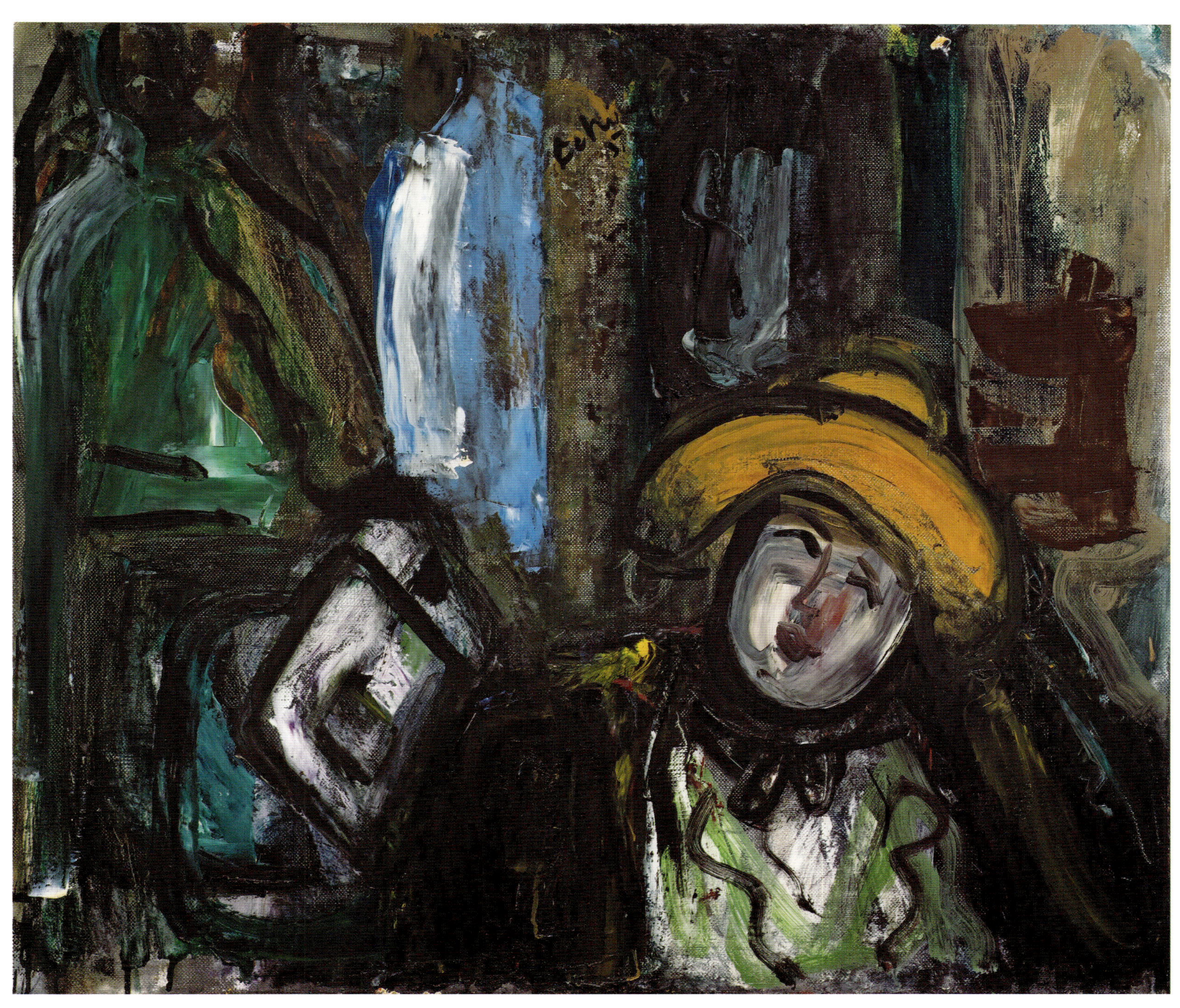

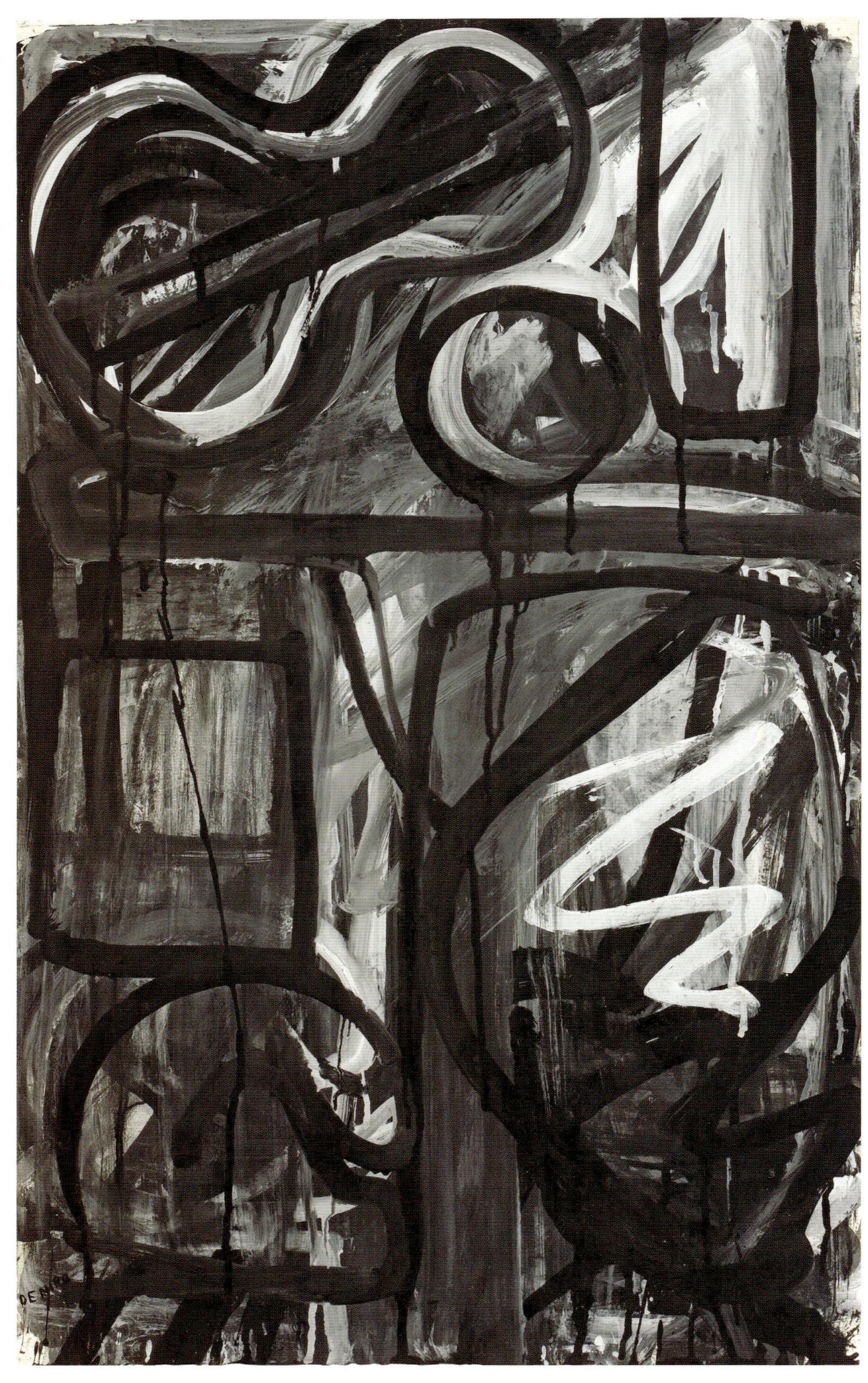

35. **Still Life with Dog**, 1958–59. Gouache and ink on paper, 30¼ x 18¼ inches

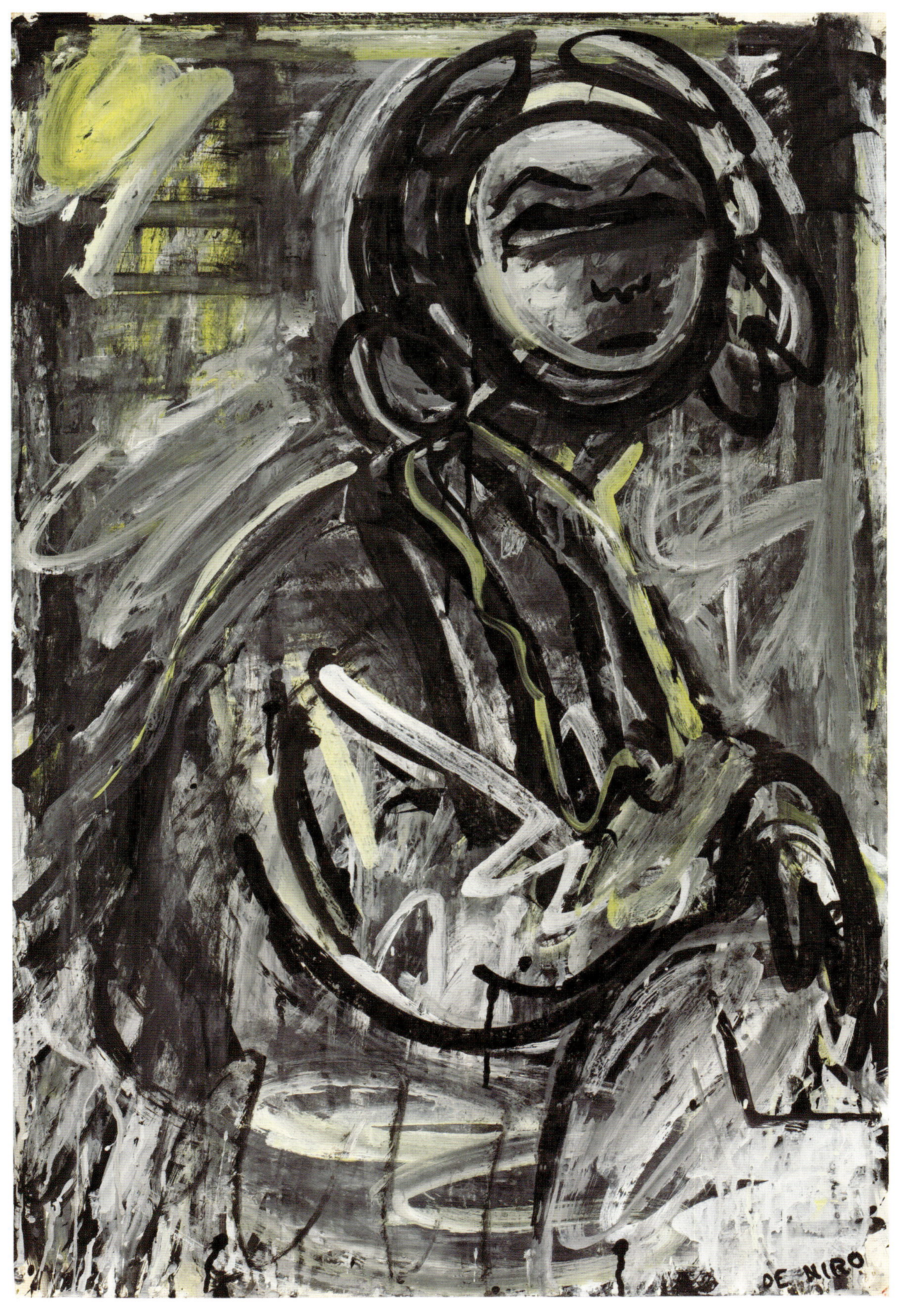

36. **Lola Montez with Cigarette**, 1958–59. Gouache and ink on paper, 36 x 24 inches

37. **Portrait of Mrs. Z**, 1959. Oil on canvas, 38¼ x 34¼ inches

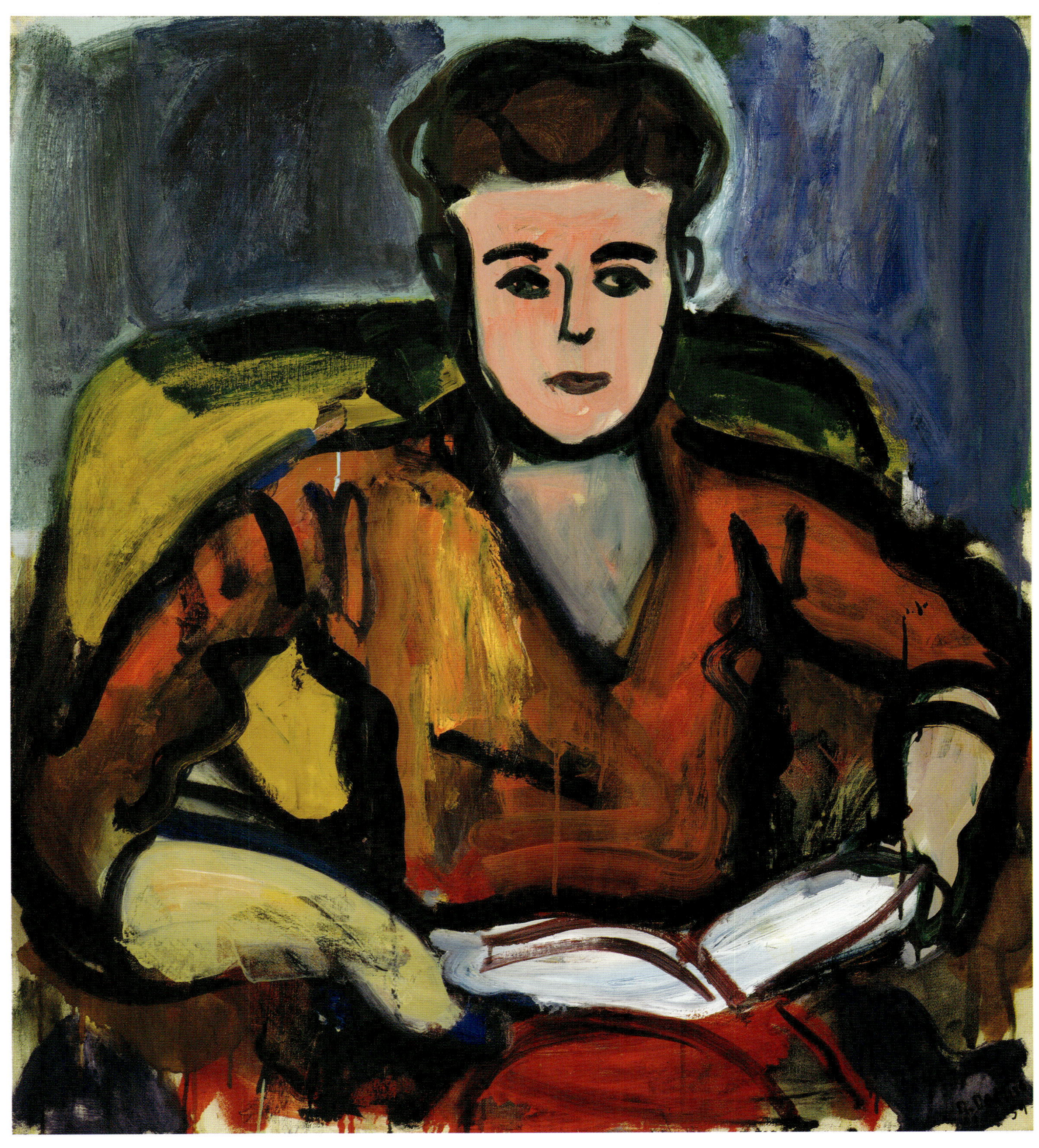

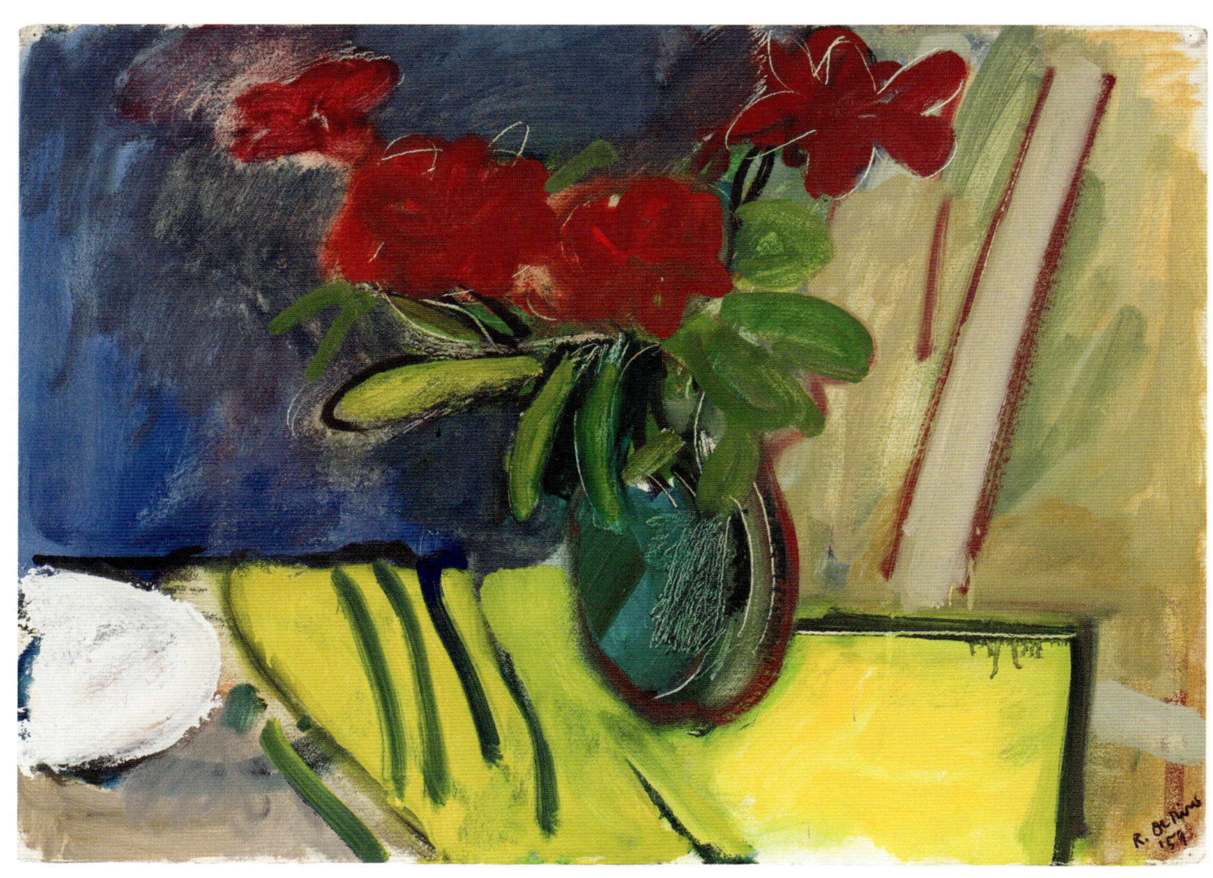

38. **Still Life**, 1959. Oil on paper, 22 ½ x 31 inches

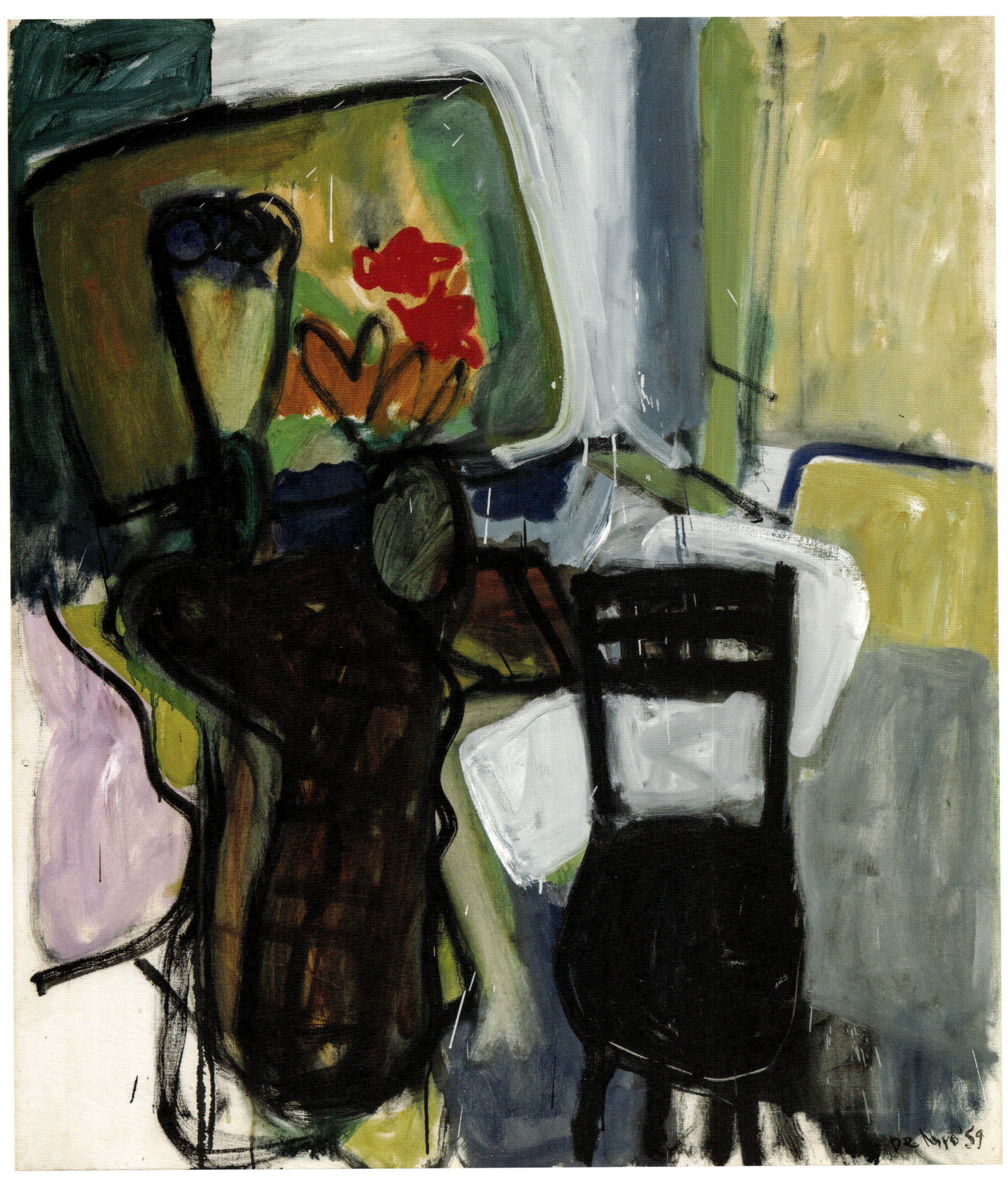

39. **Still Life and Chair**, 1959. Oil on canvas, 50 x 42 inches

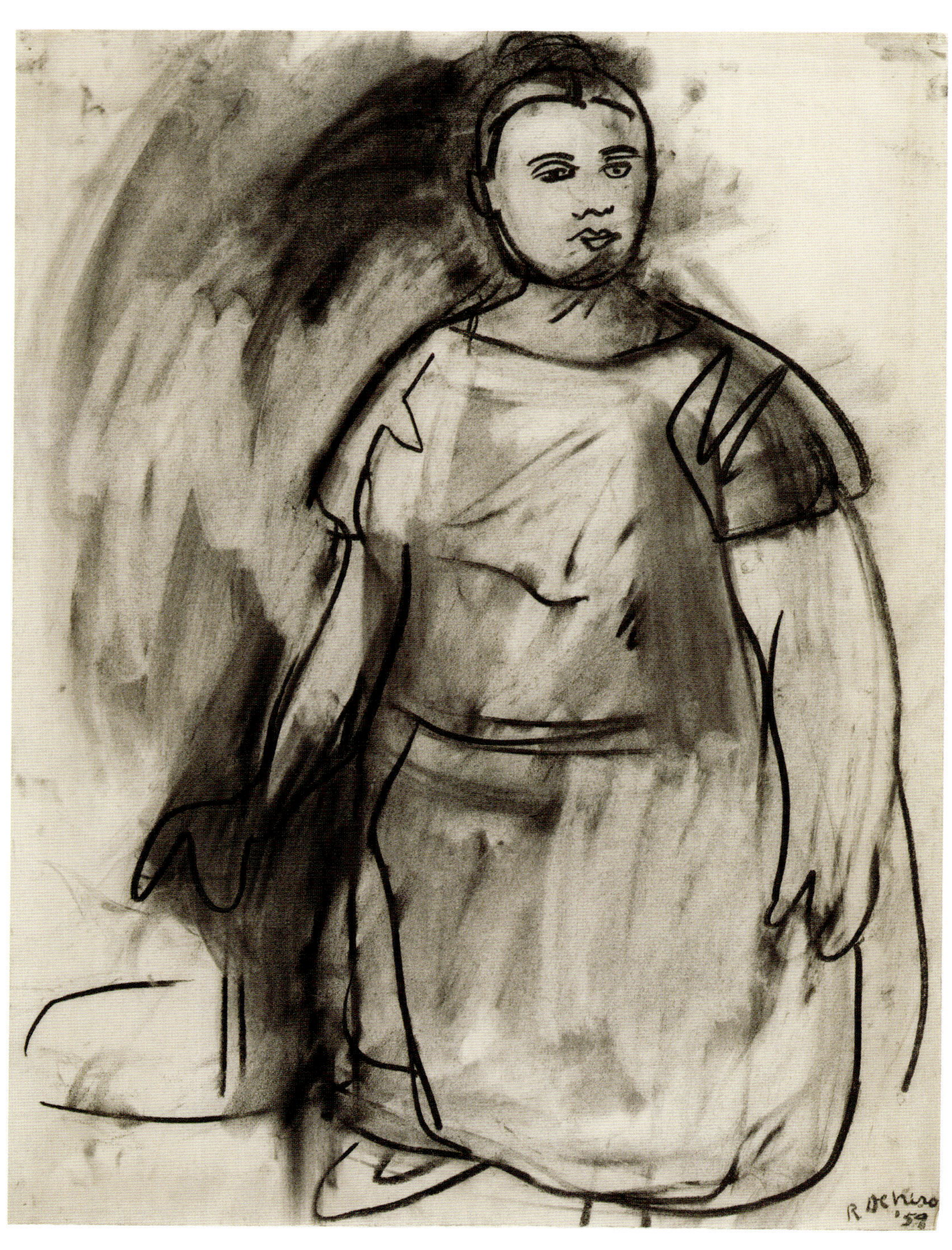

40. **Standing Woman**, 1959. Charcoal on paper, 25½ x 19¼ inches

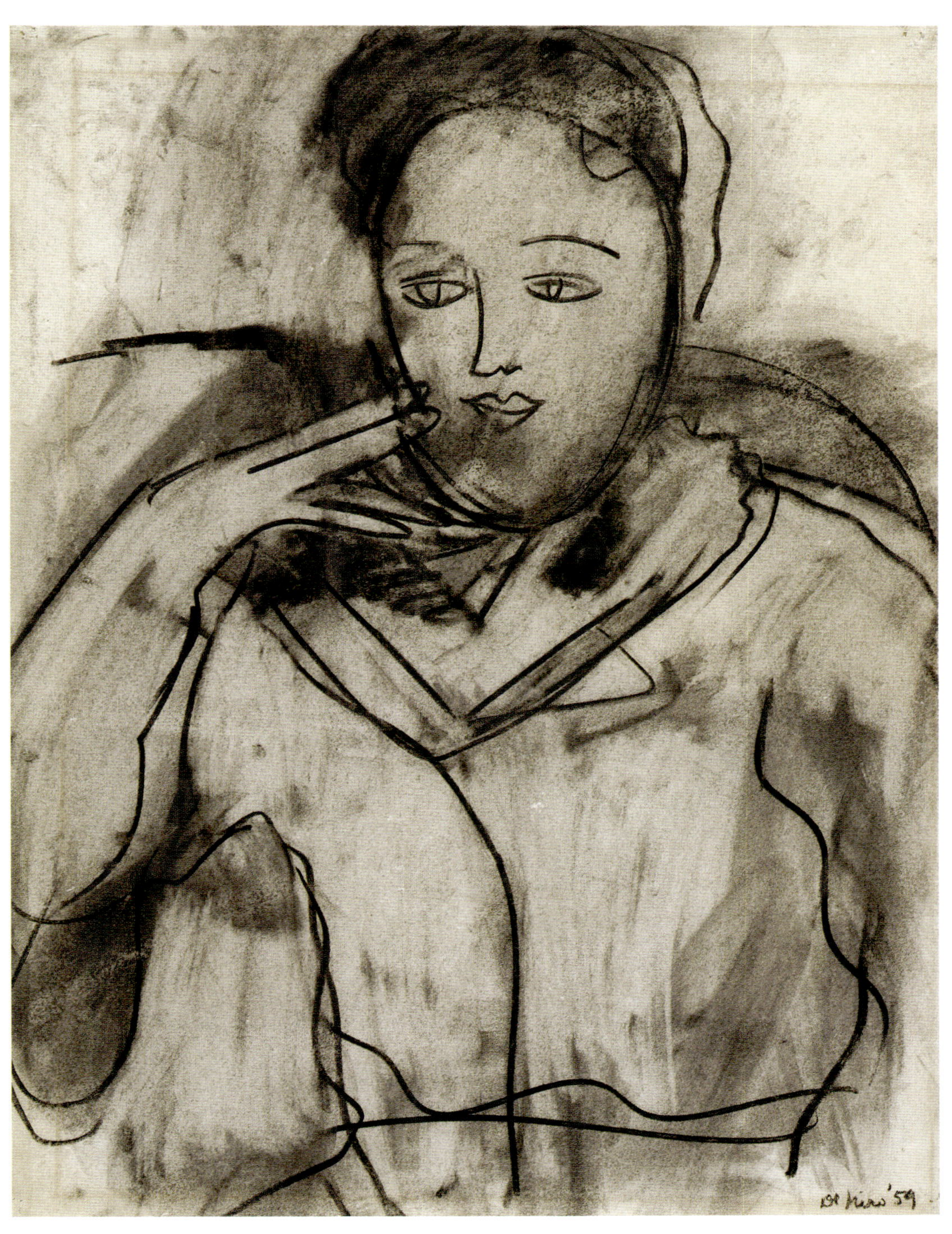

41. **Portrait of a Woman**, 1959. Charcoal on paper, 25 x 19 inches

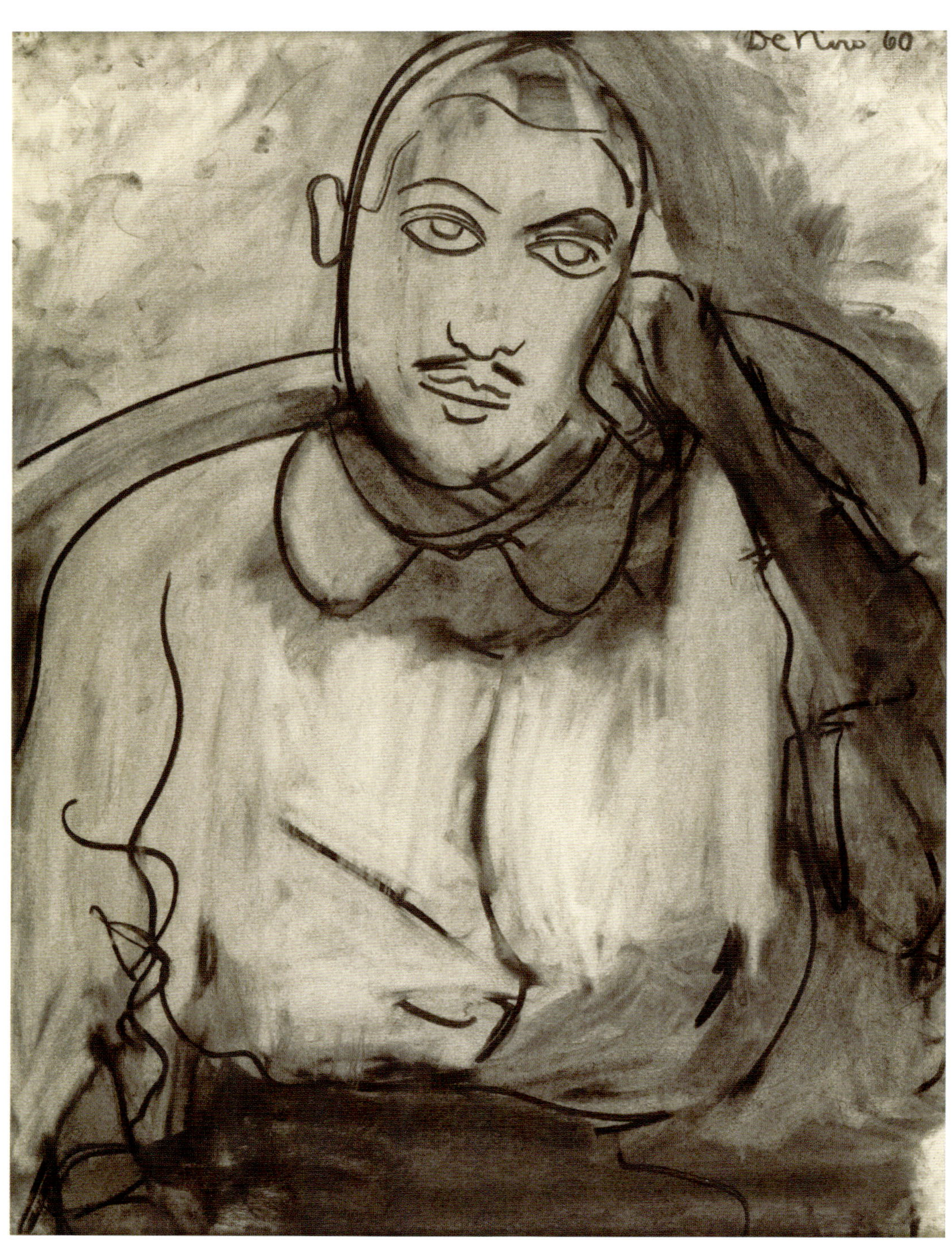

42. **Portrait of a Man with Moustache**, 1960. Charcoal on paper, 24½ x 18½ inches

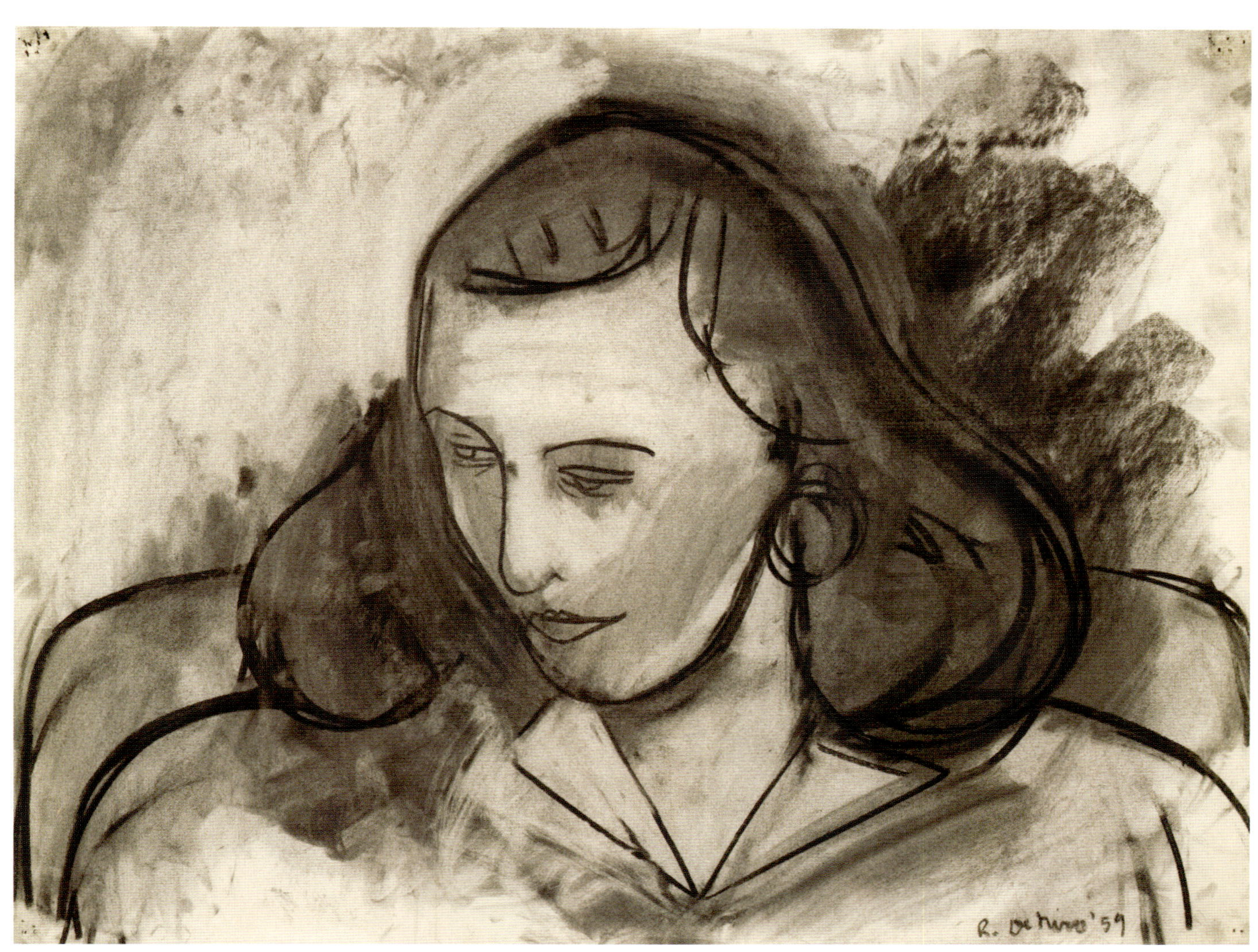

43. **Portrait of a Young Woman**, 1959. Charcoal on paper, 19 ½ x 25 ½ inches

44. **Portrait of Cynthia**, 1960. Oil on canvas, 44 ⅛ x 30¼ inches

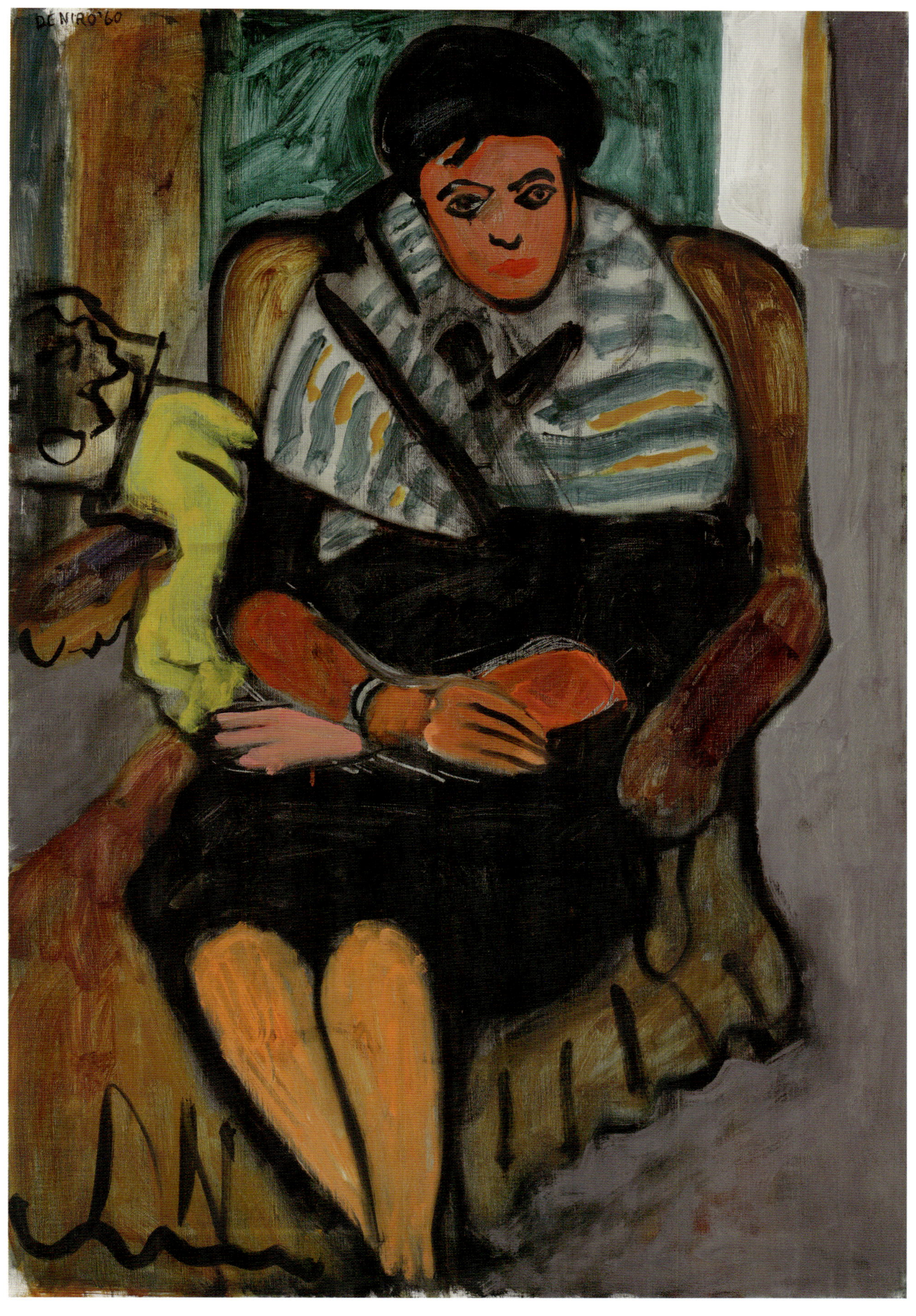
DE NIRO '60

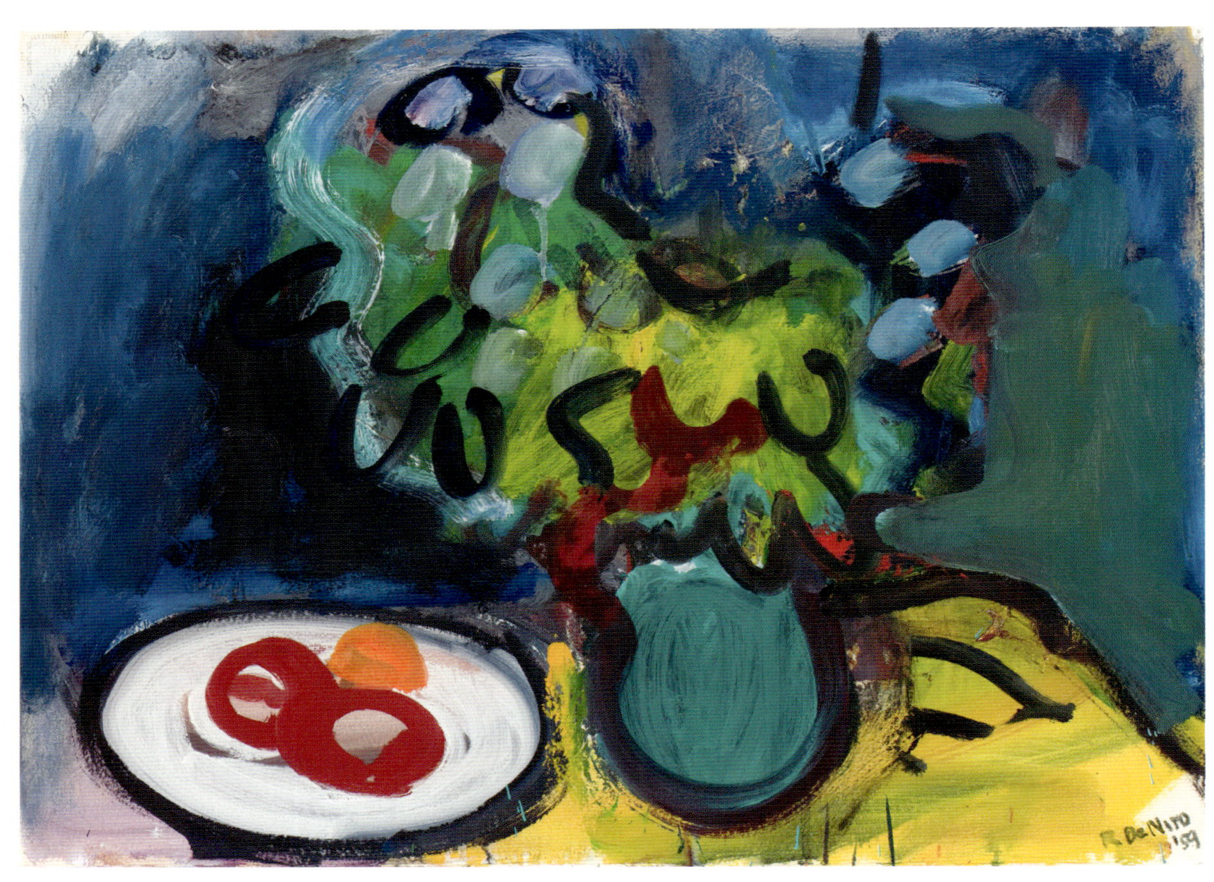

45. **Still Life**, 1959. Oil on paper, 22½ x 30½ inches

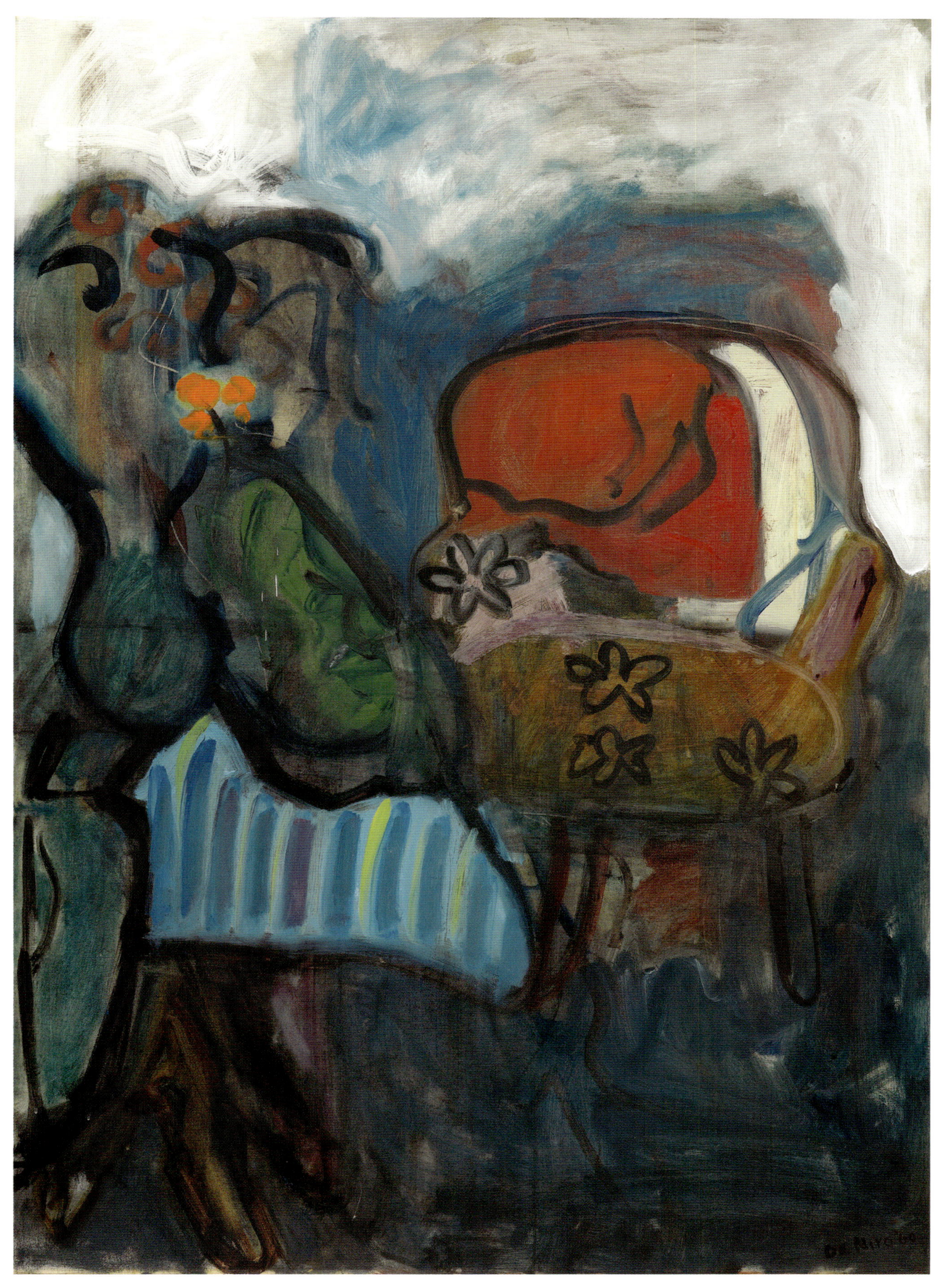

46. **Untitled (Still Life with Chair)**, 1960. Oil on linen, 54 x 38 inches

47. **Still Life with Greek Head**, 1955. Oil on canvas, 30 x 22 inches

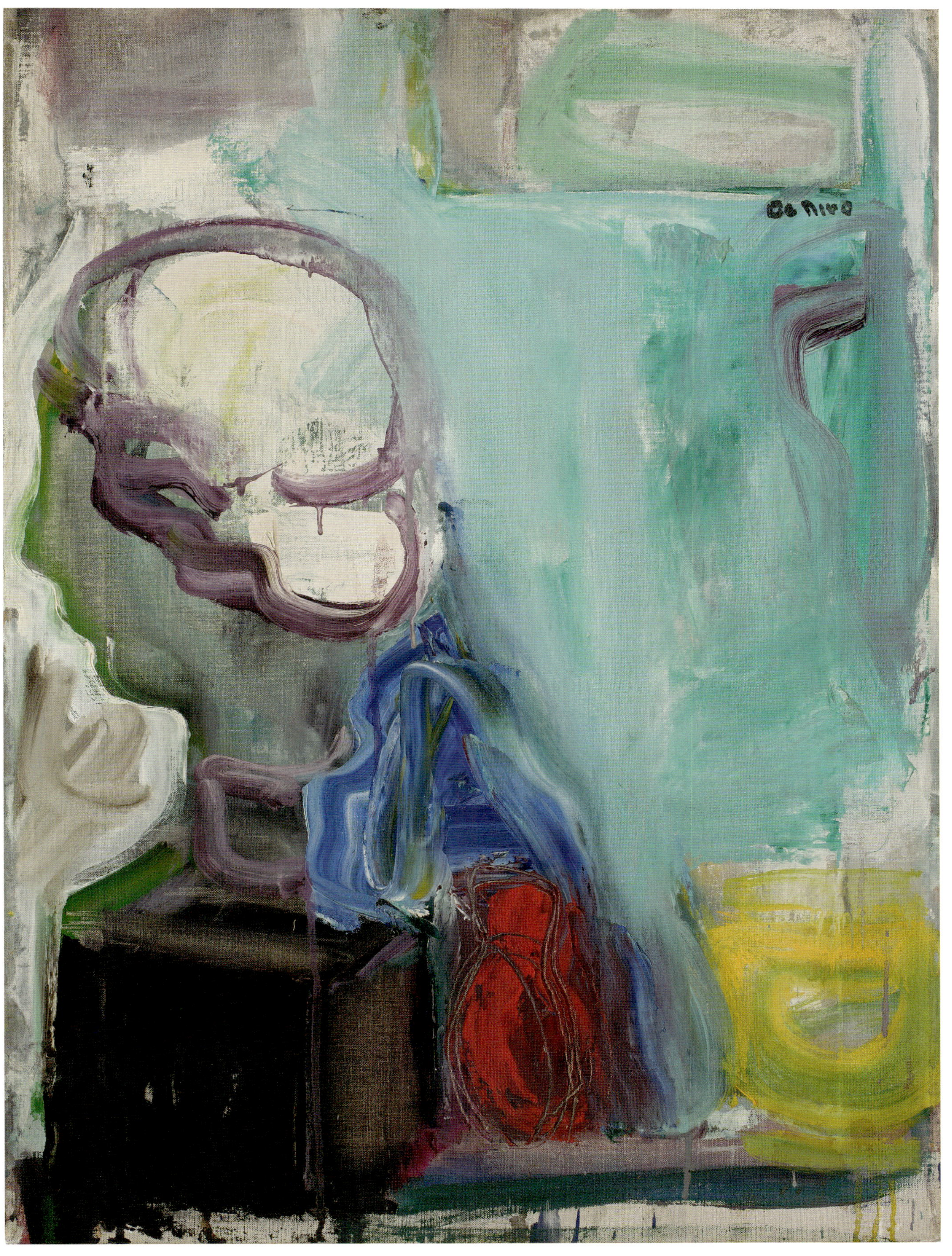
De Niro

48. **Untitled Still Life**, 1960. Oil on linen, 46⅛ x 36¼ inches

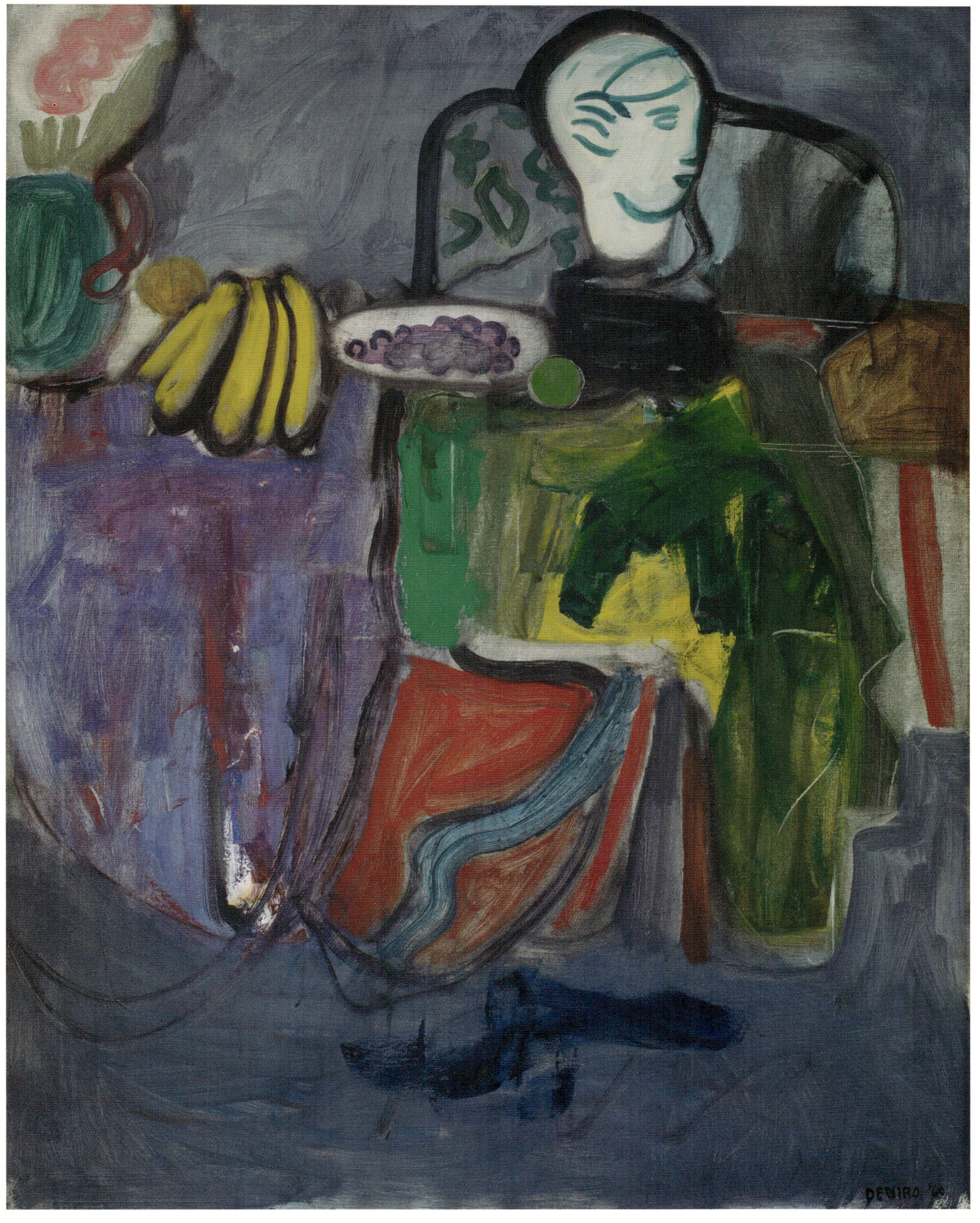

49. **Self-Portrait**, 1960. Oil and watercolor on paper, 22 x 30 inches

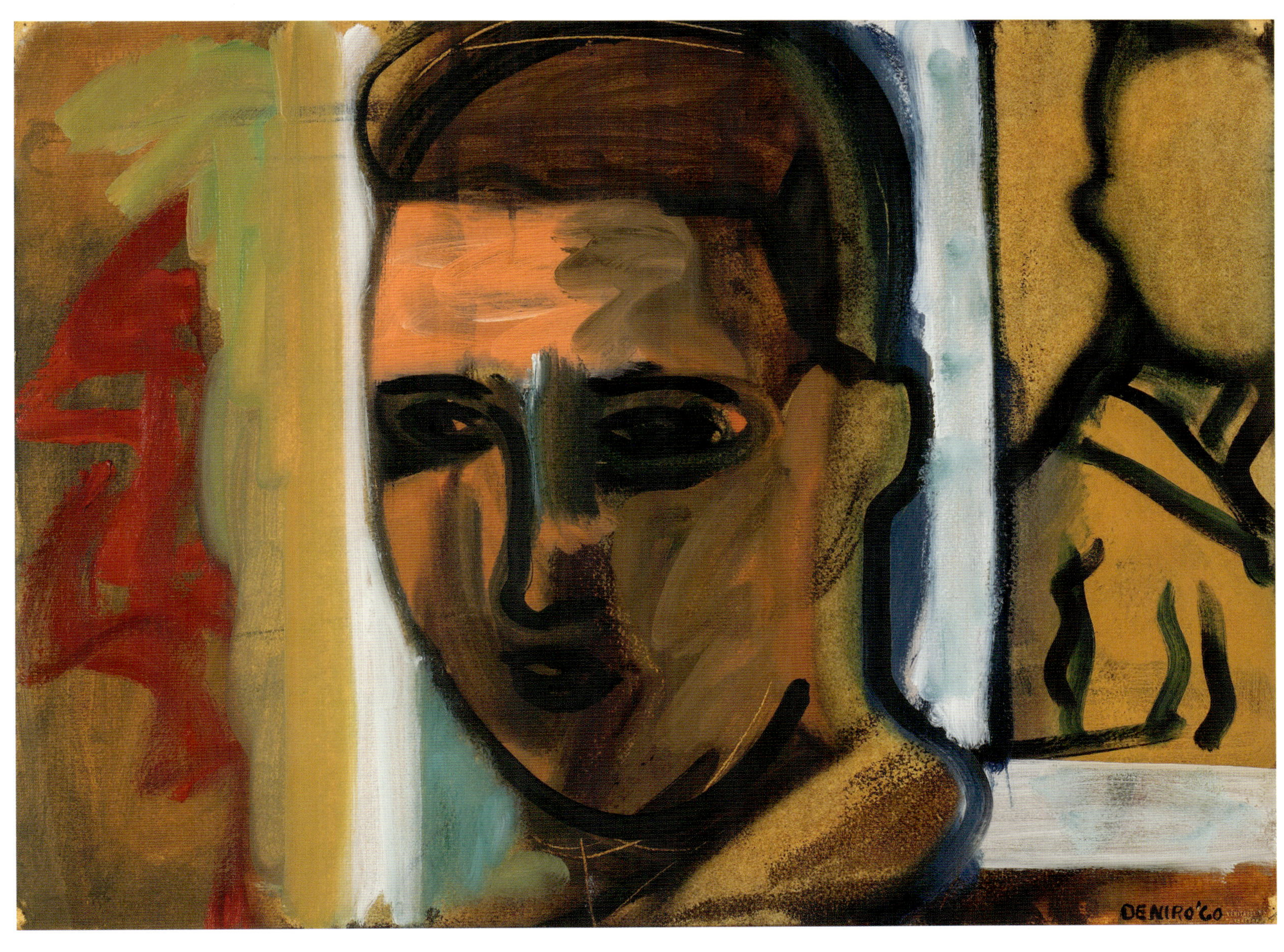
DENIRO'60

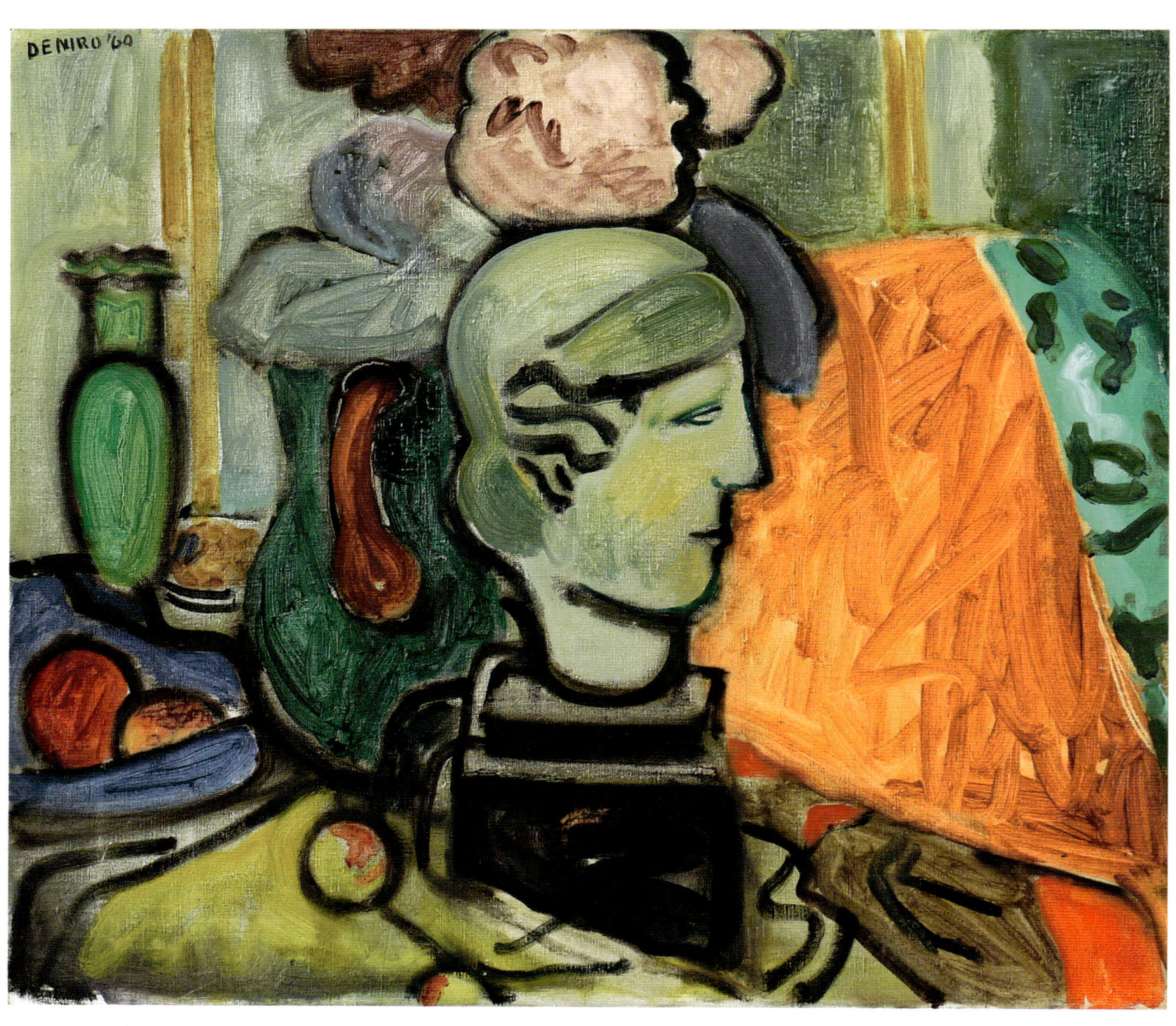

50. **Studio Still Life with Head of a Woman**, 1960. Oil on canvas, 26 x 30 inches

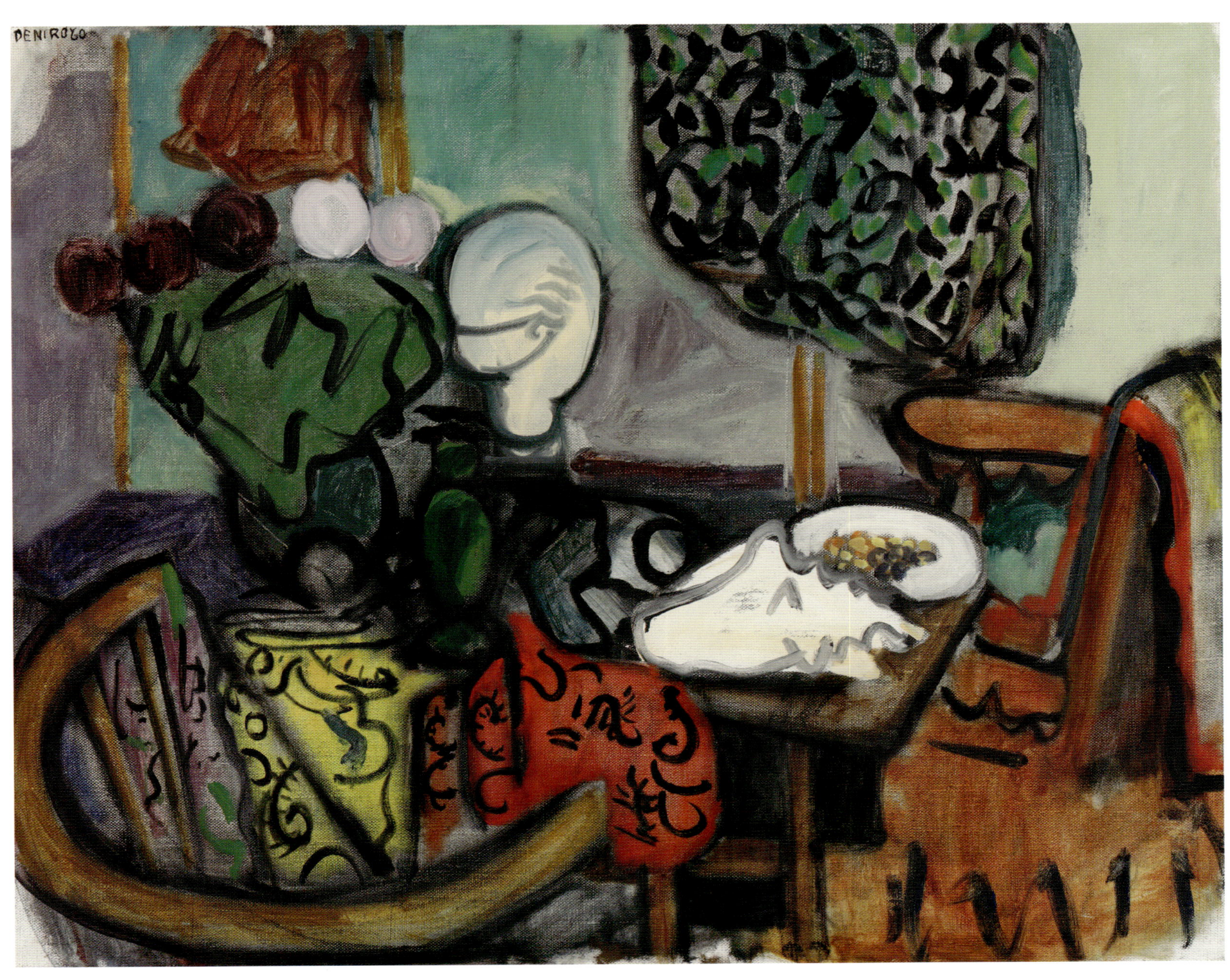

51. **Pattern Still Life #1**, 1960. Oil on canvas, 40 x 50 ⅛ inches

52. **Still Life with Fruit and Flowers on a Table**, 1961. Oil on canvas, 29 x 36¼ inches

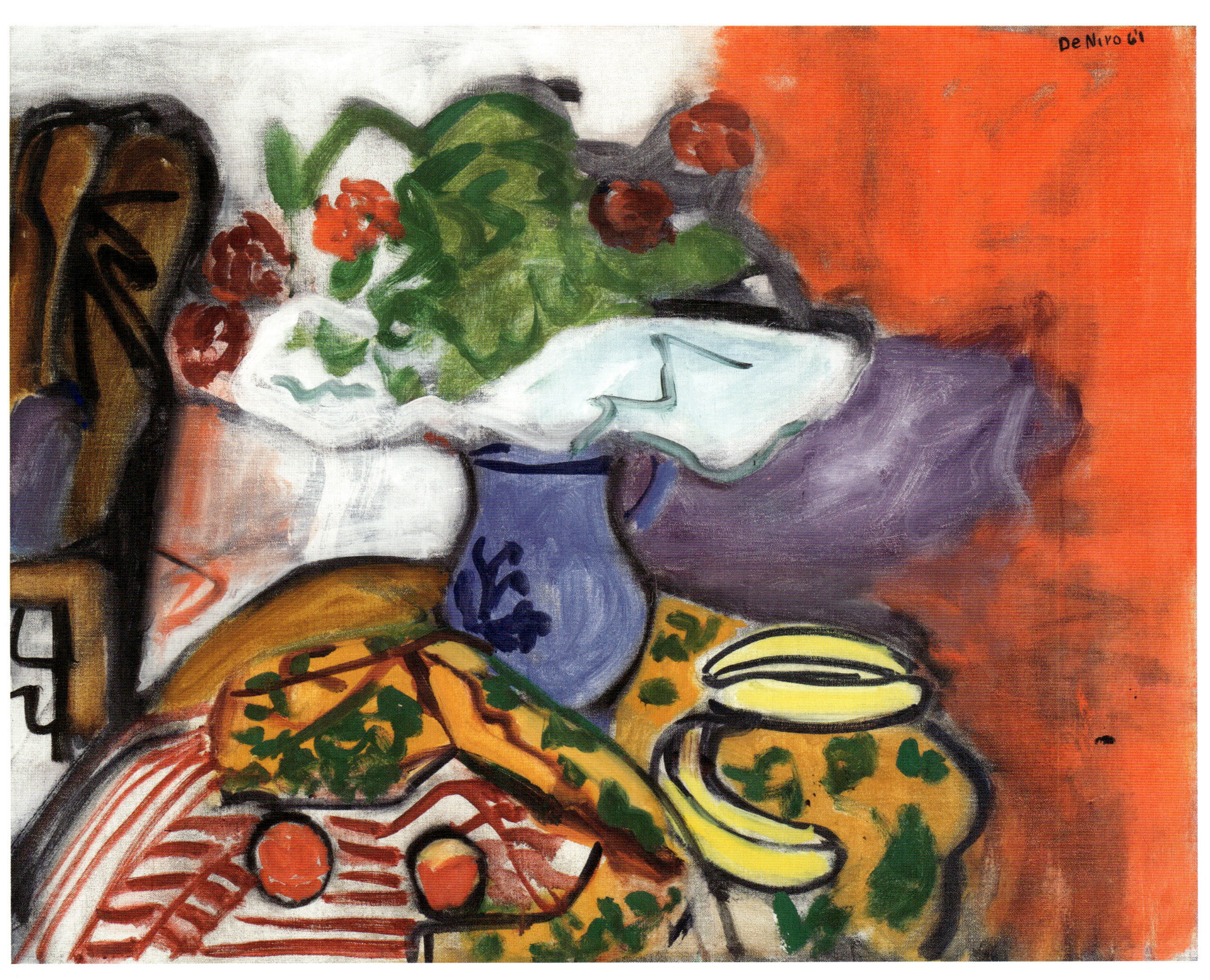
De Niro 61

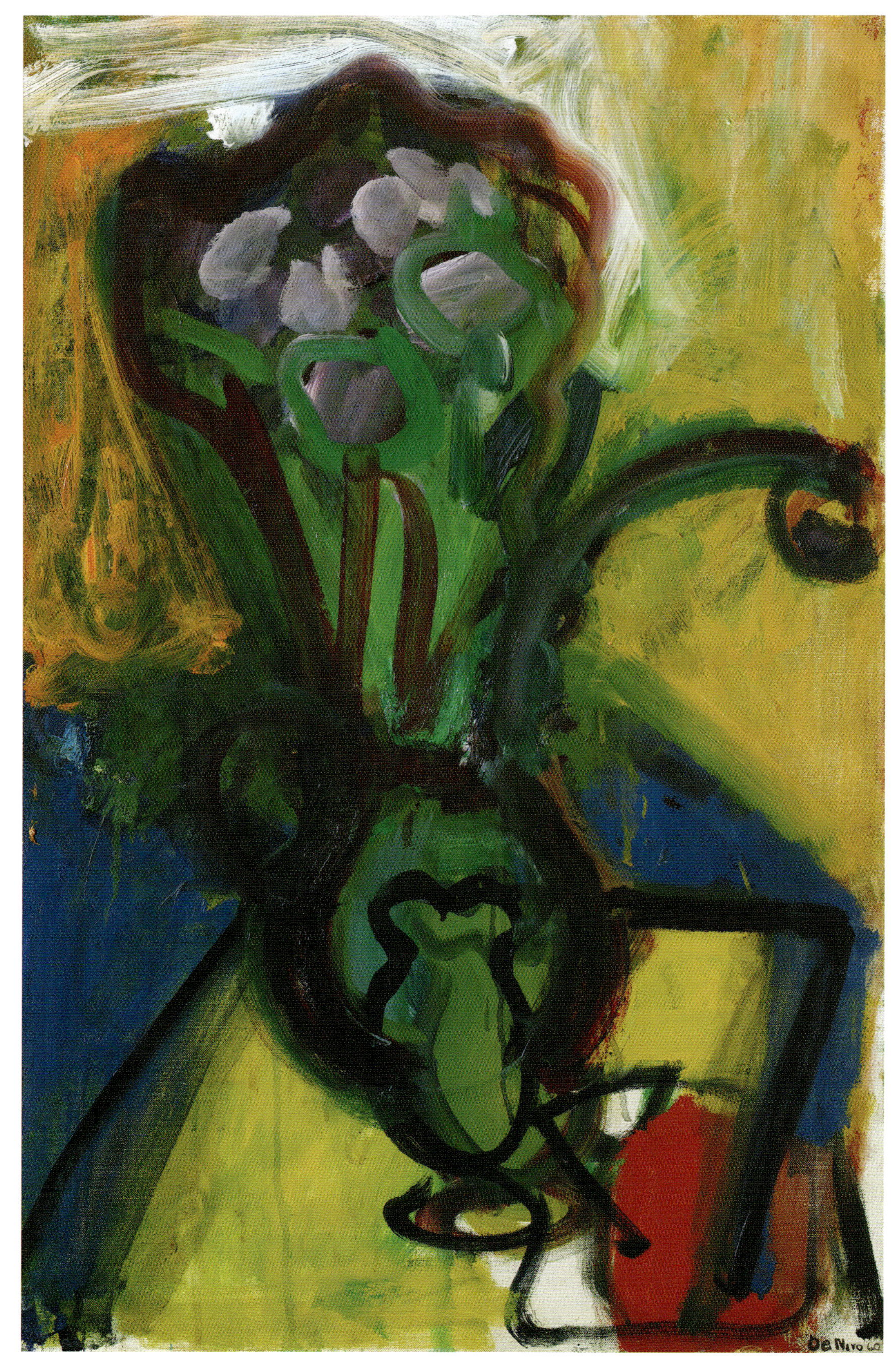

53. **Violet Flowers**, 1960. Oil on canvas, 32 x 20 inches

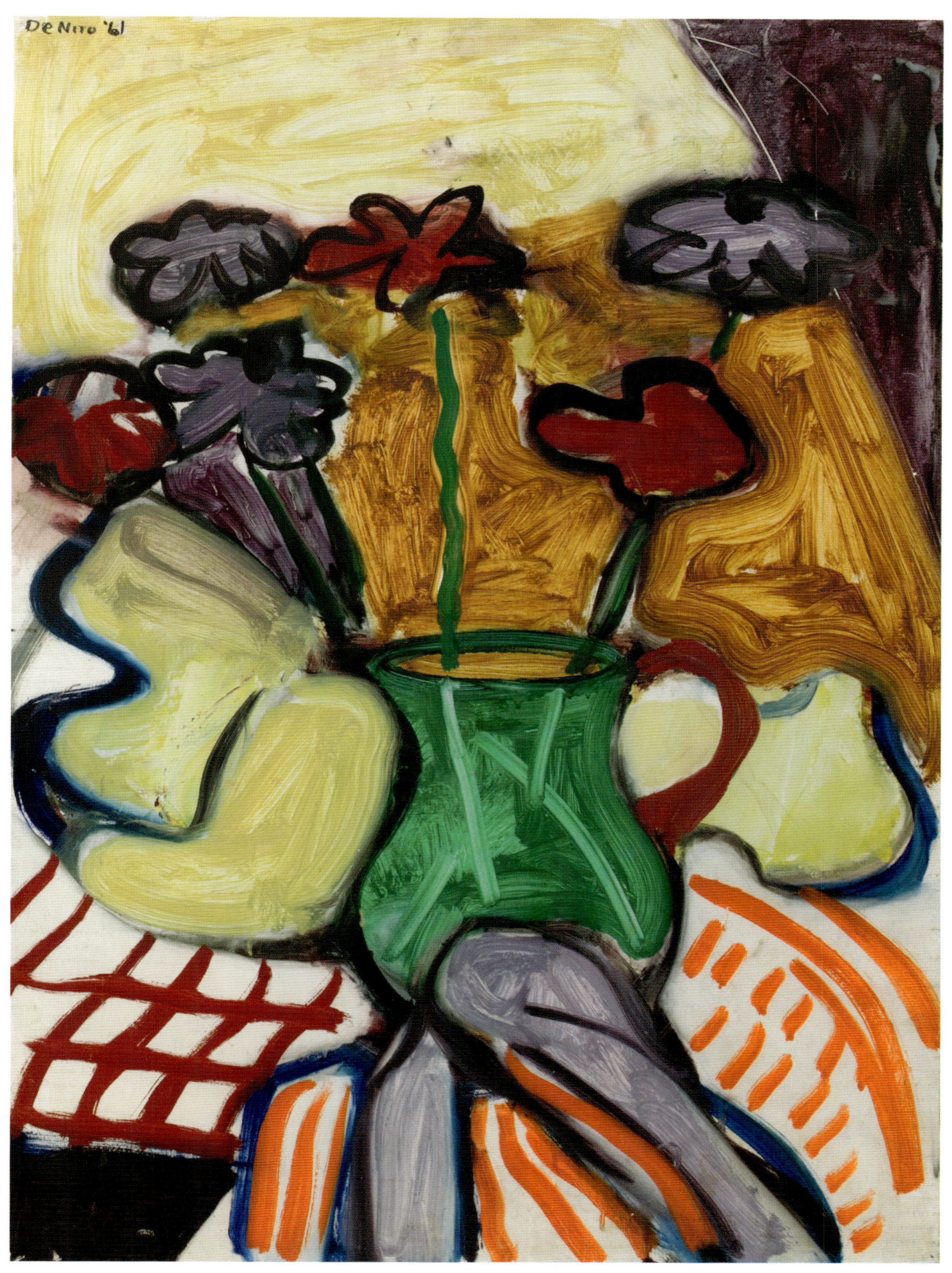

54. **Untitled**, 1961. Oil on canvas, 30 x 22 inches

55. **Woman in Red**, 1961. Oil on linen, 70 x 54 inches

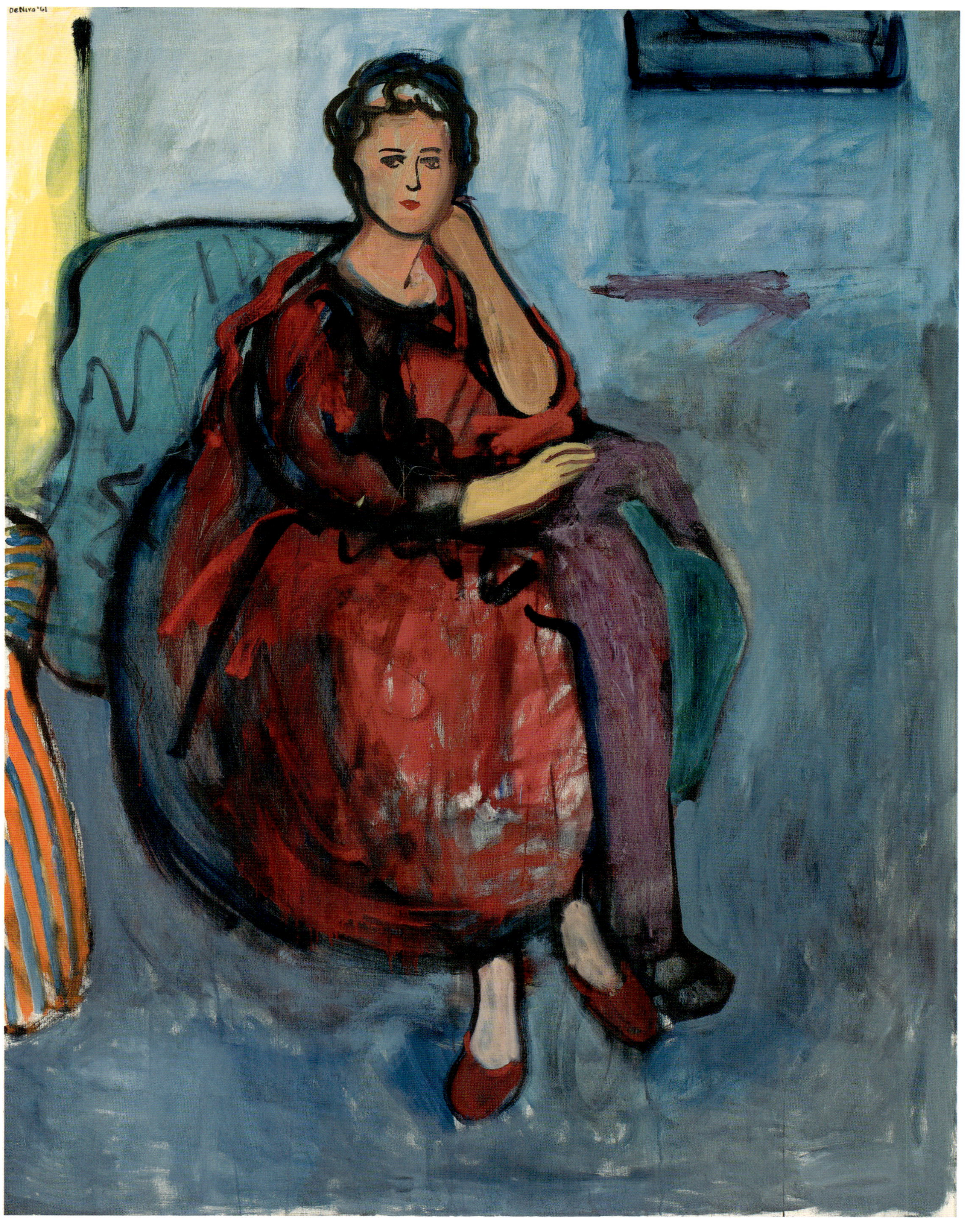
DeNiro '61

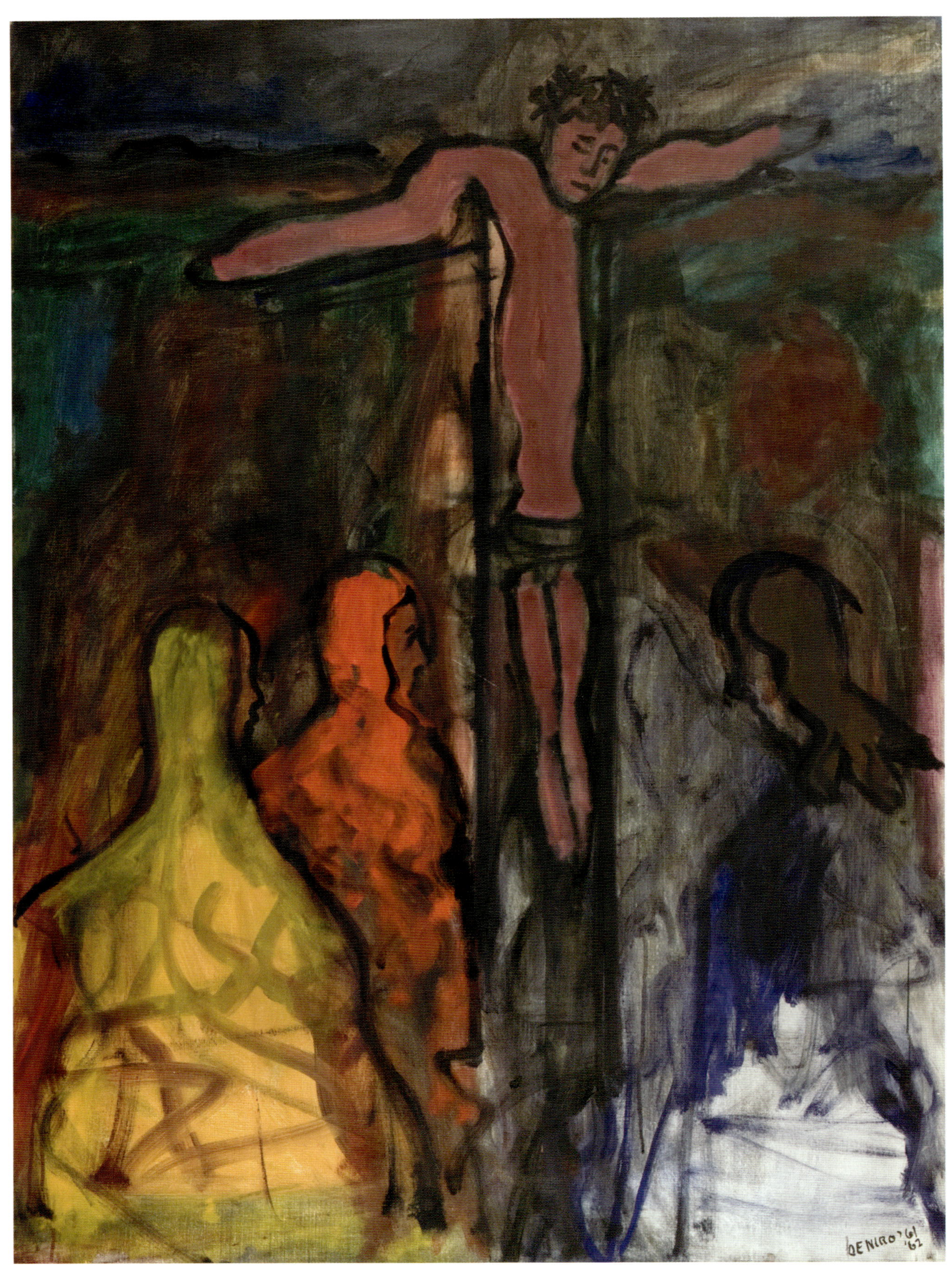

56. **Crucifixion with Three Spectators**, 1961–62. Oil on canvas, 54¼ x 38¼ inches

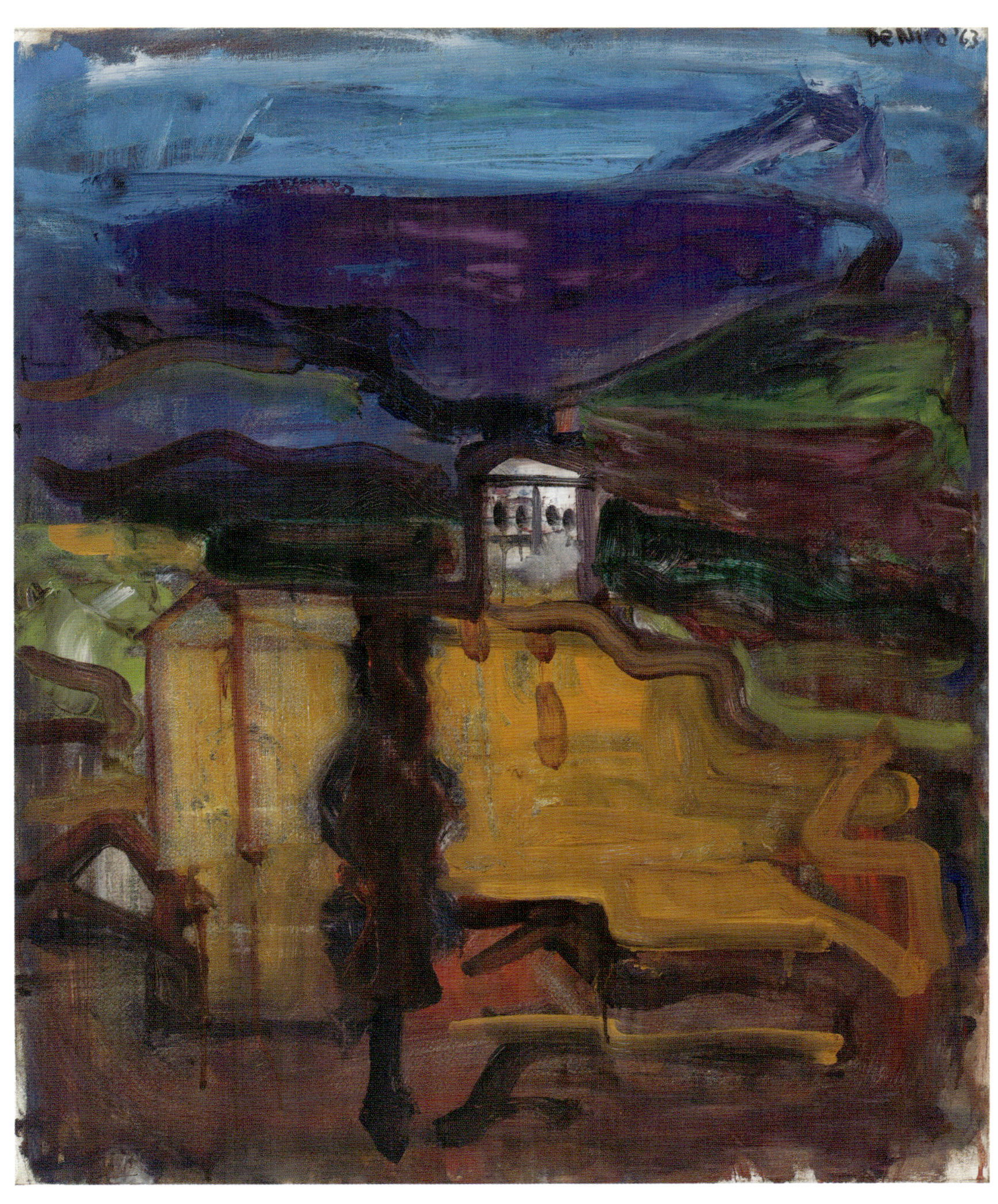

57. **St. Just en Chevalet**, 1963. Oil on linen, 28⅝ x 23½ inches

58. **Women at the Well**, 1965. Oil on canvas, 61 x 68 inches

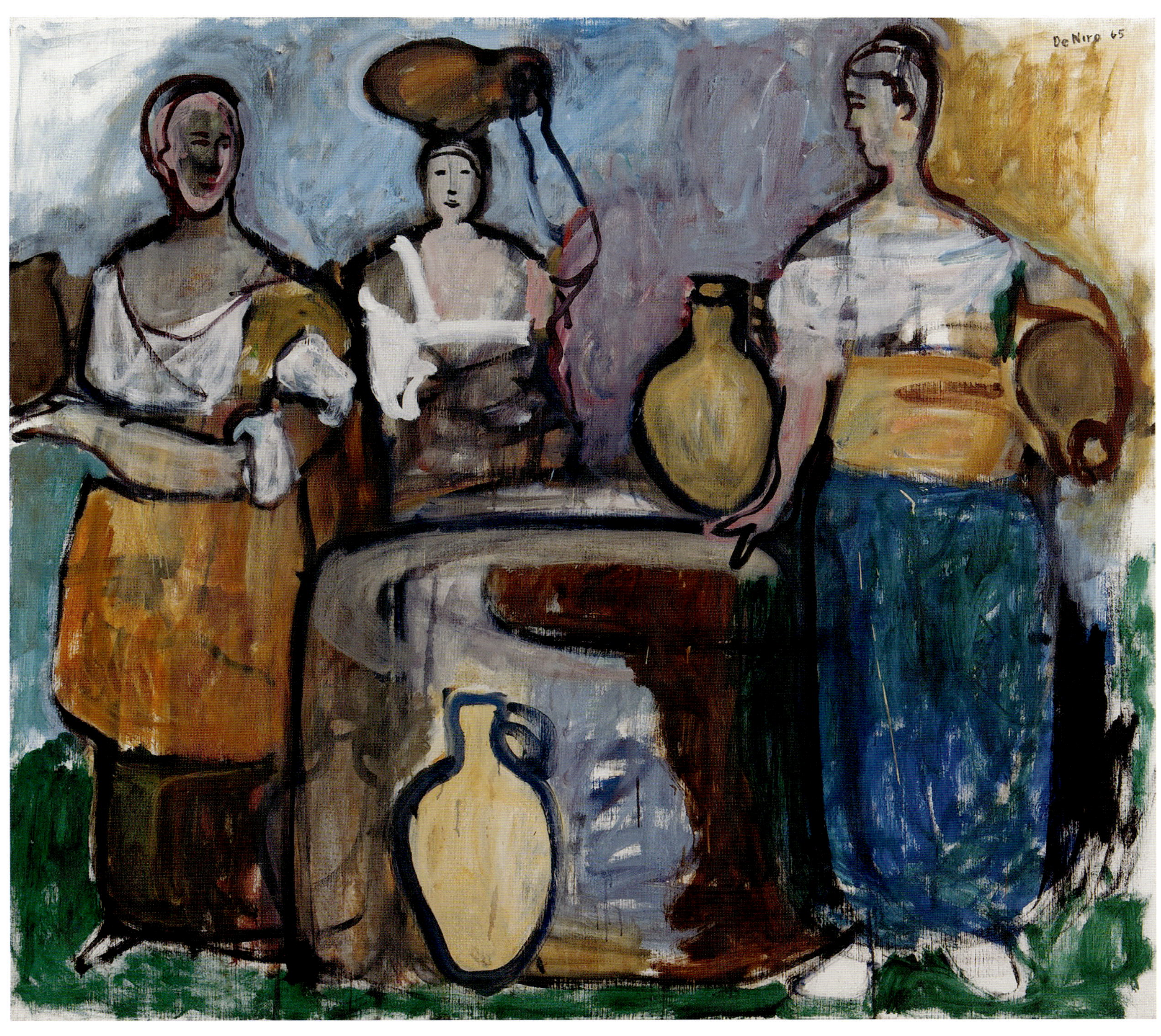
De Niro 65

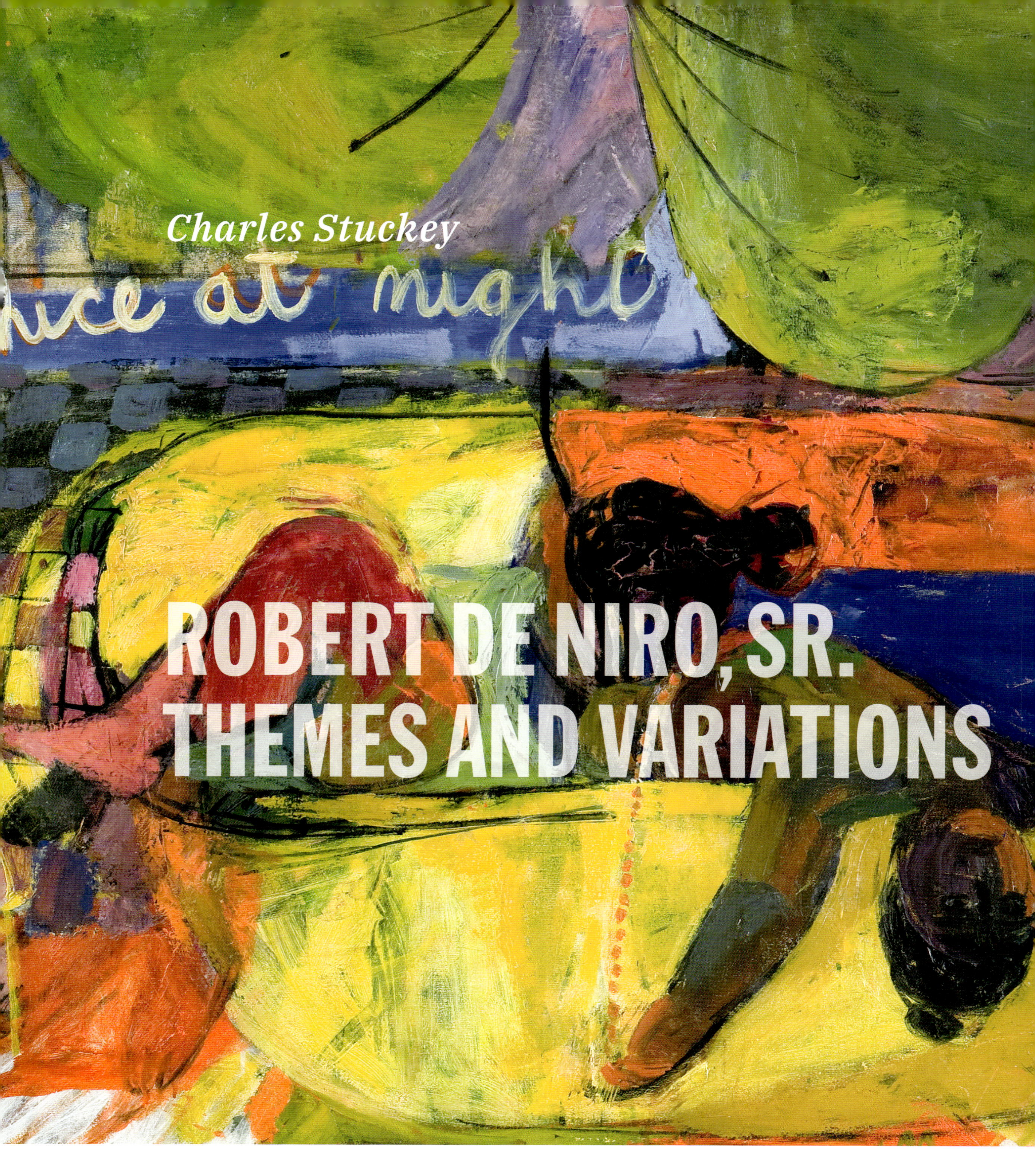

Charles Stuckey

ROBERT DE NIRO, SR. THEMES AND VARIATIONS

Venice at Night Is a Negress in Love, ca. 1942–43 (detail). Oil on canvas, 37½ x 43½ inches. Plate 2

ROBERT DE NIRO, SR., was among the most respected artists in the New York art world of the 1940s and 1950s, and afterwards he sustained a vigorous career as an esteemed veteran of those bygone days during and after World War II when American artists struggled as misunderstood outsiders. De Niro was engaged one way or another with many of the legendary figures of that era—Josef Albers, Hans Hofmann, Tennessee Williams, Anaïs Nin, Peggy Guggenheim, Clement Greenberg, Jackson Pollock, Willem de Kooning, Tony Smith, Larry Rivers, and Frank O'Hara. Writing from Paris, where he settled in 1961 to consolidate the new art-for-art's-sake style that he had begun to develop in the late 1950s, De Niro felt supremely confident: "I know I am the best painter of the epoch and I will fight my way to the top by every honest means if it takes everything I've got."[1] But like many of his equally ambitious contemporaries, Grace Hartigan and Larry Rivers among them, De Niro has too often been omitted from accounts of the so-called New York School, as if his art had stalled somewhere on the art-history highway.

De Niro's solo exhibitions, starting in 1946 and appearing regularly after 1951, enjoyed distinguished critical response from first to last. If New York museums overlooked his work, it was nonetheless especially well represented in two important museums outside the city. In 1962, E. George Poindexter gave his collection of 1950s American art, including nineteen works by De Niro, to the Montana Historical Society, holdings that were complemented locally after Poindexter's death in 1974, when his widow, the dealer Elinor Poindexter, gave many more works from their collection to the Yellowstone Art Museum, also in Montana. Her gift coincided with the opening of the Hirshhorn Museum and Sculpture Garden in Washington, DC, in 1974, a showcase for the enormous modern art collection assembled by Joseph Hirshhorn, who, starting in 1959, had acquired nearly fifty works by De Niro.

One of De Niro's earliest loyal supporters, *Art News* editor Thomas B. Hess, wondered in a 1976 review in *New York* magazine how broader recognition could possibly have been withheld from the artist, whose talent and ambition surely rivaled those of the by-then widely celebrated Andy Warhol. "De Niro's world is caught up in the timeless paradise-cum-torture-chamber of the artist's studio. And in this territory, he's as daring as any of

1. Robert De Niro, Sr., to Virgina Zabriskie, ca. 1961, Zabriskie Gallery Records, 1951–2010, Archives of American Art, Smithsonian Institution, Washington, DC.

the fashionable hotshots."[2] Two years later, when Hess was appointed consultative chairman of the Department of Twentieth-Century Art at New York's Metropolitan Museum of Art, it seemed as if De Niro's status might get an overdue boost, but his advocate died of a heart attack after only a few months on the job. Meanwhile, the artist had the crucial moral support of his son, the actor Robert De Niro, Jr., who in the 1970s and '80s received increasing acclaim for his films. As part of a real-estate complex development, De Niro, Jr. opened the Tribeca Grill in 1990 and persuaded his father to provide works of art—in the format of a unique and emblematic installation—for the venue. This gave De Niro, Sr., already dying from prostate cancer, the rare distinction of having something like his own private museum. If the display there has a fault, it is the lack of any works from the 1940s and '50s. The following text is an account of how De Niro, not without struggle with his own demons, emerged as an important New York School figure during those two decades, formulating the aesthetic approach and exploring the themes that would fuel his long career.

BORN IN SYRACUSE, NEW YORK, IN 1922, Robert De Niro, Sr., who later considered himself a prodigy, started to make art at age five, and by age eleven was admitted to adult art classes at the Syracuse Museum of Fine Arts. Unfortunately, nothing of his childhood art survives except a few mentions in local newspapers, documenting such early successes as a prize for a soap sculpture titled *The Family* in 1936, when he was fourteen. Already an outsider, De Niro as a teenager set off in search of the best art schools. Much later, in 1976, De Niro recalled that during the summer of 1938, studying in Gloucester, Massachusetts, with Ralph M. Pearson, he designed a stage set for Eugene O'Neill's drama *Anna Christie*, a work that for some mysterious reason was to remain an inspiration for him throughout his life.[3] The following year, age seventeen and lacking financial resources, De Niro attended the summer session of the Hans Hofmann School of Fine Arts, run by the legendary German art teacher in Provincetown, Massachusetts. Hofmann had trained in Paris before World War I, absorbing firsthand the innovations of Picasso, Matisse, and the earliest twentieth-century avant-garde. Himself an experimental painter in both expressionist and completely abstract modes, Hofmann was the most important mentor of the New York School artists to emerge during World War II. His wide-ranging, abundantly colorful art was a revelation to De Niro, and from that point on he belonged to Hofmann's close-knit family of students.

For a start, Hofmann encouraged De Niro to apply to the ultraprogressive Black Mountain College in North Carolina, where from 1939 to 1940 De Niro studied free of charge with the former Bauhaus professor Josef Albers. School records make clear how quickly Albers realized De Niro's discomfort in social situations and his problematic superiority complex.[4] Fellow students remembered De Niro as resentful of all authority, once, after a run-in

2. Thomas B. Hess, "Warhol and De Niro: Modesty Is the Best Policy," *New York*, December 6, 1976, 97–98.

3. Sidney Fields, "De Niro's Dad Artist," *The San Antonio Light*, December 26, 1976, 11.

4. Typewritten report from Josef Albers, December 1939, Black Mountain College Records, Student Files, Western Regional Archives, State Archives of North Carolina, Asheville.

with Albers, throwing everything in the room out of a window, his paints included, and leaving the school.[5] Nevertheless, after a difficult first semester, De Niro impressed Albers as an A student. No works of art survive from these student years.

During the summer of 1940, De Niro resumed studies in Provincetown with Hofmann, and sought financial support from the abstract German artist Hilla Rebay. Like Hofmann, Rebay had studied in Paris before World War I and was immersed in the avant-garde prior to settling in New York, where she helped Solomon Guggenheim establish the Museum of Non-Objective Painting in 1939. The intermittent financial support provided by Rebay encouraged De Niro to drop out of Black Mountain in the fall semester of 1940 and move to New York, where he was welcomed at Hofmann's school at 52 West 8th Street. The eighteen-year-old De Niro was quickly adopted by Virginia Admiral, a twenty-five-year-old fellow student. A left-wing political radical with a passion for avant-garde literature and film while a student at the University of California, Berkeley, Admiral arrived in New York in the summer of 1940 and quickly joined up with her college friend, poet Robert Duncan, who introduced her to the French novelist and amateur psychoanalyst Anaïs Nin, likewise new to New York. Nin soon enlisted first Admiral and then De Niro to help her write erotica.[6] Challenged by such intellectual colleagues, De Niro quickly developed his intense, lifelong passion for French avant-garde literature, and a sense that his destiny was to live in France.

No less an artist than a poet at this stage of his life, Duncan had been refused admission to Black Mountain College in 1939. Now Duncan responded to Admiral's new friend sexually and was reciprocated. Unconcerned about De Niro's promiscuity, Admiral invited him to live with her in her apartment at 30 East 14th Street, and in the summer of 1941 they went together to Provincetown. In her famous diary, Nin recorded how De Niro agonized over his fling with Duncan, thinking it an insurmountable obstacle to his relationship with Admiral.[7] Nin also mentioned that De Niro visited one of the houses where O'Neill lived in Provincetown. His subsequent obsession with the film version of *Anna Christie* may be connected to O'Neill's heroine's agony over her sexual past as a disqualification for true happiness. After Pearl Harbor, De Niro, as a single male, was eligible for the draft, and despite his guilt he married Admiral at the progressive Judson Memorial Church in New York in 1942. To supplement the monthly stipends sent by Rebay, De Niro worked with his Provincetown acquaintance Tennessee Williams as a waiter at the Beggar Bar in Greenwich Village.[8]

Very few of De Niro's works from the 1940s have survived. Some half a dozen charcoal drawings of seated nudes, probably life models who posed at Hofmann's school, are generally thought to date from around 1940–42. All are given a Cubist treatment, with

5. Martin Duberman, *Black Mountain: An Exploration in Community* (New York, NY: E.P. Dutton & Co., Inc., 1972), 72, 429.

6. Anaïs Nin, *The Diary of Anaïs Nin: Volume Three, 1939–1944*, ed. Gunther Stuhlmann (San Diego, CA: Harcourt Brace Jovanovich, 1969), 151.

7. Ibid., 128.

8. Shawn Levy, *De Niro: A Life* (New York, NY: Three Rivers Press, 2014), 28.

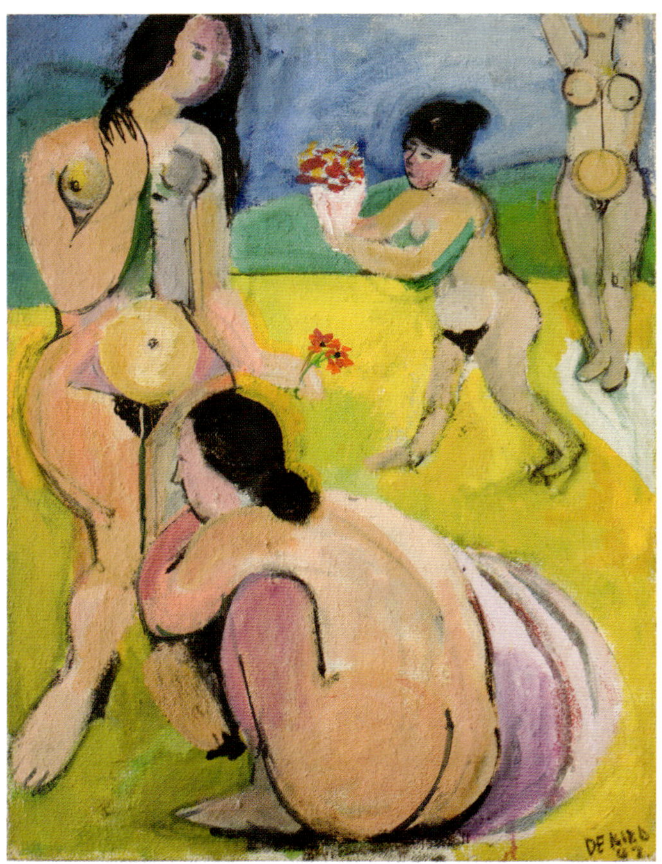

LEFT: FIGURE 1
Robert De Niro, Sr.
Figures on a Yellow and Blue Background, 1942
Oil on linen
34¼ x 26¼ in.
(88.3 x 66.7 cm)
The Estate of Robert De Niro, Sr.

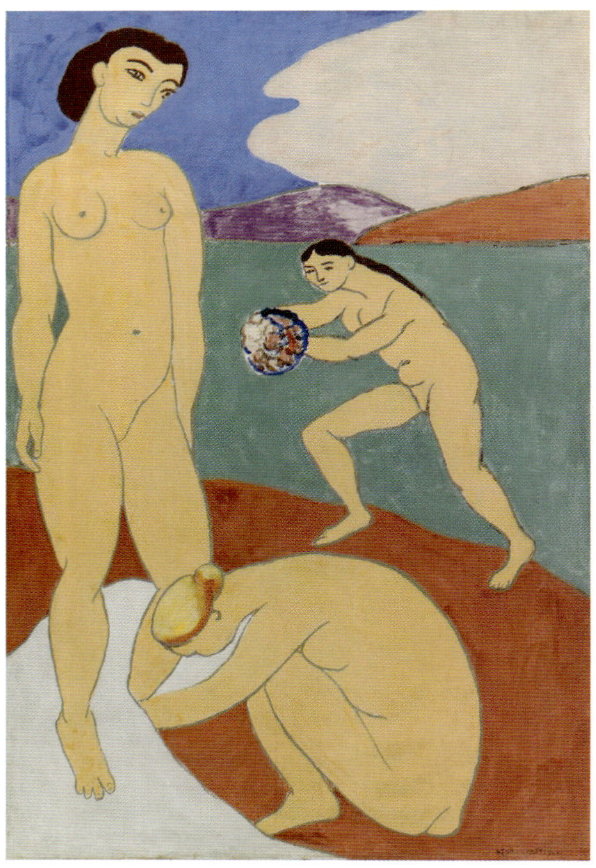

RIGHT: FIGURE 2
Henri Matisse
Le Luxe II, 1907–8
Distemper on canvas
82 x 54¾ in.
(209.5 x 139 cm)
Statens Museum for Kunst, Copenhagen

diagrammatic lines superimposed on the models' bodies and studio furnishings to emphasize otherwise invisible spatial structures. The two surviving paintings dated 1942 come as a big surprise, considering how completely out of step they are with the art of Hofmann and other leading New York painters of the early 1940s. Opulently colored in the spirit of Paul Gauguin or Pierre Bonnard, these operatic works all address female sexuality. Charmingly inept in their drawing, they appear suffused with impertinence, if not humor. *Figures on a Yellow and Blue Background* (1942, FIG. 1) is a pastiche based on a reproduction of Henri Matisse's *Le Luxe II* (1907–8, FIG. 2), evidently supplemented by life models with pubic hair taking the original poses. Already, at age twenty, De Niro saw the grouping of female nudes as an essential subject and Matisse as a fountainhead for the modernization of traditional art genres with an abstract attitude toward drawing and color. No less notably, this intensely colorful painting is the first example of De Niro's lifelong devotion to the idea of basing his avant-garde paintings on preexisting images, whether famous paintings or film stills, the way a jazz musician might improvise on familiar melodies.

More Gauguinesque in its decadence, *Reclining Nude with Attendant* (PLATE 1) shows the back of a topless African servant holding a mirror to a melancholy reclining pink-and-blonde nude with the sort of cartoonish, curvy limbs featured in 1930s works by Matisse and Picasso. The setting is rich with color and pattern, but the narrative is unclear, although its essence had enough importance for De Niro that he kept the work throughout his life. At age fifty-four, De Niro published a nostalgic illustrated book entitled *A Fashionable Watering Place* that included poems he had written around 1941, one of which is about a woman with a flower behind her ear. As an epigram for his sentimental poem, De Niro cited with erudition a line condensed to the repetition of the word "rose" by the nineteenth-century French poet Charles Cros.

De Niro went so far as to inscribe a line from a 1923 poem by gay French polymath Jean Cocteau in white script across the surface of *Venice at Night Is a Negress in Love* (PLATE 2). Larger than either of the paintings dated 1942, it is just like them in its boldly colored, cartoonish style. Presumably a takeoff on Bonnard's paintings of white nudes in bathtubs, De Niro here depicts a nude black corpse sprawled in a tub and mounted by a black cat. As props he provides a bird cage and a string of pearls, motifs that will reappear frequently in his mature art. From start to finish, De Niro's art offers a rich subject for gender studies.

Although De Niro and Admiral were equally enthralled by vibrant color, his commitment to figuration sharply differentiated his paintings from her emphasis on near total abstraction in art. Indeed, he maintained a skeptical attitude toward complete abstraction despite a job provided by Rebay as a handyman and night watchman at the Museum of Non-Objective Painting at 24 East 54th Street, the earliest avatar of the Solomon R. Guggenheim Museum.[9] The position came with health benefits for Admiral, then pregnant. De Niro lost no time in persuading Rebay to hire Pollock, ten years his senior, who began work there in May 1943.[10] That same month both Pollock and Admiral, though not yet De Niro, were included in a group exhibition at the highly publicized Art of This Century gallery, presided over by Solomon's niece Peggy Guggenheim. She would acquire one of Admiral's 1941 abstractions displaying the sort of bold color harmonies championed by Hofmann.

Robert De Niro, Jr. was born in July 1943, and the family moved to the top floor at 200 Bleecker Street in Greenwich Village. Hans Hofmann was the boy's godfather. In 1944, Admiral continued to have more success than De Niro. The Museum of Modern Art acquired a blue abstraction that was included in another group show at Art of This Century in the spring (FIG. 3). But when Rebay saw works by De Niro somewhere a few months later, she was unhappy that he had so little benefited from being around the collection at the Museum of Non-Objective Painting. "I saw your paintings," she told him in a letter, "and I think they are a waste of canvas and color and everything."[11] Her remarks must have helped to prompt a drastic change in his art, which grew ever more abstract, if never completely nonrepresentational.

9. Levy, *De Niro: A Life*, 29.

10. Ibid.

11. Hilla Rebay to Robert De Niro, 7 July 1944, Hilla Rebay Records, Box 3018, Folder 48, Solomon R. Guggenheim Museum Archives, New York, NY.

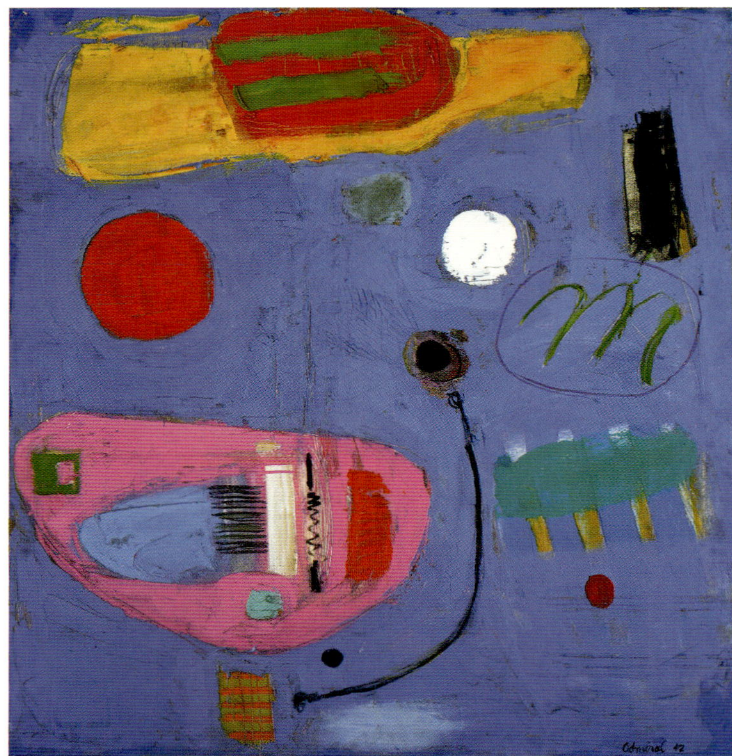

FIGURE 3
Virginia Admiral
Composition, 1942
Oil on canvas
36 x 34 in. (91.4 x 86.4 cm)
Museum of Modern Art,
New York

By October 1945, when both Admiral and De Niro had works in a group show at Art of This Century, they had separated as a couple, although they shared parenting and sometimes made family appearances together. De Niro was prolific on his own, with ten paintings ready for a prestigious solo exhibition at Art of This Century in April 1946, including one abstraction, three figure paintings, four still lifes, and two paintings with titles referring to writings by André Gide and Alfred Jarry, signs of his ongoing intellectual commitment to French literature. Apparently lost, the *Still Life with Plaster Cast* on the exhibition checklist is the earliest documented version of what would become one of De Niro's most abiding themes—meditations on the artist's studio as the locus for creative fulfillment, with an eye to tradition. Reviewing the show in *The Nation*, the now legendary critic Clement Greenberg praised De Niro's drawing, but complained about his hot, violent color derived from Matisse. In his mention of deep madder red placed against yellow in one of the paintings, Greenberg was probably referring to a still life preserved today in Montana titled *Still Life* (ca. 1946; PLATE 3), one of only two works to survive from this ambitious show. Although the loose drawing and saturated color recall the 1942 works, this still life signals a dramatic shift toward abstraction. Only vestiges of a chair, table, and room are evident as rhythmic background for the deftly scribbled flowers in a white vase placed nonchalantly on the floor. A little notice published in the May issue of *Art News* referred to arrangements of "circular and oval shapes, warmly colored, into handsome vaguely sexual patterns."[12] This seems to refer to the yet more abstract still life dated 1946 (PLATE 4), which

12. Unsigned, "Abstract Painting," *Art News*, May 1946, 64.

could correspond to several of the titles on the gallery checklist: *Still Life*, *Woman in Armchair*, or *Abstraction*. With characteristic, if somewhat perverse, playfulness, De Niro made an abstract flourish at the very center of this composition, leaving its purpose uncertain. Perhaps it represents a vase on a table, or the bodice of a woman posed on a chair, or maybe it's simply an explosion of twisting colored lines and rounded shapes having no representational reference.

Around this time a fire at Admiral's loft, where De Niro stored paintings, destroyed many of his early works. De Niro refers to the recent fire in a letter that he wrote in October 1948 to the celebrated Columbia University art historian Meyer Schapiro, himself a painter, to request a recommendation for a Guggenheim Fellowship.[13] Although De Niro failed to obtain the fellowship, in the spring of 1950 he was included in the Kootz Gallery's important *New Talent* group exhibition, organized by Greenberg and Schapiro and bringing together twenty-three artists, among them Elaine de Kooning, Franz Kline, Larry Rivers, and Grace Hartigan. Reviewing this show in the May 1950 issue of *Art News*, Thomas B. Hess, the magazine's editor, confided his wish to "buy and carry home Robert de Niro's seemingly haphazard but precisely calculated scattering of flowers . . . ,"[14] another early work that has so far been impossible to identify. Following this success, Hess and Schapiro provided De Niro with ongoing support. When De Niro wrote to Schapiro on October 30, 1950, he was living at 540 West Broadway and had just started a school of his own, one of a number of fly-by-night projects he undertook after Rebay discontinued any financial support.[15]

The opinions of Hess, Schapiro, and/or Elaine de Kooning may have influenced dealer Charles Egan's decision to offer De Niro a solo exhibition at his small gallery at 63 East 57th Street, then showing such notables as Willem de Kooning, Kline, and Joseph Cornell. Thanks to illustrated reviews of De Niro's first solo exhibition there in February 1951, we can identify several paintings that excited critical enthusiasm, including the ambitiously scaled *Moroccan Women* (PLATE 14).[16] This was among the works purchased from the show by Andre Vanden Broeck, the scholarly son of a leading Wall Street investor, who donated them to the Everson Museum in De Niro's hometown of Syracuse in the early 1980s.

With *Moroccan Women* it is finally possible to situate De Niro in close relationship to the quickly evolving New York art world. The painting is partly a response to Willem de Kooning, the leading abstract figurative painter in the late 1940s, who first exhibited one of his "Woman" series in a group show in October 1950 (FIG. 4). Of course, De Niro was familiar socially with both de Koonings, who sometimes used photographic images as inspiration for abstract paintings, as did Kline. De Niro's decision to base this large

13. Robert De Niro, Sr., to Meyer Schapiro, October 1948, Meyer Schapiro Papers (1921–91), Rare Book & Manuscript Library, Columbia University in the City of New York. All subsequently cited letters to Schapiro are also located within this holding institution.

14. Thomas B. Hess, "Seeing the Young New Yorkers," *Art News*, May 1950, 60.

15. De Niro, Sr., to Meyer Schapiro, 30 October 1950.

16. The piece is illustrated in *Art News*, February 1951, 49.

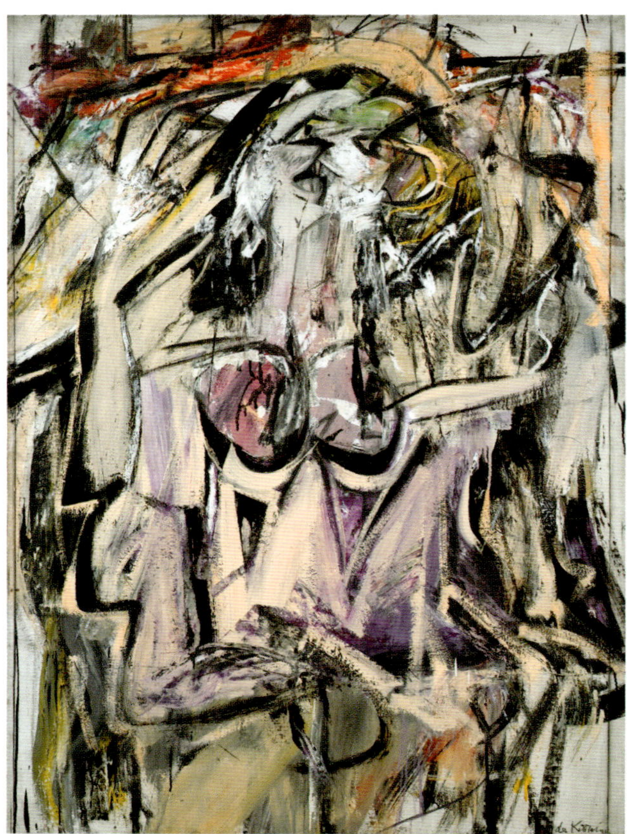

FIGURE 4
Willem de Kooning
Woman, 1949–50
Oil on canvas
64⅛ x 46 in.
(162.9 x 116.8 cm)
Weatherspoon Art Museum, UNC Greensboro, Lena Kernodle McDuffie Memorial Purchase, 1954

OPPOSITE, LEFT: FIGURE 5
Karl Bissinger
Dancers Resting at Bahia Palace, November 8, 1949
Karl Bissinger Papers, University of Delaware Library, Newark

OPPOSITE, RIGHT: FIGURE 6
Joseph Cornell contemplating *The Crystal Mask*, one of his boxed assemblages (since destroyed), ca. 1939–40
Joseph Cornell Study Center, Smithsonian Institution, Washington, DC

Abstract Expressionist painting orchestrated in tones of purple and pink on a small black-and-white photograph was not especially unusual, nor was it mentioned in reviews of the exhibition.

Surprisingly, *Moroccan Women* is based on a photograph by Karl Bissinger, published in the inaugural (February 1950) issue of *Flair*, which shows resting Shikhat dancers at the Palace of the Bahia in Marrakesh (FIG. 5). Perhaps for De Niro the photograph had some connection to his early Gauguinesque harem paintings. Without access to Bissinger's photograph for comparison, however, viewers struggle to find the women in De Niro's dogmatically anti-photographic painting. The work is both representational and abstract, showing disconnected body parts, no matter how distorted, intermingled with loose abstract color accents that read as emotional annotations.

De Niro's 1951 exhibition at the Egan Gallery included oils, gouaches, and charcoal drawings, setting a pattern that the artist followed throughout his career. Besides appealing to collectors with different price ranges, this exhibition strategy stressed the essential role of drawing in his practice as an experimental artist. Curiously, De Niro never seems to have based any of his paintings in whole or in part on one of his own related drawings, though he dramatically emphasized in his paintings how essential drawing was to his process. The perverse relationship between photography and abstraction is again at issue in another work from the 1951 exhibition, a riotously colorful gouache based on a still

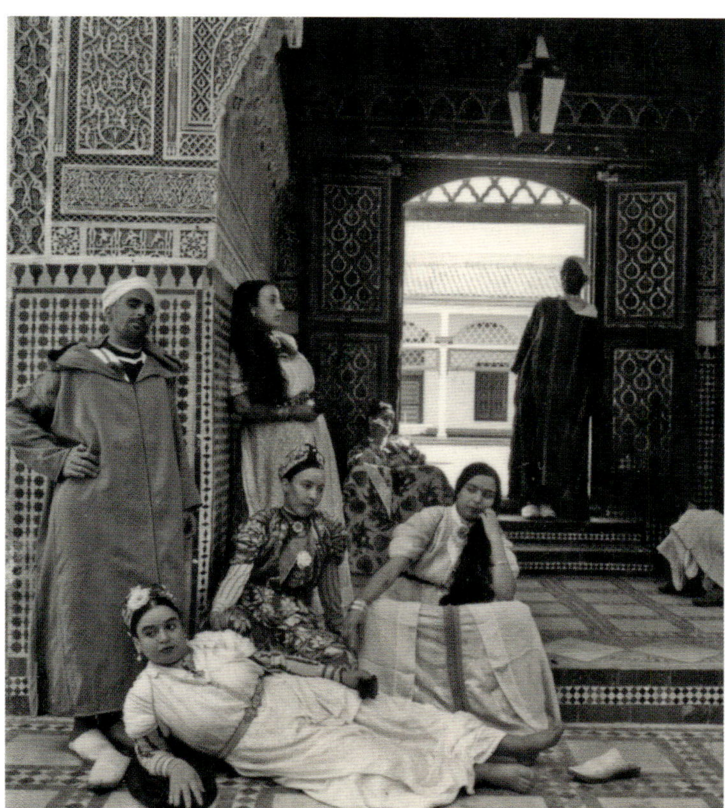

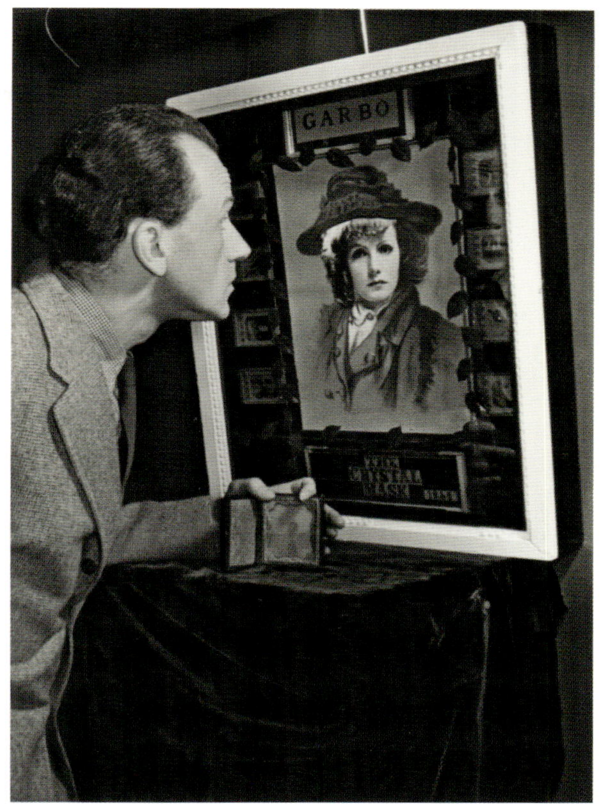

from the 1930 film version of *Anna Christie* showing a troubled Greta Garbo wearing a cloche hat and ribbon choker as she sits alone at a bar table with a whisky and a ginger ale. As the Bissinger photograph evokes famous Orientalist paintings like those by Delacroix, the film-still source image seems closely related to the tradition of early genre paintings of modern life, from Édouard Manet, Edgar Degas, Henri de Toulouse-Lautrec, and Vincent van Gogh to Pablo Picasso. Like a rambunctious child with a coloring book and a box of crayons, De Niro transformed his melancholy source with madcap strokes of garish color that, in an excited effort to represent the famous face, obliterates it. Whether or not he took inspiration from Cornell, who had devoted one of his hallmark collage/assemblage boxes to Garbo (FIG. 6), or from Willem de Kooning, who had dedicated a 1947 abstract painting to the memory of the actress Carole Lombard, De Niro's simultaneous appropriation and distortion of a publicity image for a movie star helped set the stage for such photography-minded artists as Warhol, Robert Rauschenberg, and Gerhard Richter, who around 1960 made the representation of photography a paramount issue for avant-garde art. As if he needed to refer to them constantly, De Niro kept his source photographs on display in his cluttered studio, using them as the basis for the frequent variations he painted over the course of the next four decades. Taken together, De Niro's paintings based on a particular source image bring to mind Picasso's variations on specific Old Master paintings, such as his 1954–55 series based on Eugène Delacroix's *Women of Algiers*.

In *Art News*, Hess wrote about the 1951 exhibition with enthusiasm: "[De Niro] must now be ranked among the best of the younger artists.... Working on ambitiously large surfaces with an ambitious technique, De Niro succeeds in keeping every inch of the canvas alive—spinning the spokes of a parasol with yellow gashes; letting purples or oranges cascade down or push up and across a studio interior."[17] Although the studio interior mentioned by Hess cannot be identified today, a relatively large, bright oil of a faceless seated woman with a parasol survives. This painting (PLATE 10) pulses with multicolored free brushstrokes that sometimes denote parts of the subject, but just as often do not. As far as is known, this work is not based on a specific source image.

Nor is the smaller, square-format, bust-length image of a blonde woman with a rose behind her ear titled *Portrait of Virginia (Portrait of the Artist's Wife)* (PLATE 15), which seems to correspond to a comment in a review of the show in *Arts Digest* that De Niro's paintings of women were like "sunbursts and explosions," somewhat lacking in "compositional solidity."[18] In keeping with the two paintings discussed previously, this close-up image of Admiral's face is a blank, her features scarcely discernible under a flurry of vermilion accents. Given the prominence of landscape painting in De Niro's work after 1960, it is noteworthy that the 1951 exhibition contained his earliest surviving example in that genre, a bold yellow gouache like a child's messy drawing (De Niro's own child was now seven), with rudimentary signs for sailboats overwhelmed by jabbing brushstrokes of every color that came to hand. This work, titled *P-Town* (ca. 1950; PLATE 9), surely testifies that, despite Rebay's lament, De Niro did in fact absorb the windswept abstract revelations of Kandinsky at Guggenheim's museum during the time he worked there. Beyond that, we can only guess that this 1951 exhibition included other works in this same exuberant style, such as the painting of a seated male with an orange hand and a strangely darkened head, titled *Untitled (Seated Man)* (ca. 1950; PLATE 12).

Around this time, Vanden Broeck's dancer girlfriend agreed to pose for De Niro and his friends Al Kresch and Rivers, who were making clay figure sculptures on armatures. A jazz musician who studied with Hofmann after the war, Rivers shared De Niro's esteem for French painting from Gustave Courbet to Pierre Bonnard and was a determined advocate of representational art in the face of a powerful consensus that modern painting's true destiny was complete abstraction. Like De Niro, Rivers was a father who was separated from his son's mother to pursue other partners, male as well as female. De Niro managed to sell one of these early sculptures, today unknown, to a collector in Connecticut, thanks to the intervention of the architect Tony Smith, himself determined by the early 1950s to make abstract paintings and sculptures.[19]

17. T.B.H. [Thomas B. Hess], "Robert de [*sic*] Niro" *Art News*, February 1951, 49.

18. B. K. [Belle Krasne], "Robert De Niro," *Arts Digest*, February 1, 1951, 19.

19. Unedited transcript, interview with Al Kresch, from *Remembering the Artist Robert De Niro, Sr.*, a film by Perri Peltz and Geeta Gandbhir, HBO Productions, 2014.

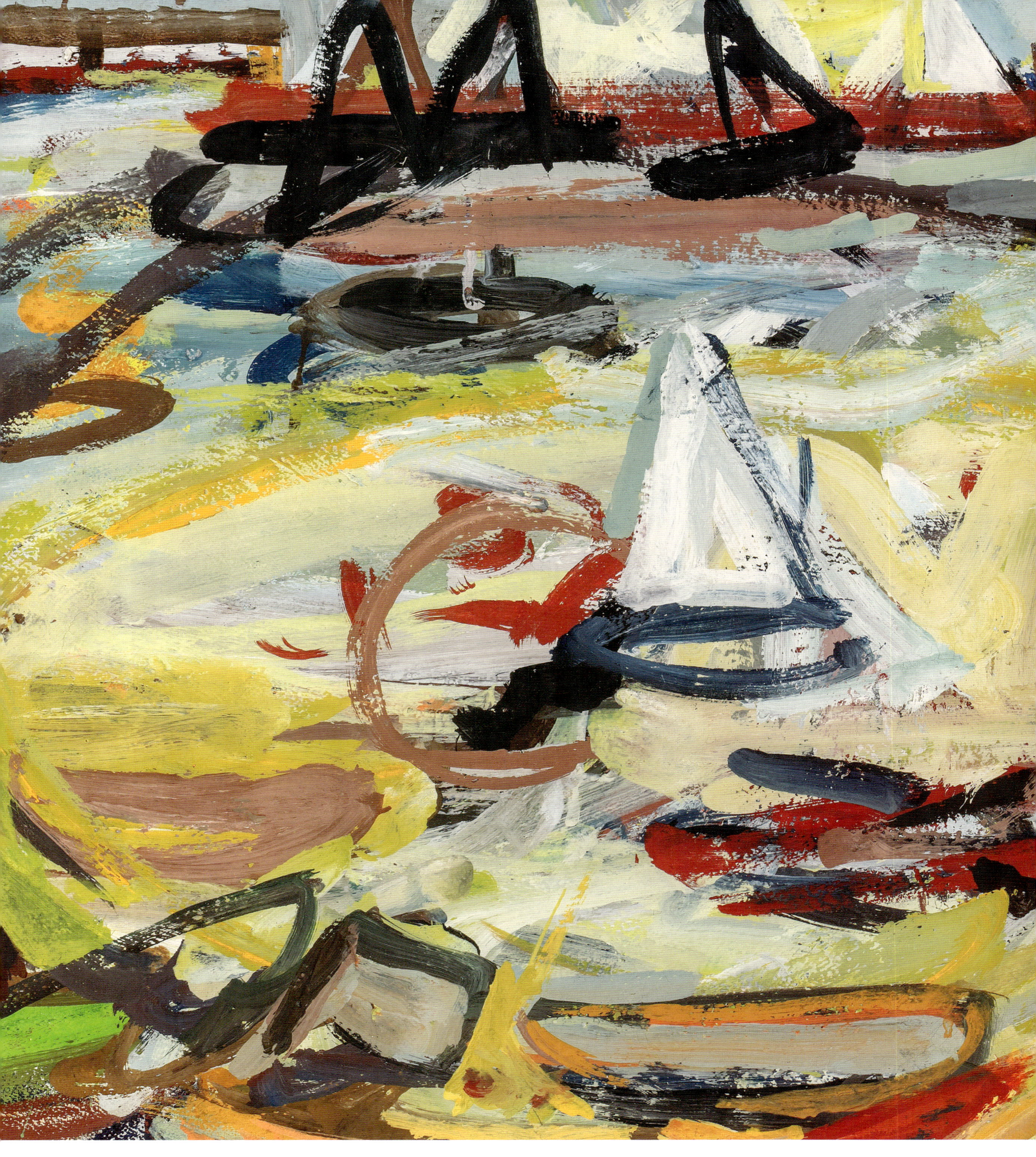

P-Town, ca. 1950 (detail). Gouache on paper, 17½ x 23½ inches. Plate 9

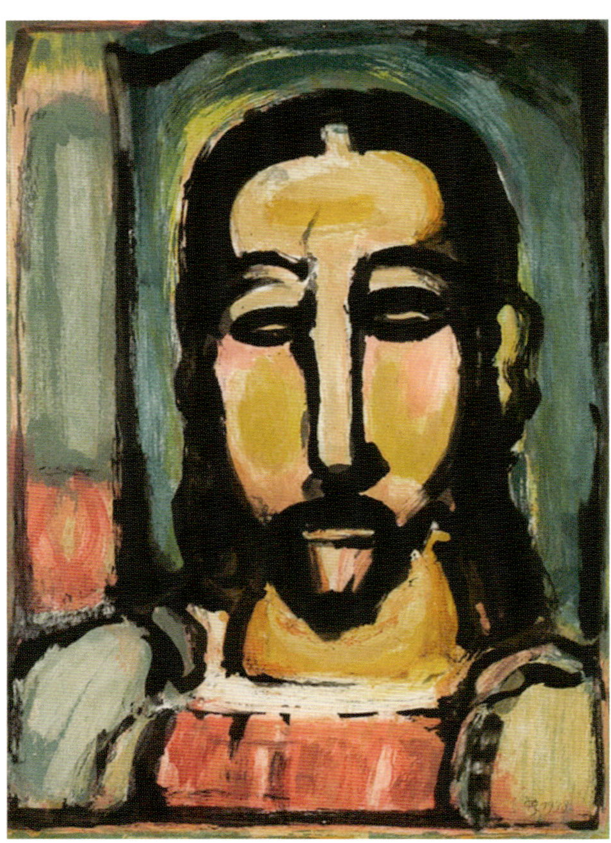

FIGURE 7
Georges Rouault
Christ de Face, from
Les Fleurs du Mal, 1938
Color aquatint on wove paper
12 x 8½ in. (30.5 x 21.6 cm)
Private Collection

OPPOSITE, LEFT: FIGURE 8
Robert De Niro, Sr.
Self-Portrait, 1977
Oil on canvas
34¼ x 28 in. (87 x 71.1 cm)
Private Collection

OPPOSITE, RIGHT: FIGURE 9
Edvard Munch
Self-Portrait in Hell, 1903
Oil on canvas
32$\frac{5}{16}$ x 26 in. (82 x 66 cm)
Munch Museum, Oslo

Already, in a somewhat manic July 1951 letter to Smith, De Niro confided his never-realized desire to leave the Egan Gallery and join the Tibor de Nagy Gallery, where his next show was scheduled to take place in March 1952.[20] By then he hoped to be settled in Paris, if only he could raise enough money. Rivers and Hartigan were already associated with Tibor de Nagy, and De Niro was eager to increase his sales. But he quickly antagonized the gallery's director, John Bernard Myers, who recalled: "The disparity between De Niro's big talent and his character was too great for me to handle."[21]

Postcards sent by De Niro to Schapiro in January 1952 are desperate appeals. Hoping that Schapiro could help him find buyers, he confessed that he and Rivers, with whom he had become very close, had stolen from Rosenthal's art supply store, where they both worked, because there had been no sales at the Egan Gallery.[22] De Niro was still working as a delivery man for Rosenthal's in December 1952 when he wrote to thank Schapiro for including him in *Contemporary Religious Art and Architecture*, an exhibition presented at the Union Theological Seminary on Broadway, December 1–16, 1952, with ninety works on religious themes by such artists as Marc Chagall, Richard Pousette-Dart, Ad Reinhardt, and Georges Rouault.[23] Although Rivers had been at work on a painting of *Christ's Agony in the Garden*, it was not included in this exhibition, which took place only a month after he slit his wrists. De Niro's persecuted mind-set at the time seems evident from his decision to exhibit a slightly larger than life bust-length *Self-Portrait* (PLATE 13). As in his 1950 paintings, the

20. Robert De Niro, Sr., to Tony Smith, 16 July 1951, Tony Smith Estate, New York, NY.

21. John Bernard Myers, *Tracking the Marvelous: A Life in the New York Art World* (New York, NY: Random House, 1981), 174.

22. Robert De Niro, Sr., to Meyer Schapiro, January 1952.

23. Robert De Niro, Sr., to Meyer Schapiro, December 1952.

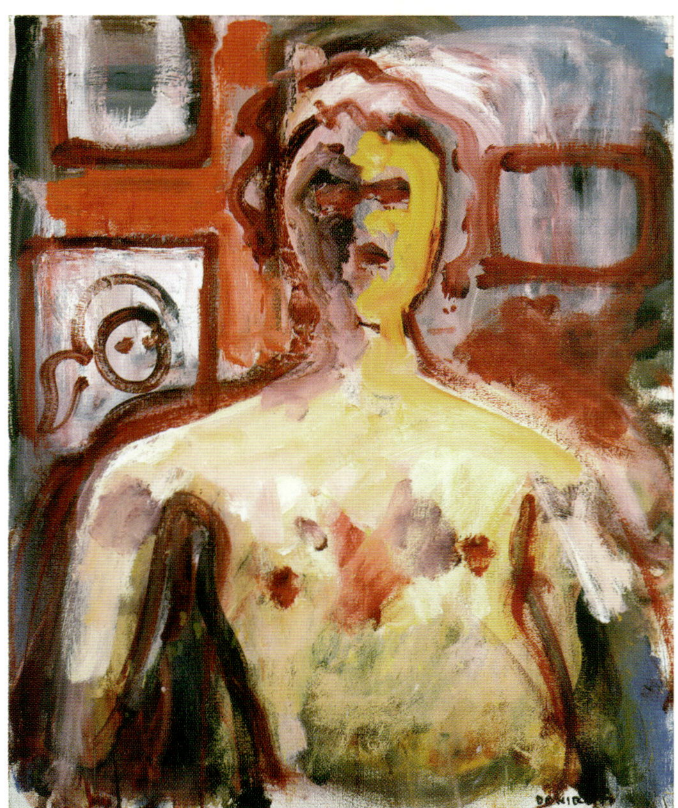

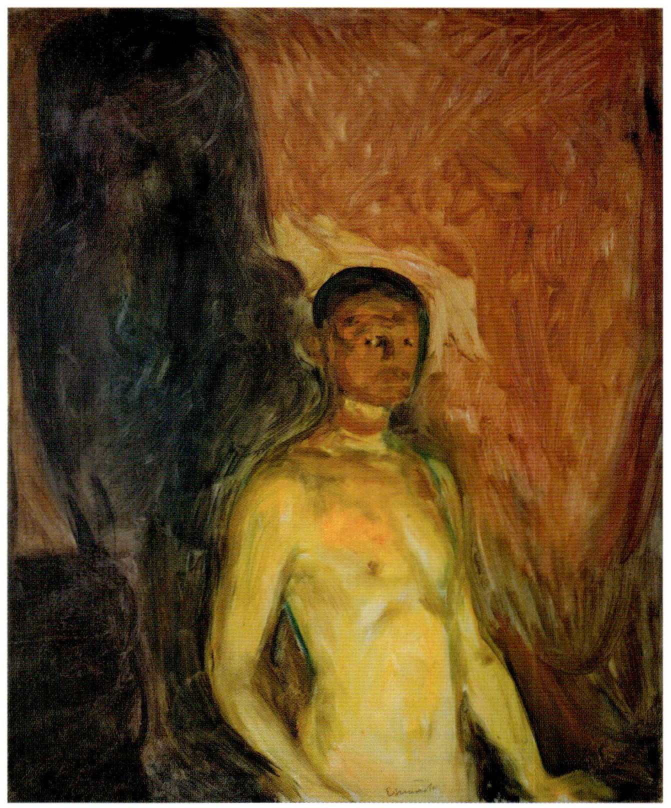

face is nearly blank. His eyebrows and the bridge of his nose are indicated by no more than thick, dark perpendicular lines, so that the badly bruised face doubles as a dripping blood-red vision of the cross. In keeping with his source image, a 1938 aquatint by Rouault (FIG. 7), De Niro depicts himself wearing a tunic, albeit underneath a sports coat, and a red scarf. The red halo indicates De Niro's appreciation for the paintings of Edvard Munch, whose secularized *Madonna* (1894) with a red halo was included in a retrospective at the Museum of Modern Art in the summer of 1950. Presumably painted around the same time, a smaller self-portrait by De Niro with a bruised, bloody face (PLATE 21), today at the Montana Historical Society, has a similar red halo.

On March 30, 1953, the Chicago collector Muriel Kallis Steinberg (later Newman), who already owned paintings by de Kooning, Kline, and Pollock, bought De Niro's religious *Self-Portrait* of 1951 from the Egan Gallery, along with a box by Cornell. Newman lent her collection to the Metropolitan Museum of Art in 1981 to announce her promised gift, and for the first time De Niro was represented in the collection of a major New York museum. Seeing the emotionally supercharged work after eighteen years, De Niro was upset by how it had darkened and lost its chromatic vibrancy. Consequently, he asked Newman to trade her painting for a more recent *Self-Portrait* made in 1977 (FIG. 8) and to return the earlier one so that he could destroy it. He pointed out that other collectors had agreed to similar trades of late works for early ones.[24] Fortunately, Newman ignored the suggestion.

24. Martica Sawin, "No. 36 Self-Portrait. 1951," *Abstract Expressionism and Other Modern Works: The Muriel Kallis Steinberg Newman Collection in The Metropolitan Museum of Art*, Gary Tinterow, Lisa Mintz Messinger, and Nan Rosenthal, eds. (New York, NY: The Metropolitan Museum of Art; New Haven, CT: Yale University Press, 2007), 115–116.

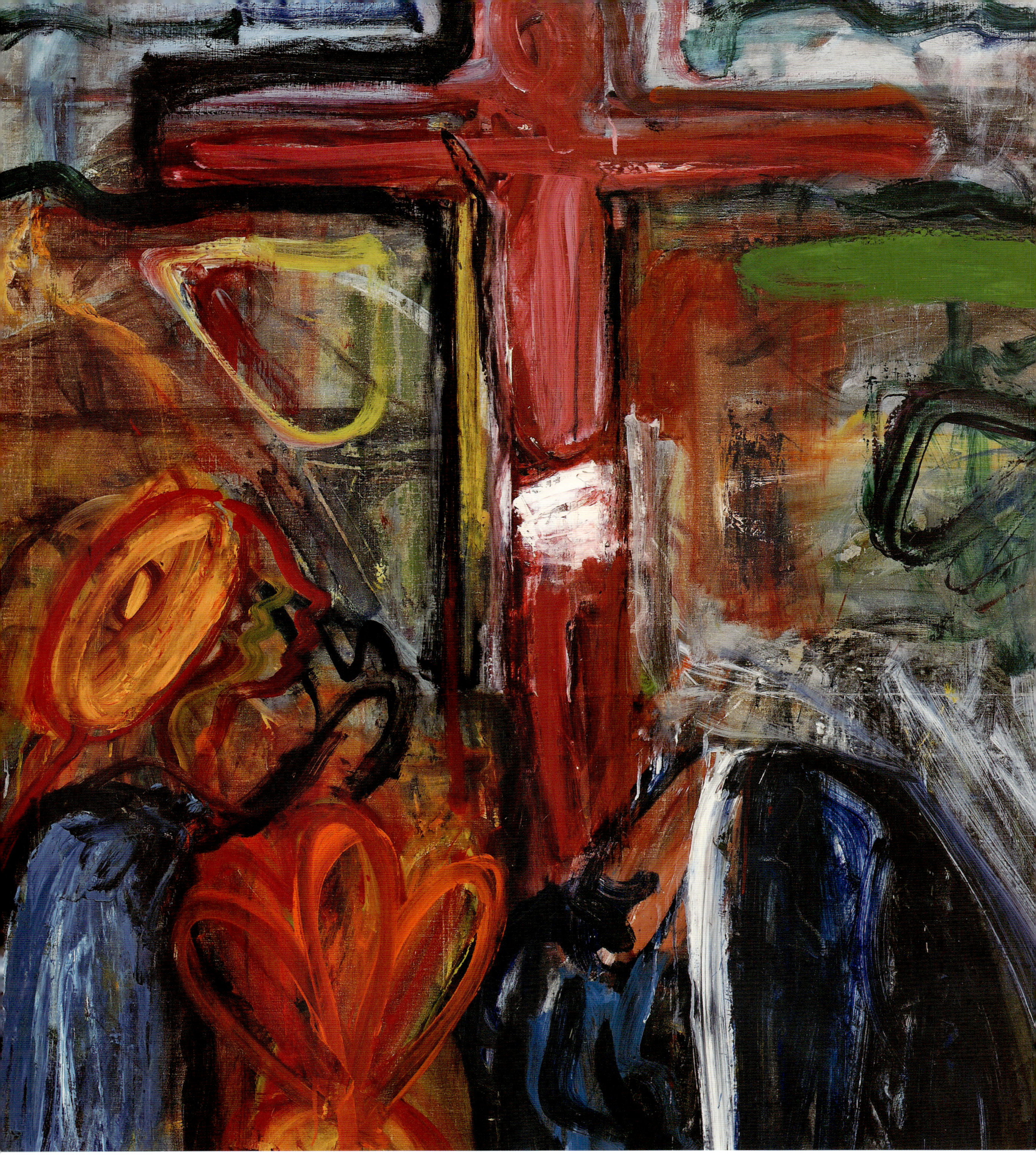

Crucifixion, 1954 (detail). Oil on canvas, 59 x 46 inches. Plate 19

In the 1977 *Self-Portrait* that he offered to Newman, De Niro presents himself bare-chested in his red studio, in the spirit of Munch's famous *Self-Portrait in Hell* (1903, FIG. 9). Visible behind him on the studio wall like guardian angels are two of his drawings, one representing Garbo in *Anna Christie*.

Placing his work in museums was a concern for De Niro. Museum status was no longer an issue for him as of 1952, again thanks to his guardian angel Schapiro, who convinced the newly organized Museum Purchase Fund, sponsored by Gloria Vanderbilt Stokowski, to purchase his first painting of the Crucifixion for $1,000 (PLATE 18). The Purchase Fund's mission was to buy works from emerging artists selected by experts like Schapiro with the intention of giving them to museums. The Fund's acquisitions of works by fourteen artists, including Rivers, Joan Mitchell, and Philip Guston, made up a touring exhibition in 1954, and De Niro's *Crucifixion* was donated to the Rosicrucian Museum in San Jose, California, by 1956.[25] Based on images of the subject by Rouault in which the cross extends to the four edges of the composition, De Niro's delirious painting is dominated by a faceless, blood-red Christ in a bright white loincloth, and wide, slashing yellow and red brushstrokes, visible more as visual rhythms than as any recognizable setting. Graphically agitated, the agonized figure of Mary at the left all but dissolves into long vertical strokes of white, black, and deep red. This *Crucifixion* was the first of dozens of versions of the theme, both oil paintings and watercolors, that the artist made for the remainder of his career, sometimes based on specific Old Master works. It is worth noting that during the 1950s such prominent postwar, avant-garde abstract painters as Mark Rothko, Barnett Newman, and Robert Rauschenberg addressed spiritual awareness in some of their completely abstract art, while museums in Europe and in this country were buying more traditional religious paintings by artists such as Salvador Dalí.

The announcement for De Niro's second solo exhibition at the Egan Gallery, in May 1953, is illustrated with a drawing rather than a painting. Introducing another theme that De Niro would treat repeatedly in years to come, the drawing is based on a reproduction of a daguerreotype by the pioneering American photographers Albert Sands Southworth and Josiah Johnson Hawes. Visible on the wall in 1957 photographs of De Niro's studio, the daguerreotype portrays the notorious Irish dancer and courtesan Lola Montez, who came to the United States in 1851 after an infamous affair with Ludwig I of Bavaria. What particular interest she held for De Niro is anyone's guess, but none of the themes that obsessed De Niro over the years seem arbitrary. Adopting an influential mode developed in the 1930s by Picasso and Matisse to record the artist's processes as attentively as the nominal subject, De Niro's drawing includes erasures as well as preliminary scribbles

25. After the museum changed its mission in 1966 to specialize in Egyptian art, De Niro's ambitious painting was deaccessioned.

overdrawn with more decisive outlines, even elementary facial features. De Niro made drawings in this same style for the rest of his life, incorporating the sequential stages of his response to a subject, as he believed drawing to be an ongoing, necessarily imperfect search for perfection.

Aside from the drawing of Lola Montez, the Egan Gallery exhibition announcement lists seven works by title. One whose theme is charged with perverse family relationships, *Lot Leaving Sodom*, has since been lost. Perhaps the works titled *Boy Reading* and *Boy with Guitar* were memory images of his nearly ten-year-old son. One of three still lifes, *Straw Hat with Flowers* (ca. 1952–53; PLATE 17) is the only work from this exhibition that can be identified today. Seemingly painted in hurried abandon, the rich colors applied in wide stripes like finger paints, sometimes scraped on with a palette knife, the work shows a wide-brimmed yellow hat in close-up, with semi-legible red flowers on either side. Overall, the scene is blurry and emphatically melancholy. Indeed, one way to look at this mysterious still life is to see the hat as pulled down over a head, of which only the purple chin is visible, though this purple patch might just as well be read as the leg of a small table. Whatever the case may be, De Niro associated such hats with working outdoors on landscapes, and he shows himself wearing just such a hat in a manic red-and-yellow *Self-Portrait of the Artist at His Easel* done in 1985 (PLATE 110).

On August 22, 1953, De Niro wrote to Schapiro at length, suggesting that Gloria Vanderbilt could perhaps now provide funds to support him for a year. In the letter he also confided that Admiral was threatening suicide. As if no one was helping him, he complained, "De Kooning walks across the street when he sees me—apparently I make him feel guilty." Presumably fully aware that his slashing expressionist intensity and off-key colors had counterparts in works by Grace Hartigan, he informed Schapiro that the Museum of Modern Art had just acquired her painting *The Persian Jacket* (1952, FIG. 10).[26] By November, De Niro's depressed outlook was less under control, and he threatened to kill Schapiro if anything happened to his son.[27] Apologizing to Schapiro, the painter's mother explained that De Niro was undernourished from poverty and overwrought with anxiety about Admiral, who had custody of the boy.[28] Indeed, the couple opted to divorce officially that year.

De Niro's final exhibition at the Egan Gallery (February 24–March 19, 1955) featured a peculiar composition with two adjacent blank-faced, graphically elementary figures in reddish jackets, one standing and the other seated, with flanking zones of sky blue as daringly minimal suggestions of the outdoors. The painting's title, *Bonjour Mr. De Niro* (ca. 1955; PLATE 30), refers knowingly to a famous work by the French Realist Gustave Courbet painted exactly one hundred years earlier to show the artist greeted by his foremost

26. Robert De Niro, Sr., to Meyer Schapiro, 22 August 1953.

27. Robert De Niro, Sr., to Meyer Schapiro, 18 November 1953.

28. Helen De Niro to Meyer Schapiro, 3 December 1953.

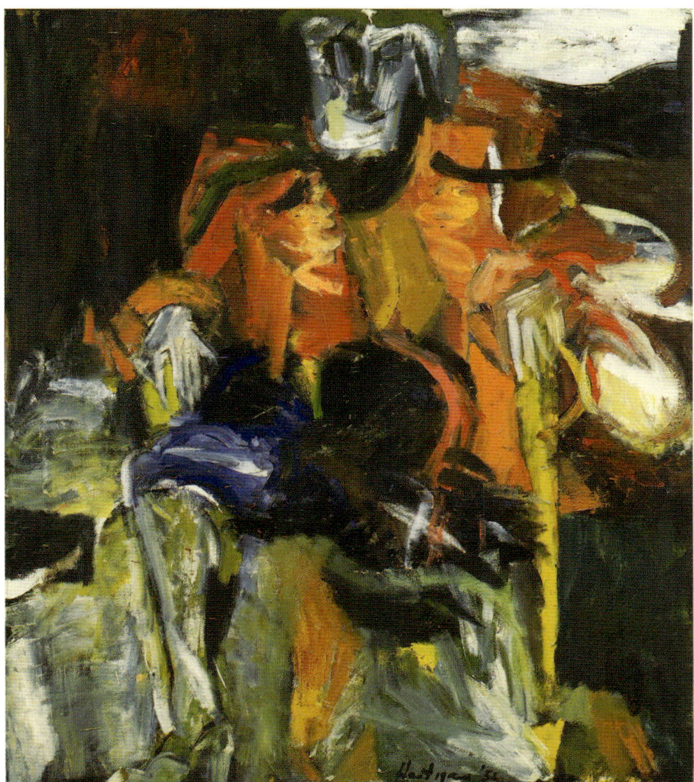

FIGURE 10
Grace Hartigan
The Persian Jacket, 1952
Oil on canvas
57½ x 48 in.
(146 x 121.9 cm)
Museum of Modern Art,
New York

patron, a reference that might be understood by Rivers or Schapiro, both familiar with Courbet's art. It is difficult not to consider the painting as an oblique double portrait of De Niro with George Poindexter, who acquired it for his collection destined for Montana. Egan's gallery assistant, Elinor Poindexter, was about to take over his gallery space as her own, and her collector husband offered De Niro a monthly stipend in exchange for works.

Newly hired by the Museum of Modern Art, the poet Frank O'Hara, who had been Rivers's lover and was especially close to Hartigan, wrote enthusiastically in the March 1955 issue of *Art News*: "Robert De Niro is one of the most original and powerful younger painters showing today, and each show of his is an event."[29] O'Hara admired two mysterious large works with female nudes, now at the Montana Historical Society, because "the intensity of the paint application . . . sweeps and fills the figures, pressing against the earth as if rain were gradually washing them into the sea, a rain of rich color which is very controlled and autocratic, almost negligently applied."[30] No source image of paired nudes is known for either of these offbeat paintings, but they ought to be understood in relationship to contemporaneous explicit nudes that Helen Frankenthaler and Rivers made in defiance of good taste. Anything but explicit, suggesting the ghosts of Old Master nudes from Giorgione to Cézanne, De Niro's crude, featureless figures are likewise meant to challenge expectations, their nudity strangely dissolved and obscured by the assertive brushwork. The backgrounds in these paintings are at once

29. F. O'H. [Frank O'Hara], "Robert De Niro," *Art News*, March 1955, 53.
30. Ibid.

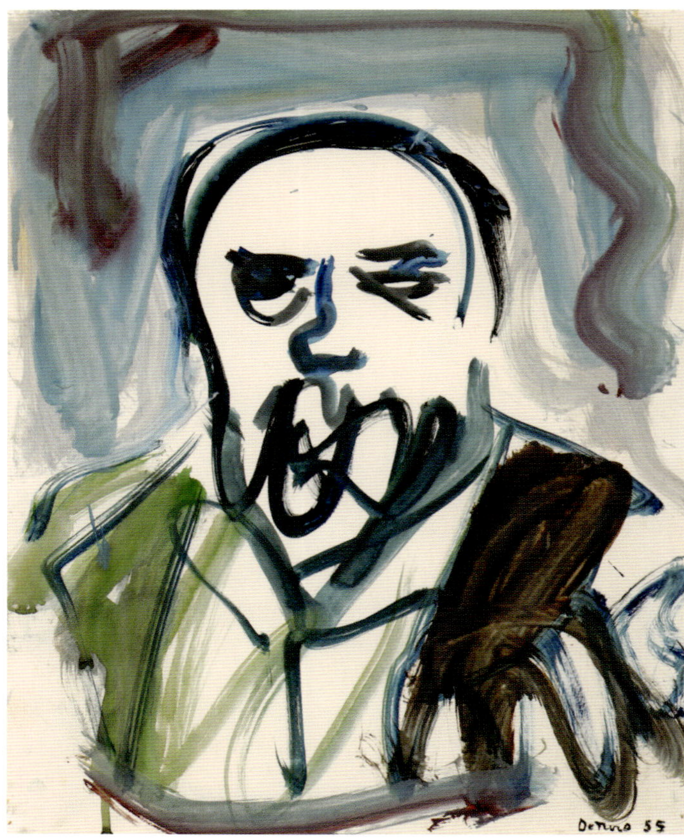

FIGURE 11
Robert De Niro, Sr.
Verlaine, 1955
Watercolor on paper
20 x 14¾ in. (50.8 x 37.5 cm)
Montana Historical Society, Poindexter Collection, Helena

illegible and bold, and the relationship, if any, between the figures and the mood of somewhat nightmarish agitation is left unresolved.

For the young critic Martica Sawin, writing in *Arts Digest*, "The most ambitious work is a large *Crucifixion* in throbbing sour color, the plumes of the helmet providing a gaudy note of temporal triumph against the deep blue shape of the sorrowing mother, beneath the painfully attenuated lines of the cross."[31] Although the earlier 1952 *Crucifixion* was previously exhibited in a group show, what this later *Crucifixion* reveals is De Niro's very unusual decision to show works on the same theme over and over. Starting at this time, these revisited themes became a constant in his practice. Of the four remarkable figures in this compact composition, none is stranger than the bruised Christ figure with the bright white cloth to cover his sex. He is so emaciated and rigid as to be barely distinguishable from the cross itself, and the reds and purples, adjacent to the yellow and orange of the helmet, intensify an upsetting visual dissonance.

De Niro's final Egan Gallery exhibition was also notable for still lifes of various objects arranged along a mantelpiece, a few roughly legible as studio props—a black fan, a vase, and a small plaster reproduction of the Venus de Milo. The two still lifes that were reproduced to illustrate reviews cannot be located today, but the 1955 exhibition may have included several other fascinating studio still lifes dated 1954, such as two brilliantly colorful variations on a single composition (*Still Life with Plaster Statue* [PLATE 23] and

31. M. S. [Martica Sawin], "Robert DeNiro [*sic*]," *Arts Digest*, March 15, 1955, 23.

Guitar, Plaster Statue [PLATE 24]). Slightly less abstracted in the larger version, the constituent elements of these two works, observed close-up but with little concern for accuracy, include a guitar at the left and, at the center, a plaster cast of a sculpture of a woman posed like Matisse's *La Serpentine* (1909), the first bronze cast of which is now in the Museum of Modern Art collection. De Niro was surely aware that Matisse sometimes included images of his sculptures in paintings of his studio. Now lost, the sculpture represented so vaguely in the foreground of these still lifes may well be a cast of the already mentioned work that De Niro made in the early 1950s. If so, these two interrelated still lifes are the only documentation of this work. Although few specific elements can be identified with confidence, De Niro's still lifes offer a glimpse of the artist's laboratory and so convey his presence by proxy no less than does his hallmark style, with every loose line and color accent nervously, if not insistently, adjusted to accord with all the others.

George Poindexter acquired an exciting floral still life executed in pastels and dated 1955, but it is uncertain whether this work appeared in the final Egan exhibition or in De Niro's subsequent solo show at the Poindexter Gallery in June 1956. The vase and the yellow flowers represented by freehand circles both appear insubstantial, as does the table supporting the arrangement, outlined repeatedly and loosely with red, white, lavender, and blue lines. The dynamic blue shadows dominate what could be described as an apparition of a still life, recalling the way that shadows stand out in a photographic negative. Among the thirty-three oils and drawings that comprised his first exhibition at the Poindexter Gallery, a highly abstracted portrait in watercolor, very loosely based on a photograph of the French poet Paul Verlaine, had special appeal for the critic Parker Tyler, who recalled that De Niro had previously exhibited a less abstract portrait of the same subject (FIG. 11).[32] In this case, the Francophilic De Niro chose a theme with obvious personal resonance for him: Verlaine had abandoned his wife and baby son for the young poet Arthur Rimbaud. Rivers likewise identified with this *poète maudit*, the iconic misunderstood visionary.

In early July 1956, on the occasion of De Niro's show at the Poindexter Gallery, *Newsweek* ran an informative profile of the artist. "[De Niro] is an artist caught up in an old, if somewhat neglected tradition. He is lean and brooding and he has frequently gone hungry for want of artistic compromising, caught as he puts it in the squeeze between conventional representation and all-out abstraction in the painting world, he finds no quarter with either camp."[33] During a visit to his studio on lower Broadway, with source images tacked to the wall alongside his own works, the writer explained that no one else among De Niro's contemporaries made "deft and bold portraits, without commission and without sitter, from movie stills and yellowing nineteenth-century photographs. Verlaine, the French

32. P. T. [Parker Tyler], "Robert De Niro," *Art News*, Summer 1956, 53.

33. Unsigned, "Art: Up from the Frenzy," *Newsweek*, July 9, 1956, 59–60.

symbolist poet, keeps silent company with Greta Garbo, rendered full face and [in] profile [in] her famous roles of 'Anna Christie' and 'Camille.'"[34] One wonders if the artist's now twelve-year-old son took notice of his father's erudite appreciation of vintage film.

Lost today, the painting of Garbo in *Anna Christie* that is reproduced on the announcement for the June 1956 Poindexter show marks a return to a theme that De Niro had last visited six years previously. This painting shows the same scene he had depicted earlier: Anna sitting alone at a table, attended by the bartender Larry. The faces of both figures are blank, as if to stress the artist's lack of interest in actors and plot, both irrelevant to the compositional structure evident in the source film still.

This detachment did not inform the drawings of Garbo in the show; however, one of them was reproduced in reviews. Here, De Niro shows a close-up of the actress in the same role, her facial features smudged with melancholy shadows that capture her mystique with elegant economy. According to reviews, another drawing showed Garbo in profile playing the title role in the 1936 film *Camille*, which was based on the nineteenth-century best seller by Alexandre Dumas *fils*. Two masterful drawings of Garbo in profile have survived, both rendered in charcoal and chalk in keeping with the tones of some presumed (but unknown) source photograph in which the actress holds a large bouquet (PLATES 32, 33). In strict profile, the actress appears stoic, quite unlike the quickly sketched profusion of flowers, mostly just outlined blossoms and leaves, that animate the shadowy mood.

Critics unfamiliar with the first Egan show in 1951 referred to De Niro's landscapes and drawings of seated Moroccan women as a new theme. But like the image of Garbo, these figures, based on Bissinger's photograph, belong to a repertoire that De Niro now embraced, the way contemporaries like Jasper Johns around the same time were creating multiple variations of favorite themes like the flag or numerals in a variety of media and formats. The charcoal drawings of grouped Moroccan women in the 1956 exhibition are tours de force, close in spirit to Degas's elaborate drawings of dancers, which incorporate every stage of his artistic process, including scribbled lines to determine a silhouette, smudges, and chalk highlights. It is not known whether the large 1956 painting on the Moroccan women theme that was purchased in 1962 by Joseph Hirshhorn was included in the Poindexter exhibition (FIG. 12).

It seems that De Niro's decision to make works in repertoire appealed to serious collectors wanting significant examples of each of his key themes. The review of the exhibition in the June 1956 issue of *Arts* mentions a *Still Life with Greek Head* only to say that it had less

34. "Art: Up from the Frenzy," 59–60.

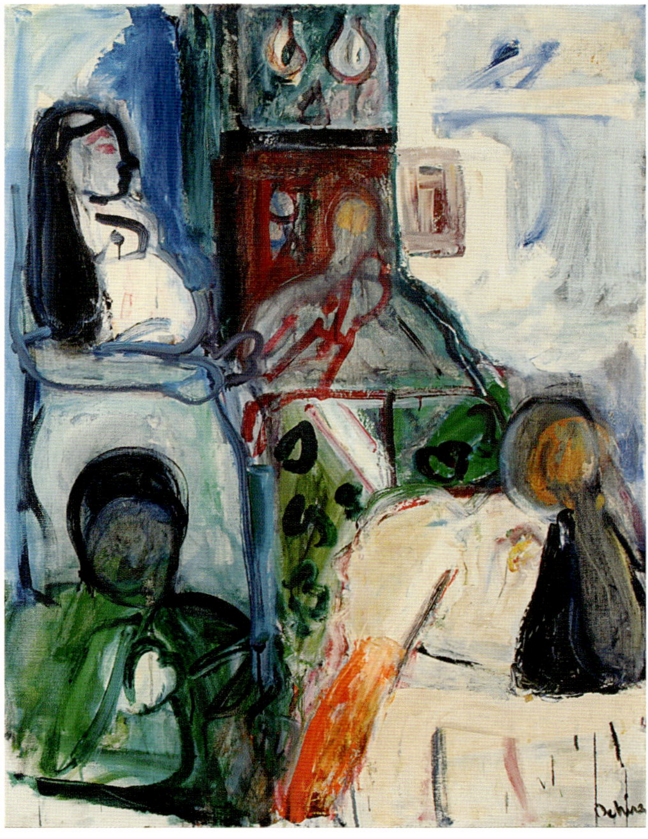

FIGURE 12
Robert De Niro, Sr.
Moroccan Women, 1956
Oil on canvas
48 x 36½ in. (121.9 x 92.7 cm)
Private Collection

appeal than the virtuoso drawings.[35] But it is important to note that the life-sized plaster cast of the head of Aphrodite after Praxiteles had now joined the artist's set of established themes. Photographs taken at the end of 1957 show leaning against his studio walls two new still lifes that include a plaster head, as well as the plaster cast itself placed on the floor. Judging from the loosely applied yellows, blues, and greens that De Niro orchestrated for the variations introduced in the mid-1950s, he took old-fashioned satisfaction in evoking and extending the rich modern tradition of still lifes featuring sculptures, carried on from Cézanne to Matisse and Picasso.

Predictably, De Niro was soon at odds with the Poindexters, and predictably he turned for help to Schapiro and Hess. Apparently, it was Schapiro who introduced De Niro to Hirshhorn, who at the time was assembling one of the most comprehensive contemporary art collections in the United States.[36] As editor of *Art News*, Hess sent Eleanor Munro to write a lavishly illustrated feature article on De Niro's studio practice, part of the magazine's popular series "So-and-so paints a picture," which documented the evolution of an artwork from start to finish.[37] Presumably it was the artist who chose to chronicle the development of not one but a whole group of new works on the Crucifixion theme, to which he claimed to have already devoted "about six gouaches and several oils." In the opening paragraph of "De Niro Works on a Series of Pictures," Munro stresses that De Niro chose to limit himself to several "inexhaustible" themes, listing, in addition to

35. J. R. M. "Robert De Niro" *Arts*, June 1956, 58.

36. Robert De Niro, Sr., to Meyer Schapiro, 18 November 1953.

37. Eleanor C. Munro, "De Niro Works on a Series of Pictures," *Art News*, May 1958, 38–41, 48, 50.

the Crucifixion, Moroccan women, Anna Magnani, and Garbo as Anna Christie—all based on source images. Photographs for this article, taken by Rudy Burckhardt over the course of several visits, show a studio cluttered with art supplies and works in progress on all of these themes, with source photos on display here and there for reference.[38]

Munro included a detailed account of the artist's autobiography as a child prodigy and later autodidact in French, and she noted that tennis, chess, and metapsychology were among his interests, adding that the artist "has several times turned his life upside down and now wants 'peace and quiet' for his painting and himself."[39] About his studio practice, Munro explained that "returning to the canvas again and again over a period of weeks, De Niro will simplify, cover large areas with flat strokes of the palette-knife, scrape huge sections bare with a turpentine-soaked rag, and draw broad, outlined forms with one of his Rubens brushes."[40] But as Munro tried to keep track of the developing works for her text, De Niro, speaking as a self-persecuted perfectionist, declared his dissatisfaction with these works and the majority of his previous variations on the Crucifixion theme. No mention was made of popular interest in the subject, in films like *The Robe* (1953), for example, or of veteran artist Barnett Newman's series, begun that year, of fully abstract paintings on the Stations of the Cross.

Curiously enough, no image of the great Italian actress Anna Magnani has been identified as such among De Niro's surviving works, although she seems to be the subject of the drawing, commissioned in 1957, that is illustrated in Munro's article. Magnani won an Oscar in 1955 for her performance in Tennessee Williams's *The Rose Tattoo*. In 1958, it would have certainly been more modern-minded of De Niro to have focused on his images of movie stars for this *Art News* article, rather than on his variations on the Crucifixion theme, which he referred to as a frustrating "shipwreck" for himself artistically.[41] Since De Niro was among fifteen artists selected by Hess to be in a group exhibition at the first Spoleto Festival of Two Worlds in June 1958—along with Hartigan, Rivers, and Rauschenberg—he could not have been oblivious to the growing interest in images from popular culture in contemporary art.

In the same year, as De Niro prepared for a solo exhibition at the small Virginia Zabriskie Gallery, where Schapiro helped arrange his representation, he received the patronage of the Longview Foundation, established in 1958 by Hess and his wife, Audrey, to benefit artists more admired by their fellow artists than supported by collectors. Schapiro and Hofmann were among the judges selecting work. When the Longview Foundation's collection was exhibited at the Whitney Museum of American Art in June 1959, five works by De Niro from 1957 and 1958 were included. Subsequently donated to the International

38. Munro, "De Niro Works on a Series of Pictures," 38–40.

39. Ibid.

40. Ibid.

41. Ibid.

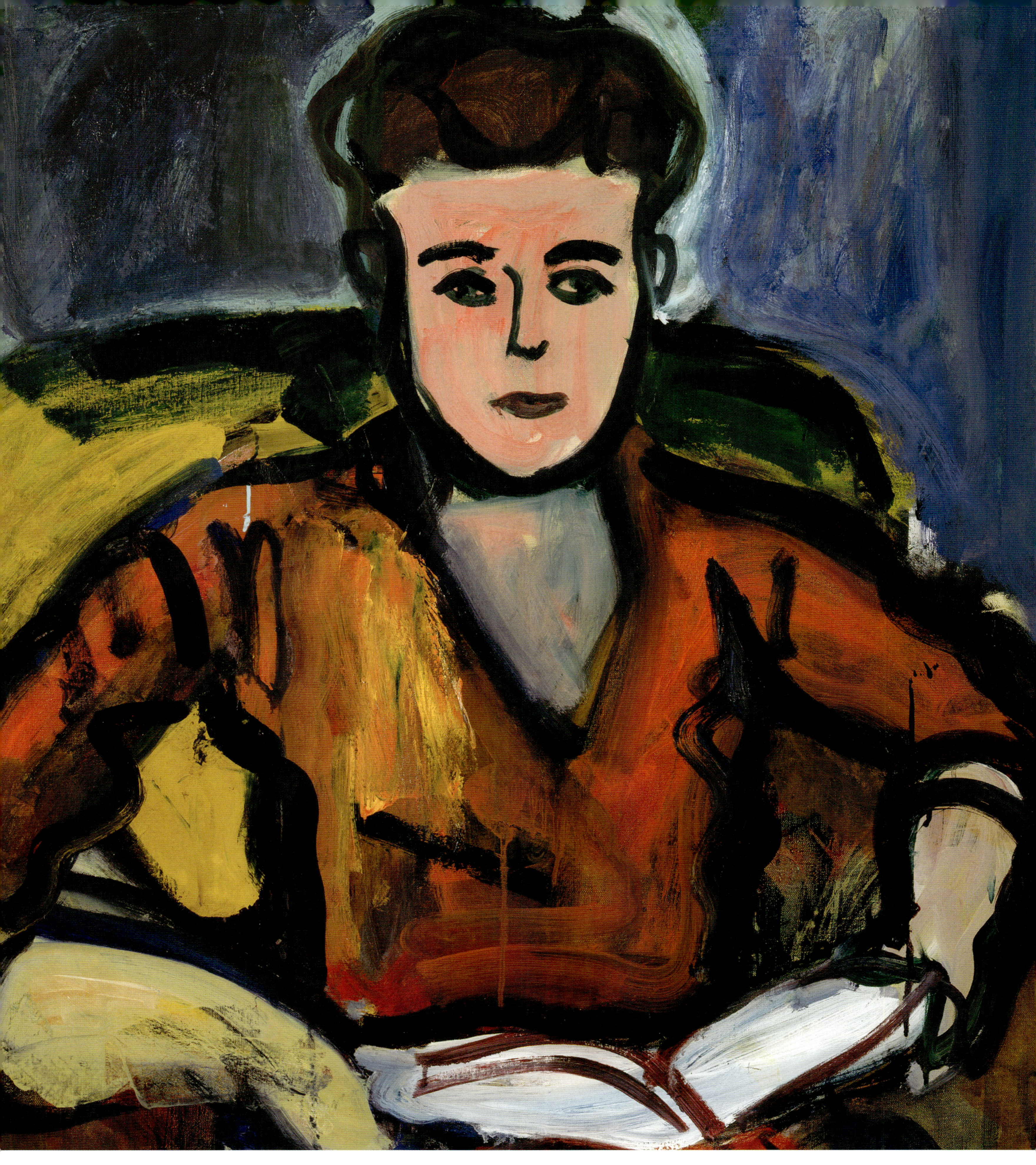

Portrait of Mrs. Z, 1959 (detail). Oil on canvas, 38¼ x 34¼ inches. Plate 37

Ladies' Garment Workers' Union in New York, these important early works unfortunately can no longer be located. In addition to his earliest painting of the Descent from the Cross, this group included examples of all of De Niro's essential themes, some as paintings, others as elaborate exhibition drawings—a Crucifixion, a Garbo, a Moroccan women, a still life.[42]

A drawing was reproduced on the announcement for De Niro's October 1958 debut exhibition at the Zabriskie Gallery, which would represent him for the next dozen years. French poetry enthusiasts perhaps realized that this drawing depicts a precious documentary photograph of the outcast Verlaine wearing a broad-brimmed hat and seated alone at a bar table in the spirit of Garbo's Anna Christie. As a self-portrait by proxy, this scribbled homage represents a fantasy that De Niro would soon be able to live out, when Zabriskie agreed to support him as an expatriate artist in Paris. It is not known whether the exhibition included the painting of Garbo in *Anna Christie* visible on the studio wall in Burckhardt's *Art News* photographs. Based as much on moody modern-life paintings by Toulouse-Lautrec and Munch as on a film-still source, De Niro's composition omits as unimportant both the tabletop on which Garbo leans and the head of the waiter in the background. Here the emphasis is on her hat, no longer a cloche as in the still, but rather a broad-brimmed straw design, its solar color at odds with Garbo's shadowy lunar face and the nocturnal mood of melancholy. Reviewing the exhibition in *Art News*, the poet James Schuyler neglected the paintings, except to say that two still lifes dominated. But he wrote enthusiastically about the drawings. "De Niro's drawings are a major phase of his work and not merely an adjunct of his paintings. The charcoal rubbed to soft silvers, the black, smoothly jagged line dropping like slow lightning, their finish and control escape expertise because his style is so personal. That, and the means he uses, disassociating line and tone (or, in his oils, line and color) so that the elements can always be grasped both as themselves and as a part of what they compose."[43]

Although whether any of them had been in the October 1958 exhibition is unknown, in March 1959, Zabriskie sold five works to Hirshhorn, one a brand-new portrait of herself titled *Portrait of Mrs. Z* (1959; PLATE 37), and in April she sold him two still lifes. Perhaps impressed by the Longview Foundation's support for the artist, Hirshhorn quickly became a force in De Niro's career on a par with Schapiro, with whom he consulted. During the next decade, Hirshhorn acquired De Niro's paintings and works on paper in depth, as he acquired the works of other contemporary artists—with the evolving intention to create a museum of modern art on the National Mall in Washington, DC, an ambition ratified by Congressional approval in 1966.

42. See *Project 1*, exh. cat. (New York, NY: Whitney Museum of American Art, 1959).

43. J. S. [James Schuyler], "Robert de Niro," *Art News*, November 1958, 12–13.

An exhibition limited to De Niro's drawings and watercolors inaugurated Zabriskie's new gallery space at 36 East 61st Street in June 1960, and it was followed just months later, in October, by a show of his new paintings. Included in this second exhibition were two self-portraits in oil on paper that Hirshhorn acquired, one vertical in format, the other horizontal. Now successful and planning to settle in Paris, De Niro in these interrelated works presented himself nostalgically as a boy with short hair, something like the prodigy he was as a student in Syracuse. He incorporated the vertical self-portrait into the composition of the horizontal one (1960; PLATE 49), where it appears reflected over his shoulder on the wall behind him, blank-faced and golden. By contrast, the simplified, masklike features of the primary self-image are pensive and darkened with shadow. Mostly, the October exhibition featured variations on De Niro's favorite still-life arrangements, with fruits and flowers under the gaze of his plaster head of Aphrodite in a setting rich with patterned fabrics. Hirshhorn immediately acquired the largest of these.

In their pervasive Matissean mood, these works clearly anticipate De Niro's decision to abandon his hard-won status in the New York School in order to fulfill his longstanding dream of joining the School of Paris, as he finally did in April 1961, when he settled in France as a successful artist. Unsurprisingly, given his depression, De Niro was hardly less of a misfit in Paris than he had been in New York. His turbulent years in France and his eventual repatriation as a veteran modernist deserve a separate careful study. However, in many ways De Niro's New York School years provide the foundation and template for understanding the last three decades of his remarkable career. It was in these early years that De Niro found his own way, based on source images, to synthesize representation and abstraction. What's more, the repertoire of themes that he developed in the 1950s served as the basis for the constant variations that preoccupied him right up to the end. De Niro's masterful later images of *Moroccan Women* (1968; PLATE 70) and *Anna Christie Entering the Bar* (1976; PLATE 97), as well as the *Last Painting* (1985–93; PLATE 113), all on display at the Tribeca Grill, are nothing less than a recapitulation of his 1950s artistic identity. No matter how painful those formative years were at times for him, the concerns and strategies he developed then were what sustained him as an artist.

PAINTINGS & DRAWINGS 1966–1993

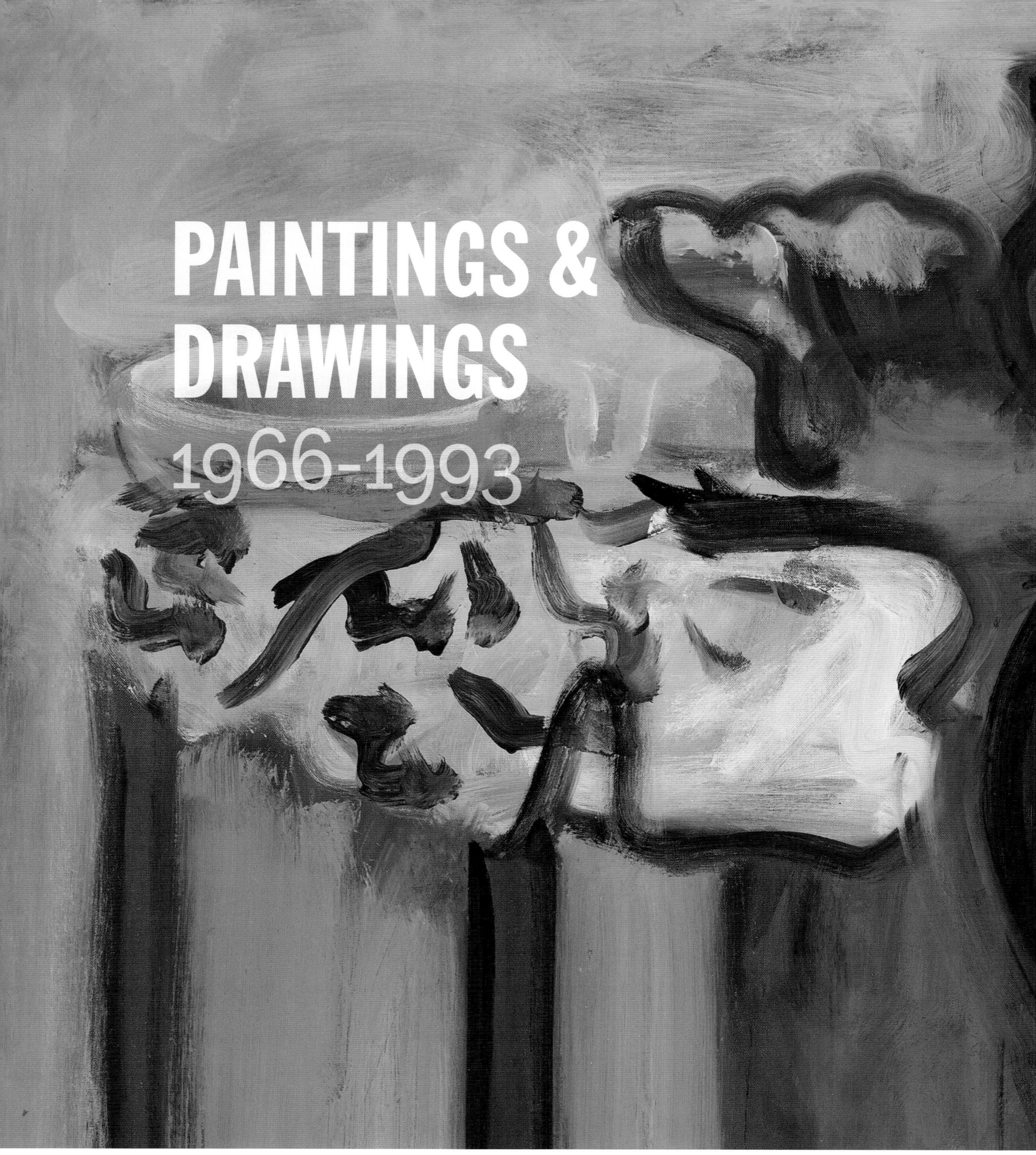

Man in Blue Sweater, 1967 (detail). Oil on linen, 38 x 48 inches. Plate 62

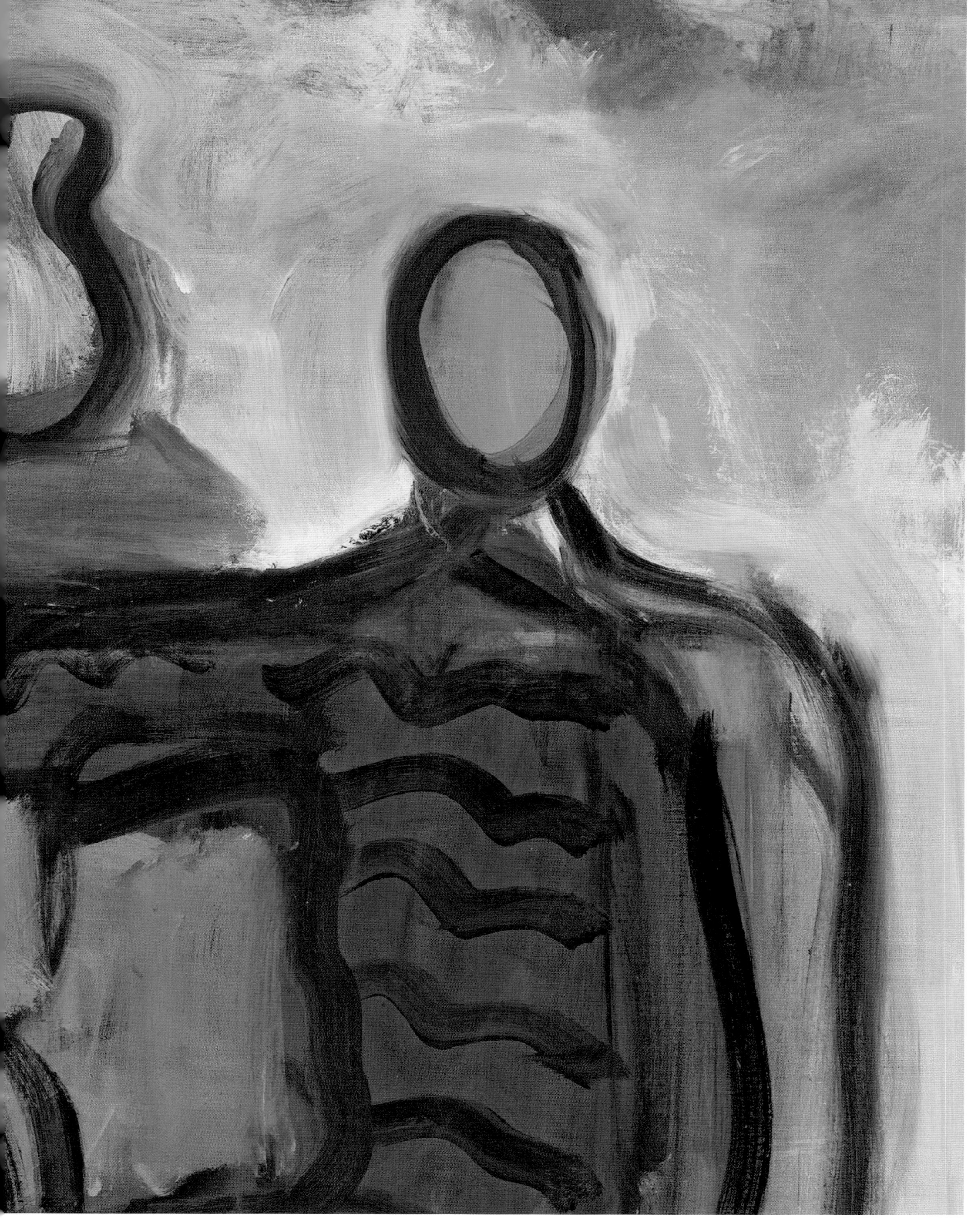

59. **Women at the Well**, 1966. Oil on canvas, 64 x 70 inches

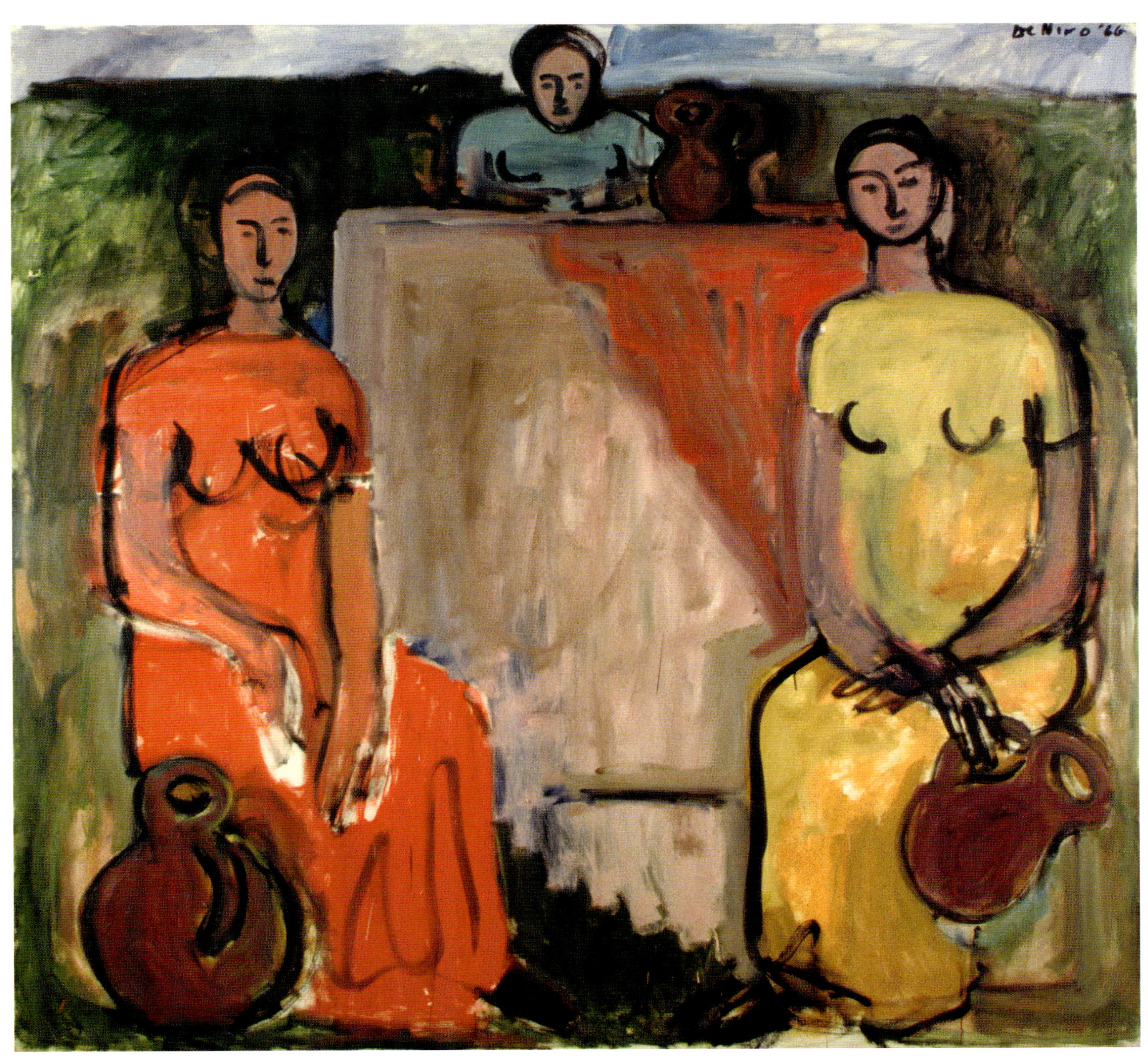
DeNiro '66

60. **Flowers in a Blue Vase**, 1966. Oil on canvas, 28 x 36 inches

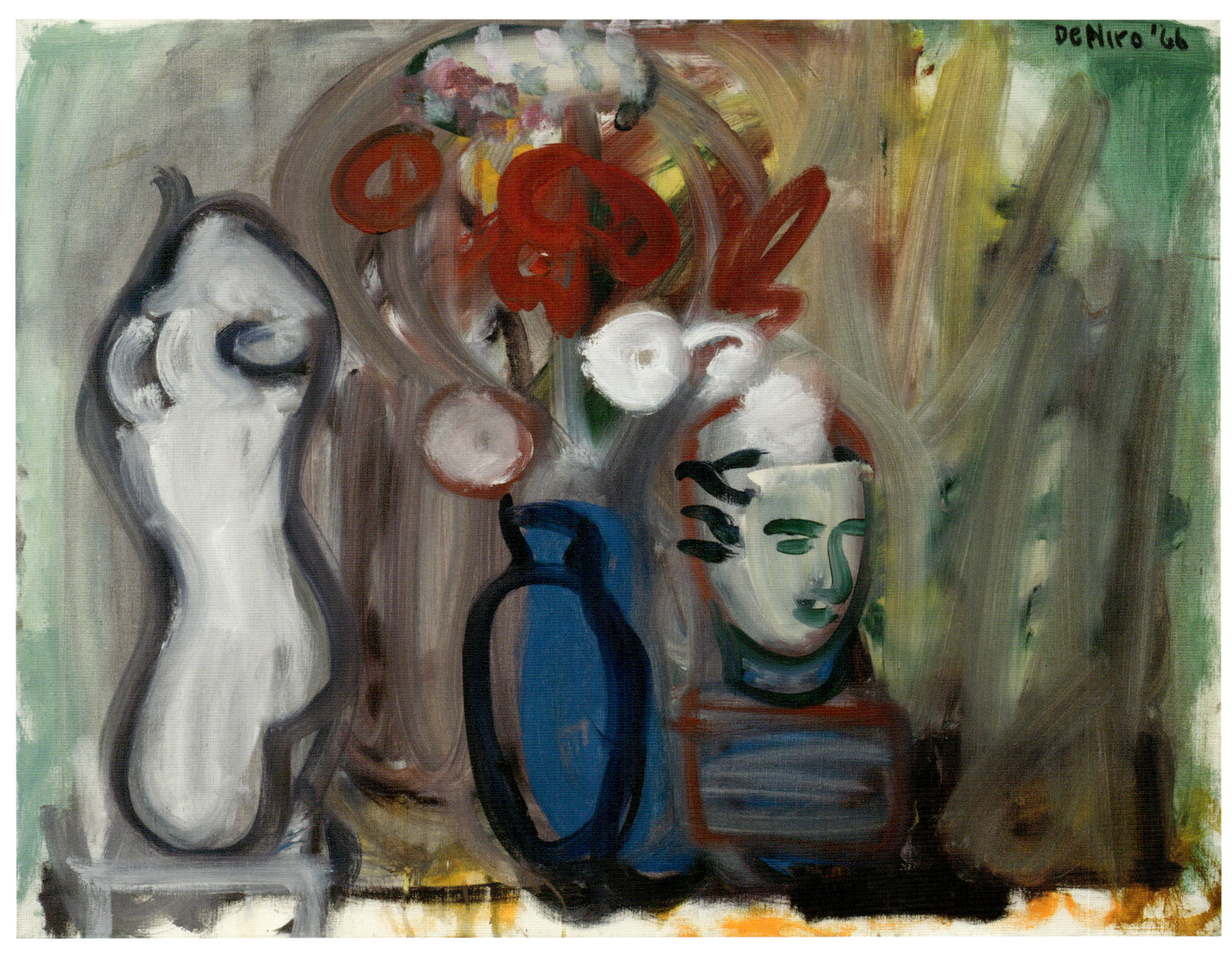
DeNiro '66

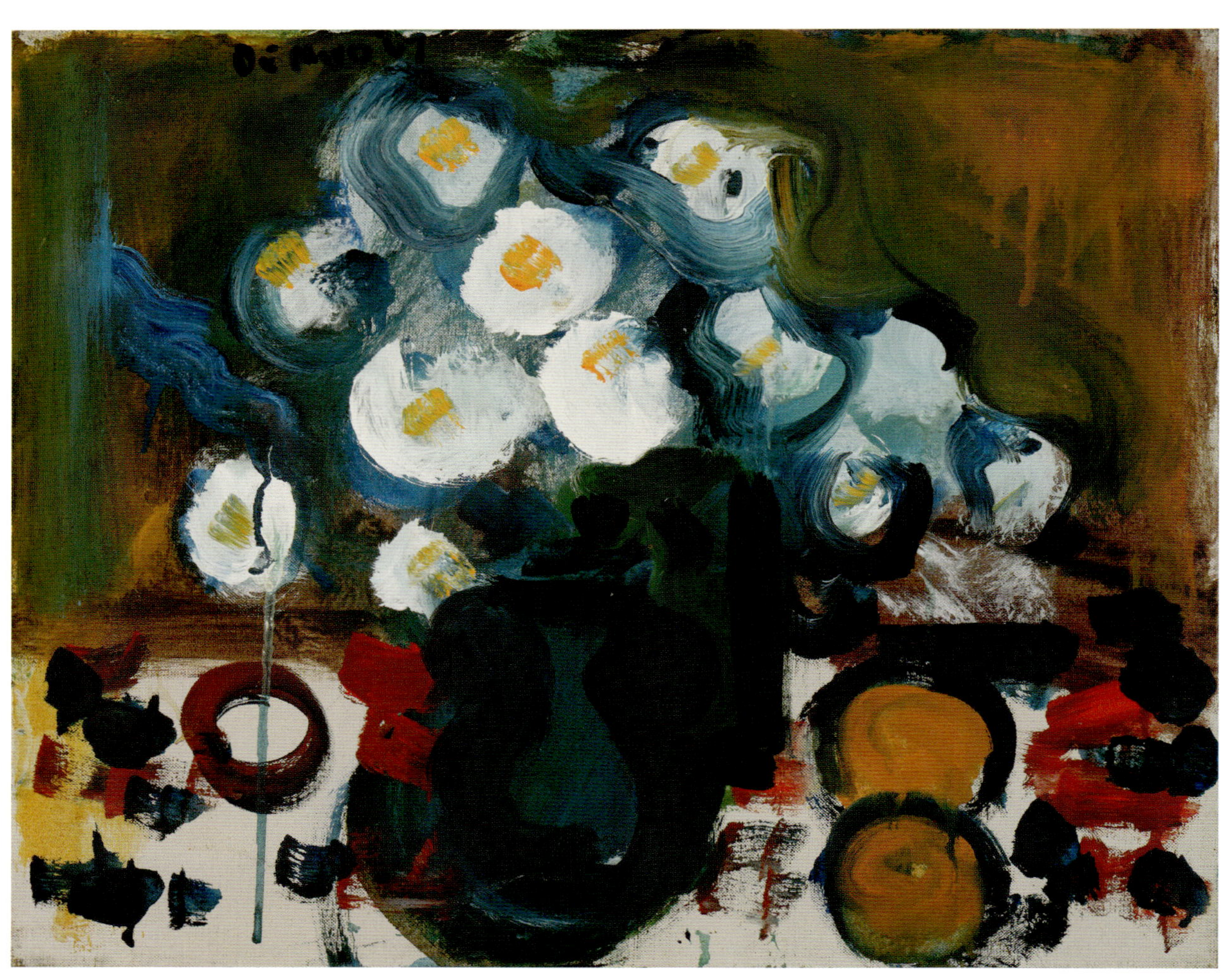

61. **Two Vases: Flowers**, 1967. Acrylic on canvas, 16 x 20 inches

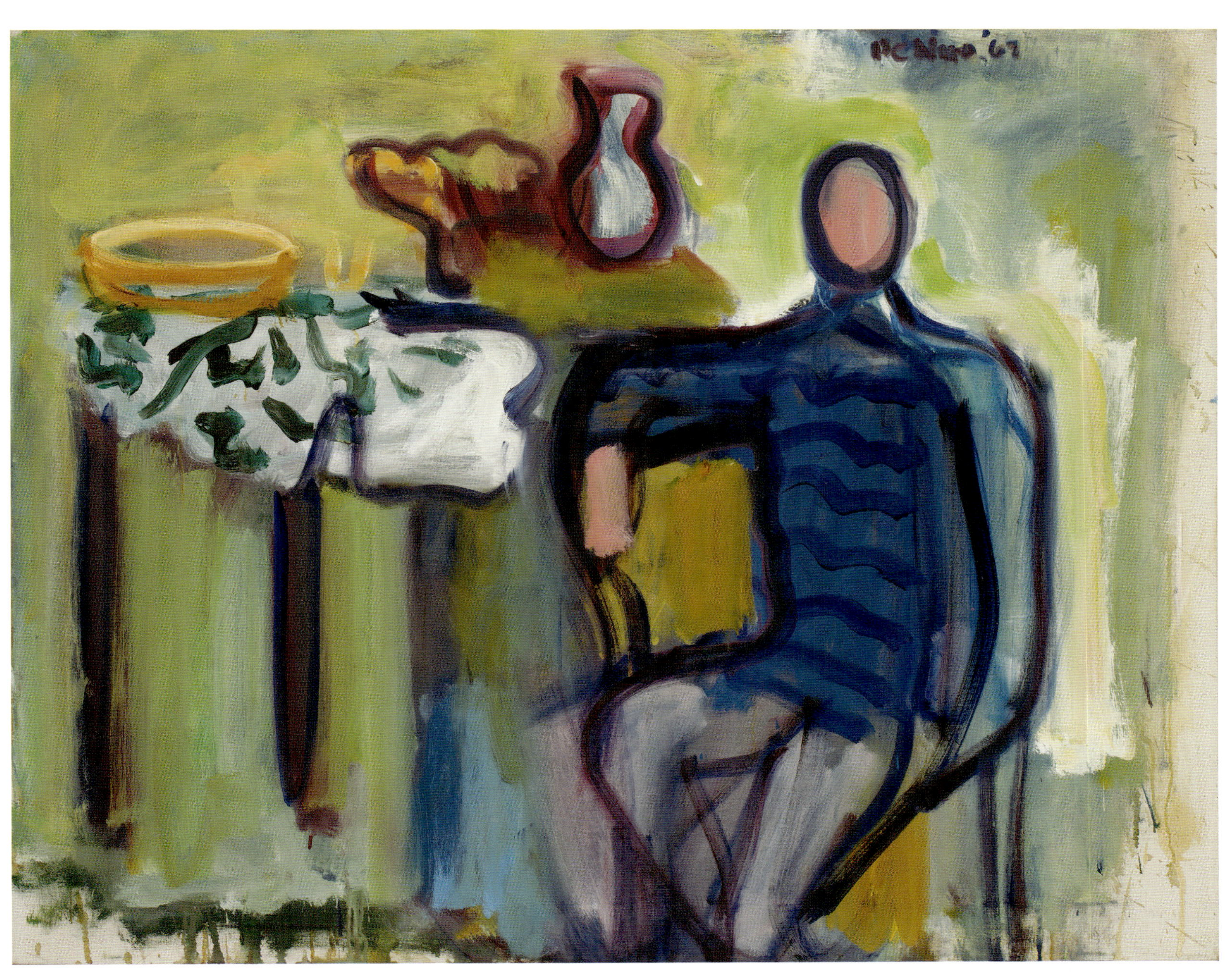

62. **Man in Blue Sweater**, 1967. Oil on linen, 38 x 48 inches

63. **White Building from Blue Porch**, 1968. Oil on canvas, 30 x 32 inches

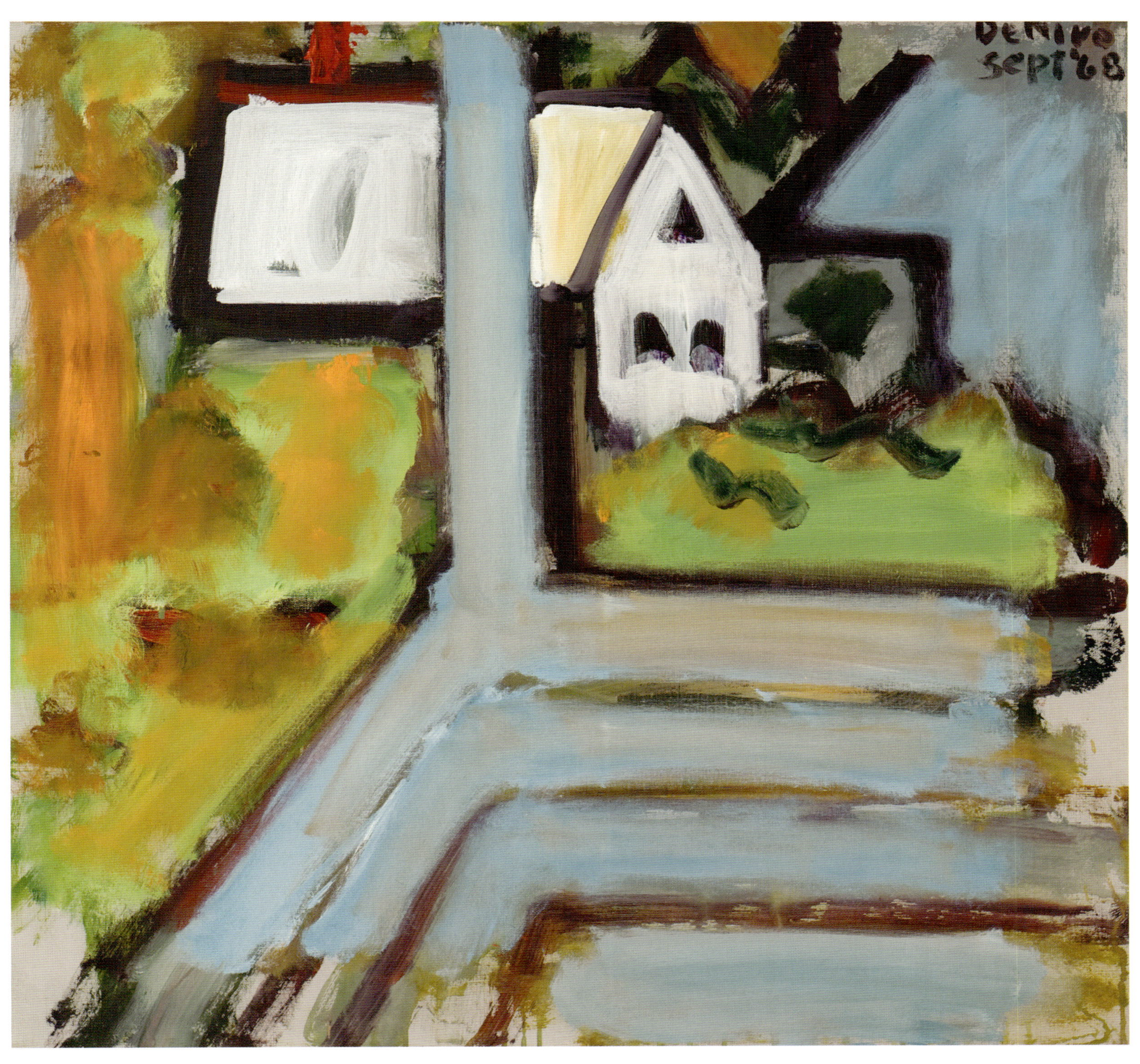
DeNiro
Sept'68

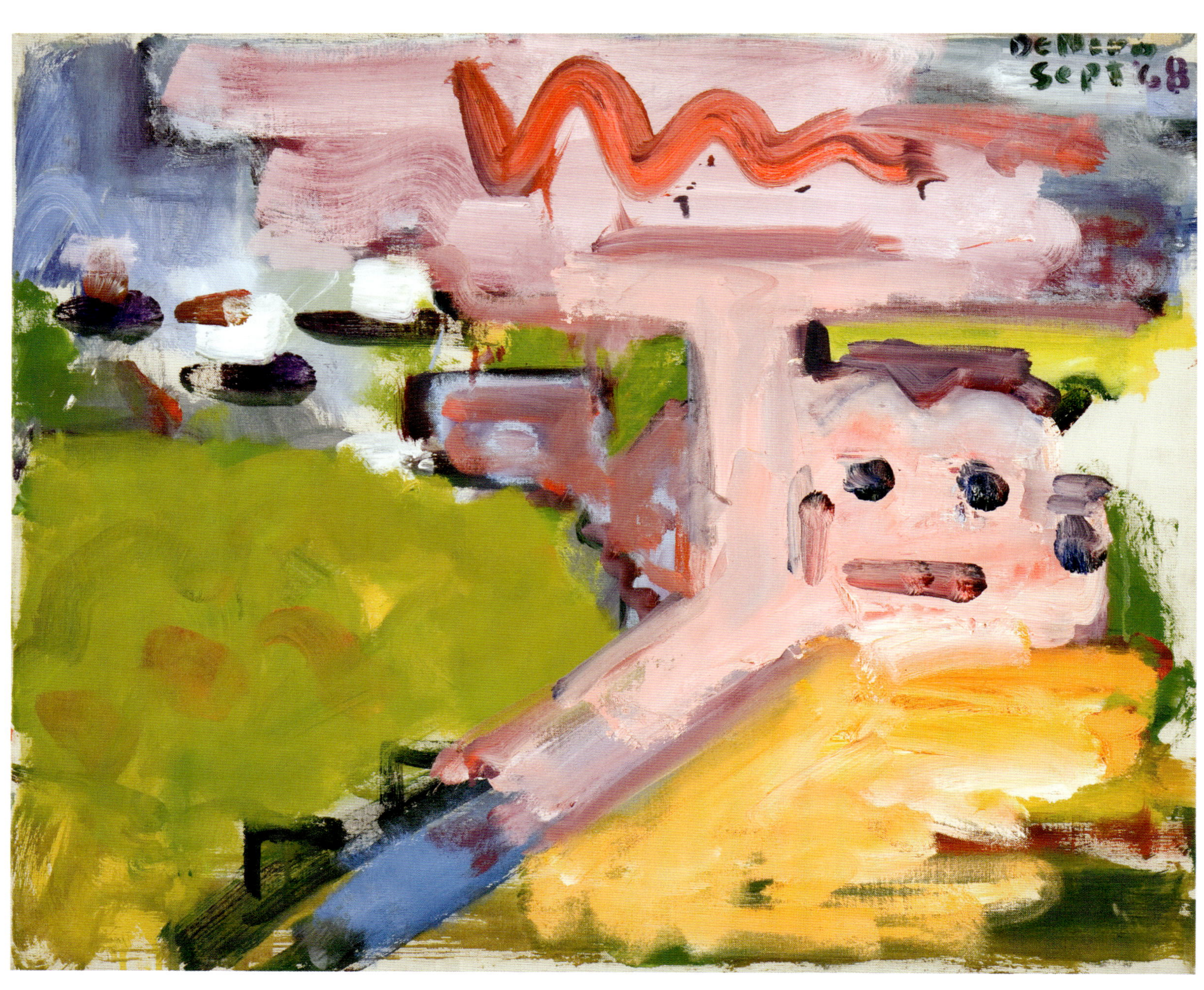

64. **Buildings in a Landscape**, 1968. Oil on canvas, 24 x 30 inches

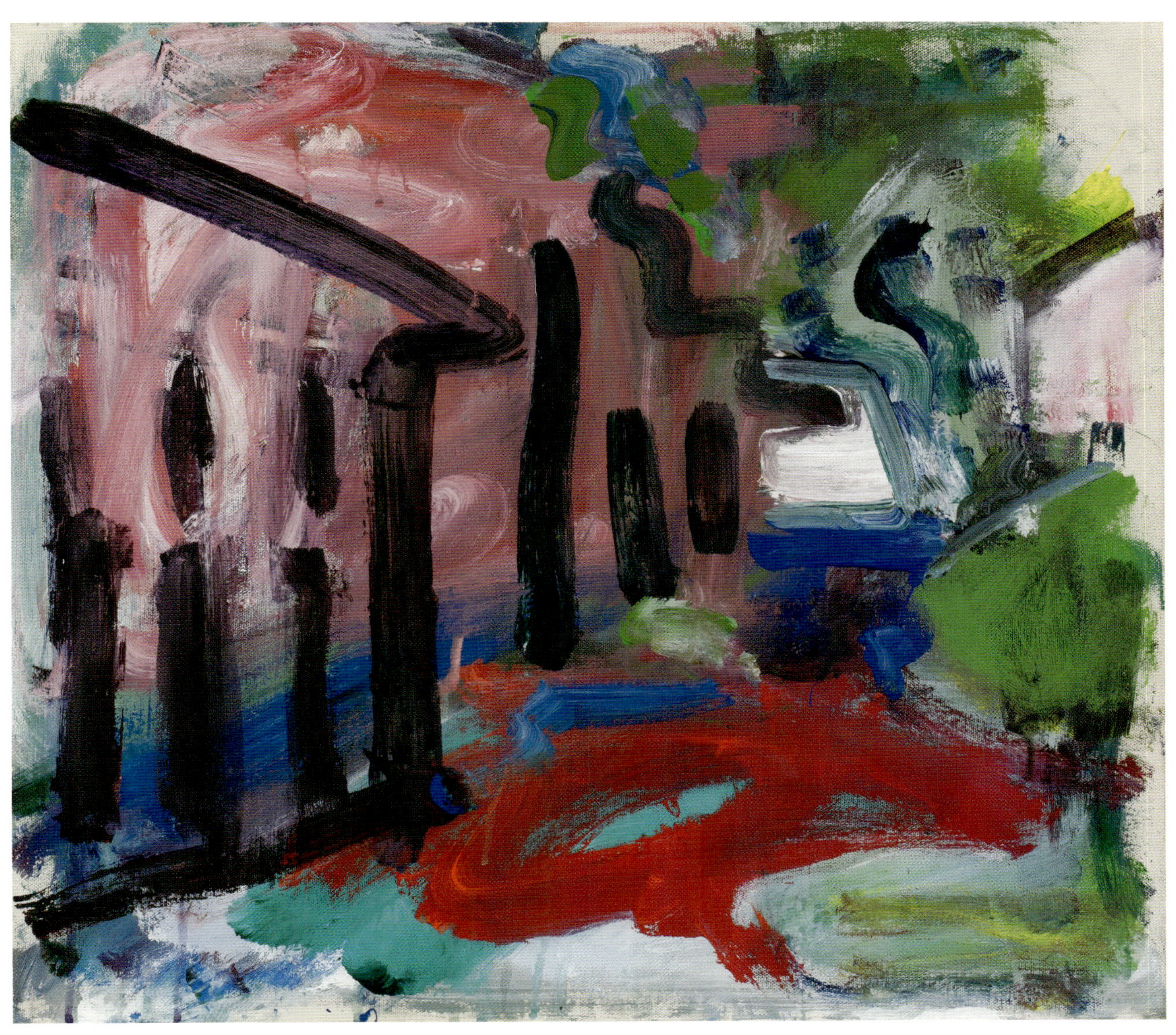

65. **Side View of Houses and Street**, 1967–69. Oil on canvas, 17¾ x 20 inches

66. **Autumn Landscape with House**, 1968. Oil on canvas, 30¼ x 36 inches

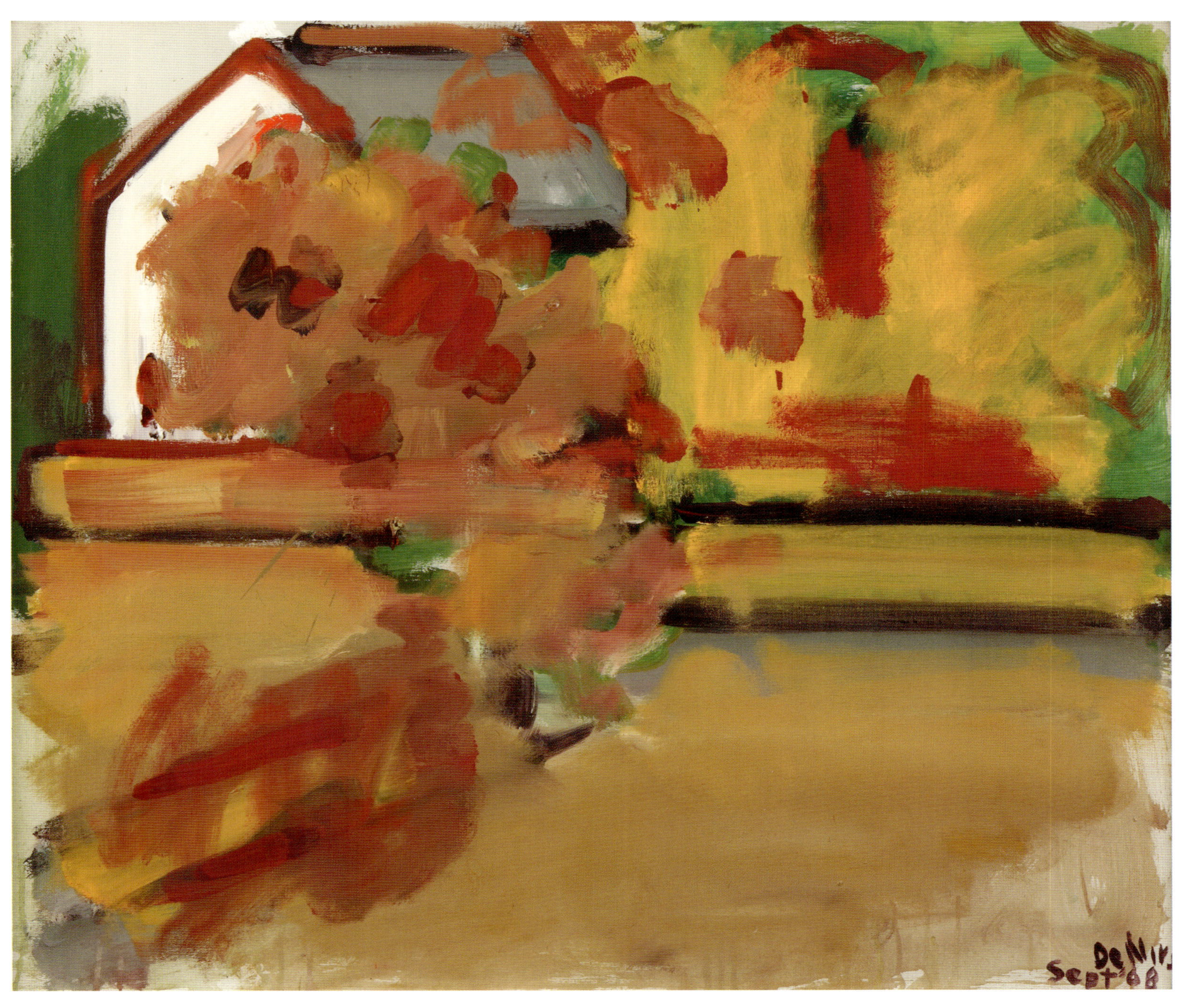

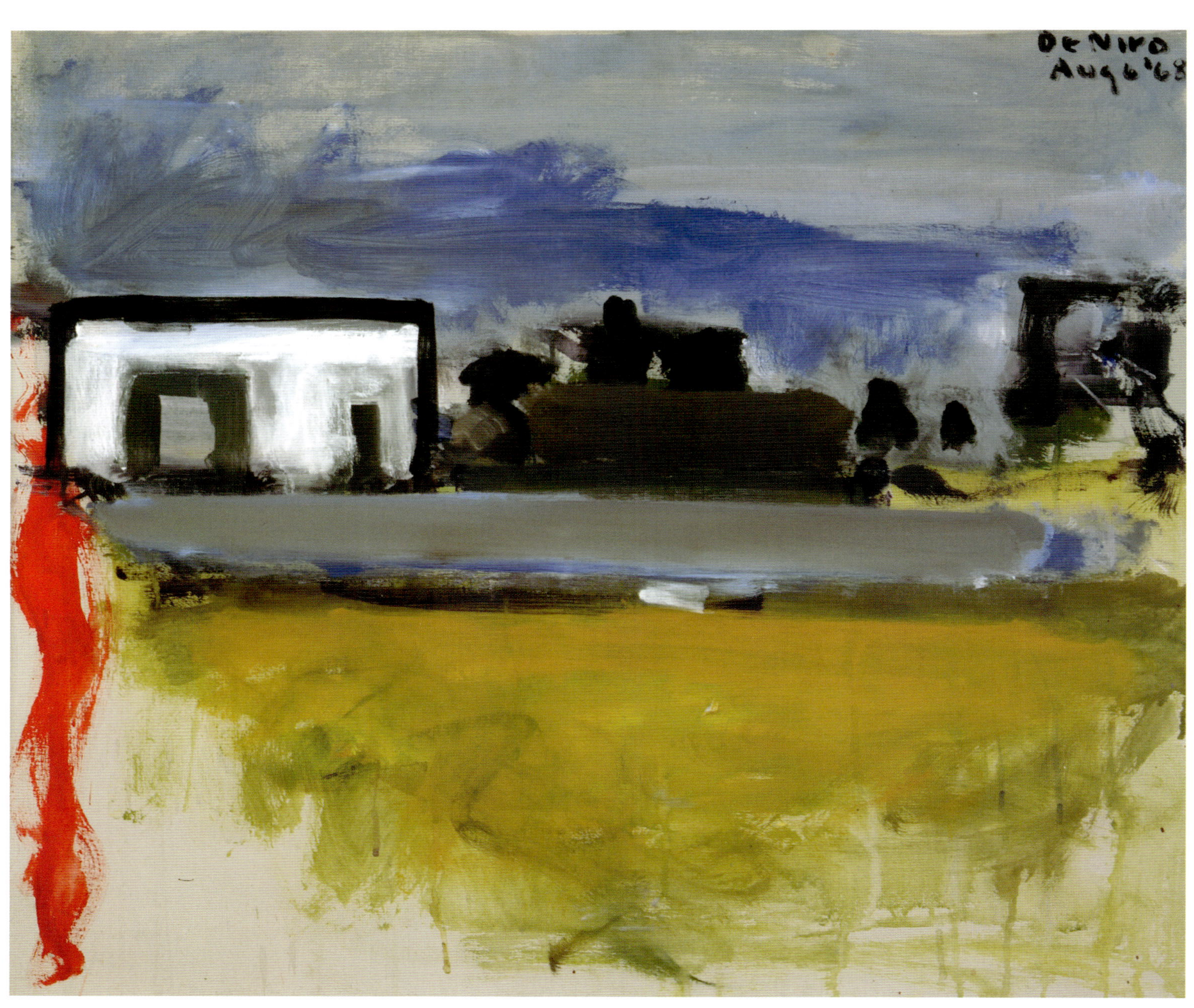

67. **Landscape with White House**, 1968. Oil on canvas, 28¾ x 33 inches

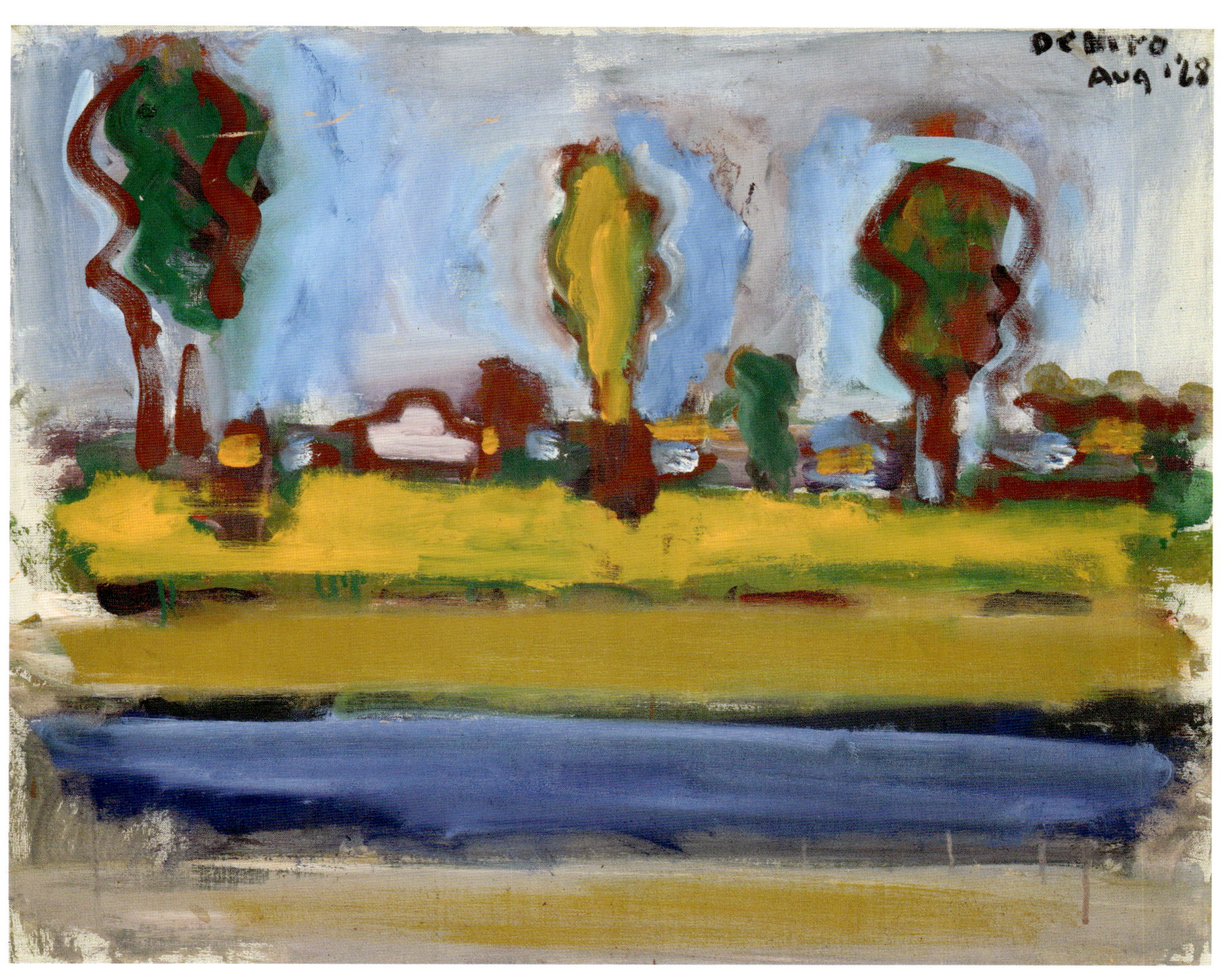

68. **Autumn Landscape**, 1968. Oil on canvas, 24 x 30 inches

69. **Untitled Landscape**, 1968. Oil on linen, 30 x 34 inches

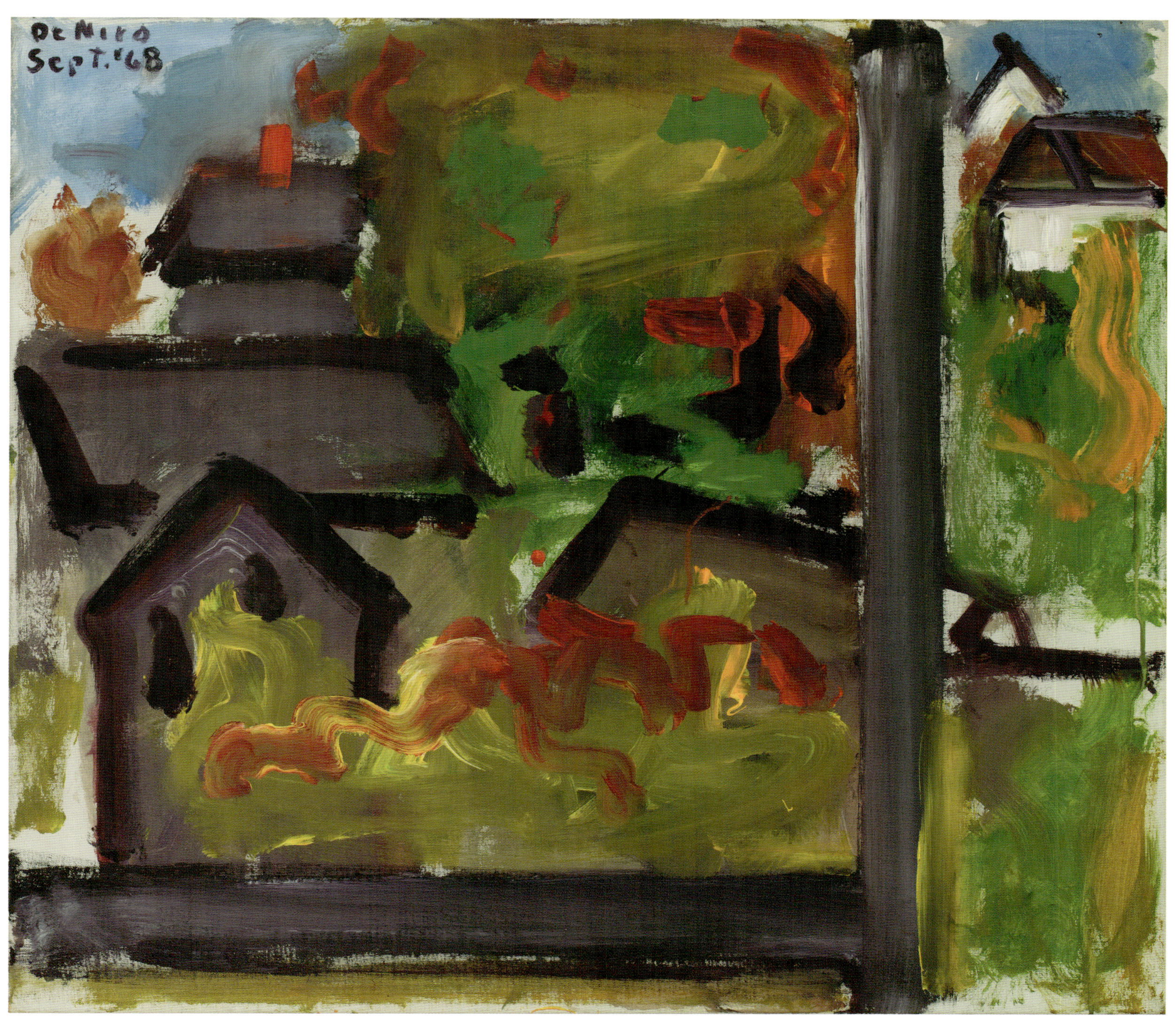
De Niro
Sept. '68

70. **Moroccan Women**, 1968. Oil on canvas, 68 x 64 inches

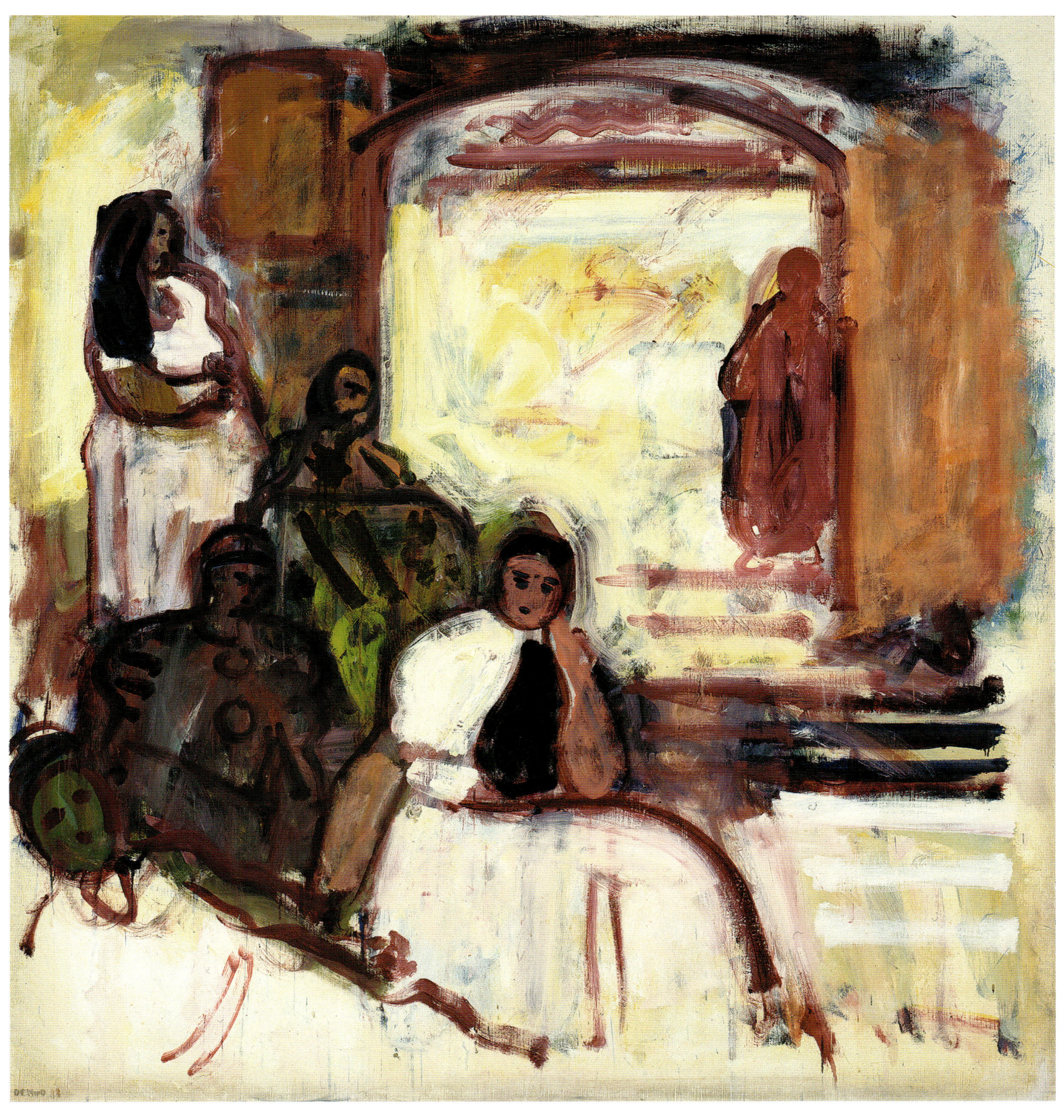

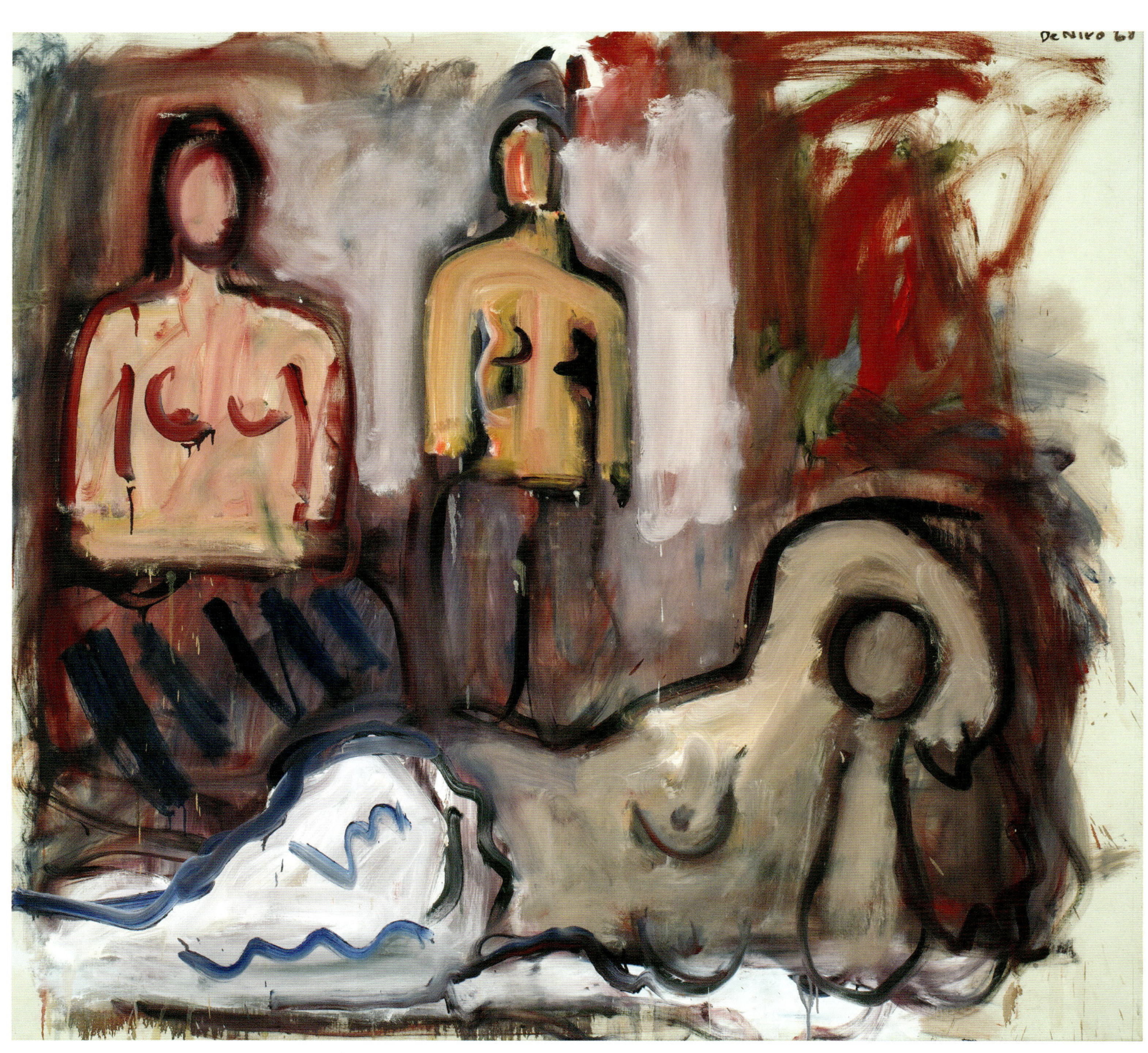

71. **Three Women**, 1968. Oil on canvas, 64 x 70 inches

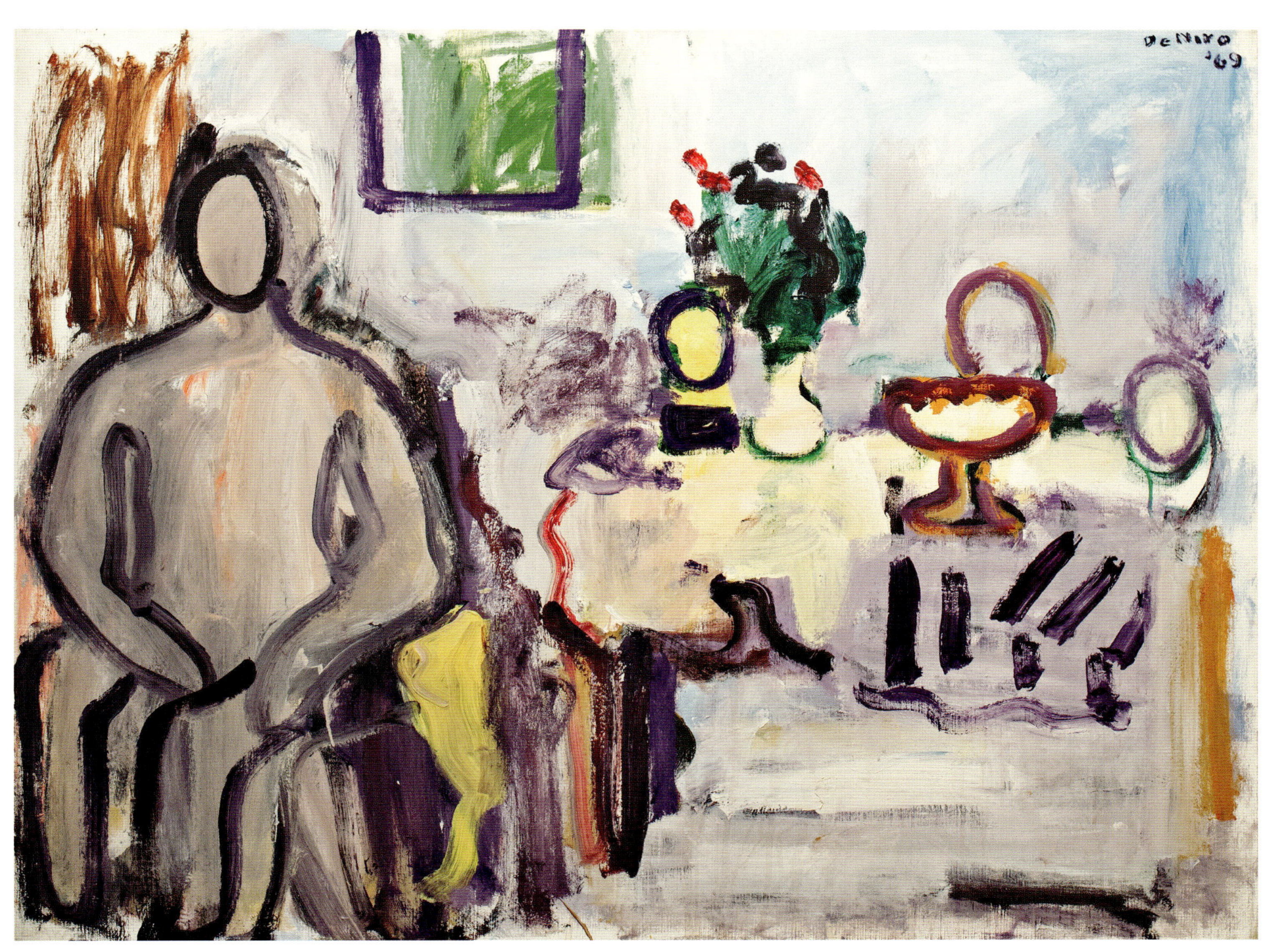

72. **Woman at Table**, 1969. Oil on canvas, 42 x 56 inches

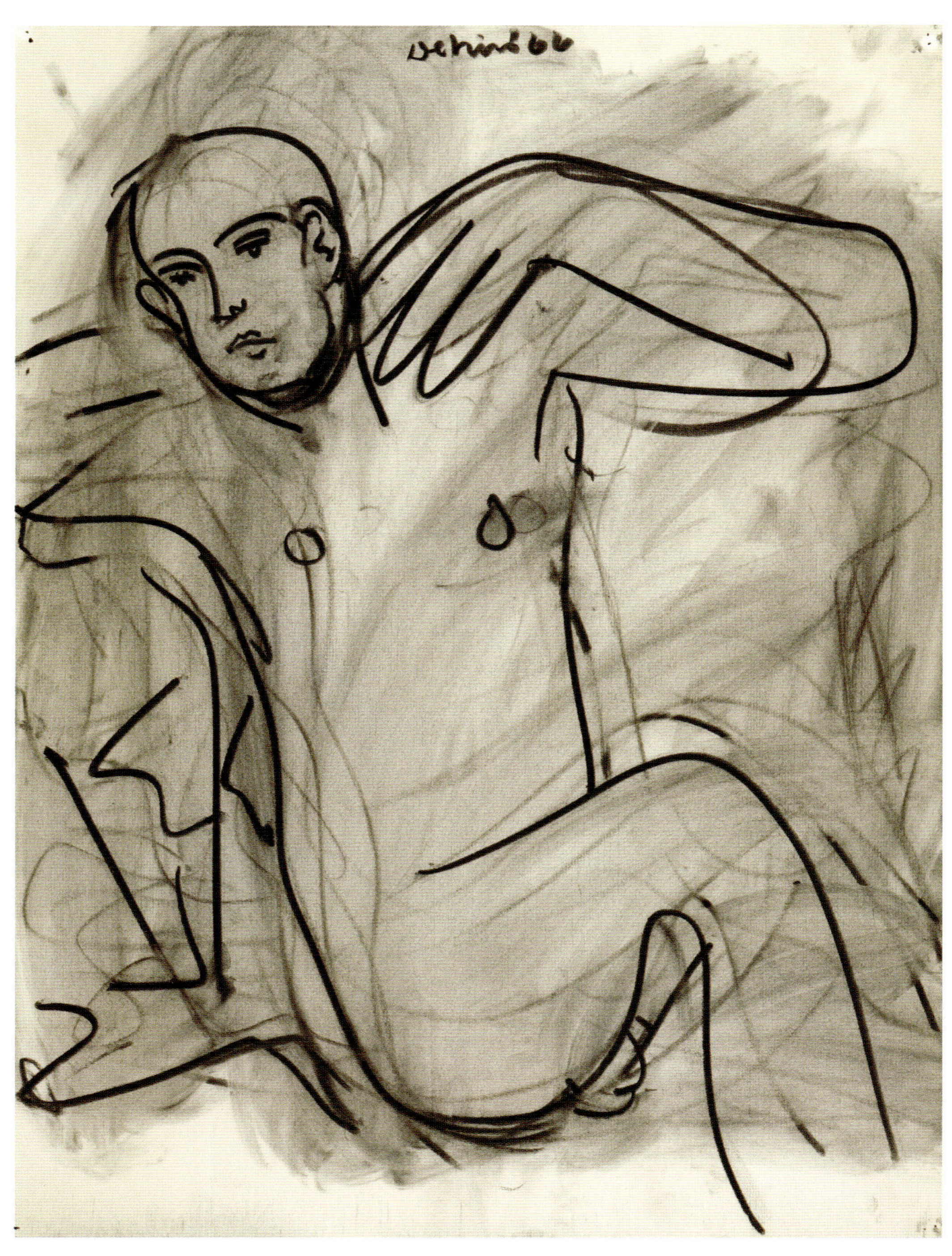

73. **Male Nude**, 1966. Charcoal on paper, 25½ x 19 inches

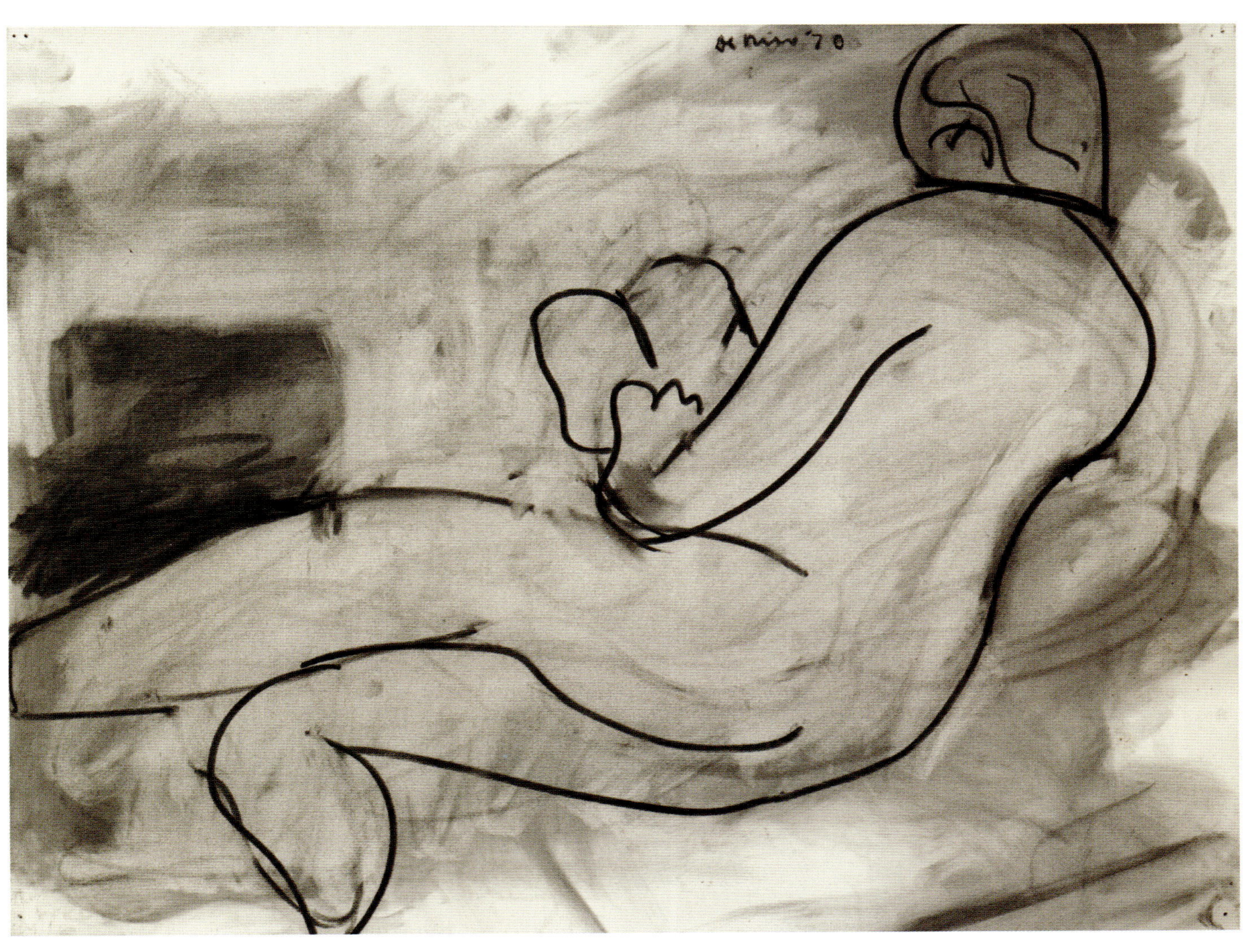

74. **Reclining Figure Reading a Book**, 1970. Charcoal on paper, 19½ x 25½ inches

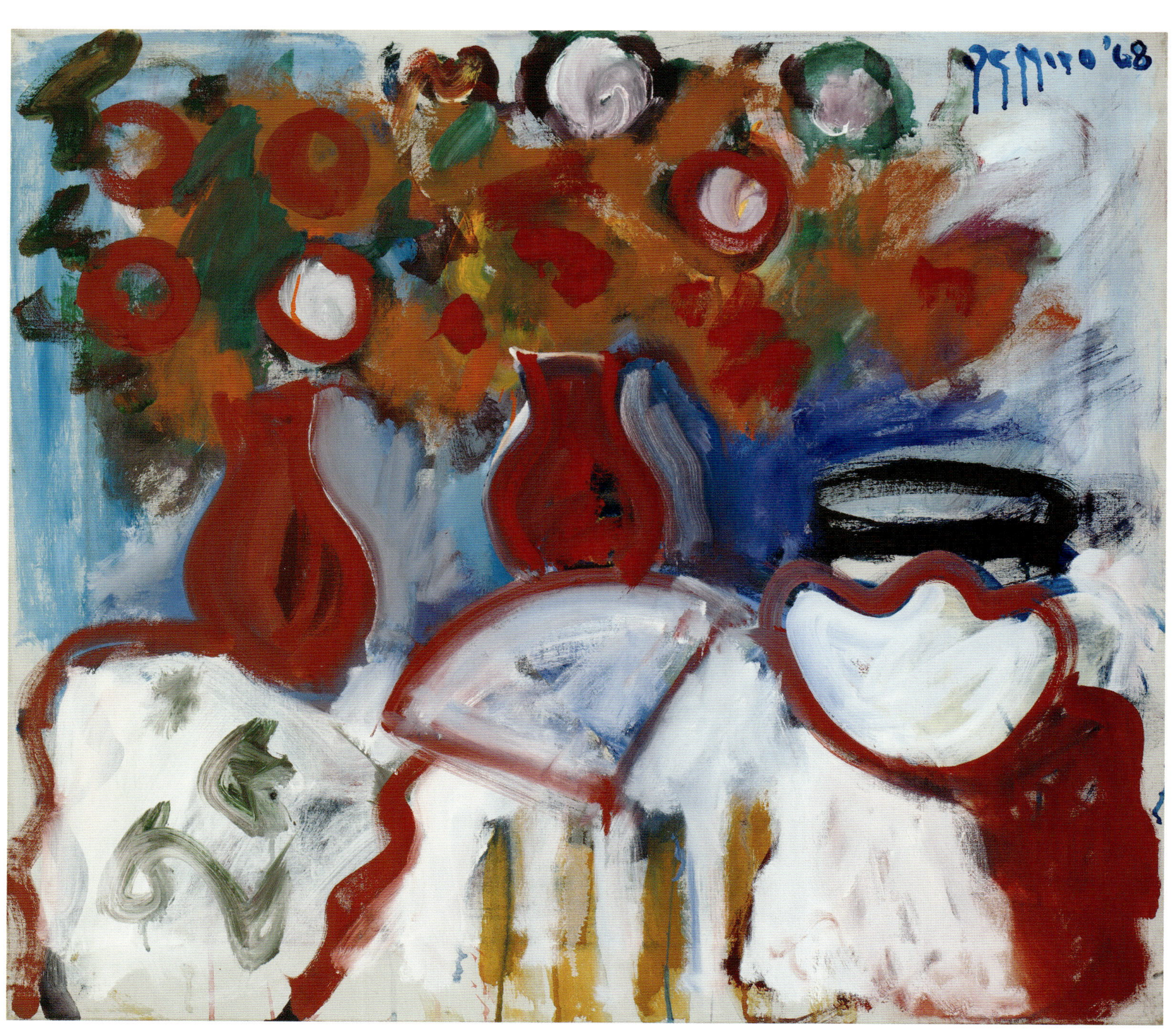

75. **Table Still Life with Red Vases, Fan and Bowl**, 1968. Oil on canvas, 30 x 34 inches

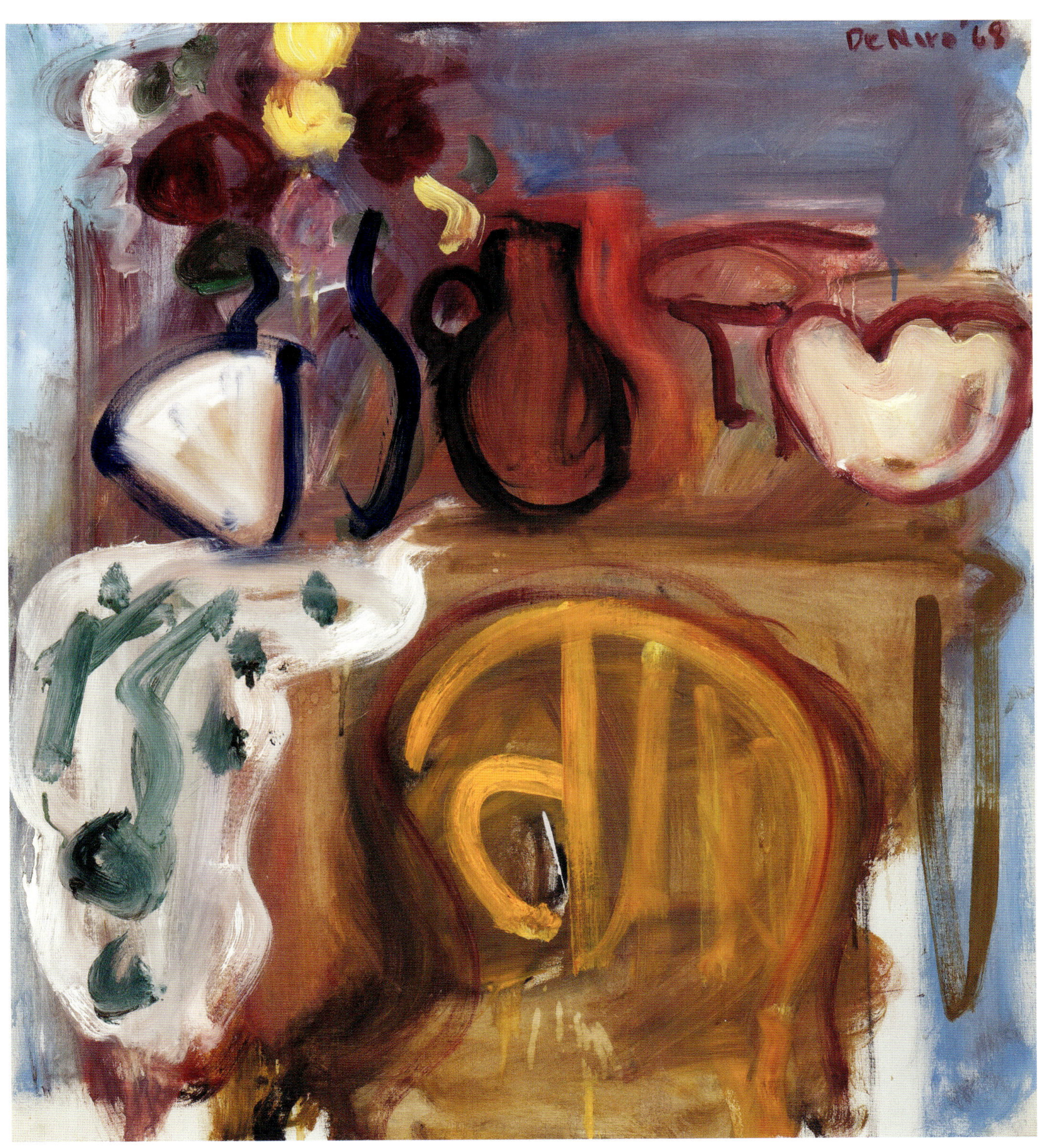

76. **Studio Interior with Yellow Chair and Vase of Flowers**, 1968. Oil on canvas, 34 x 30 inches

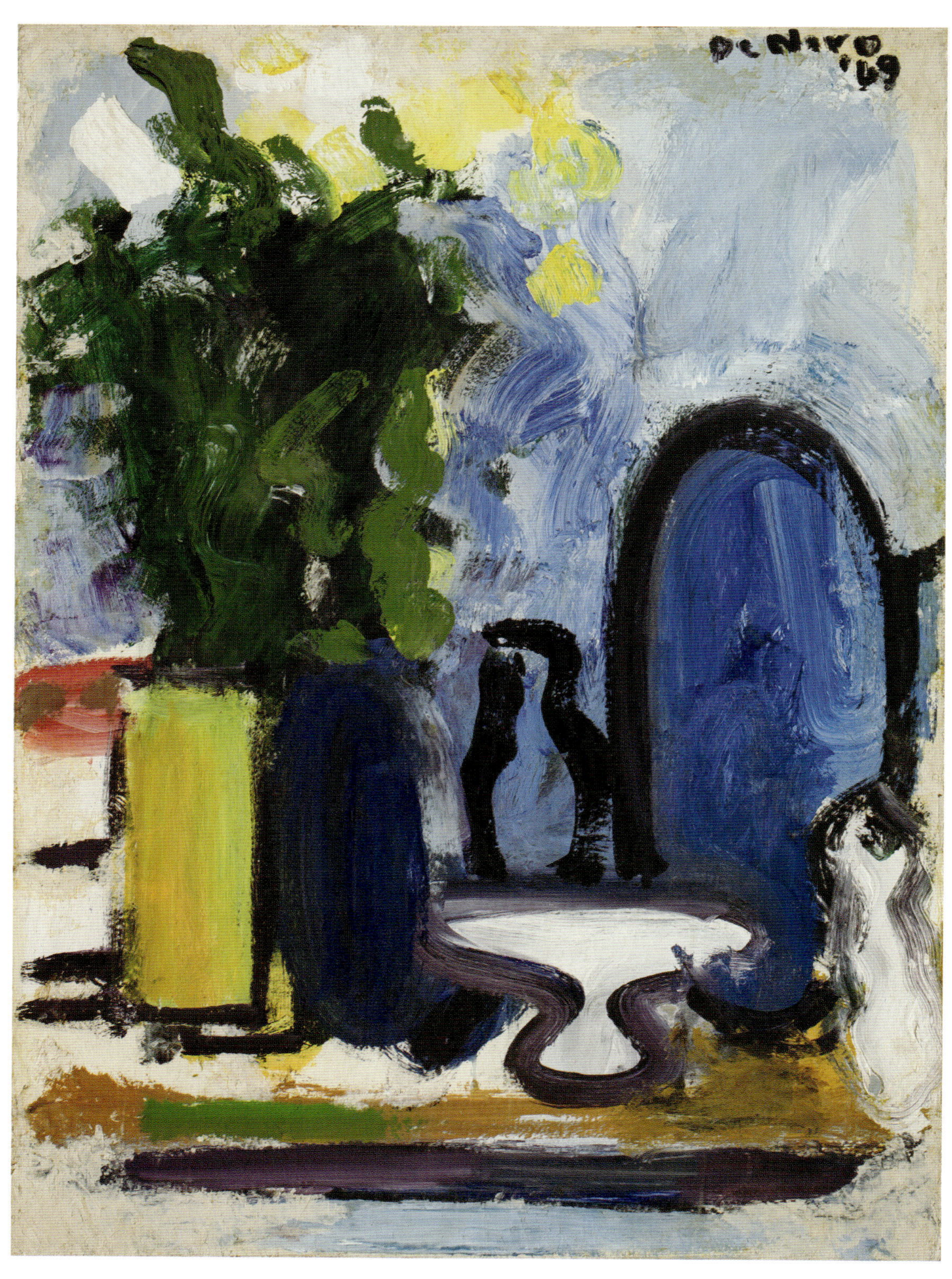

77. **Still Life with Flowers, Vase and Tazza**, 1969. Oil on Masonite, 30 x 22 inches

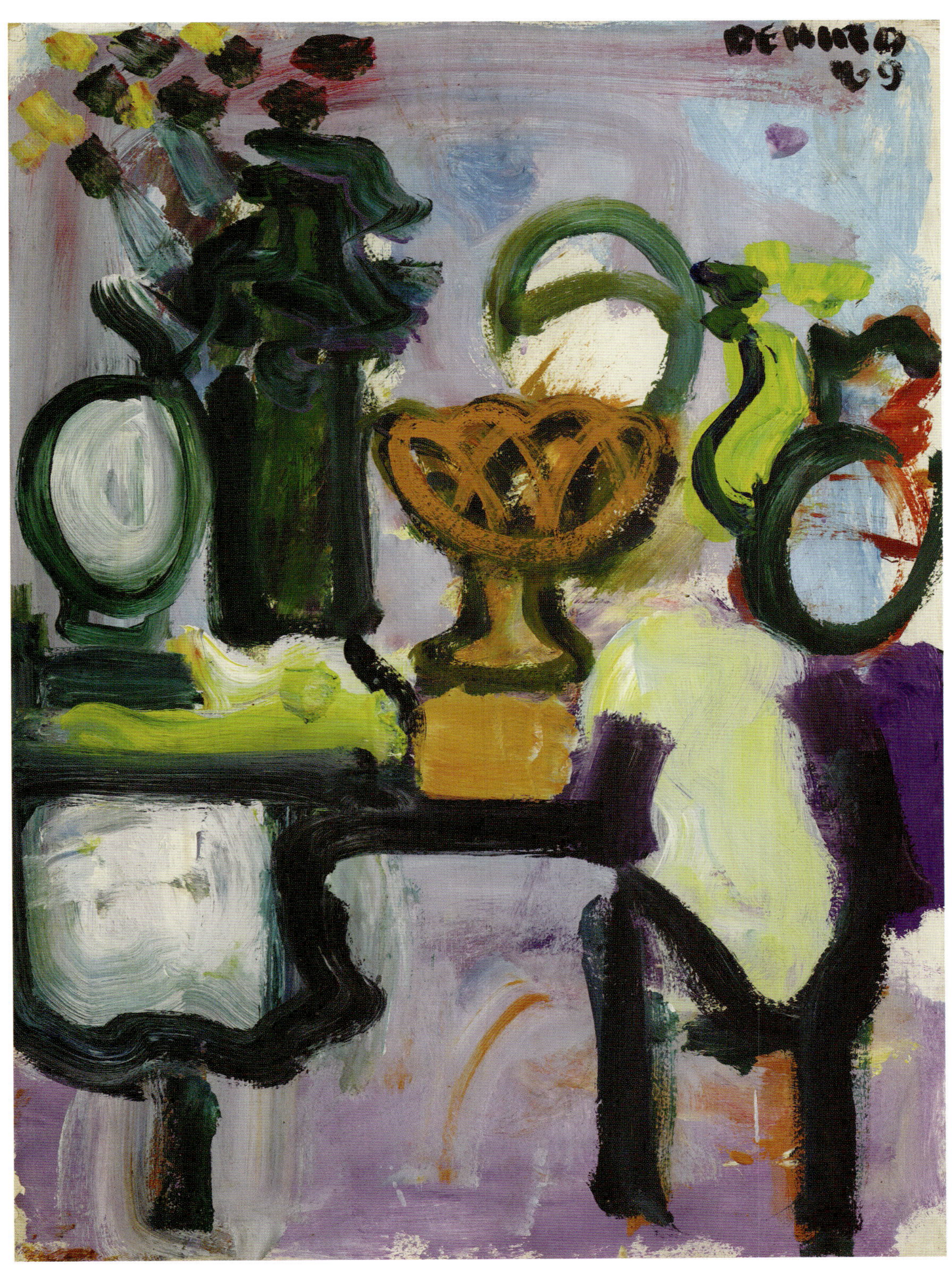

78. **Interior Still Life**, 1969. Oil on panel, 30 x 22 inches

79. **Red House with Blue Door**, 1970. Oil on panel, 30½ x 33¾ inches

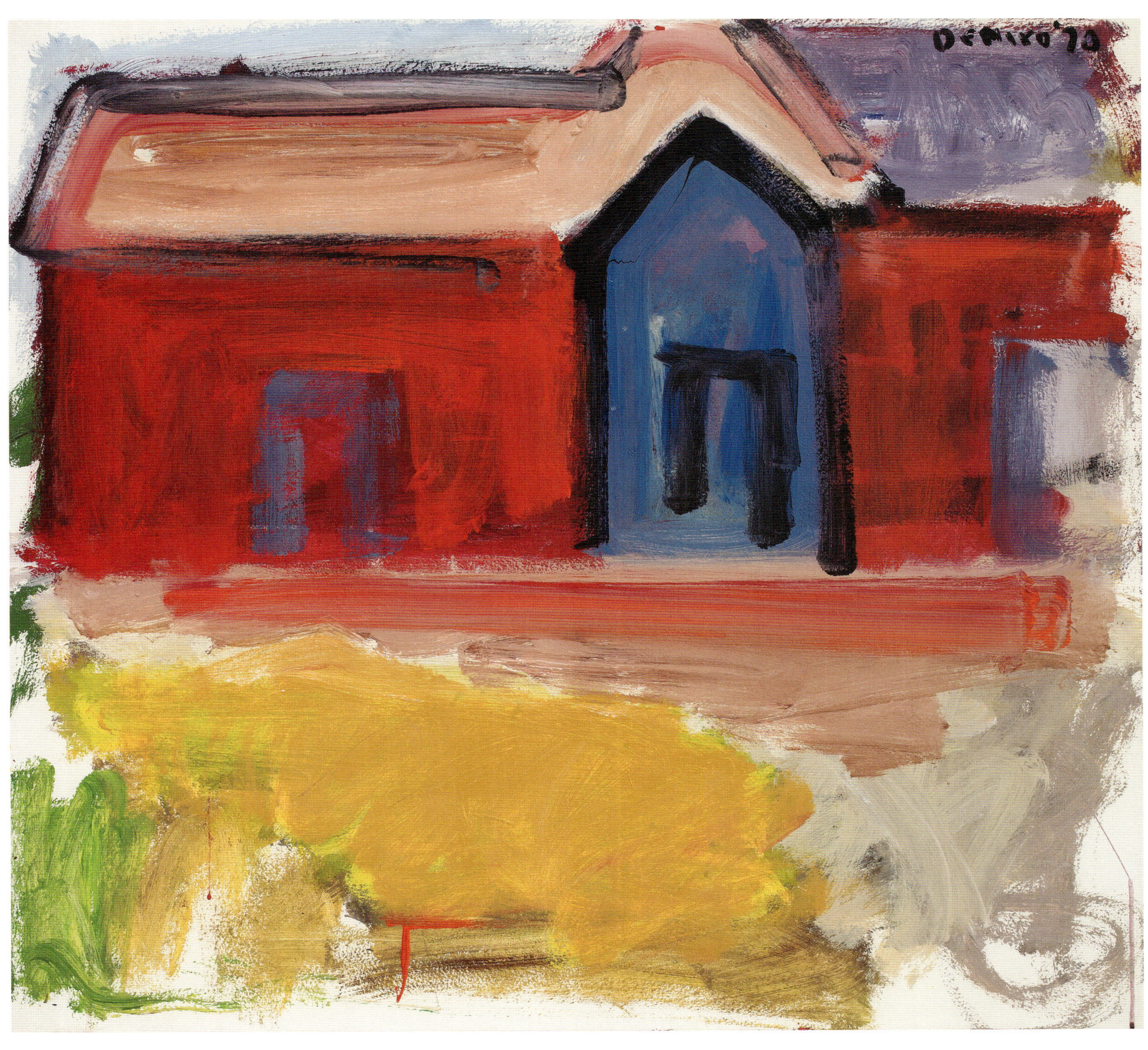
DENIRO '70

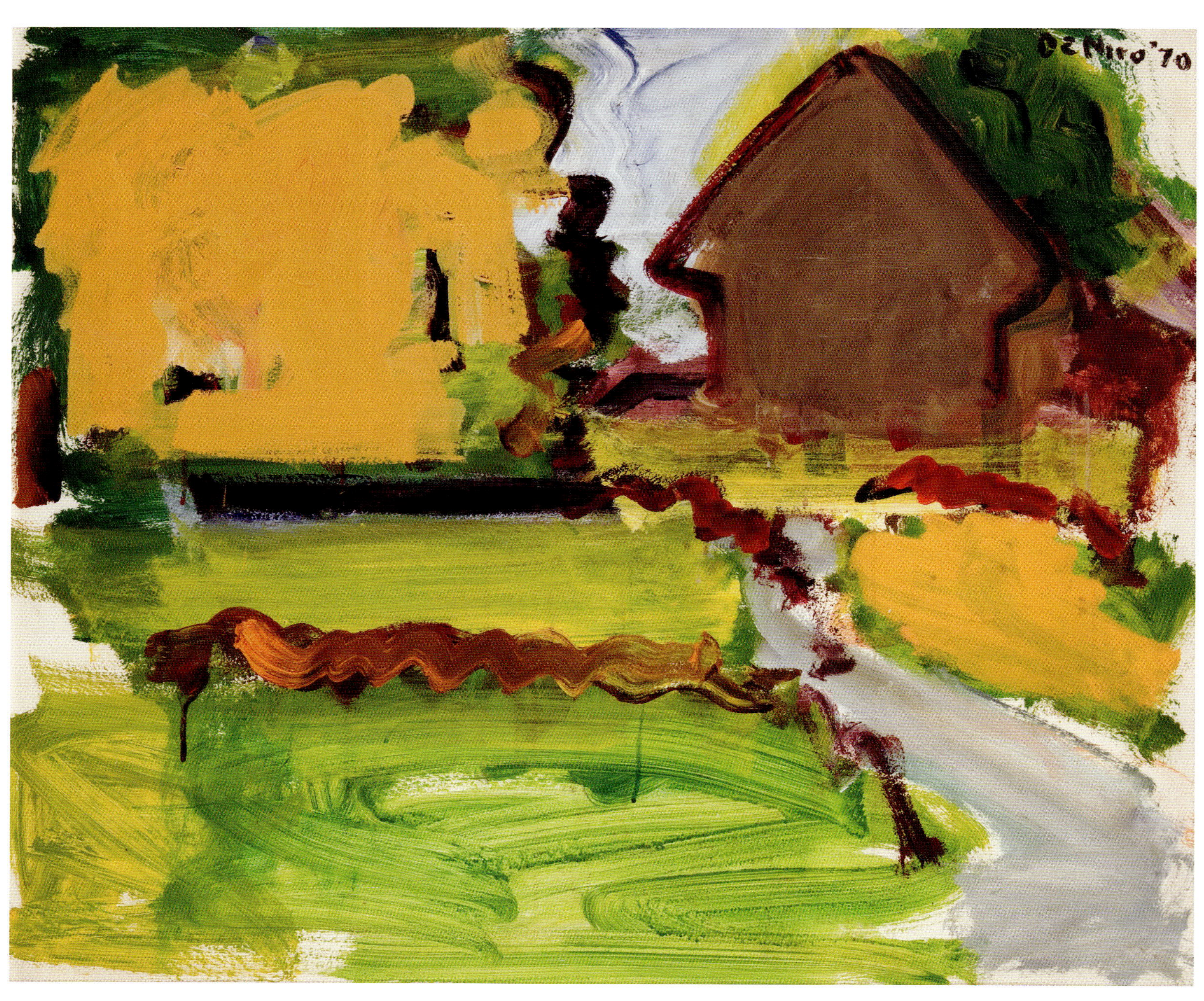

80. **Autumn Landscape with House**, 1970. Oil on panel, 30 x 36 inches

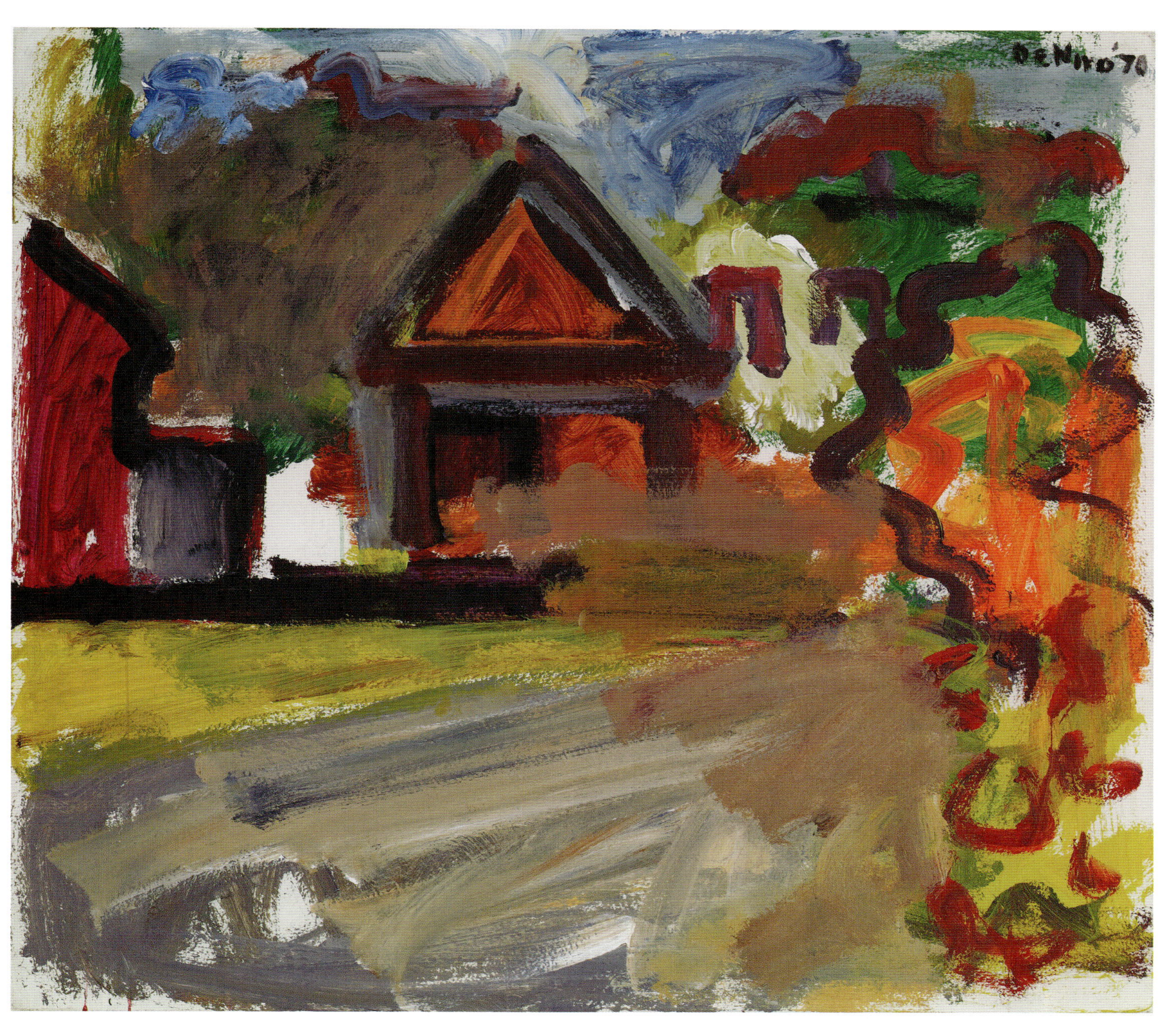

81. **Landscape with Two Buildings**, 1970. Oil on canvas, 30 x 34 inches

82. **Still Life**, 1970. Oil on canvas, 30 x 24 inches

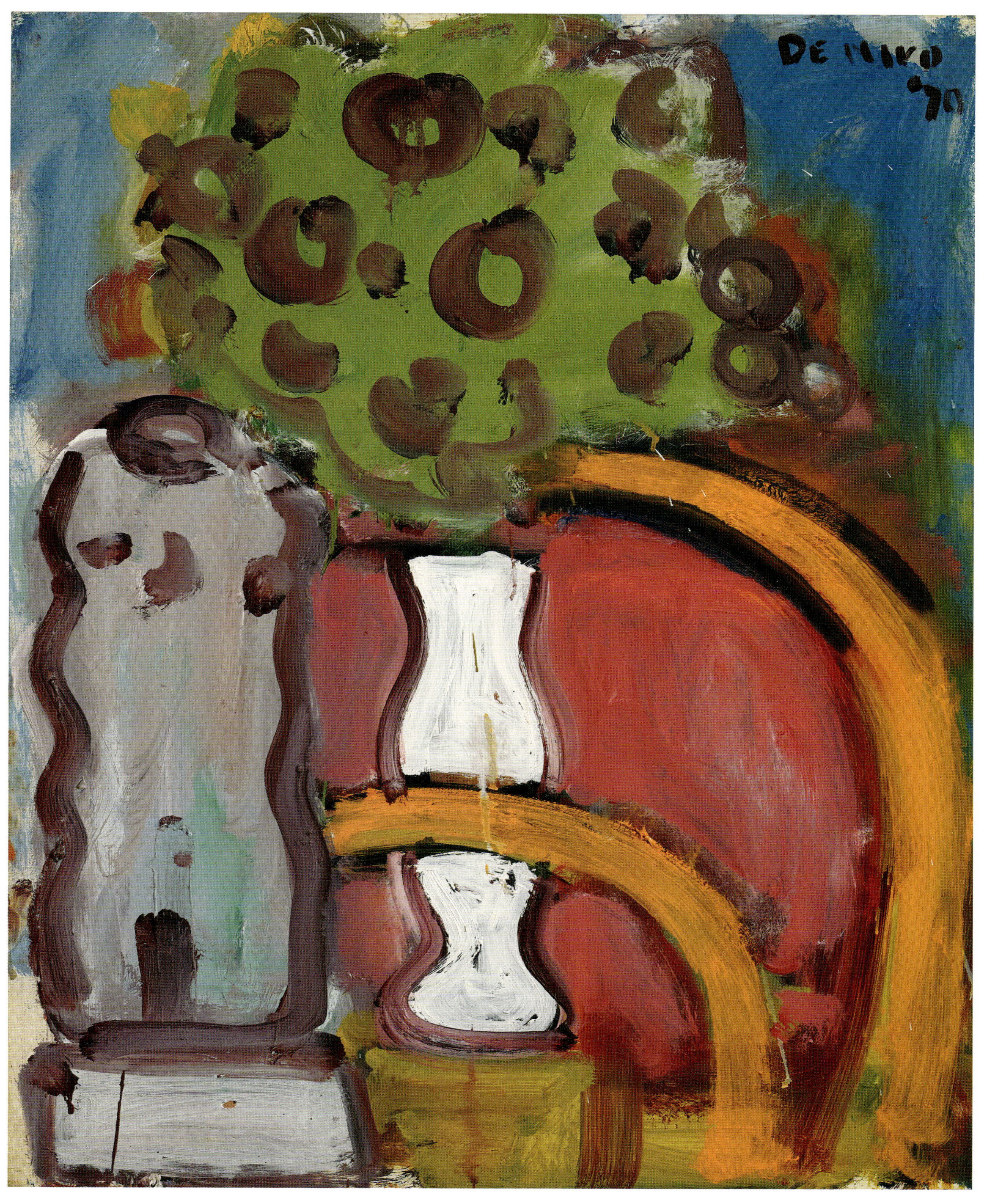

83. **Seated Nude with Green Pants**, 1970. Oil on canvas, 36 x 28 inches

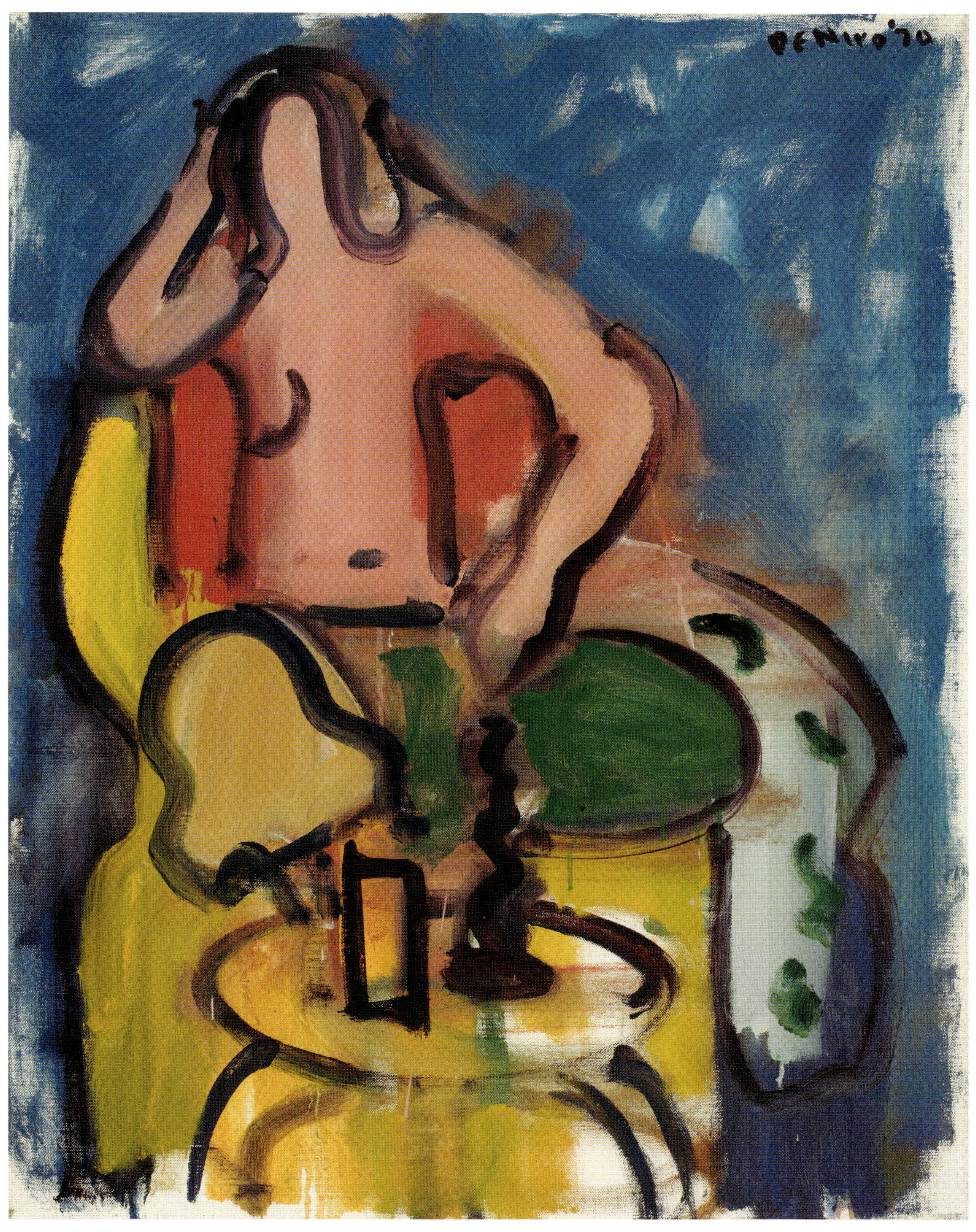
DENIRO'70

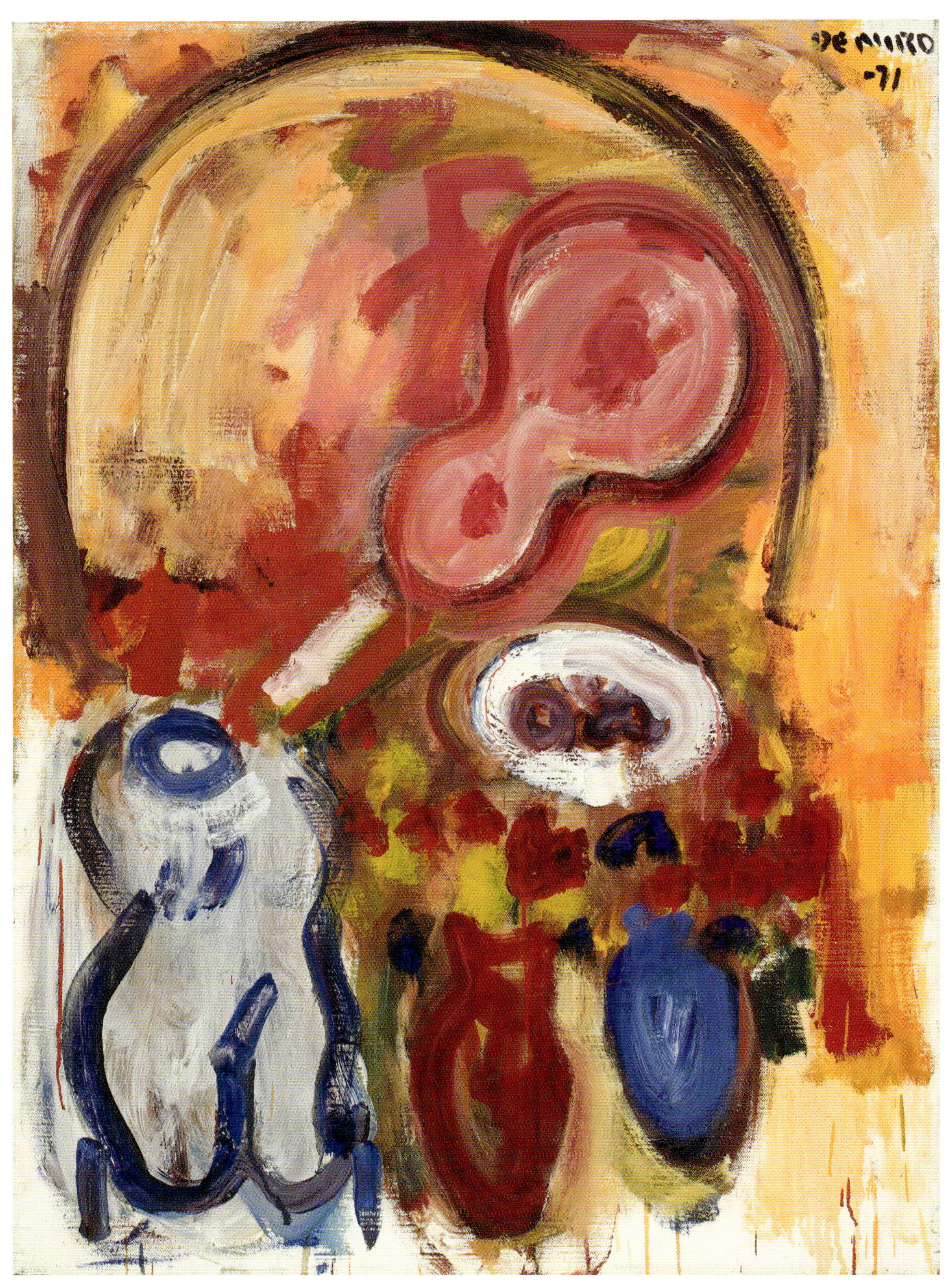

84. **Still Life with Guitar, Torso and Two Vases**, 1971. Oil on canvas, 38 ½ x 27 ¾ inches

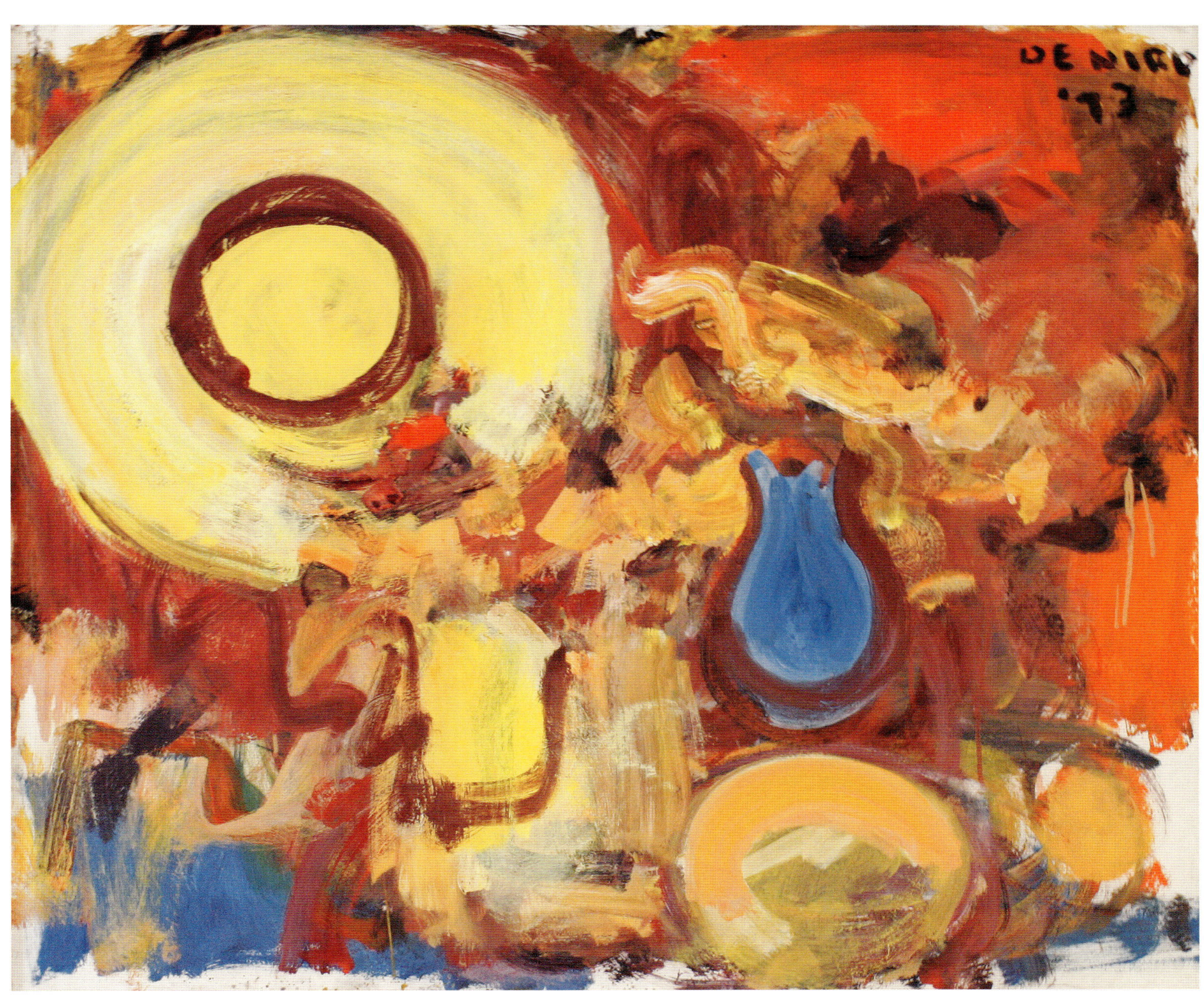

85. **Yellow Hat**, 1973. Oil on board, 30 x 36 inches

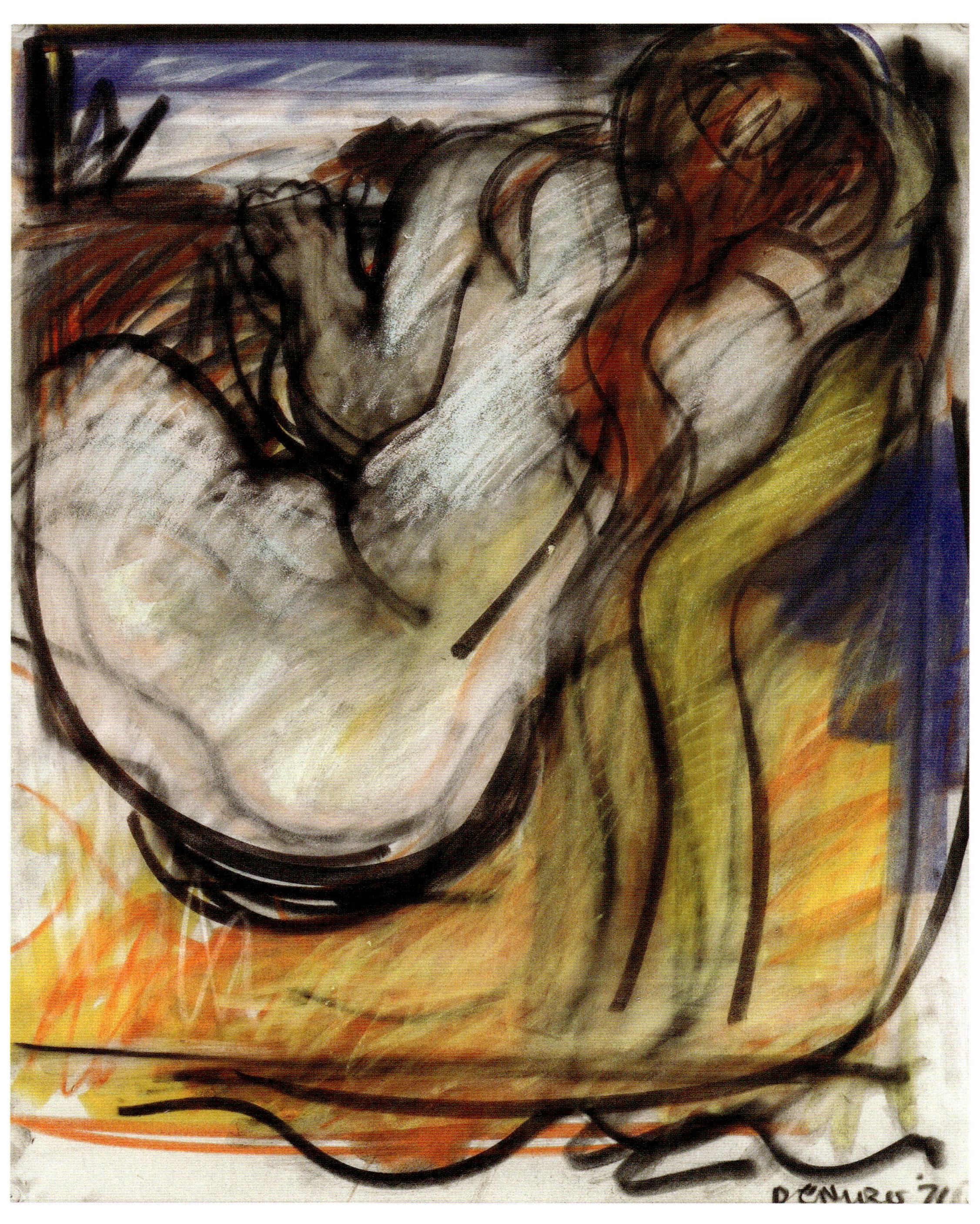

86. **Female Nude Seen from Behind**, 1971. Pastel on paper, 24½ x 19½ inches

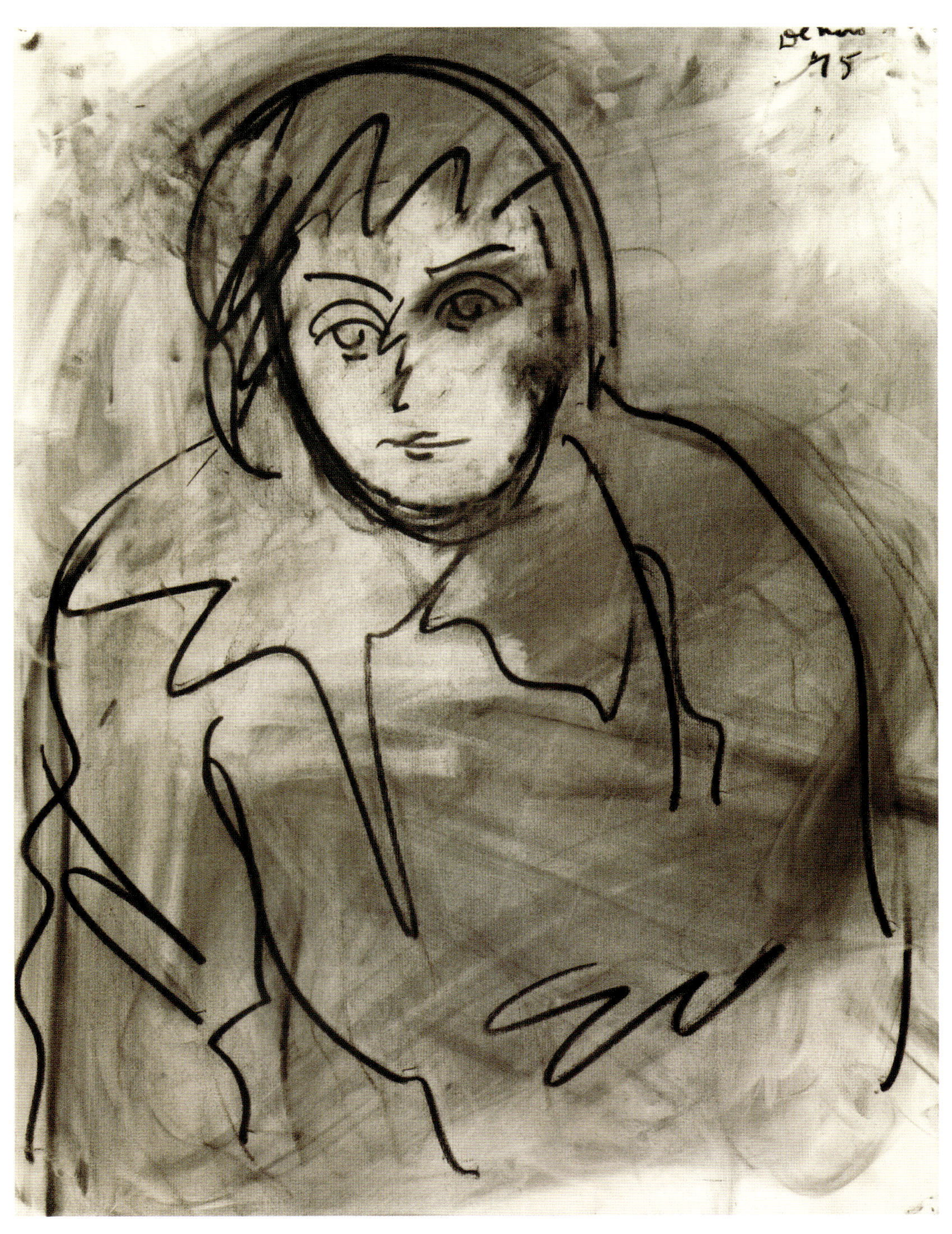

87. **Portrait of Elaine de Kooning**, 1975. Charcoal on paper, 25 x 19 inches

88. **Black Statuette**, 1975. Oil on fiberboard, 30 x 36 inches

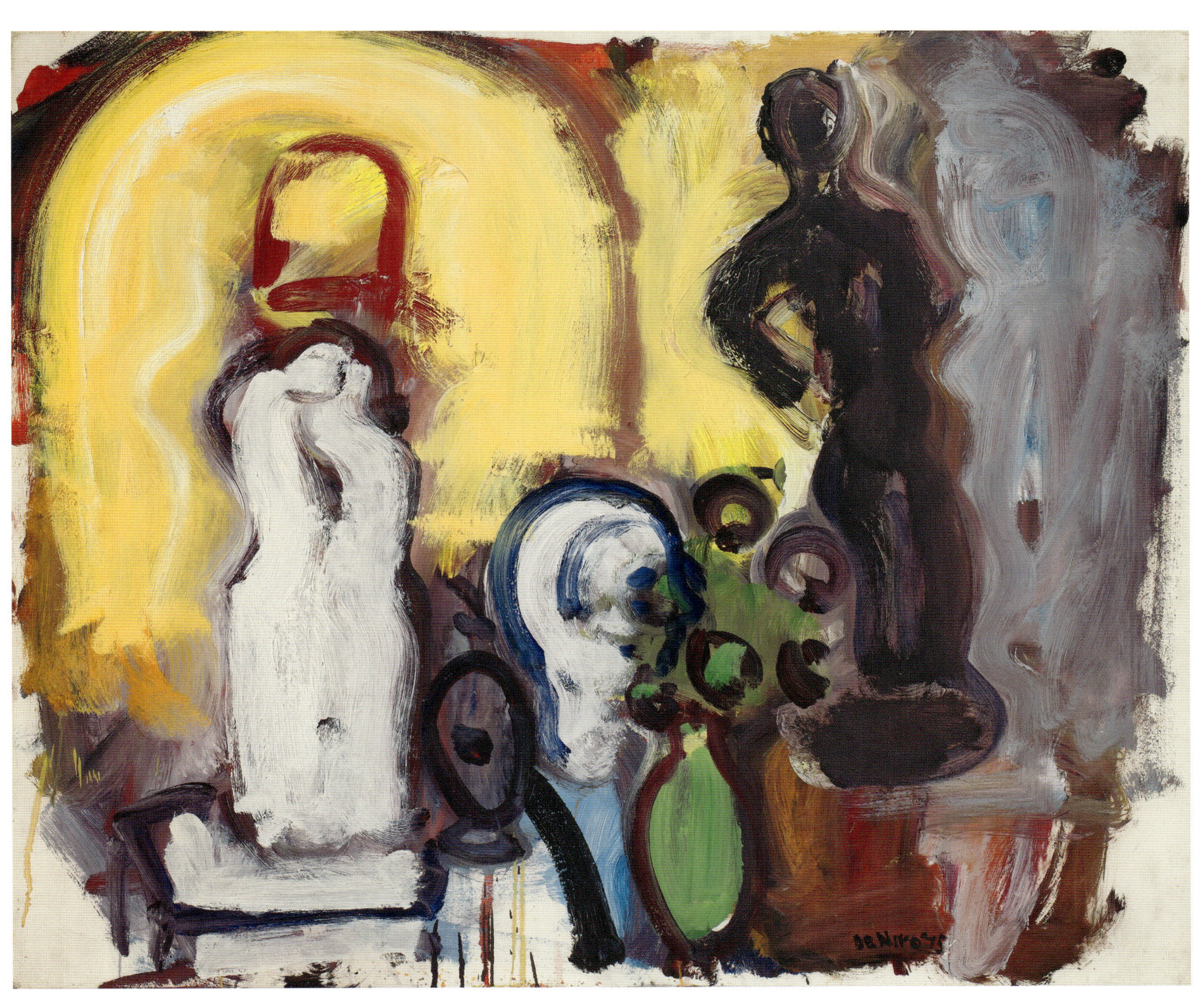

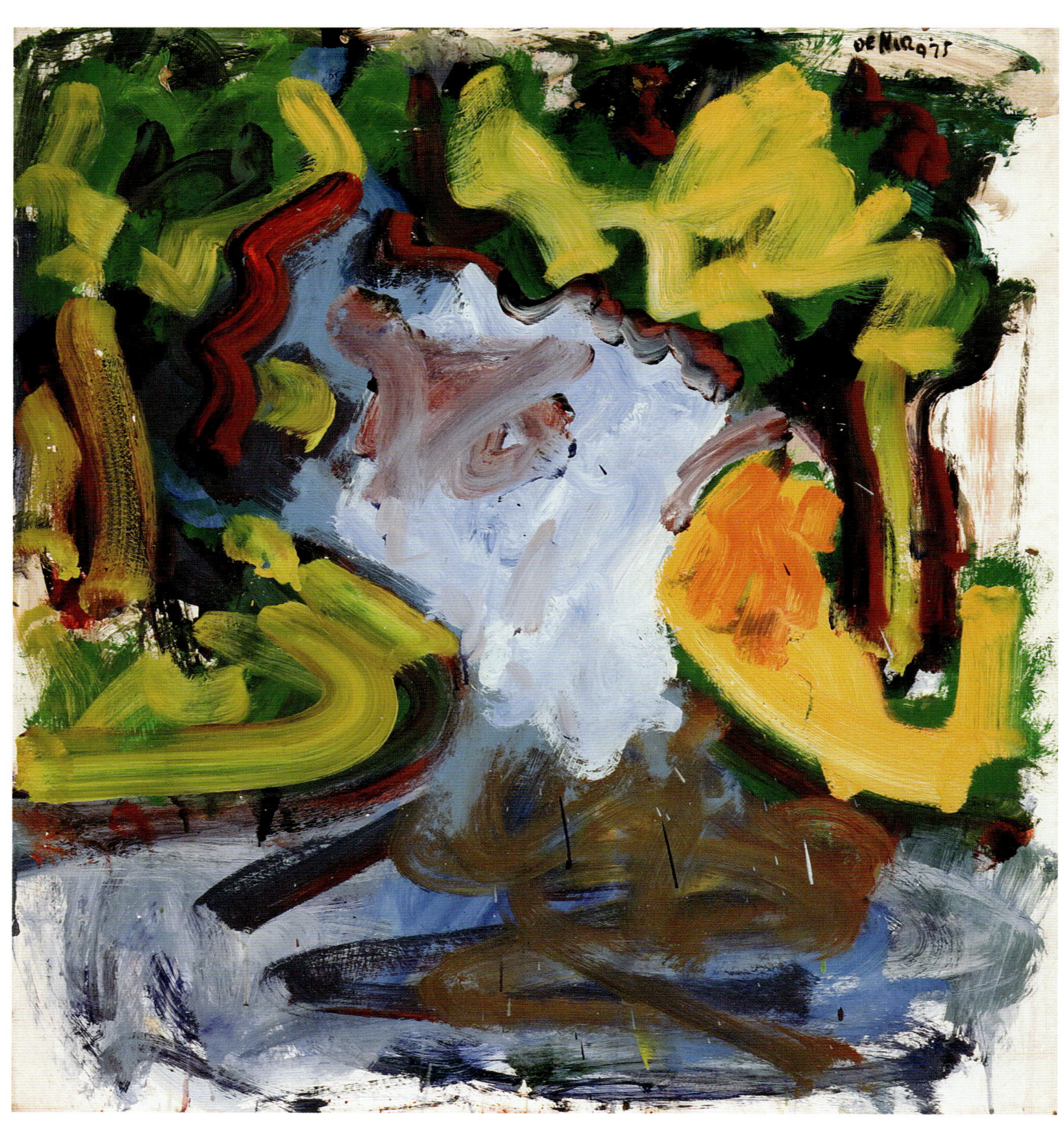

89. **Landscape with Pond**, 1975. Oil on Masonite, 30 x 28 inches

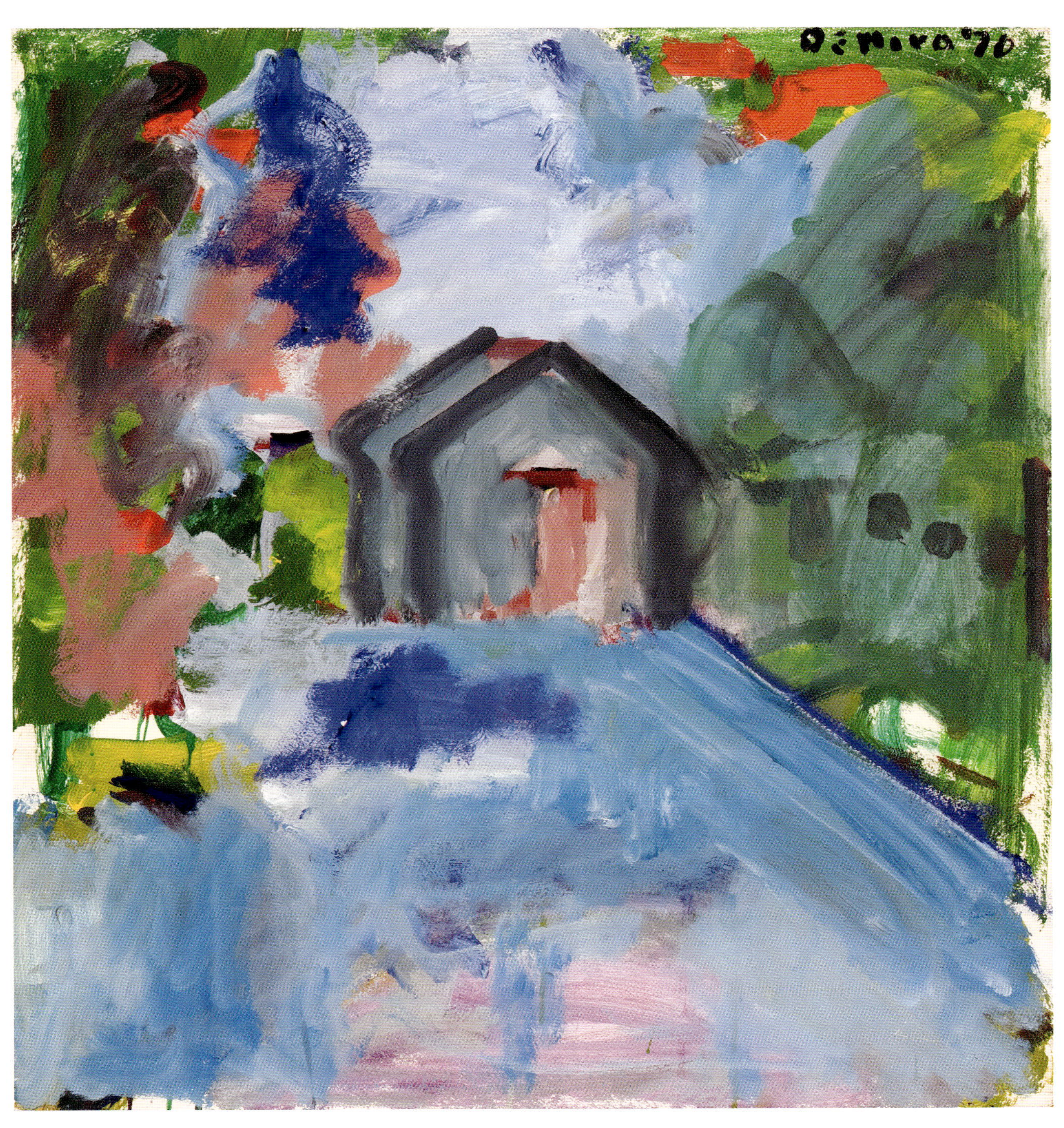

90. **Gray Barn in Blue Landscape**, 1976. Oil on Masonite, 30 x 28 inches

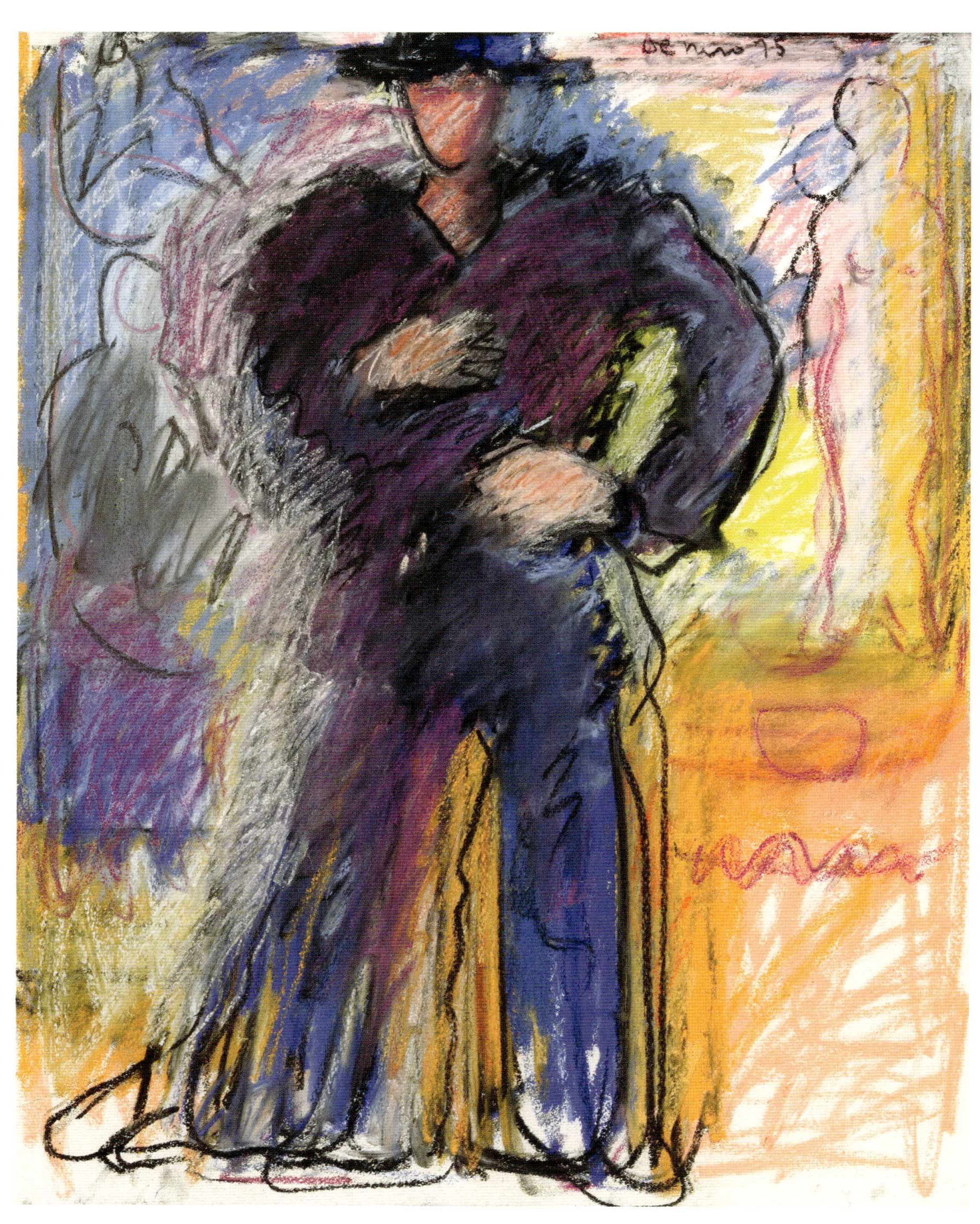

91. **Standing Male in a Toreador Hat**, 1975. Pastel on paper, 29 x 23 inches

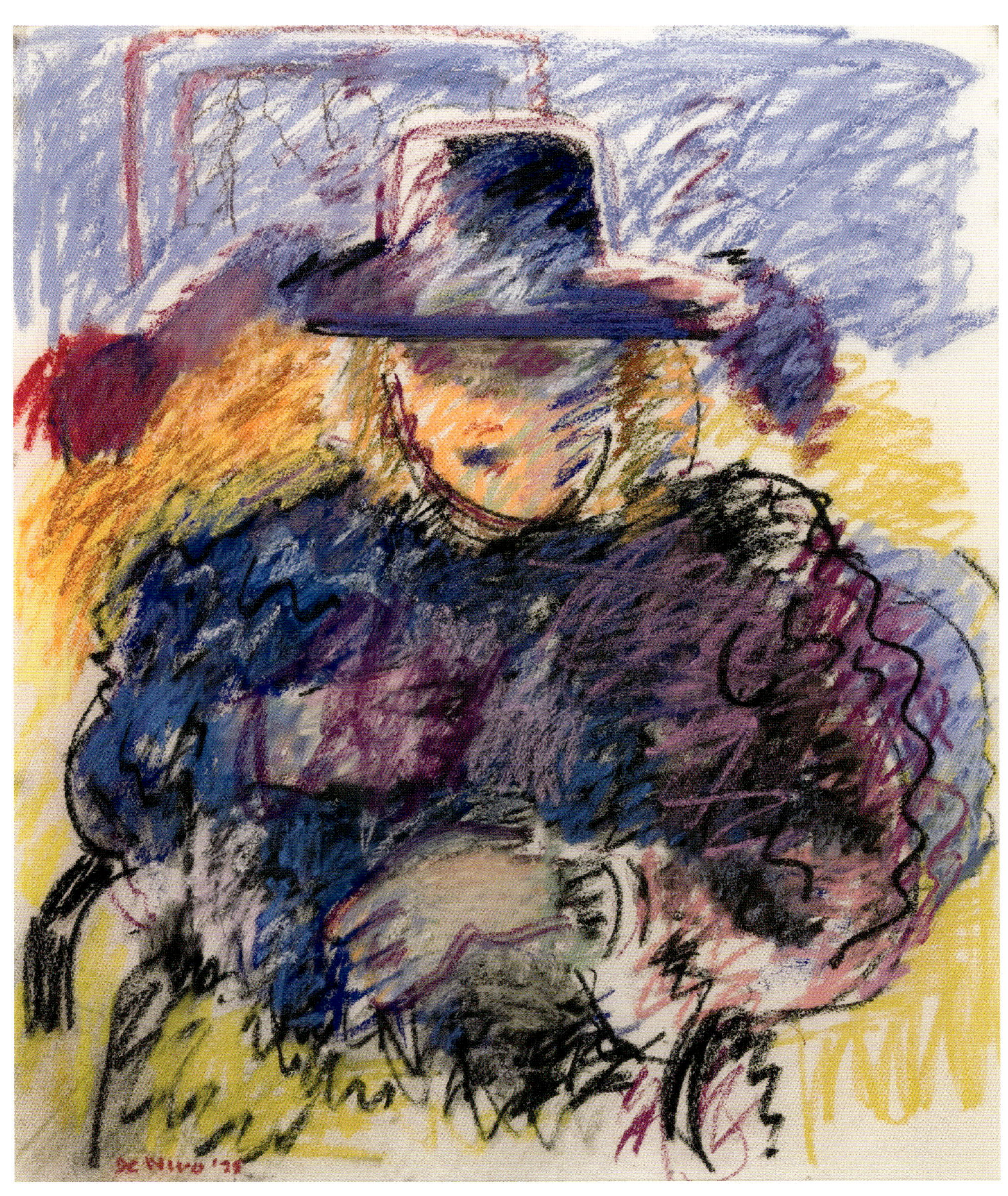

92. **Girl with a Toreador Hat and Feather Boa**, 1975. Pastel on panel, 35 ½ x 29 ½ inches

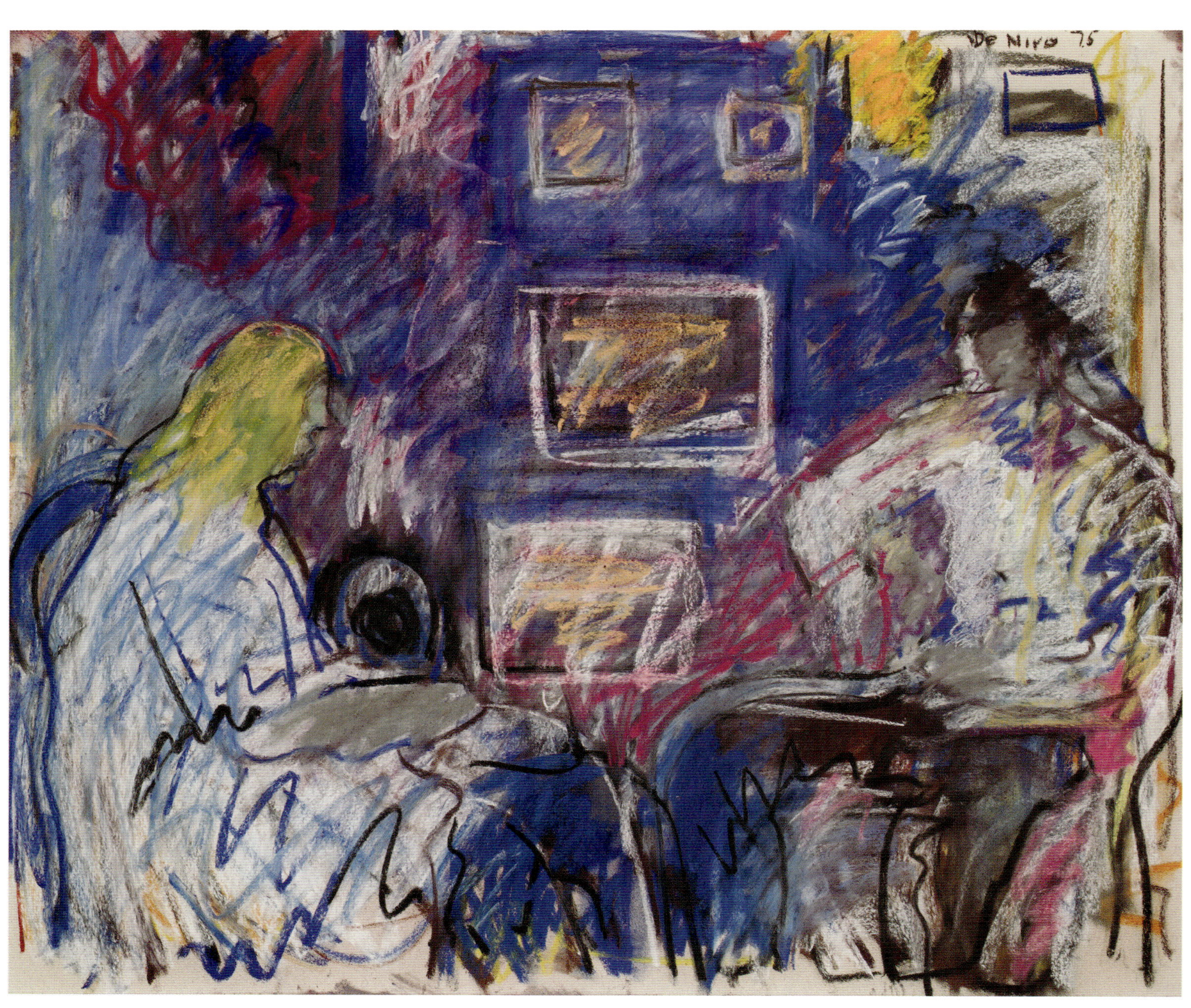

93. **Figures Seated before a Screen**, 1975. Pastel on paper, 29½ x 35 inches

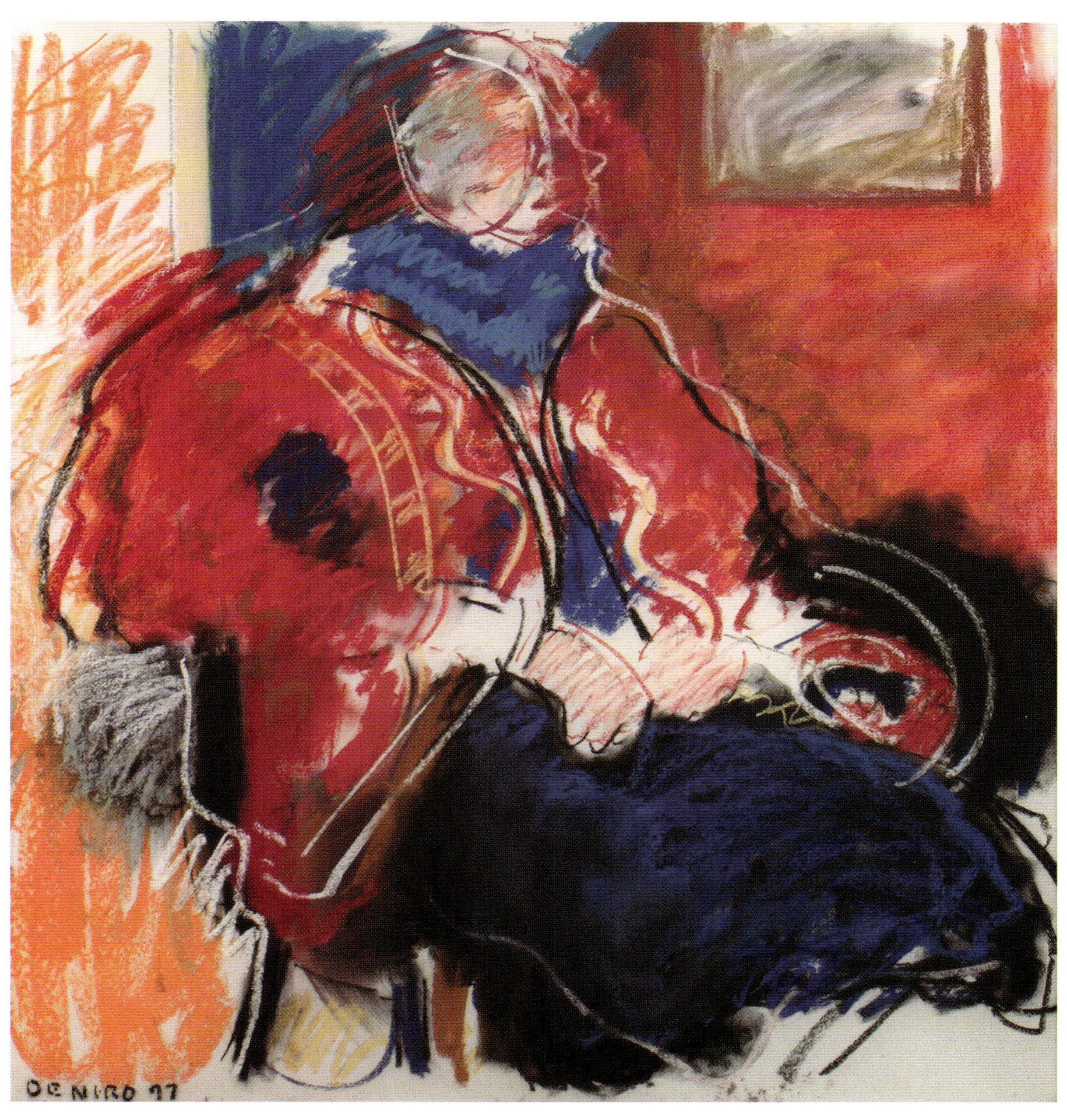

94. **Seated Figure, Red Jacket**, 1977. Pastel on board, 30 x 28¾ inches

95. **Figure in a Hat with Rubber Plant**, 1976. Oil on canvas, 50 ½ x 60 inches

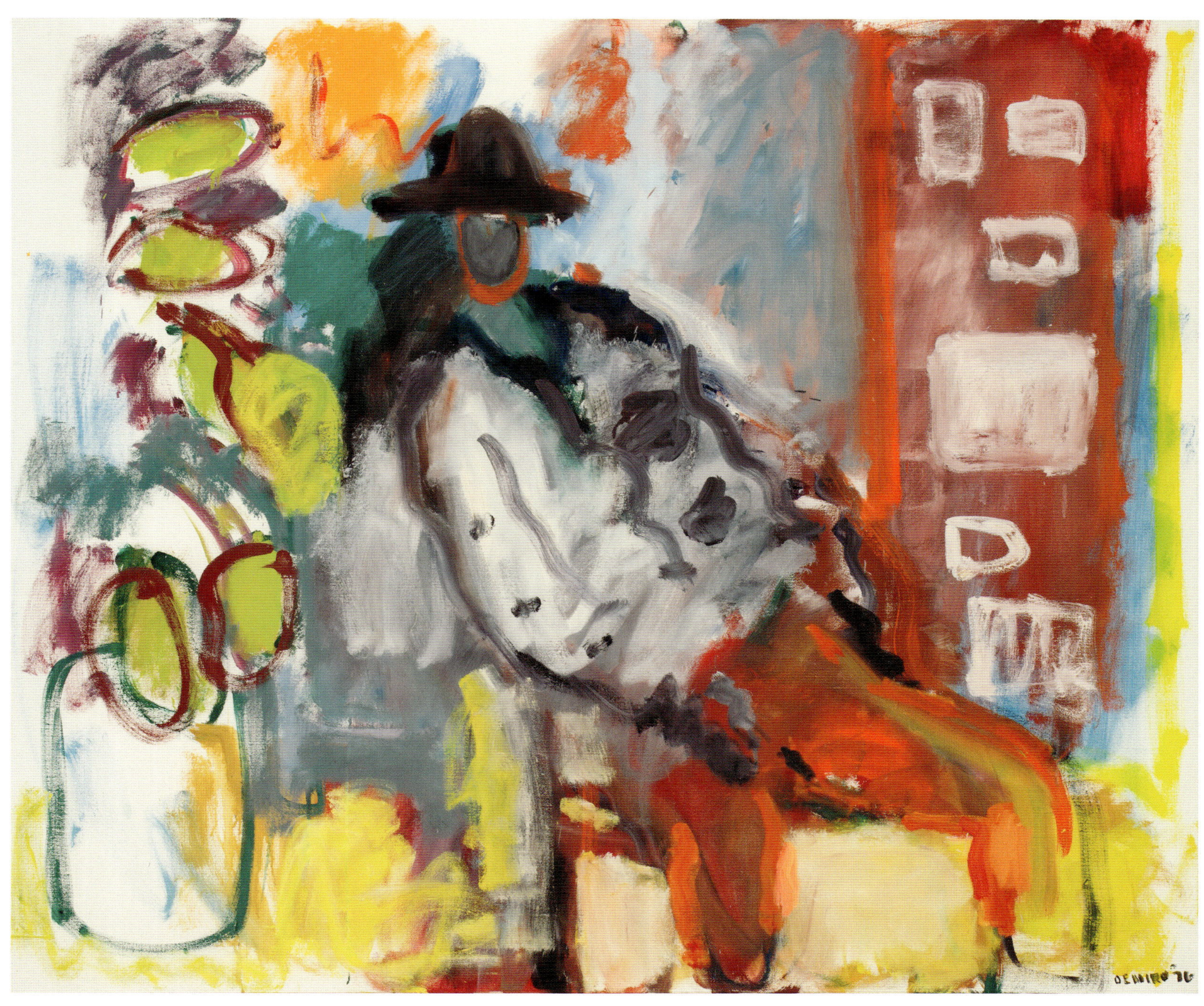
DENIRO '76

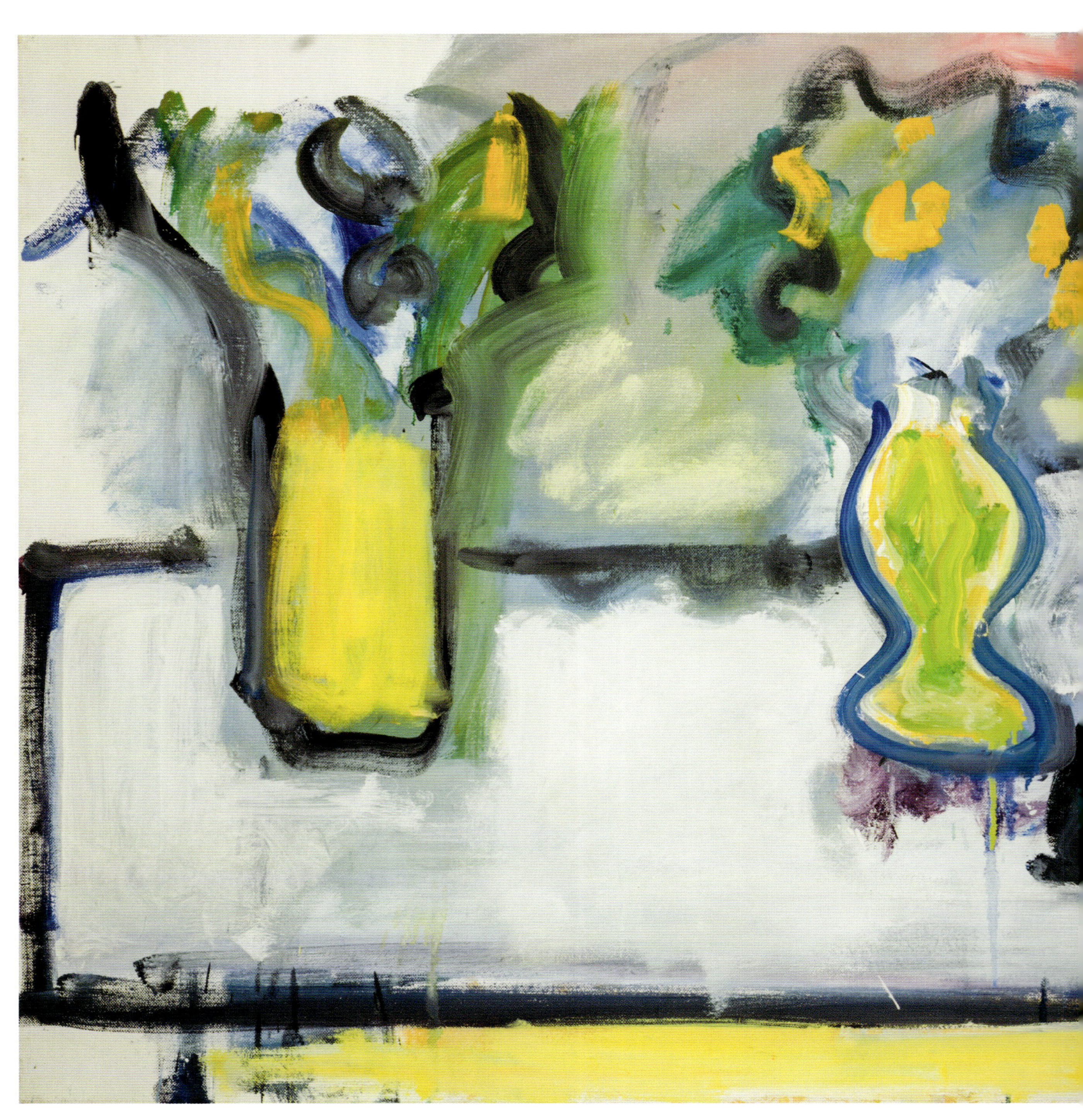

96. **Still Life with Flowers and Eggplant**, 1976. Oil on canvas, 30 x 60 inches

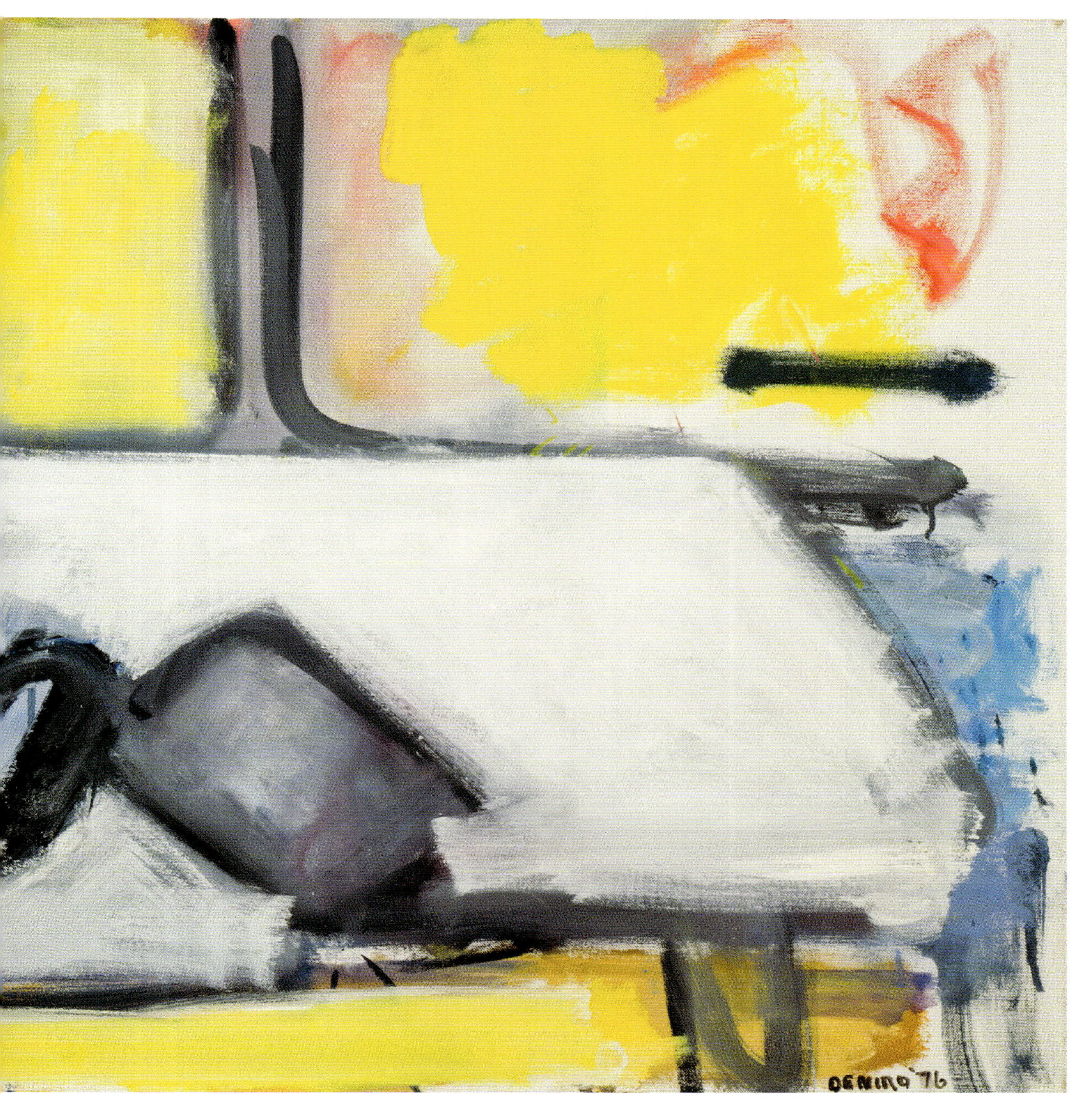
DENIRO '76

97. **Anna Christie Entering the Bar**, 1976. Oil on canvas, 62 x 50 inches

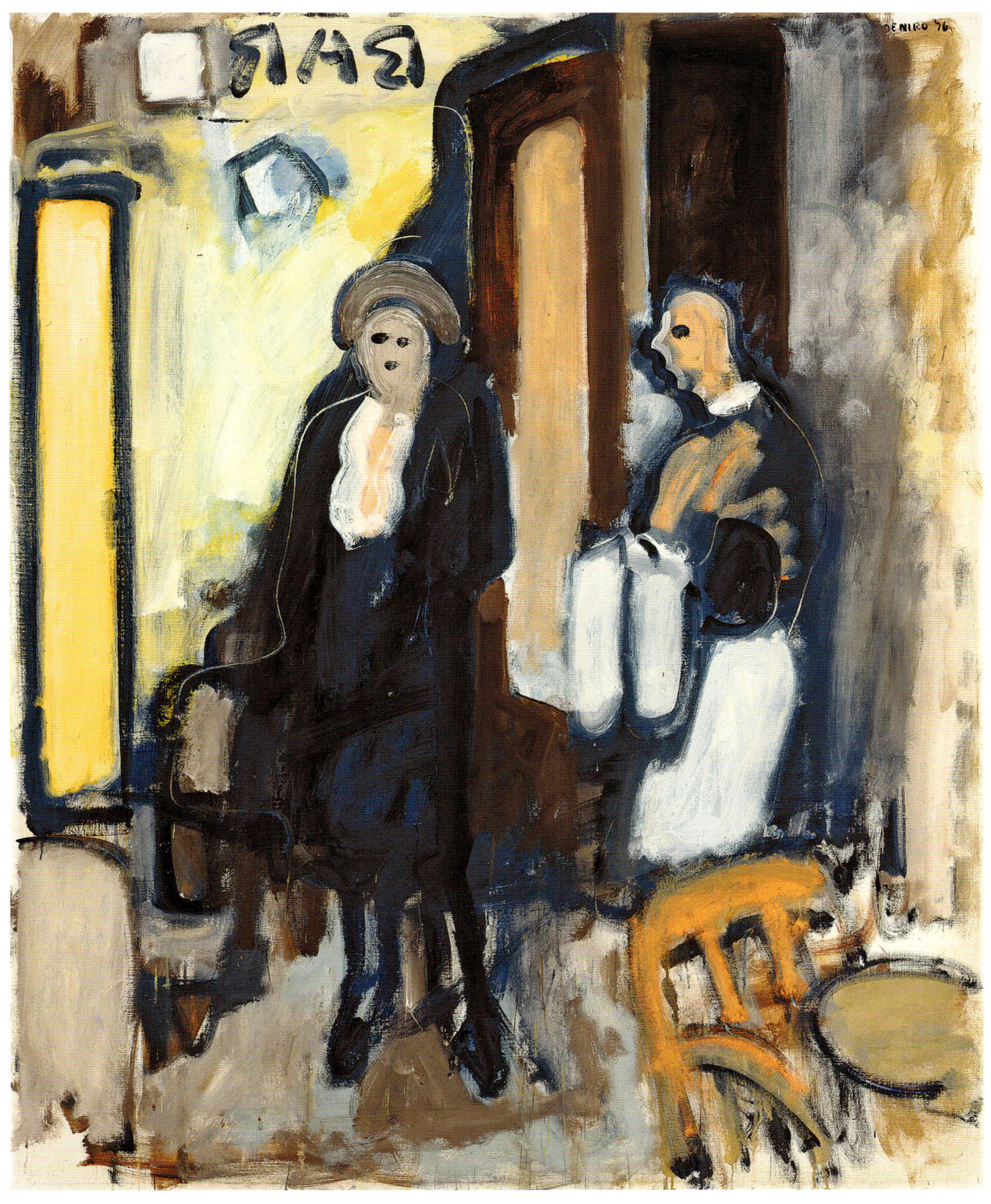
DENIRO '76

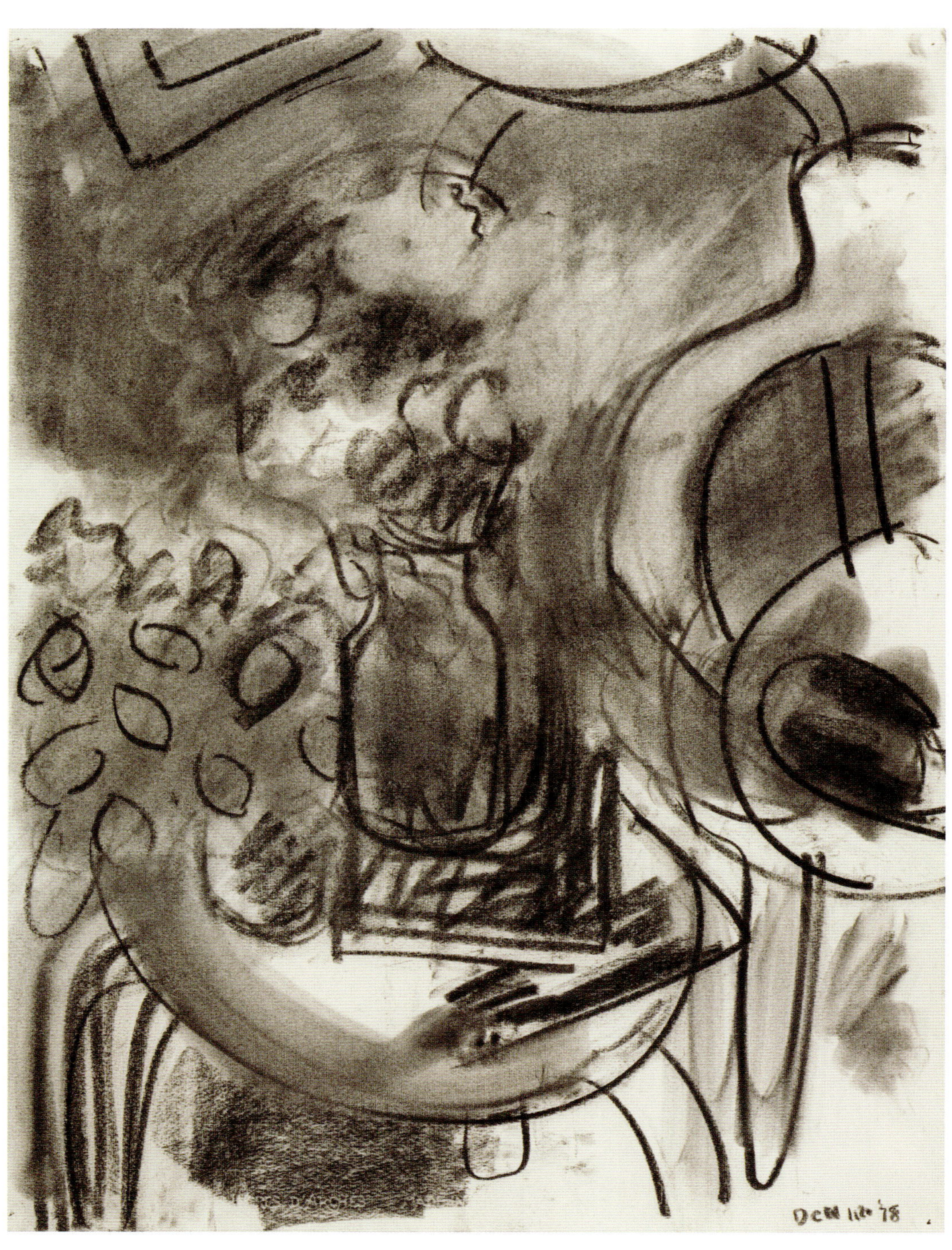

98. **Vase of Flowers**, 1978. Charcoal on paper, 25½ x 19½ inches

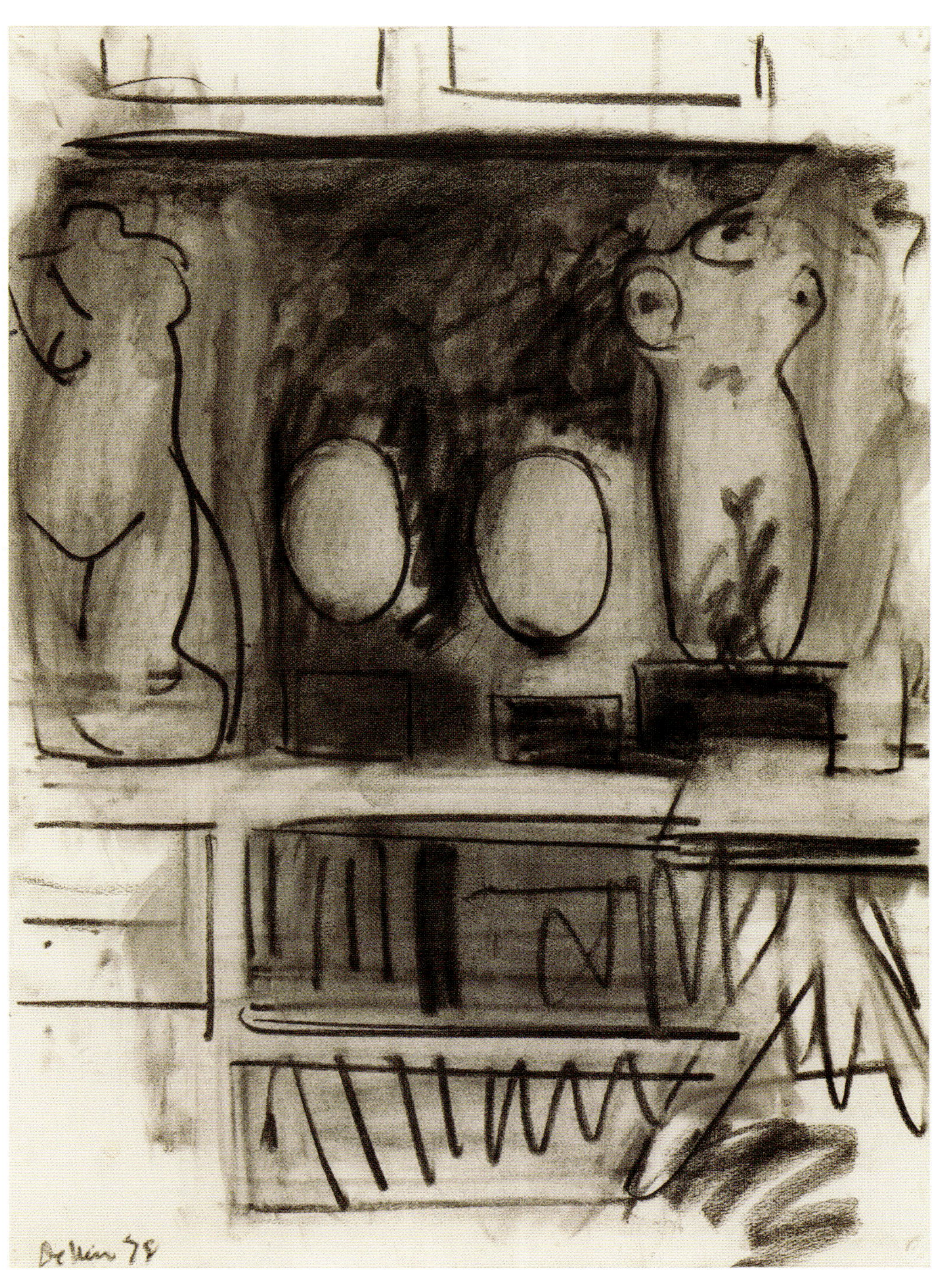

99. **Studio Drawing with Two Torsos and Two Busts**, 1978. Charcoal on paper, 25 ½ x 18 ½ inches

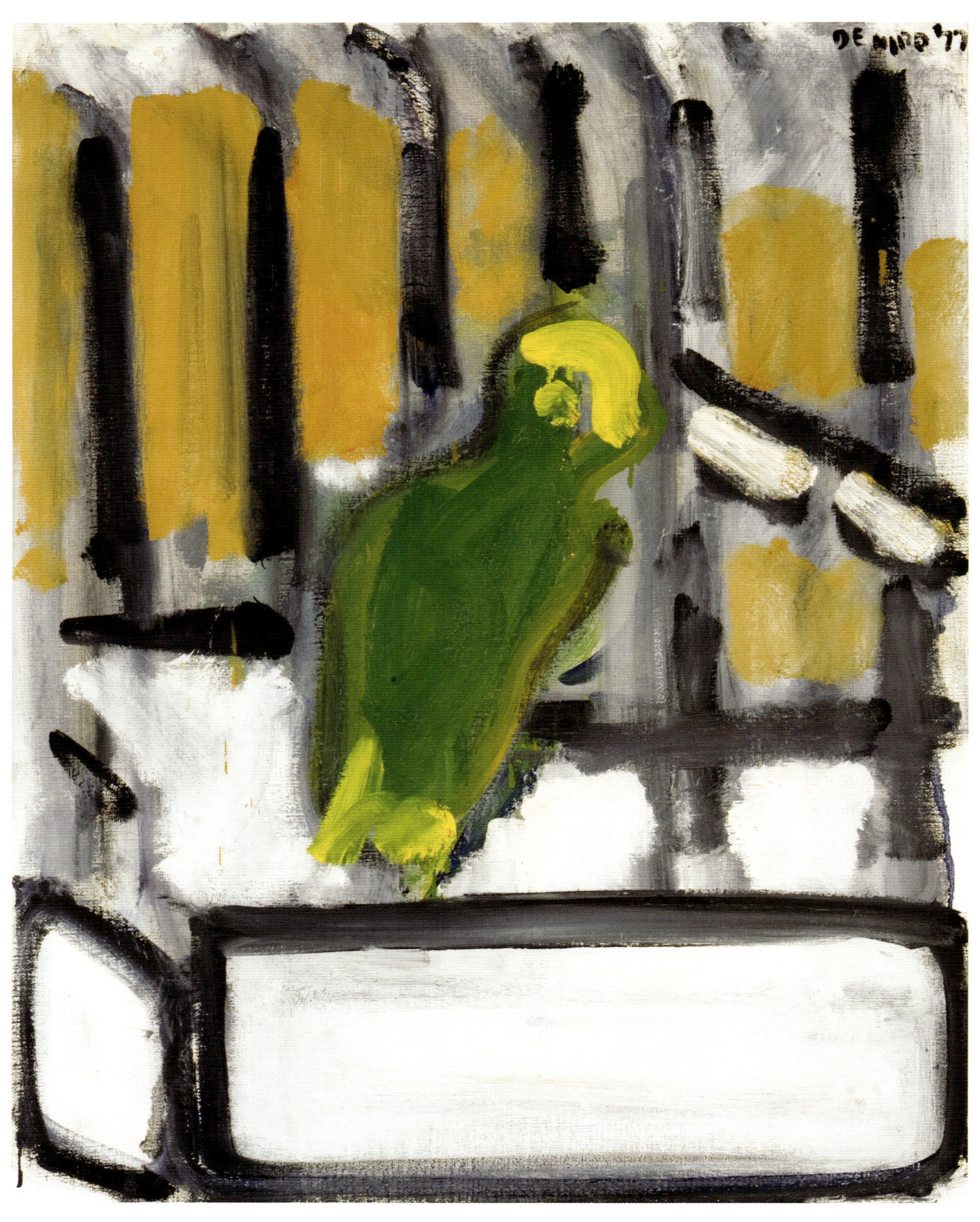

100. **Green Parrot**, 1977. Oil on canvas, 30 x 23¾ inches

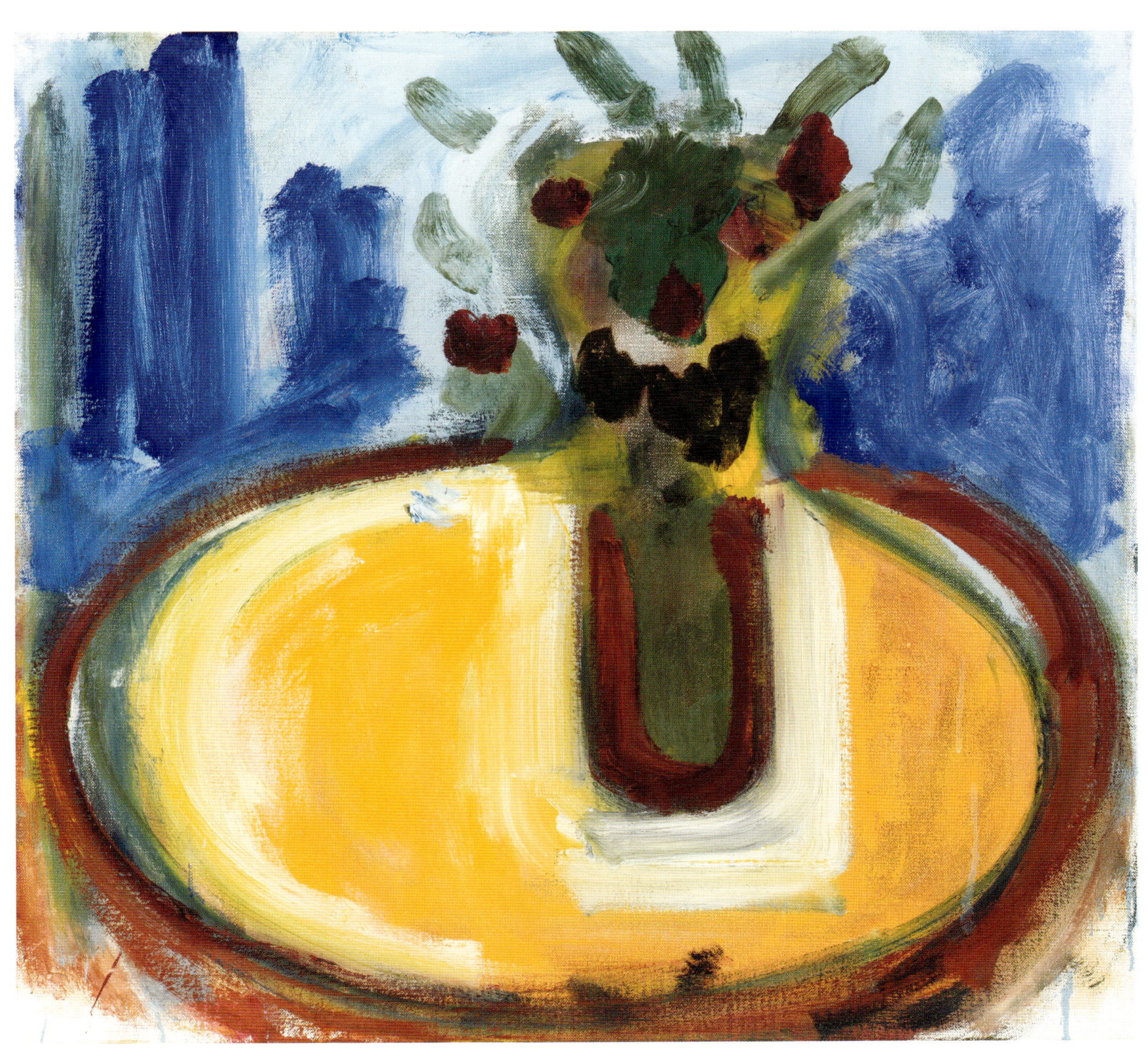

101. **Roses on Table**, 1979. Oil on canvas, 24 x 26 inches

102. **Moroccan Women**, 1979. Oil on linen, 64 x 53 inches

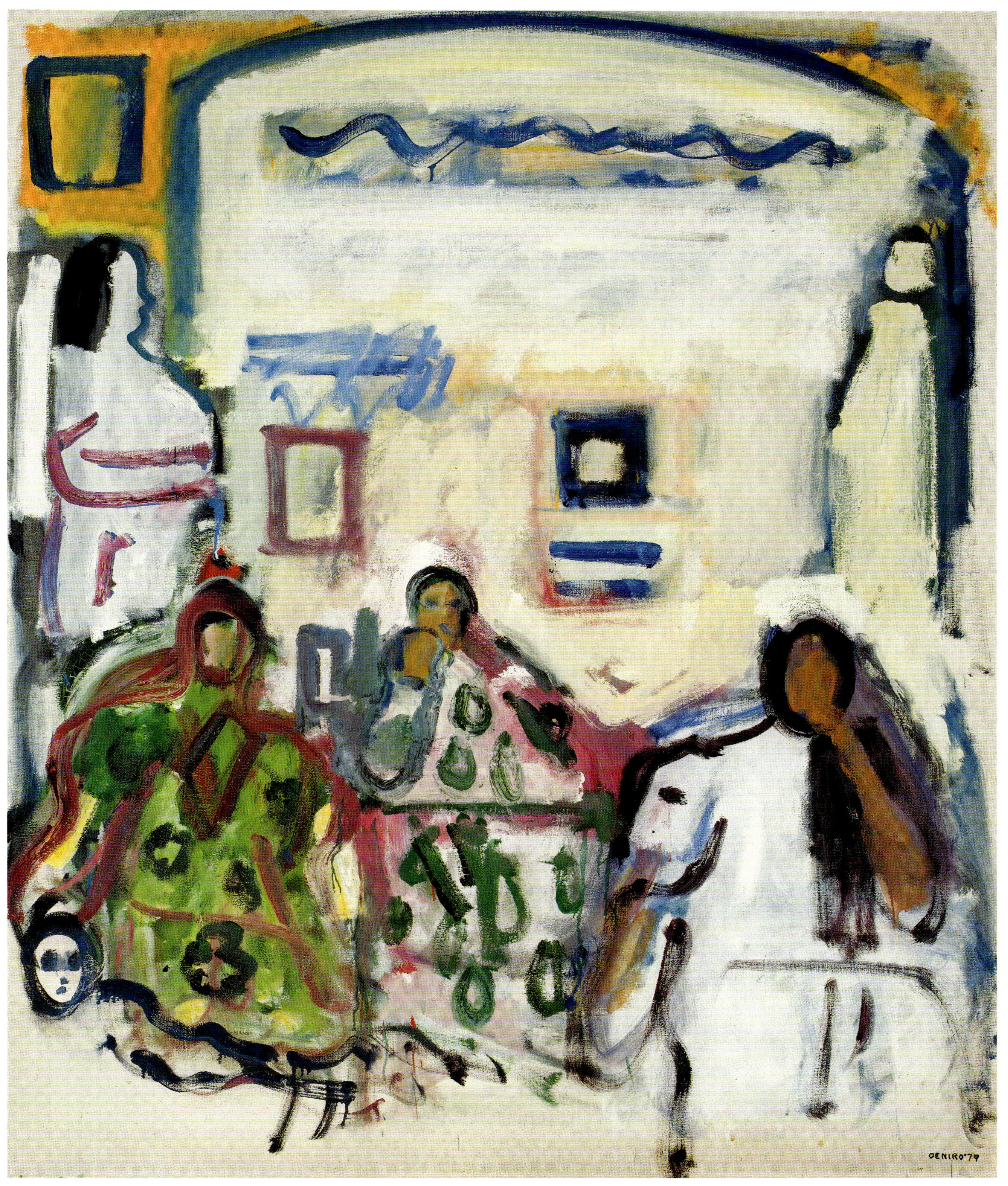
DENIRO '79

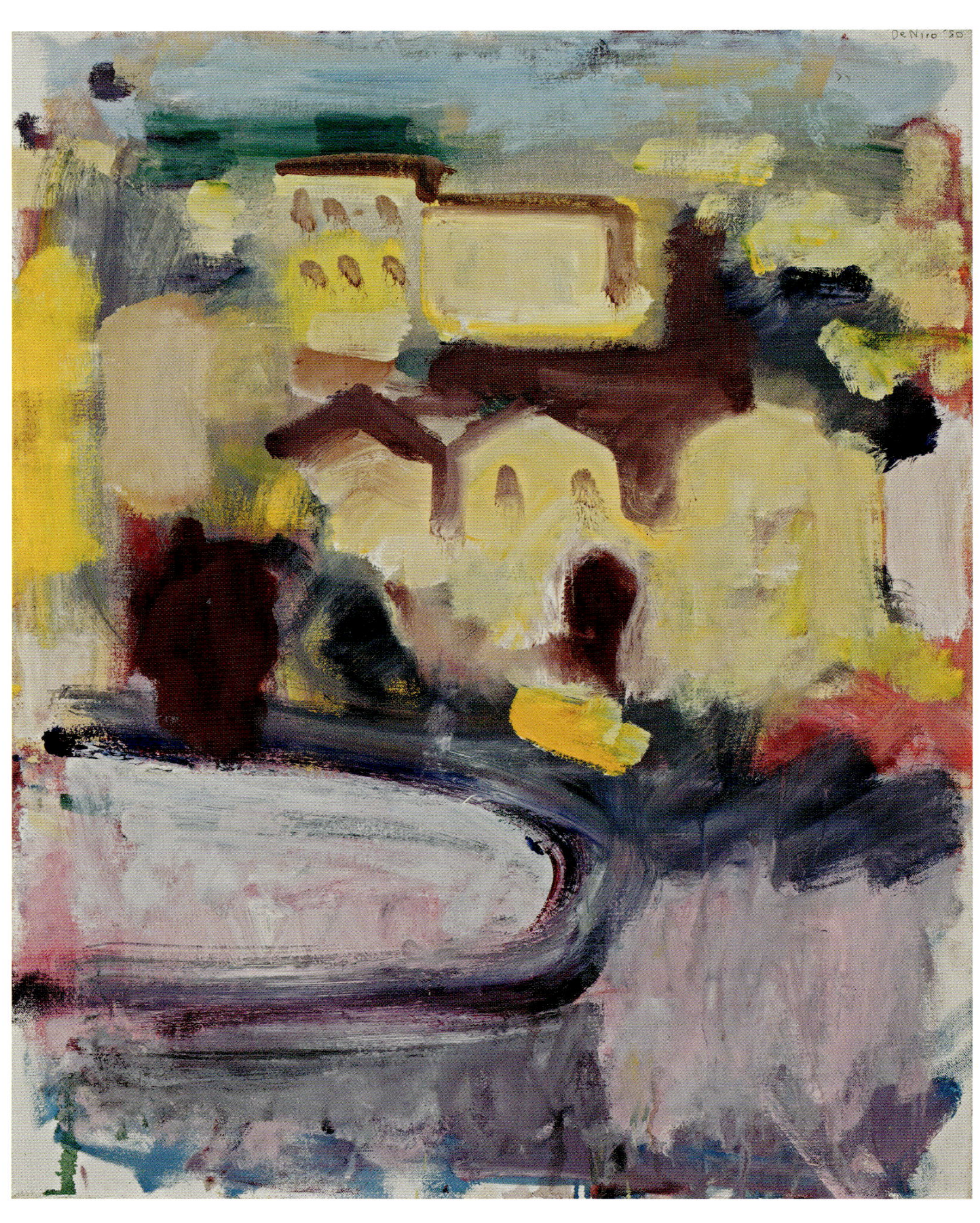

103. **Looking towards Downtown San Francisco from Bernal Heights**, 1980. Oil on canvas, 30 x 24 inches

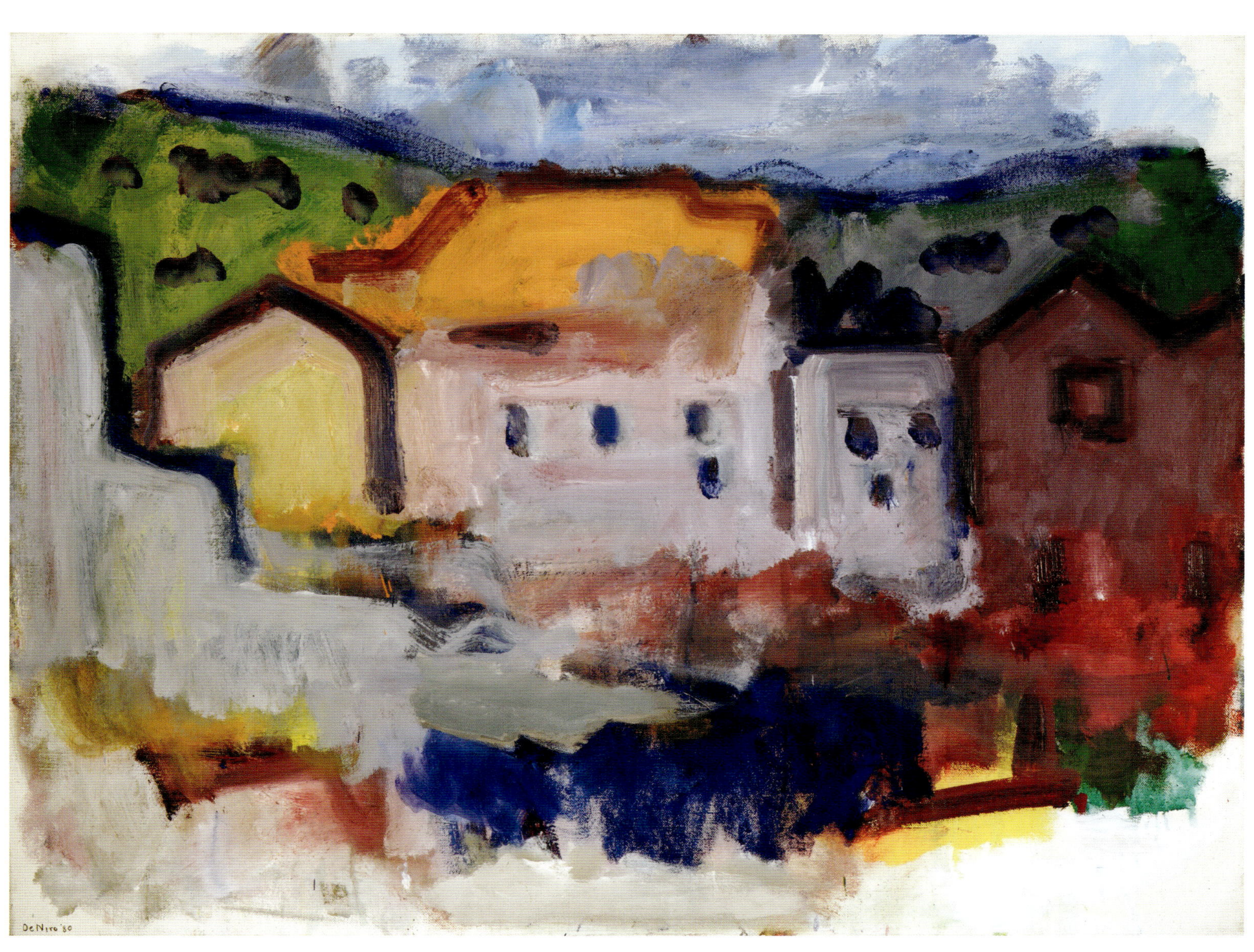

104. **Landscape with Houses** (verso **Houses on Folsom Street**), 1980. Oil on canvas, 30 x 40 inches

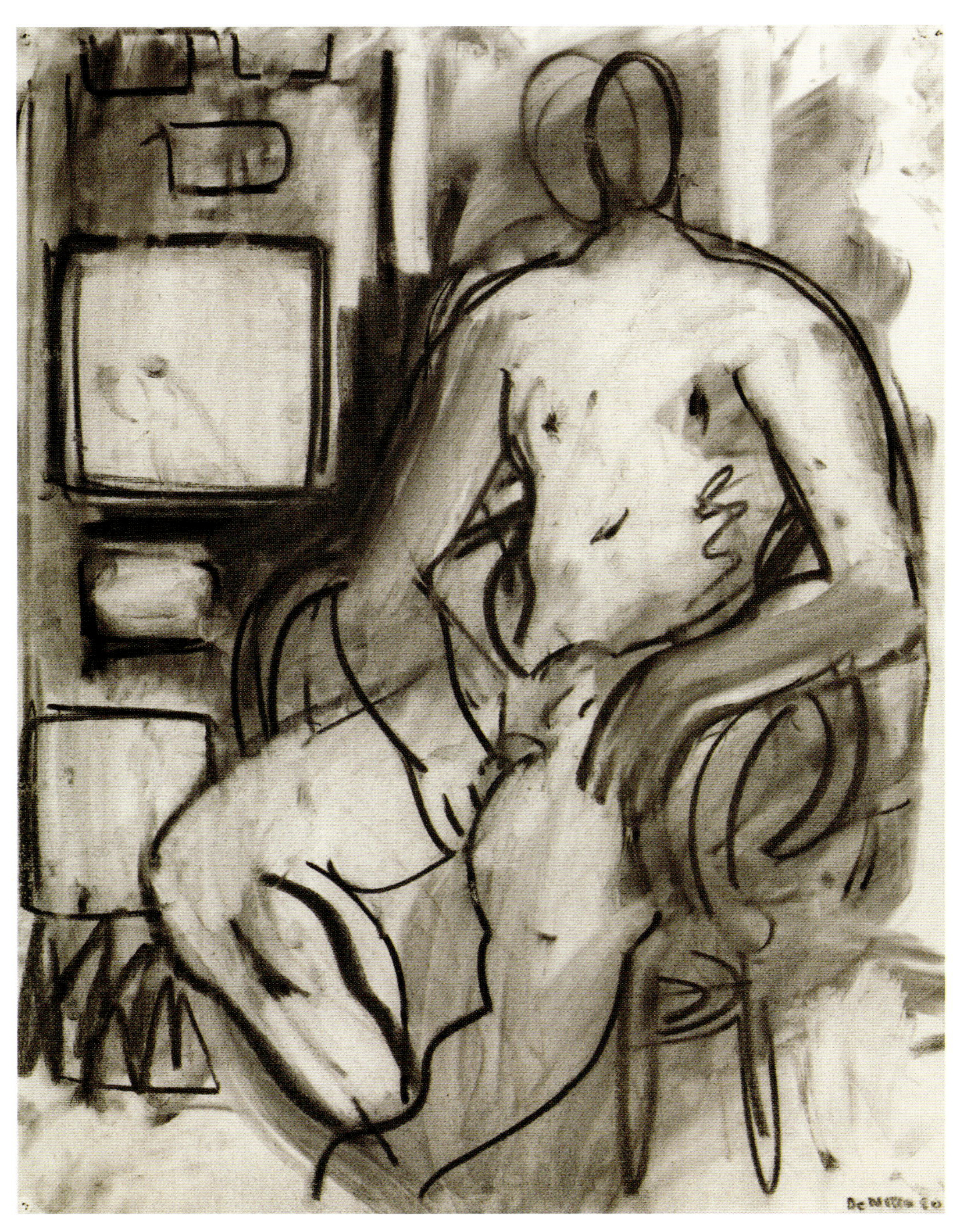

105. **Seated Male Nude with Studio Pictures**, 1980. Charcoal on paper, 25 ½ x 19½ inches

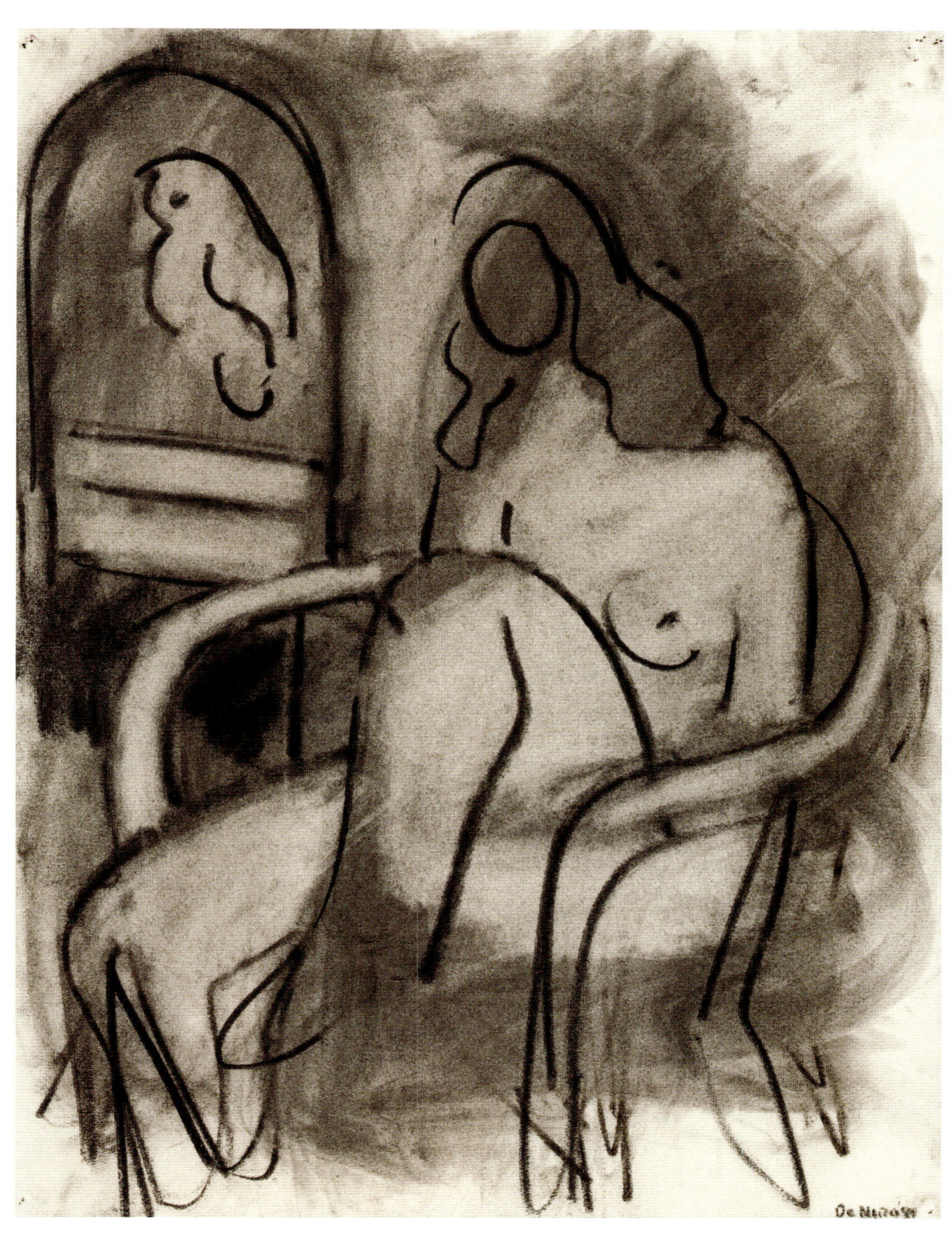

106. **Seated Female Nude with a Parrot**, 1980. Charcoal on paper, 25½ x 19½ inches

107. **Bird Cage, Two Vases and Flowers**, 1981. Oil on linen, 40 x 30 inches

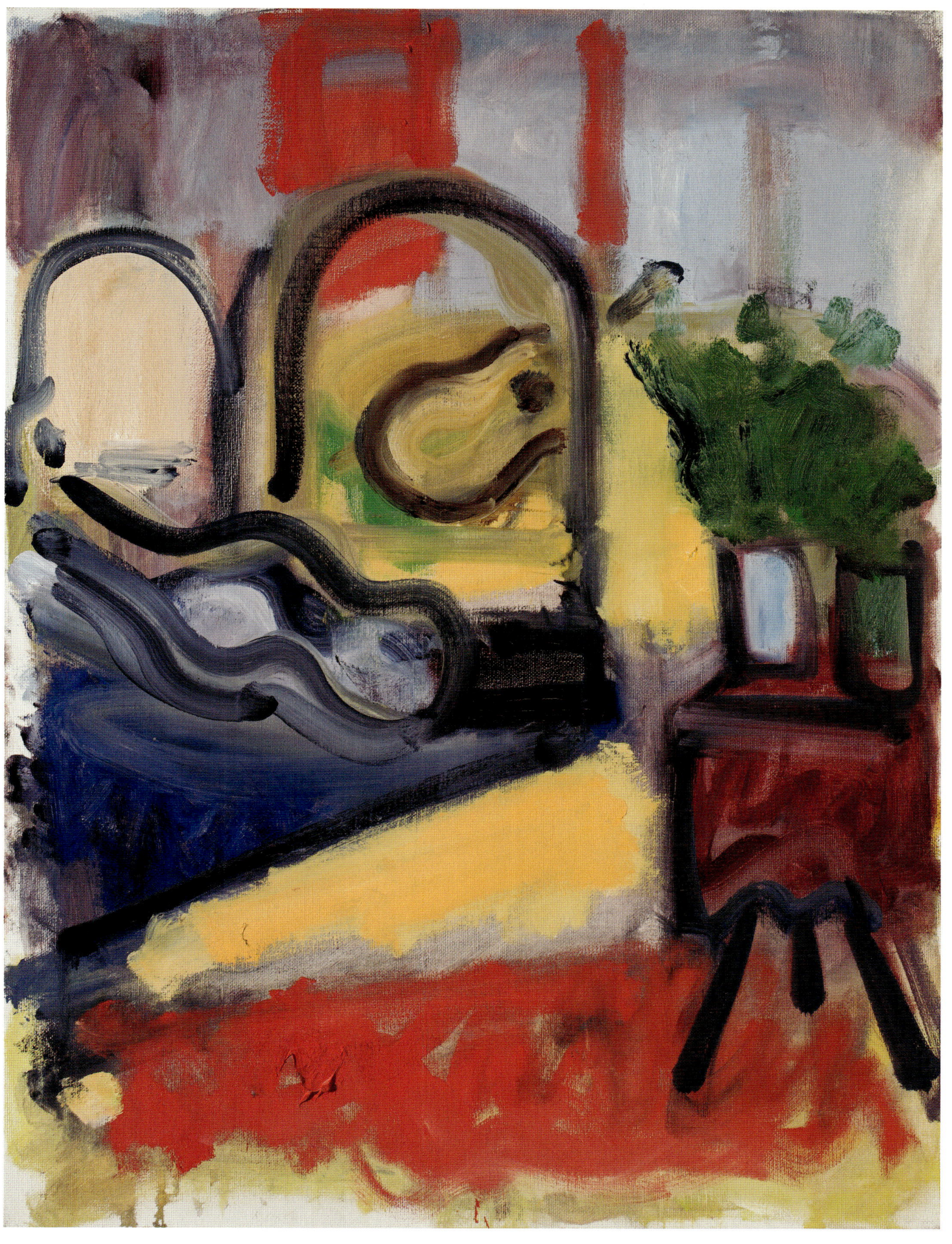

108. **Crucifixion with Four Spectators**, 1982. Oil on canvas, 54 ¼ x 48 ¼ inches

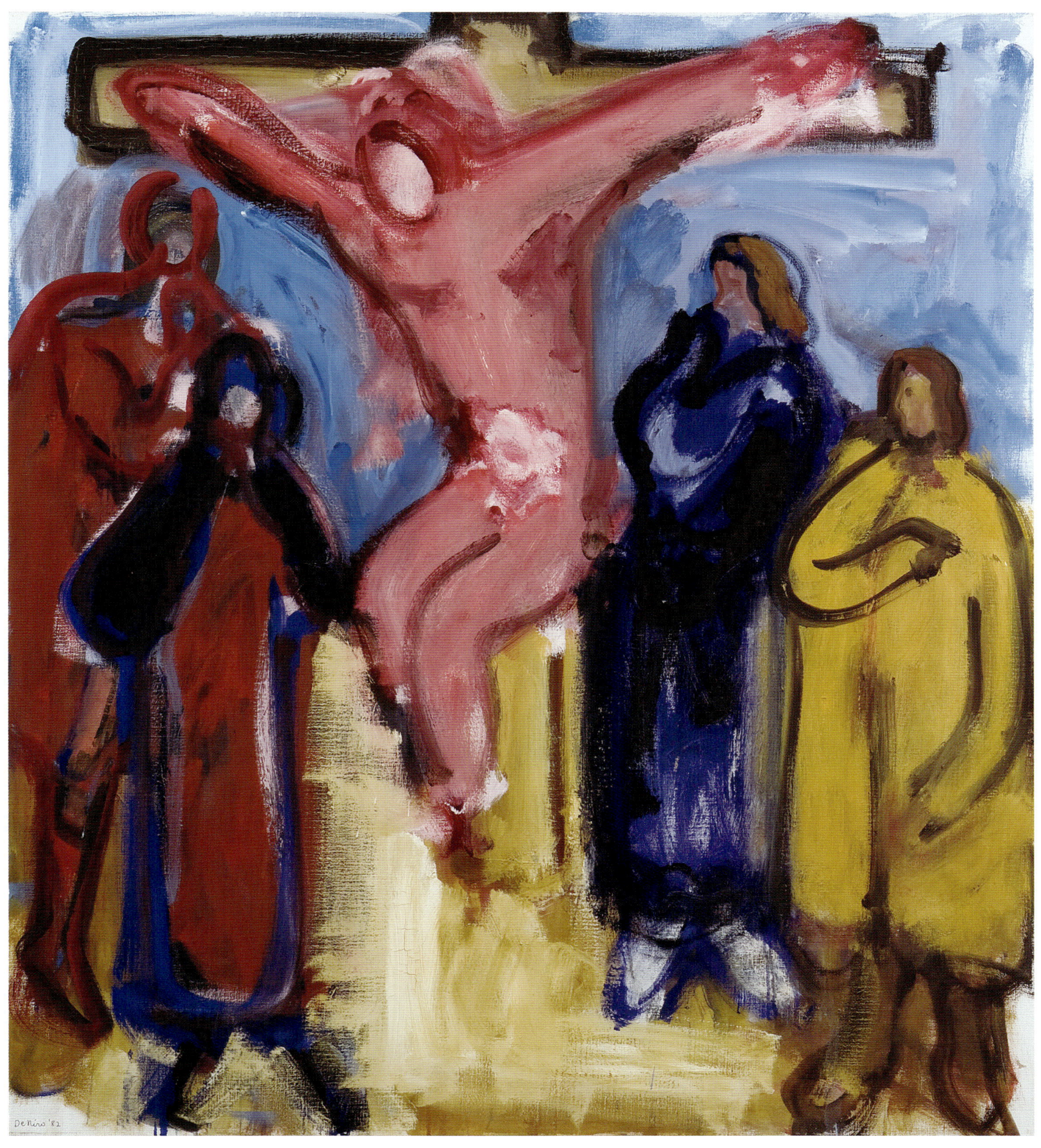
DeNiro '82

109. **Moroccan Women**, 1984. Oil on linen, 70 x 76 inches

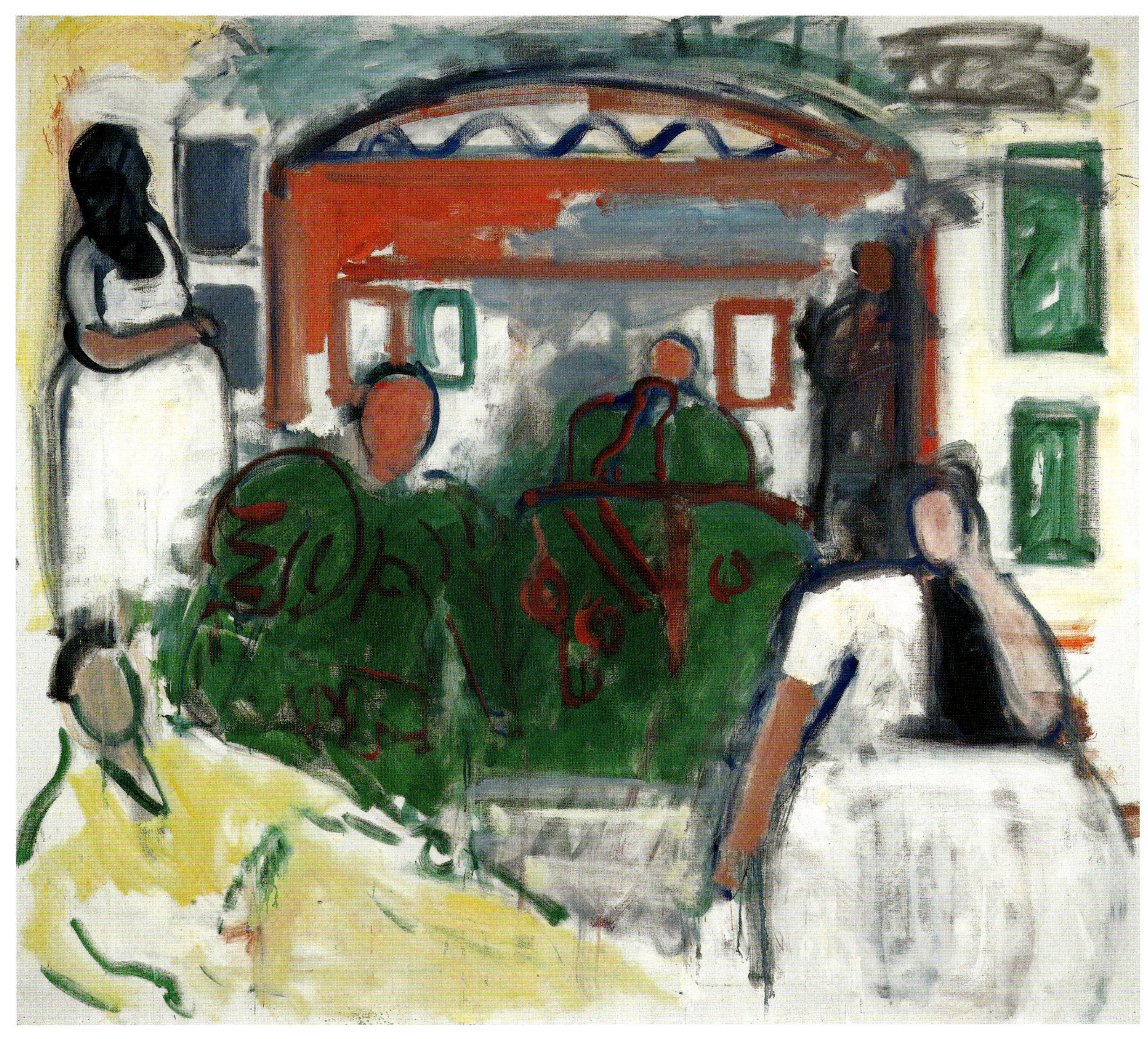

110. **Self-Portrait of the Artist at His Easel**, 1985. Oil on canvas, 40 x 30 inches

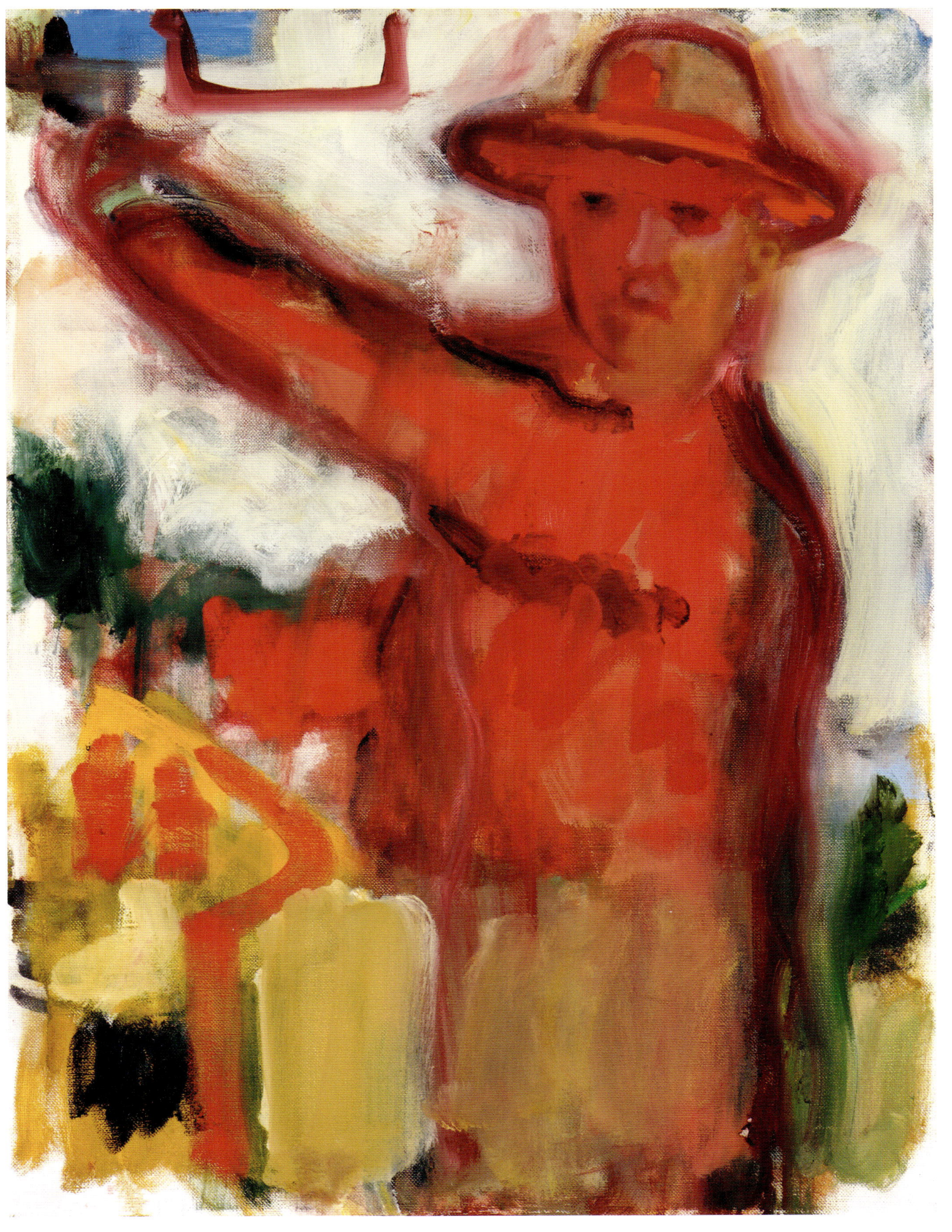

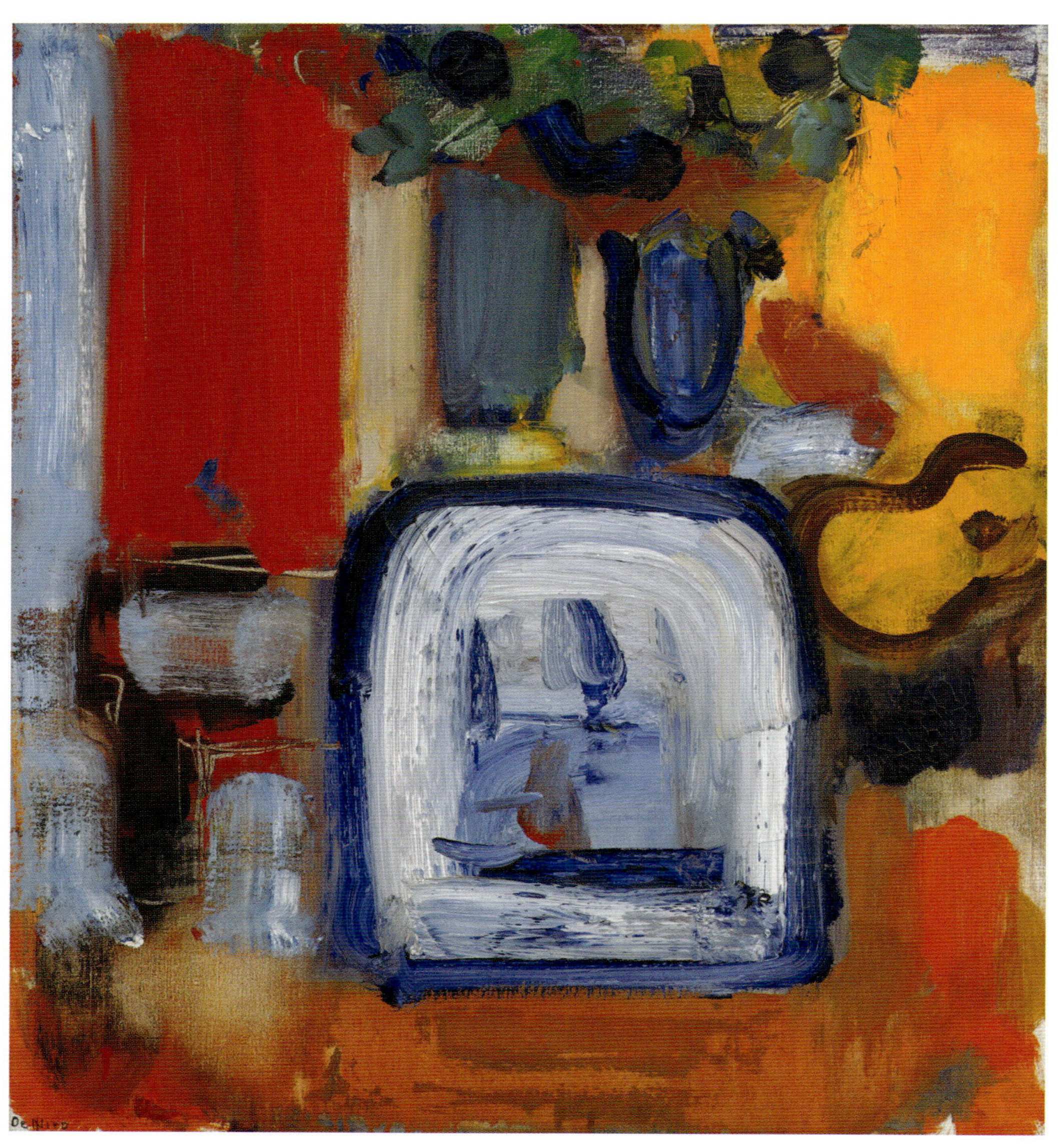

111. **Still Life with Bird Cage, Guitar, Flowers**, ca. 1980s. Oil on canvas, 22⅛ x 20⅛ inches

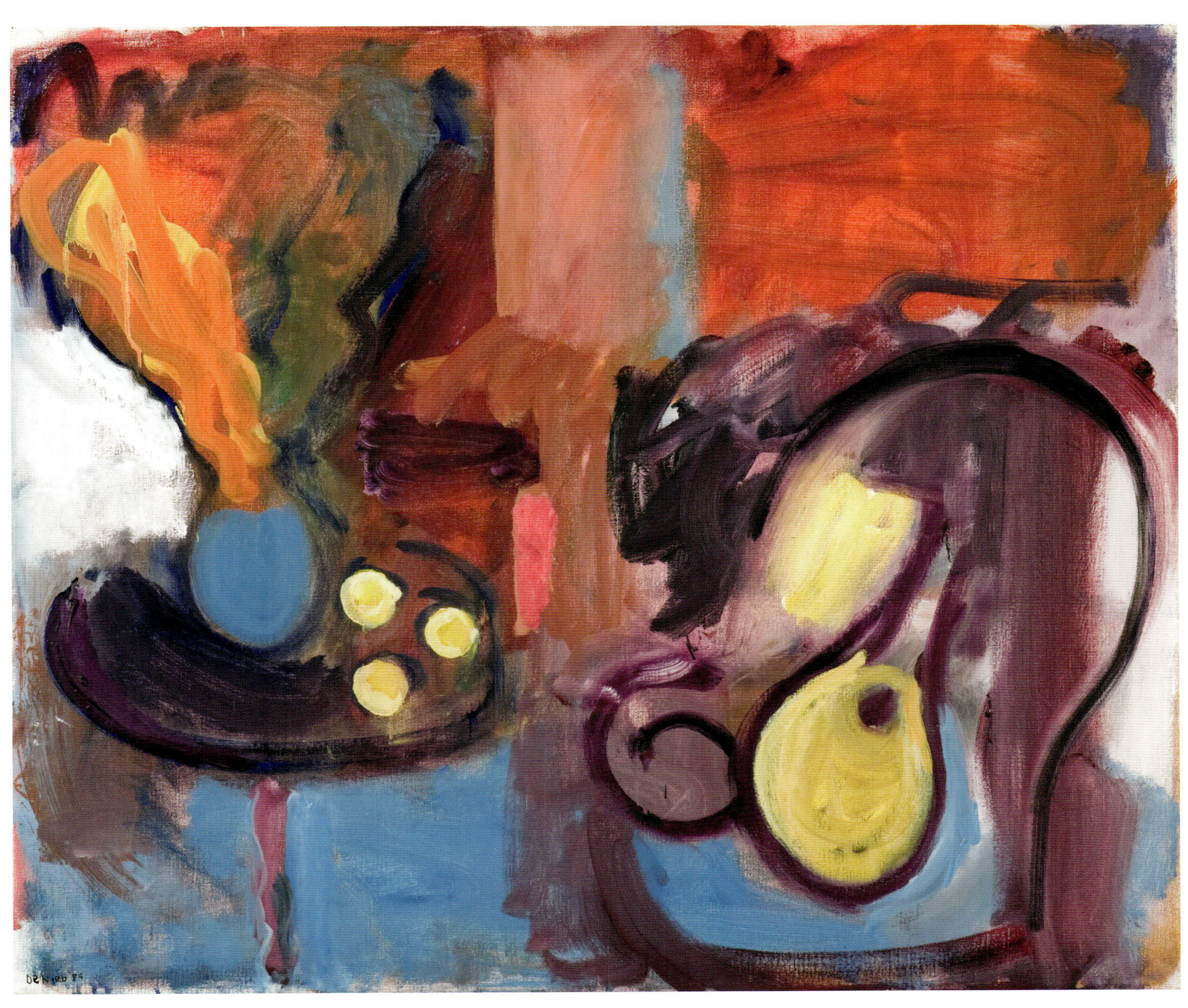

112. **Still Life with Vase of Flowers, Lemons, Chair and Guitar**, 1989. Oil on canvas, 34 x 40 inches

113. **Last Painting**, 1985–93. Oil on canvas, 60 x 48 inches

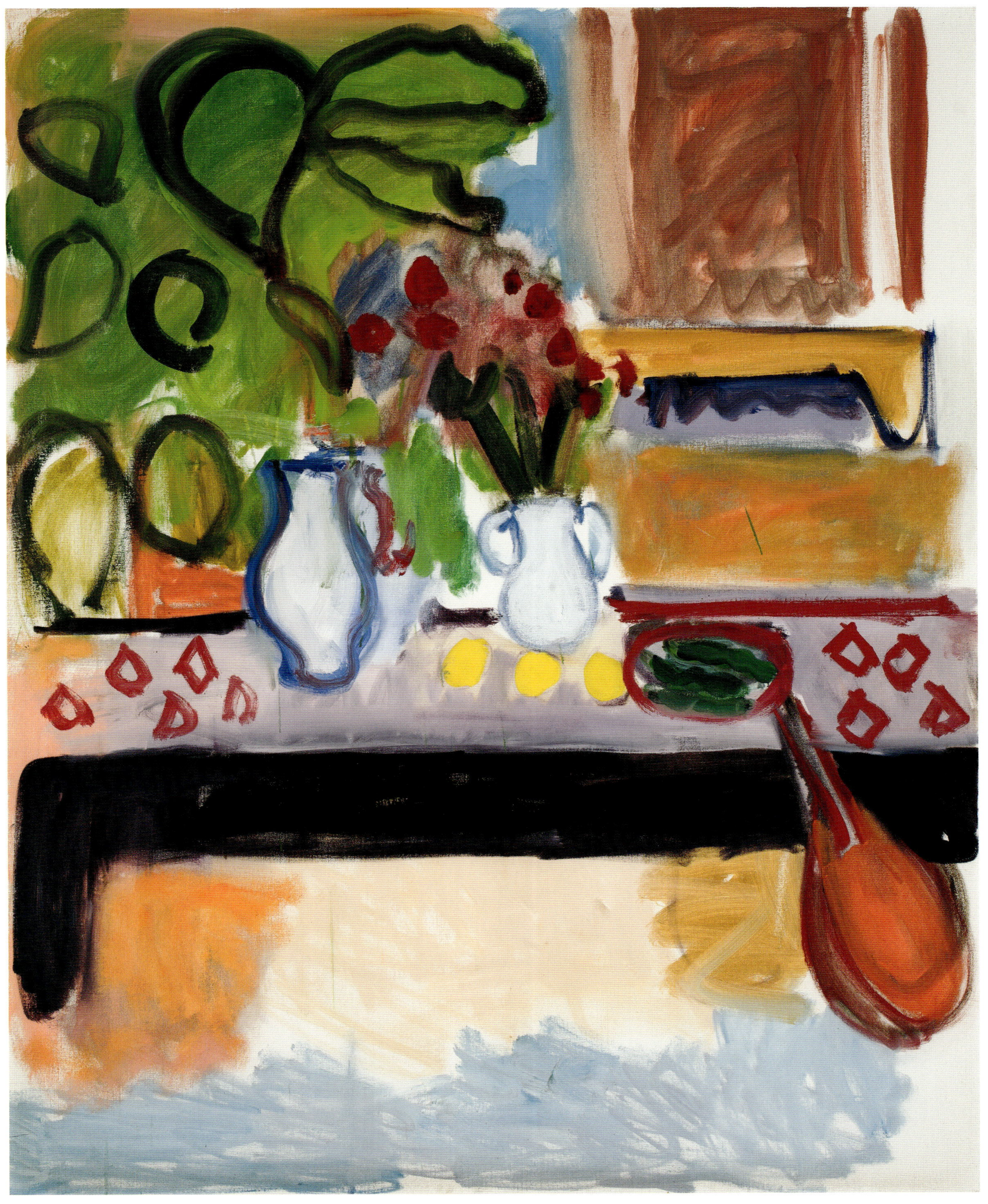

Robert Kushner

COLOR: INTOXICANT OF CHOICE

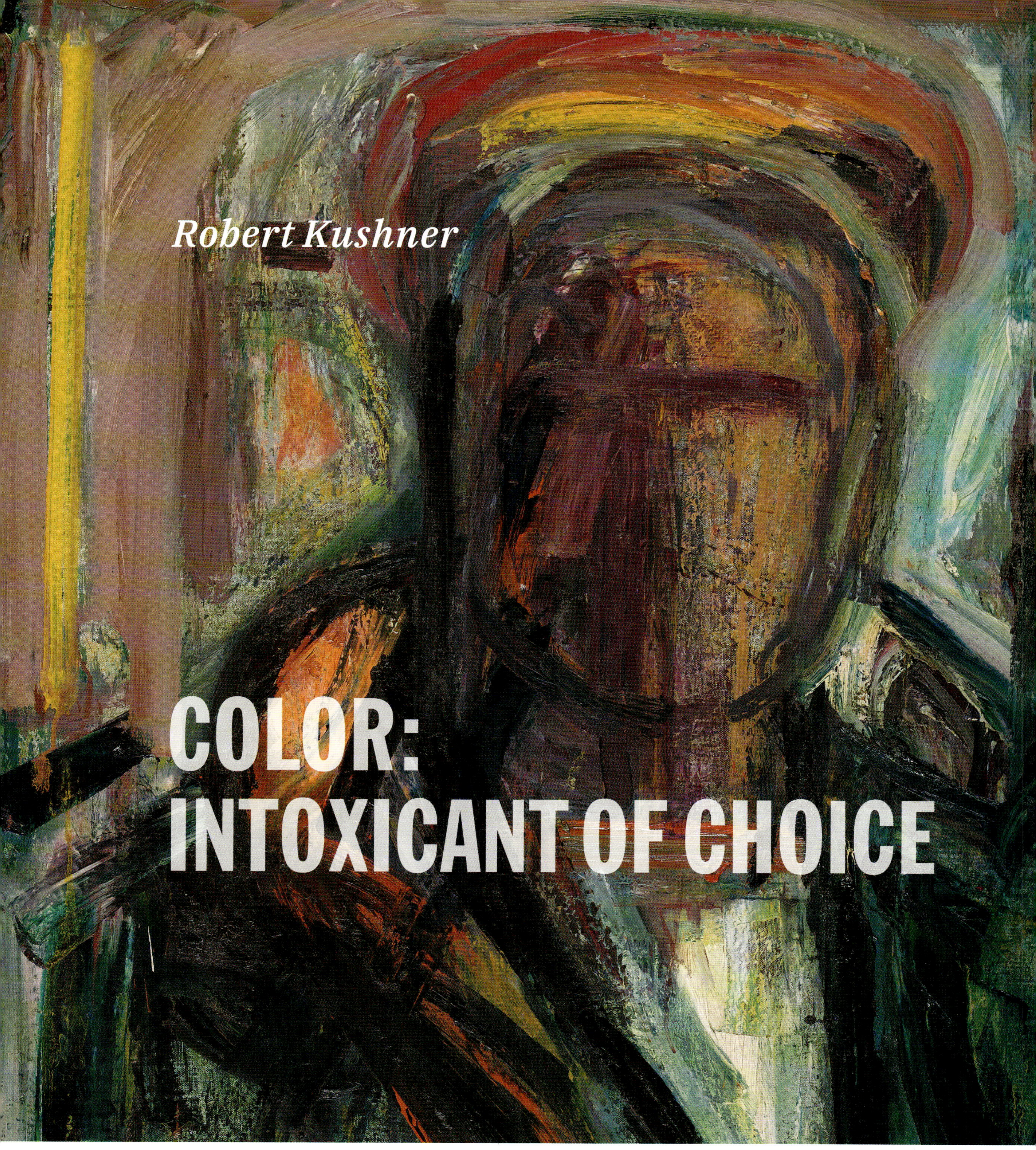

Self-Portrait, 1951 (detail). Oil on canvas, 35⅛ x 30 inches. Plate 13

OTHER ESSAYS IN THIS BOOK DEAL WITH Robert De Niro, Sr.'s, chronology, his writing, his journals, but I want to take a brief meander, a slow read of three particular paintings from different moments in De Niro's life. This essay is not a definitive discussion of his entire production. I have omitted whole bodies of the artist's work and discussion of medium—drawing, painting on paper, landscape, sculpture, images of celebrities, and Crucifixions. Addressing just these three personal choices allows me to enter into the aspects of De Niro's work that I like and admire the most.

SELF-PORTRAIT (1951)

When he painted this *Self-Portrait* (PLATE 13), De Niro was twenty-nine. He had already received considerable attention, both as a child prodigy and as a precocious student of his mentor and noted teacher, Hans Hofmann (1880–1966). De Niro was on the cusp of wider recognition, and he was trying to support himself and his young son. This painting is somewhat brutal, and when it is viewed as a self-portrait, it is even more disturbing. Brash gestures and gutsy paint handling, both present in this work, was the name of the game in 1951. To the first-generation Abstract Expressionists, unfussy, rough brushwork introduced the viewer to a newfound postwar aesthetic. De Niro signed on with gusto. The paint is applied with a ferocious barbarism that today seems somewhat mannered. However, when this painting is viewed in person, it still carries a wallop. Paint is applied with a wide brush in strong colors. Layers of paint have been scraped off, not with a narrow palette knife but with what appears to be a wide putty knife. The knife leaves marks as decisive and gestural as the brushed-on paint itself. The trail of the knife's path through the wet paint leaves significant lumps of oil paint clinging to the edges of the dragged gesture.

The painting is a series of angular, jarring shards. The thick scum of paint around the edge of the canvas is evidence that the painting was painted and repainted numerous times. Already De Niro has taken an interest in color, and even though the colors showing through are almost like memories, they are beginning to assert themselves as an important part of his artistic artillery. Traces of putty brown, gray green, phthalo green, and alizarin crimson lie atop and beneath the defining lines of deep green and black.

The painting is more of an attack than a caress. In painting a self-portrait, did he conceive of himself as his own psychic assailant? Does he feel that he is under attack by the art world? Or is he the victim of his own personal and internal world? De Niro paints fast, wipes out, repaints. His brush dances over the surface in repeatable rhythms that we reexperience in the finished canvases. There are home movies of De Niro at a later date, painting with confidence and breakneck speed. There are also films of Jackson Pollock gracefully dripping skeins of paint onto the horizontal canvas. De Niro is more like a toreador. In these films he is poised, attentive, and lithe. His attack is bold and fast. He seems to be dancing in relationship to the canvas. De Niro liked to dance and was known as a skilled social dancer. His sense of rhythm and movement in life is at one with his physical approach to the canvas. As his work develops over time, this obsession with rapid paint application continues to be an essential element of his style. It almost becomes part of the subject matter.

The most disturbing component of this painting is the face. Painted, scraped, repainted, it is left as a dull red-brown stain on the raw canvas. The face is nearly featureless, ultimately left as no more than a T. There is only the brusque geometry of a vertical facial midline and a horizontal demarcation for the eyes, with an implication of light falling from the upper right.

Is this abstraction a re-creation of the artist's face as a Christian cross? Is he seeing himself as persecuted, alone, a man of sorrows? At this point in his life, he is a father, separated and eventually to be divorced. He has been around the greats of the Abstract Expressionist movement, but perhaps he wonders whether he is indeed able to measure up. But he is also slightly detached, both socially and artistically, a bit apart from the greater art-world dialogue. Does he feel isolated from the hetero-machismo of the Cedar Tavern gang? Separated by his now acknowledged homosexuality from the ultra-straight art world of the AbEx pioneers?

Should we view this self-portrait as a contemporary interpretation of *ecce homo*, Jesus as the human embodiment of life's sorrows? It is interesting to compare this painting with the powerful religious imagery of Georges Rouault (1871–1958). Rouault, two generations older than De Niro and a stalwart exemplar of the School of Paris, was quite well known and still working at that time. The strong, frontal gaze consisting of a set of shapes held together by bold black lines, epitomized in Rouault's style, was a potential

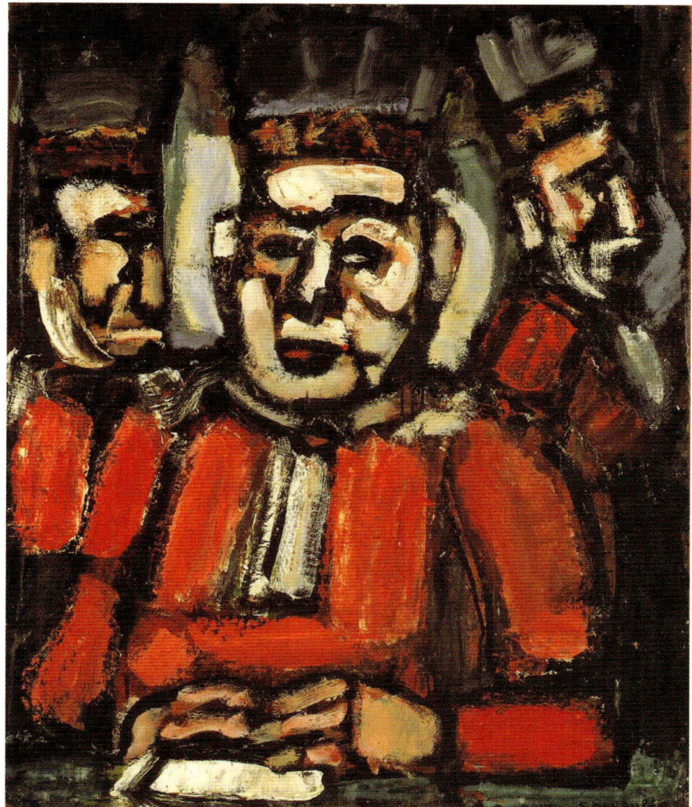

FIGURE 1
Georges Rouault
The Three Judges, 1936
Oil on board mounted
on mahogany panel
33 x 26¼ in. (81.3 x 64.1 cm)
Tate Galleries, London

source for this painting (FIG. 1). The French artist infused a Modernist aesthetic with his deeply felt religious conviction, which is echoed by De Niro in this self-portrait. What does the presence of a red, yellow, and orange circular form around the face of the self-portrait mean? It could be read as a hat or a turban. But it feels more like a halo—the hidden radiance revealed, despite the external pain of the mundane world.

Artistically speaking, an alternative stylistic source might be the late portraits of Alexej von Jawlensky (1864–1941). While more obscure than Rouault, Jawlensky might have been brought to De Niro's attention by Hofmann. Jawlensky's late "Meditation" series features extreme close-ups of faces reduced to little more than abstract rectangles, so that they become the entire image (FIG. 2). These paintings are a reduction to transcendent simplicity.

De Niro's work of this period embarked on an exploration of the wet-on-wet painting style that he continued to employ, with variations, for the rest of his life. With this technique, the entire surface is worked on at the same time. Oil paint will remain wet and workable for several days, during which time the artist can add, wipe out, scrape, and repaint at will. Colors can remain pristine, or they can mix and blend to create strange new colors on the surface of the canvas. However, once the painting is considered finished, it is difficult to make later changes that will not stand out. This technique, preferred by De Niro, provides a sense of exhilaration and immediacy, but it also puts considerable pressure on the artist to "get it right." De Niro was up for the challenge.

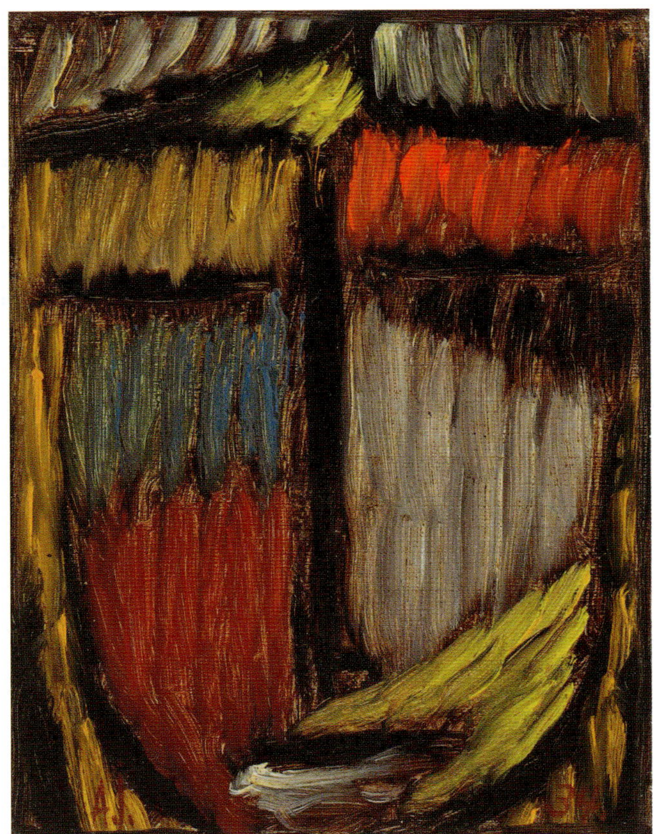

FIGURE 2
Alexej von Jawlensky
Meditation, 1934
Oil on linen-finished paper mounted on board
6¾ x 5 in. (17.1 x 12.7 cm)
Private Collection

WOMAN IN RED (1961)

As his work grew and changed, De Niro began to leave aside this anxious energy and angularity. He became more interested in forms that are looser and more curvaceous, more sensuous, with paint handling that depended on his confident, fluent brushwork. By the early 1960s, the artist, now in his late thirties, had arrived at a new way of working that synthesized his rapid gestural brushwork with a deep admiration for the vocabulary and coloristic intensity of Henri Matisse (1869–1954).

For the most part, De Niro, like Matisse, preferred to keep his themes nonconfrontational: interiors, nudes, landscapes, still lifes. His sense of provocation relied on attack and brio. *Woman in Red* (1961; PLATE 55). is part of a series of major figurative compositions. Notably, it was shown the year of its completion at the Museum of Modern Art, New York, in an exhibition titled *Recent Painting USA: The Figure*. Clearly things were going well for De Niro.

The central figure is a seated woman in a stylish red dress with a poofy skirt, her feet dangling below. The dress is a whirlwind of cadmium red brushstrokes intermixed with black under- and overpainting. The brushstrokes never coalesce to form a convincing volume for the skirt; they remain a swarm of red and black lines. The skirt could almost be a passage from a Joan Mitchell abstraction from this same era. Splashes and drips of red paint clue us to the velocity and frenzy of the execution. Color is the intoxicant of

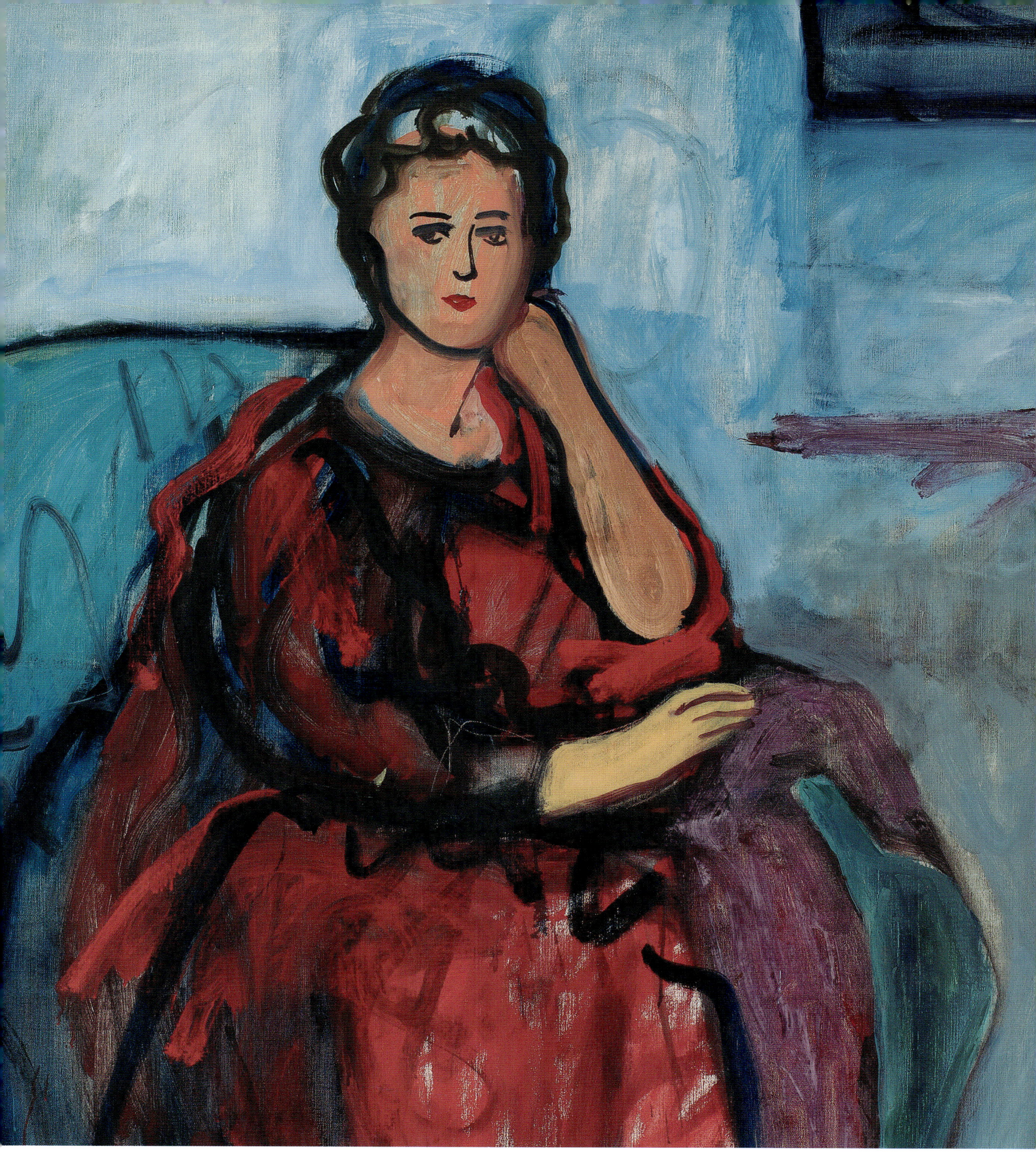

Woman in Red, 1961 (detail). Oil on linen, 70 x 54 inches. Plate 55

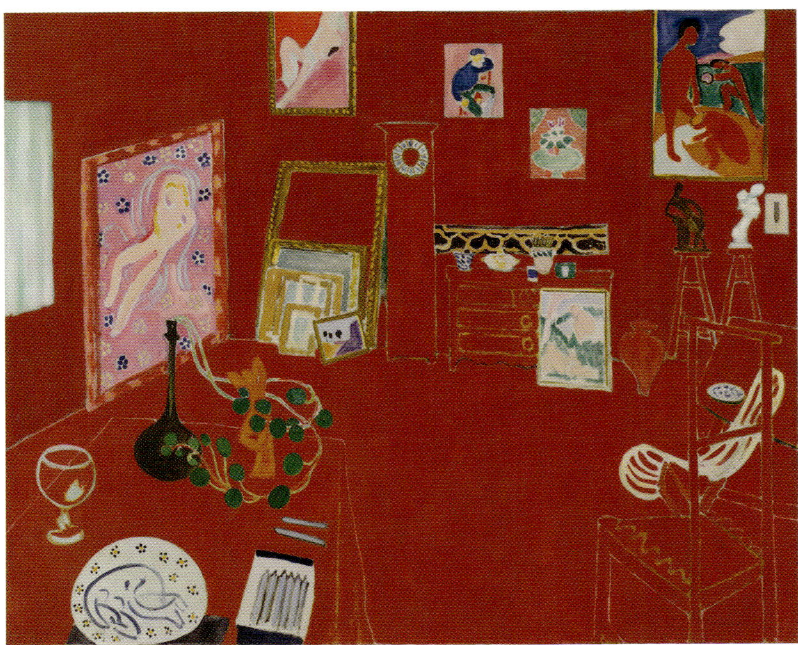

FIGURE 3
Henri Matisse
The Red Studio, 1911
Oil on canvas
71¼ x 86¼ in.
(181 x 219 cm)
Museum of Modern Art, New York

choice. Our lady is clutching a plum-purple shawl. Her chair is a complementary tourmaline green. In contrast to all the breezy energy of color and drawing, her face is rendered simply and calmly, with a staccato series of brushstrokes that coalesce into a pensive expression. Surrounding the figure is an abstract field of blue, which transitions from dusty teal to browned turquoise to cerulean to clear aqua. There is also a mauve horizontal scumble. What does it define? Perhaps the edge of the room between the wall and the floor. It does not really create a sense of space. So is it primarily a gestural form to balance the weight and color of the solid figure to the left? On the far left of the canvas, there are two other forms that enrich the chromatic dialogue. One is a splash of lemon yellow in a vertical stripe, and the other a series of cadmium orange and turquoise stripes. Perhaps they are both studio furnishings. Together they anchor the seated figure and serve as two edgy complements to the color harmony.

Compositionally, every one of these elements comes from Matisse. If De Niro's early work was concerned with a reinterpretation of the spiky angularity of Picasso and Cubism, in the intervening decade the artist has imbibed and digested the coloristic and representational innovations of Matisse (FIG. 3). In the 1950s Matisse, widely acknowledged as one of the greatest of modern painters, was a bit of a specialist taste compared with Picasso. His paintings and sculptures could be seen at the Museum of Modern Art, but many of his greatest works lay hidden in the Barnes Foundation outside Philadelphia, or at the Hermitage in St. Petersburg. Both were challenging destinations for most Matisse enthusiasts to reach. But for De Niro, Matisse became a lifeline. He emulated Matisse in his thin paint handling, drawing style (on canvas and particularly in his charcoal drawings on paper), chromatic intensity, and subject matter. The distance from *Self-Portrait* to *Woman in Red* is vast.

By this point De Niro had learned the value of painting a single layer of paint over the primed canvas. The white ground of the primed canvas shows through the relatively thin layer of paint, offering luminosity when the pigments are clean and pure. When the paint is scumbled, muddied, or repainted on the surface, a different dynamic results. Often, unnamable tertiary colors emerge from the combined brushstrokes. In *Woman in Red*, De Niro's restrained use of a black line—from the soft modeling of the hair to the throwaway squiggles on the green chair to the controlled gestures of the face—animates and unifies the entire surface.

In the middle of all this frantic brushy activity, the figure maintains her steely gaze. Her confident expression makes us wonder whether this is a studio model or a young socialite posing for a commissioned portrait. It turns out that she is a studio model, but we have the sense of a real individual embedded in the flurry of paint. De Niro seduces us with the fluid speed of his careening brush and strange, off-harmonies of radiant color. His best paintings, like this one, reveal humanizing hints of slight diffidence mixed with bravura. Spending time with a painting like *Woman in Red* reminds us of the pleasure of seeing paint skillfully applied to canvas with a balance of abandon and control.

Every era offers an artist unique opportunities as well as challenges. Certain times present larger challenges. An enormous sea change occurred in the early 1950s, after a core group of gestural abstractionists created an entirely new vocabulary, and dictated what the next step would be: action painting, Abstract Expressionism. The gospel of large, embracing formats, of unprecedentedly bold brushwork and an unfinished look was rapidly communicated around the world. De Niro rode that wave and painted brilliantly. However, to quote art historian Irving Sandler:

> What happens around 1958... really by 1962, I've always referred to it as a blood bath. There is a radical change in style. A young generation of artists—abstract painters, Pop, Hard Edge—suppress the painterly quality of their work. The energy of paint, the sweep of paint, the movement of paint—and this is really what interested De Niro, always his emphasis—suddenly this becomes very unfashionable.[1]

What is a motivated artist to do at such a time? To his credit, De Niro stuck to his guns, finding new variations of his heated, expressionist style to explore. Others did the same,

1. Irving Sandler, quoted in *Remembering the Artist: Robert De Niro, Sr.*, a film by Perri Peltz and Geeta Gandbhir, 2014.

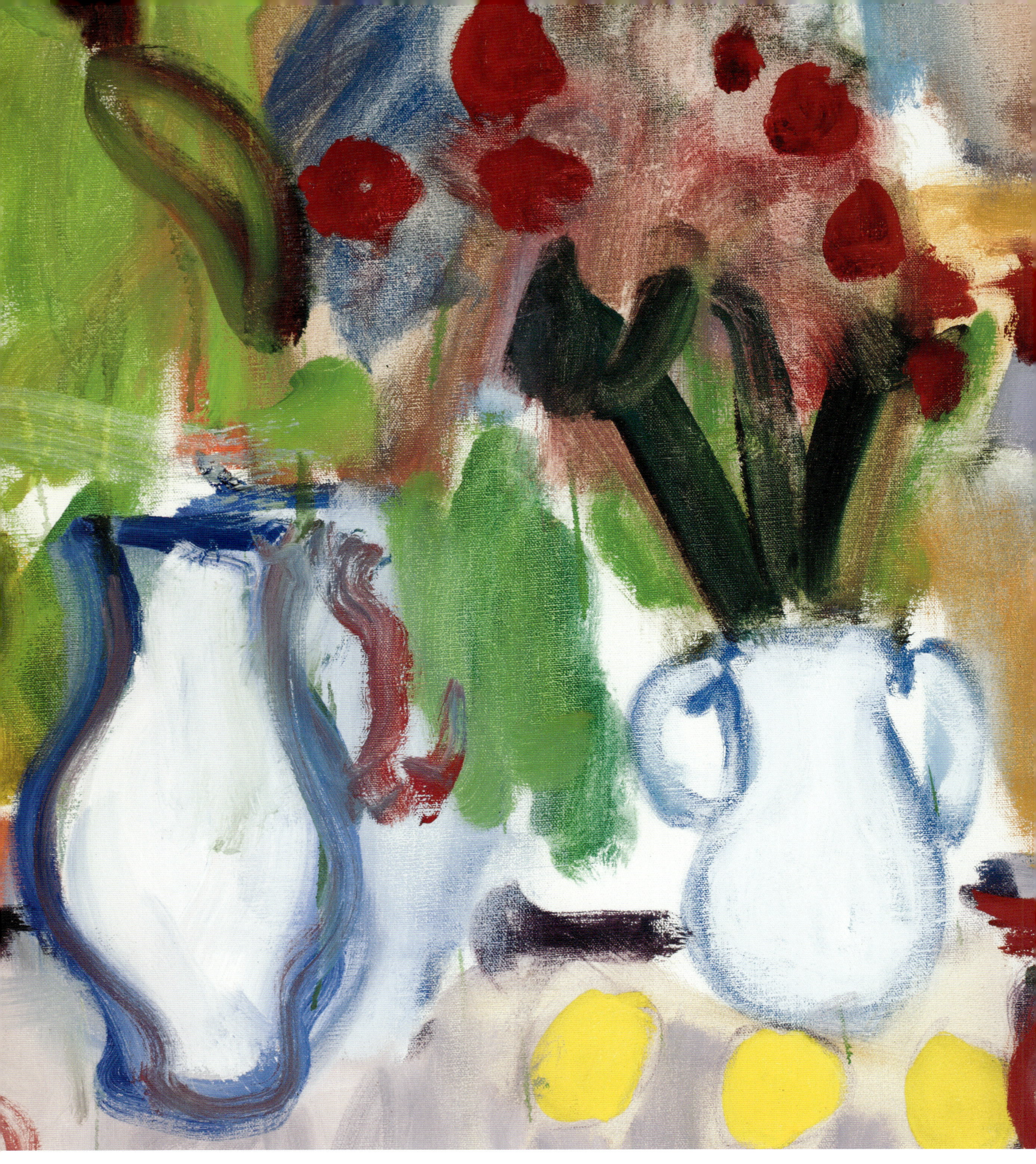

Last Painting, 1985-93 (detail). Oil on canvas, 60 x 48 inches. Plate 113

most notably Willem de Kooning and Joan Mitchell. De Niro found solace and new ideas in his subject matter, particularly the human figure. References to the works of great artists of the past, along with photo-derived subject matter, remained the core inspiration for his paintings.

De Niro asked few questions about his preferred groups of subject matter. For the most part, he adhered to the Modernist canon of figure, landscape, and still life. There is none of the irony, social commentary, or self-reflexive questioning that one would encounter with the Pop generation of artists. When there are figures, they exist only in the studio: nude or dressed, seated or standing, always roughly and quickly drawn. They are not working people, performing specific activities or enacting a narrative, rather they are studio furniture of a fleshy variety, posing for the sake of the artist's interest in paint handling, composition, and color. But De Niro is at his best when his approach is Apollonian, art for art's sake, with little or no troubling relationship to the nuanced complexities of the contemporary world.

De Niro was ten to twenty years younger than the first generation of Abstract Expressionist painters, and he joined their circle when he was barely in his twenties. From an early stage, he felt distance from the inner circle of the Expressionists, in his addition of overt subject matter and the primacy of color. He is sometimes considered a second-generation Abstract Expressionist. In many ways, his artistic approach was closer to the Jane Street Gallery group of artists (Larry Rivers, Leland Bell, Louisa Matthíasdóttir, Albert Kresch). He was closer chronologically to the Pop and Minimalist artists, but he eschewed their work. He identified with his older mentors and colleagues, their styles and their studio practices. Even though De Niro maintained Hofmann's approach to composition and painterly brushwork, one could say that he identified stylistically with Matisse, Rouault, Soutine, Manet, and the poet Verlaine. This puts De Niro's work in a slightly strange time warp, both current as well as slightly outdated, strongly American but also Francophilic at its core.

LAST PAINTING (1985–93)

Last Painting (PLATE 113) is a large summation painting—a mature expression of the issues and techniques that the artist had explored over his lifetime. I doubt that this was his last painting, as it was posthumously titled, especially due to its vigor of execution.

There is an ease and a Matissian joy to the thin, unlabored paint handling and loosely structured composition. Like most of his works from this period, *Last Painting* is painted wet on wet, with the entire surface completed in one prolonged series of sessions. When examined in person, it shows little or no repainting. It is a bravura performance.

This painting was done after De Niro's extensive series of figures in the studio and many abstracted landscapes. In the landscapes he could concentrate on the balance of strong vertical and horizontal lines and color. Here, the still life is treated as an indoor landscape, with clearly receding planes demarcated by horizontal passages of contrasting colors—blue at the bottom, then a passage of orange to peach to ochre, followed by a dynamic black horizontal table and, finally, a breakup of still life and plant forms. This ascension ends with a series of vertical slabs that delineate the back wall of the studio and the enclosure of the depicted space.

The colors sing. The purple tabletop is a fine setting for the clear yellow lemons and three humorous pickles on a red plate. A line depicting the back of the tabletop turns from black to purple and then to red and violet. There are two clusters of red diamond shapes that might be a cloth under the still-life elements on the tabletop. The logic of these color harmonies is visual and sensual. Here black is used as a color in its own right—a radiant, deep shade, not like the black lines that animate and organize *Self-Portrait* or *Woman in Red*. Either the outlines of the objects contrast strongly with the colors they define, or the forms remain unrestrained by a contour. The strong black bar is broken by a red-orange mandolin casually leaning against it. Pentimenti reveal that the mandolin was originally placed farther to the left. Where it now rests, however, it gives the center passage of the painting a perfect, off-center diagonal entry point for the sequence of events on the table's top, and it nicely breaks the insistence of the black rectangle.

There are two vases with blue outlines of slightly different tones. The forms of the vases are painted in a white that picks up traces of two shades of blue, offering very tender tones of pale color. Two vases, always side by side, recur repeatedly in De Niro's still lifes of this period. I think that they are a metaphor for loss and isolation, a code for an absent relationship, the wished-for lover, an element of life that eluded De Niro at this time. One vase is filled with red flowers; the other is empty.

The colors tied to objects are all specific to the objects depicted. The lemons are yellow; the pickles and plant leaves are green. However, when it comes to the background, De Niro's color flies with a complete abandon that sets off the jewel tones of his still-life elements. Persimmon, brilliant cadmium orange, shrill turquoise, scumbled greens and peach fill the space, creating a full-spectrum composition. In the resulting chromatic mosaic, it is the areas of color themselves, more than the dynamism and vigor of the drawing, that move the eye over the surface of the painting. This power of color to dominate and activate a composition is one of Matisse's greatest discoveries, and in this painting De Niro demonstrates how fully he has assimilated and individualized Matisse's breakthroughs.

At the top right is a rectangle of burnt sienna set off by narrow mauve stripes. In this earth-tone passage is the bass note of the painting. All the drama of the foreground is anchored by this surprisingly somber wall behind the stage set. A less sophisticated artist might have opted to avoid this dour color, but in the spectacle of pure and mixed colors that De Niro has tossed together, sienna offers sobriety and a calm foundation. The humble earth tone with its warm/cool nature sets off the purer hues and guarantees that the overall composition will not become overheated.

Behind and above the tabletop are large leaves drawn rapidly in deep green over a scumbled permanent-green ground. The leaves provide an organic, nonorthogonal grid as a foil for the straight-line structure of the tabletop. For this botanical form Matisse would probably have chosen one of his beloved *Philodendron monstera* plants, whose leaves gave him unequaled opportunity to play with positive and negative form. De Niro turns to a different houseplant—a rubber tree, with its large, fleshy, ovoid leaves resting at odd angles—to provide its own rhythm of organic forms.

Except for some of his late landscapes, this *Last Painting* is as close as De Niro comes to "Luxe, calme et volupté," the final line of Charles Baudelaire's poem "L'Invitation au voyage," and the title of a famous early painting by Matisse. Fully embodying De Niro's version of "luxury, calm and voluptuousness," this still life is an expression of mature energy, discovery, bold and seductive chromatic choices, poise, and balance. We know that this was the painting on De Niro's easel when he died, and I would like to think that he enjoyed reliving the excitement of its creation at the end of his life.

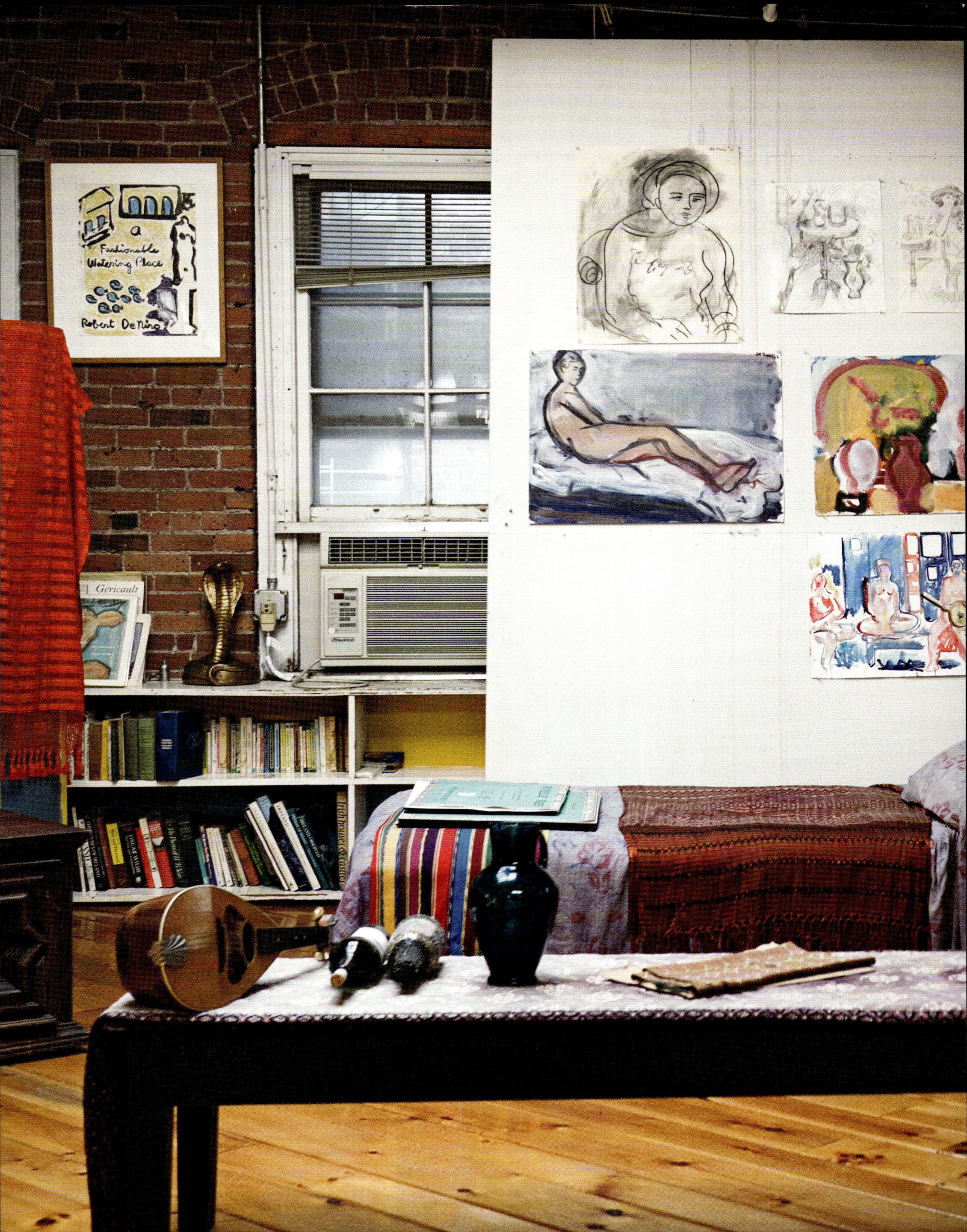
a
Fashionable
Watering Place
Robert De Niro
Géricault

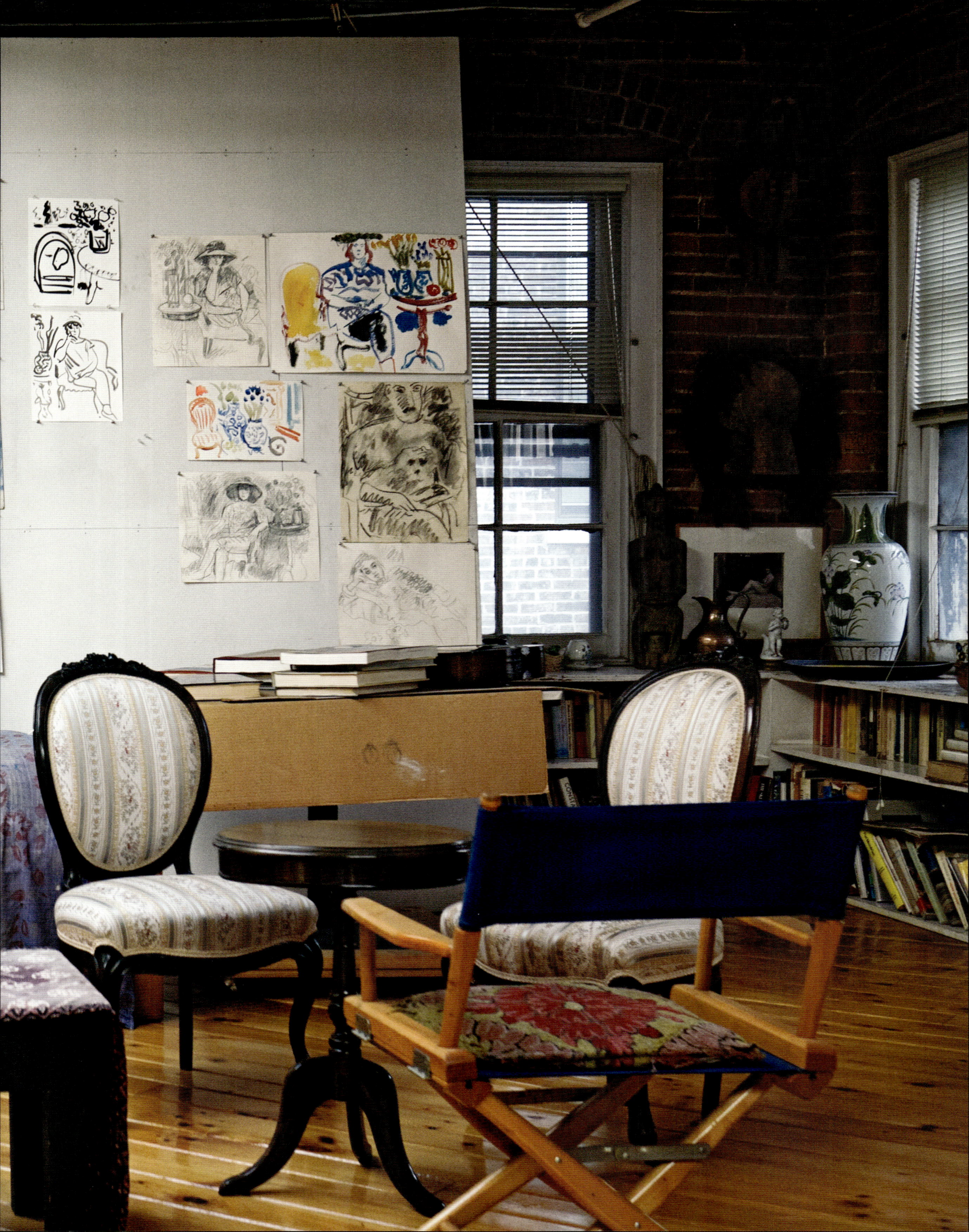

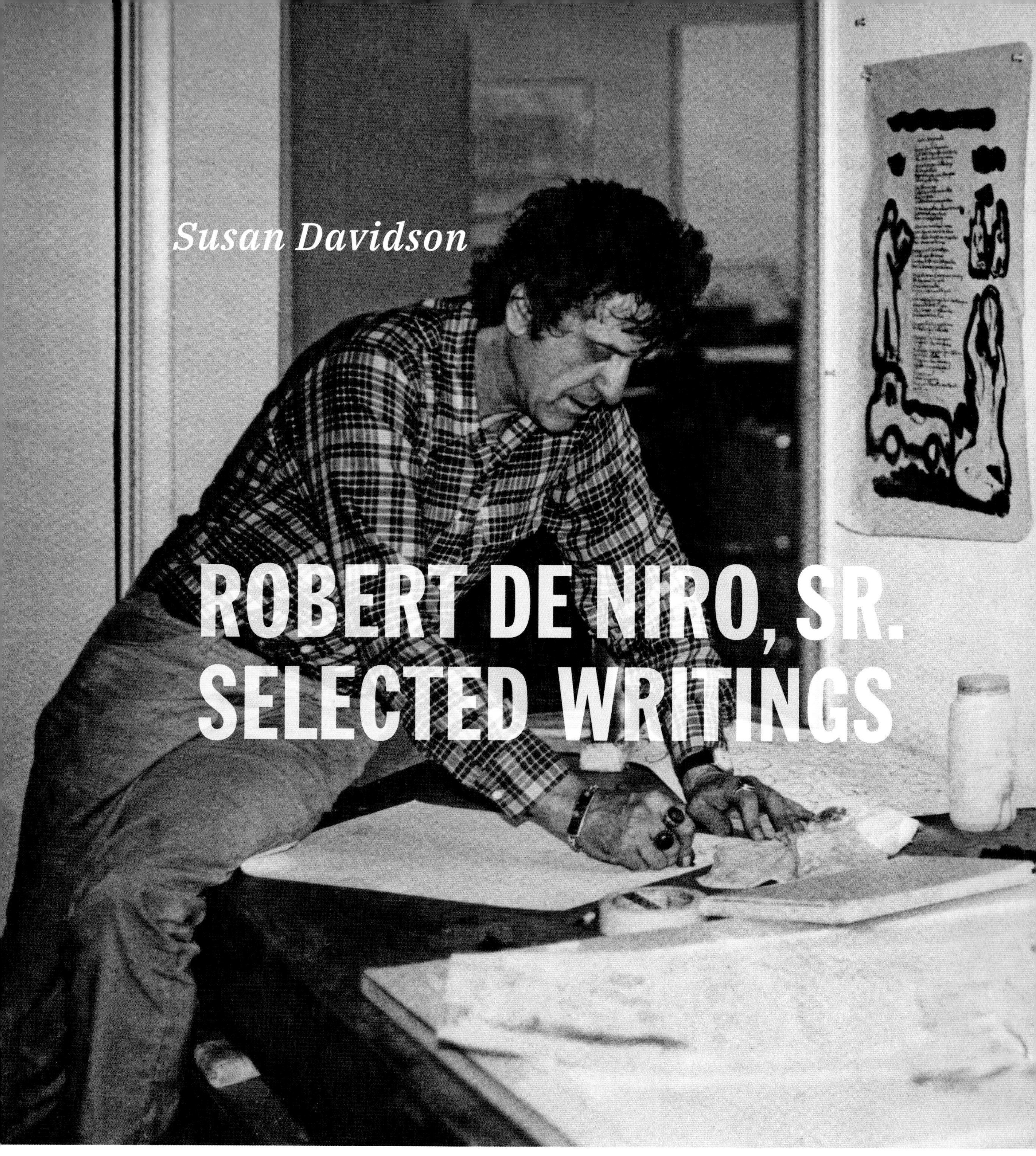

Susan Davidson

ROBERT DE NIRO, SR. SELECTED WRITINGS

Robert De Niro, Sr., working on *A Fashionable Watering Place*, ca. 1976.

Preceding pages: Robert De Niro, Sr.'s, New York studio. Photo by Brigitte Lacombe.

THE JOURNALS OF ROBERT DE NIRO, SR.

Ten Years of Personal Reflection

ROBERT DE NIRO, SR., ACHIEVED ARTISTIC RECOGNITION as a young man of twenty-four when he had his first one-man exhibition at Art of This Century during the museum/gallery's penultimate season in 1946. For the next fifteen years, the artist enjoyed a certain amount of critical acclaim through regular presentations in well-established galleries and inclusion in key museum exhibitions. As the decade of the 1960s dawned, he fulfilled his longtime desire to live and paint in France, following in the footsteps of his heroes Pierre Bonnard, Eugène Delacroix, and Henri Matisse. Little did De Niro realize that removing himself from New York just as the art world was radically changing would send him into an emotional decline that he struggled daily to overcome.

De Niro's concerns about his art and his personal life are chronicled in four notebooks he kept over a ten-year period beginning in 1963.[1] In an effort to capture the artist's voice, this text weaves De Niro's written thoughts and feelings into a summary of each year. It thus provides insight into the artist's psyche and activities during a financially difficult period in his life. One does not know why De Niro took pen to paper. It has been suggested that it was at the encouragement of his psychiatrist, Dr. Nathan S. Kline, best known for his pioneering work in treating depression with psychopharmacologic drugs, whom De Niro began to see around 1959. The entries vacillate among De Niro expressing his inner turmoil, mundane tasks related to his living and to his art, and remarks about friends, lovers, and colleagues, who often dissatisfy or irk him. The diametric predicament between De Niro's self-perceived greatness as a painter and his profound insecurity is not unusual for artists. What sets De Niro apart, however, is the artist's extreme Catholic guilt regarding his sexual orientation that favored men over women. Throughout, De Niro's journals focus on his quest for both physical and emotional love and his anxiety that he is not properly recognized as an artist. His journals are peppered with quotes from early twentieth-century French poets and philosophers that demonstrate his erudition, references to earlier masters, especially Spanish Baroque artists, and passages from movies that featured Hollywood starlets, some of whom, such as Greta Garbo, became subjects of his painting.

De Niro's journals belie the reality of his success. He was a well-liked teacher, enjoyed several exhibitions that sold reasonably well to a small group of dedicated collectors, and was a recipient of a prestigious John Simon Guggenheim Fellowship. The art world was undergoing a transformation with the advent of Pop art and Minimalism at this time, two artistic movements De Niro neither understood nor cared to participate in. He was a stalwart of realism whose paintings were redolent of bright color and formal organization. Thus, as the art world was embracing new ways of representation, becoming younger and more conceptual, De Niro held fast to an "old school" approach, one that was out of step with then-current artistic modes.

1963 De Niro spent approximately three and half years in France—from April 1961 to sometime in the late summer or early fall of 1964—first in Paris, where he steeped himself in visiting museums and the city's most important galleries. Needing to reduce his overhead, he moved to the one-street village of Gravigny in Normandy in early 1962. After a short period, he moved south to Baren in the Pyrenees, approximately 200 kilometers from the Spanish border, and, finally in February 1963, to Saint-Just-en-Chevalet in the Rhône-Alpes region. Little is known of De Niro's time in France other than a few sketchy details. He appeared to have lived frugally and painted regularly, but ultimately found himself isolated and without any true means of support.[2] On a hitchhiking trip through Europe, his son, Bobby, then about twenty years of age, spent a week with his father, where he encountered a bitterly discouraged and near-destitute parent.

It was at this moment—in 1963—that De Niro started his journal. The year's tone is less personal and shorter (just four entries in the month of April) than later journals written in New York. The first entry addresses a request from the Museum of Modern Art, which was seeking comment from the students of celebrated Abstract Expressionist Hans Hofmann.[3] De Niro penned a frank assessment of his first mentor, but upon reflection decided against submitting it out of concern for sounding resentful, recalling Mrs. Hofmann's adage once offered about Jackson Pollock: *In America, you can convince anyone of anything. By the time they find out he is not as good as they think, it will be too late.... If you say anything, they think you are jealous.*[4] Another entry was in letter format to his gallerist, Virginia Zabriskie, regarding his *best and largest painting* included in his November 1962 exhibition that she wished to sell to a private collector at a 50-percent reduction. De Niro vehemently opposed having to consider this proposal, as he had expressly requested the work be for sale only to a museum, but ultimately agreed, as he was in desperate need of money. De Niro concluded this first journal on April 29, quoting Balzac: *Hatred can turn to love, but love that has turned to hatred can never turn back again.*[5] This passage would serve as a personal mantra for De Niro to extend kindness to others in alignment with his Christian beliefs.

1964 De Niro remained in France for another year and a half before his son convinced him to return to the States following a deeply upsetting personal event: *He* [Bobby] *has always managed to visit me in Europe at the opportune moment to help me through a shock, such as the one in the Loire & to give me courage to leave an unbearable situation. It was he who practically pushed me on the plane to return to New York.*[6] This year's thirty-four entries were written nearly daily between November 15 and December 23, and narrate De Niro settling back into life in New York. Although he harbored resentment toward his gallerist for her lack of sales, De Niro recognized that *she is only like most or all dealers as far as honesty goes & she believes in me & knows more about painting than most.*[7] In his attempts to balance the inner turmoil he was suffering, De Niro harnessed his Catholicism, believing that a pious approach of steadfast prayer would save him from his demons: *God help me to salvage what is left of my life and to become a 'saint & a hero for myself' as Baudelaire said.*[8] His regular visits to Dr. Kline offered some solace, although *pills have not eliminated symptoms.*[9] De Niro trolled for physical encounters, almost obsessively, acknowledging that *domesticity & living with someone keeping regular hours is completely against my temperament, a false ideal, like looking for the perfect dealer.... As Dr. Kline once remarked, I am married to painting.*[10]

1965 & 66 About a month passed between De Niro's last entry in 1964 until he began the new year's journal with two entries on January 20 and January 21. Another hiatus ensued for about a month, before he resumed in mid-February for ten entries until March 10. De Niro's journal then became somewhat dormant for the remainder of 1965 and throughout most of 1966; just three writing spurts occurred during this twelve-month period, consisting of seven entries in the first two weeks of June, seven entries in the first two weeks of October, and six entries from late January through early February of 1966. De Niro then stopped, for unknown reasons, for nearly one and a half years before writing in his journal again.

In the entries that began in 1965, De Niro posed an existential question: *to paint is merely a desire for more comfort and a lesser social life.... What is all this worrying about whether events in one's life are accidental as Valiery* [sic] *says or that "l'hazard n'existe pas" as Léon Bloy writes. Maybe it's my mental sickness which makes me exaggerate my fatalistic and passive philosophy.*[11] Soon after De Niro closed his successful exhibition at Zabriskie Gallery of those paintings he produced in France, he found it difficult to start work on new pictures: *I am still not painting. I am filled with fear... I worry about everything... I go crazy trying to figure out what I am not supposed to understand. As Jane* [sic] *Crawford said, "there are things we are not supposed to understand."*[12] When he resumed writing in the summer, a distinctly more positive attitude emerged, and a determination to lead a more fulfilled life as an artist. *Shall I do all the oils on paper over or throw most of them out? Must have one photoed* [sic] *before June 20th for Tom Hess show.... Prayed for one hour this morning. Musts* [sic] *do this every morning. Send for other Garbo still from Camille (profile).*[13] *Must try to buy issue of Flair which contains harem interior photo from which I have done quite a few paintings and drawings.*[14] He was excited by a new challenge to work in a wholly different medium: *Virginia Z. wants me to do 3 pieces of sculpture before she departs for Italy July 1st. She will cast them there. She gave me more money than usual for art materials.... One of the sculptures will be a head of Bobby, the other two figures with or without models.*[15] De Niro showed twice at Zabriskie Gallery in 1965. Ahead of the second opening, and in spite of her support of his work, he admitted: *I really think that I must change galleries after my show beginning this October 12th. Zabriskie is headed nowhere.*[16] Yet, *Show opened with Lerner reserving a painting "Women at the Well after Murillo" for Hirshhorn purchase. Big crowd.*[17] This boosted De Niro's immodesty, prompting him to claim that the exhibition was *the best I've ever had. It did so happen, for whatever that's worth that I got very good reviews for it, too.*[18] Within two weeks, however, he reverted to his habitual paranoia, expressing his frustration with the art world: *Why have I not sold for so long when Zabriskie as she wrote me in France always sold a minimum of $300 a month's worth of my work? If part of the reason is because I've been away then why does Diebenkorn sell so much in New York when he lives in California? Or is there no parallel. I am puzzled. Or is it due to the advent of pop art as Reis suggests? If that's so then perhaps pop & op art have run their course enough by now so that I will sell from this show.*[19] The entries for the remainder of 1965 are sullen as De Niro recalled the tragic and fatal demise of his friend, which precipitated his departure from France. The reoccurrence of these thoughts may be the reason he put his pen away for an extended period. *Still plague myself with stupid questions such as why I got into such a bad state of mind in Europe which has continued this last year since I've been back & how I would have felt if I never went at all or stayed a year or less. Europe is not for me, permanently, anyway.*[20]

In the winter of 1966, De Niro commenced teaching at both the New School for Social Research and the School of Visual Arts. The engagement with young students energized him and reinvigorated his own production: *Buy ruler in morning to measure pipe for sculpture so as to get correct size wire. Get fixatif* [sic] *for charcoals.... Buy thumbtacks.*[21] In an effort to suppress his homosexual desires, he prayed for several hours a day as well as attended Mattachine Society meetings.[22] For all De Niro's angst about his sexual orientation, he truly believed prayer alleviated his guilt-ridden mental state: *Prayed in the neighborhood church for an hour this morning, and will continue to pray there... until I am cured of my mental and emotional sickness. If God doesn't want me to be homosexual (about which I have so much guilt) he will find a woman whom I will love and who will love me.* That said, he had no real intention of changing: *But I really don't want my homosexuality to be cured, although old age as a homosexual frightens me more than a little.*[23] His concern of becoming an aging queer would assume great proportion throughout the remaining journals.

1968 When De Niro resumed his journal after a one-and-a-half-year hiatus, his state of mind was significantly improved. He wrote forty-one nearly consecutive entries this year, beginning on August 15 while out of the city. He picked up his journal again when he returned to New York in mid-September, writing for a week, then skipping to the third week of October, stopping for about a month, and resuming for a few days around Thanksgiving and finally concluding with three entries written over the first ten days of December. This journal began as De Niro was finishing the summer teaching session at the University of Buffalo and heading off to Provincetown, close to where he first studied painting in 1939 as a teenager at Hofmann's prestigious school. It was a highly productive period both artistically as well as personally. He was no longer as hard on himself as in previous years. He had two solo exhibitions this year—sculptural work at Zabriskie Gallery and a showing of new paintings, sculpture, and works on paper at Reese Paley Gallery in its Atlantic City and San Francisco venues. Most validating was receiving a John Simon Guggenheim Fellowship for exceptional talent in fine arts that provided much-needed financial relief. Nonetheless, De Niro continuingly queried his lack of recognition, albeit more philosophically than angrily. *Depressing discussion of the art world so called.... Talk made me realize how little really famous and accepted and recognized I am. If that's my goal. It does seem to be one of them no matter how hard I try for more spiritual and solid ambitions. But can we really try to be spiritual or humble. Wouldn't Krishnamurti only call this another form of pride? All we can really do is to see & be aware of what is in ourselves and the world around us.*[24] He started guitar lessons, a lifelong interest, and for the first time, considered purchasing a studio or cooperative loft in which to live and work. A chance meeting with artist Elaine de Kooning, however, changed his course: *I have decided to wait and to try to get into the Westbeth housing project... to save my money for a house in North Africa, Spain or some inexpensive fishing village. I must get sculpture photographed to send to Guggenheim committee for renewal of grant right away. Painted 3 still-lives* [sic] *on paper today.*[25] De Niro was especially proud of his son's blossoming career, which brought him great joy: *Called New York and spoke to Virginia Admiral. It seems that our son Bobby is getting all sorts of movie and stage offers, if I understand her correctly and I think I did due to his acting in a recent play or movie. My little baby-doll has grown up.*[26]

1969 De Niro's journal for this year is roughly equivalent in number of entries and mood to the previous year, but extends across the full year for forty-three entries. He began on New Year's Day, writing relatively consistently every day that month. For the remainder of the winter, he contributed only six entries, with the spring yielding another ten entries in April and May. De Niro then did not write until the end of the year, penning seven entries throughout November and December. De Niro was still teaching at the New School. Throughout the year, he attended group meetings at Recovery, Inc., established by the noted neuropsychiatrist Dr. Abraham Low, an early proponent of self-help. De Niro exhibited for the first time with Grace Borgenicht Gallery in a group exhibition, *Homage to Matisse*, as a tryout for moving to her gallery; however, he would not join her roster of artists. This rejection underscored his view that he would never receive the recognition he believed was his due: *I don't know how I will be able to live, pay models, have sculpture cast & do lithographs when my Guggenheim is finished!... I was a little depressed at Freed's as he brought up examples like Eilshemius who were not recognized until after their death, even though they lived to an advanced age. Hofmann, they said, sold nothing before the age of 75.*[27] As he faced middle age, De Niro convinced himself that he was unlovable or at the minimum no longer attractive to the young men he fancied: *Obsessed with age. Will be 47 soon. That is one reason I didn't ask the boy at the bar home last nite ... Bobby, my son who will be soon in 3 movies running simultaneously in New York gave me the same advice as Dr. Kline, "Find young people who like older people."*[28]

UNDATED [1971] De Niro did not keep a journal in 1970, a year in which he exhibited for the final time at Zabriskie Gallery.[29] Although long in coming, it is possible that when the separation finally occurred, it unsettled him. He found it hard to believe he might be without representation and worried that not having any would push him further into artistic oblivion: *Va. Zabriskie doesn't want to give me a show this season and won't commit herself for next. She "likes my painting, believes in it, but I won't sell." She has 17 years of experience to buttress her beliefs, she says. I also have 17 years of experience and I don't agree with her. Reis, my agent, thinks that I should let things ride since business is so bad now, and not seek a new gallery at this time. I will see him on Monday and discuss the matter further.*[30] When De Niro resumed his journal in mid-January 1971, his attitude was decidedly more mature, as if, through his various therapies, he had resolved many of his previous plights. This year is both the most concentrated (January to April) and full, with seventy-two entries, the most of any year. De Niro was attuned with his consciousness and accepting that creativity was essential to his well-being: *Harold spoke about my belief in the irrational. I meant simply that one should seek one's deepest feelings rather than reason. That the former and true reason actually coincide. Is the desire to be a painter reasonable or unreasonable. Unreasonable, I suppose only for a non-painter.*[31] While he continued to query just about everyone and everything, he was generally more patient and accepting: *I want to be around people who are kind, loving and whom I can trust. If "perfect love castesth out fear" then this is not love. Or what I thought was such in the past. When I read Max Jacob's remark that courage was at the bottom of everything, I thought, no, love is, if one can love all the other virtues follow. But did I know then what love was or even very clearly what I meant by it. Without courage there is no love. And I am full of fear, not so much of things outside me but of the discomfort caused by my own thoughts, feelings, sensations and impulses.*[32]

Throughout this year, De Niro frequently referenced historical artists, often musing whether his own work would stand in comparison: *Yesterday I went with a poet Milton Klonsky, who was posing for me to the Marin show at the Whitney Museum.*[33] *It was great. In some of the oil seascapes the deliciousness of the application of paint for its pure sensuous quality equals the French masters.*

Someone said to me that Marin was good or great from the start.... I wonder how I would look in comparison in a retrospective. Maybe better than I think. I may imagine that my black or confused states of mind affected my painting more than they did.[34] De Niro had a burst of fatherly pride one afternoon when he encountered his son on the street (their schedules kept them from seeing each other for long periods): *He is tanned from a sunlamp—for his new movie part—and looks much better than when he returned from Italy 2 weeks ago. I wanted to run my fingers through his hair and to kiss him, but I hardly think that he would have appreciated it.*[35] His admiration was unbounded.

1972 When 1972 began, De Niro had not written in his journal for eight months and indeed for this year he contributed only five entries. These include four written in mid-January and a final one on July 1. De Niro was quite agitated in these entries and concerned that the Recovery, Inc., program he had been attending for the past few years was not helping him: *The people are too depressing and I have gotten worse since I have been in it. I would have become more depressed anyway and undoubtedly it helped me through it but now it has become a depressant in itself and I can take no more of it, at least for the moment.*[36] He questioned the validity of keeping a journal: *There is so much I have left out of this journal, almost all or anyway a lot that would be compromising to me. My laments, wailings, self pity and complaining are much greater than I have indicted* [sic] *here. My despair. My laziness. My pride. All of my sins.* He acknowledged a friend's remark that: *To talk or to think about them is to energize them, to keep them alive.*[37] Decades after his divorce from his wife, he still possessed great admiration for her: *I have come from Va. Admiral's. There is something noble in her refusal to complain, to pity herself. There is a grandeur that is touching about her. I am again indulging in my old prophecies of gloom and doom.*[38] This is one of the few entries that expresses an empathy for others.

1973 Another six months passed before De Niro put pen to paper in what would be his last journal, written over the course of January and February for twenty-five entries. One might say that the psychological treatments he had undergone over the ten years he maintained a journal resulted in greater resolve. Perhaps, too, one can attribute this acceptance to his entrance into middle age, as De Niro not only took stock of his life, but took control over his mental health. Certainly, his artistry was an essential vehicle for grounding him. De Niro was extremely focused in this year on securing his place in the art world by having more exhibitions of his artwork, garnering support where he could, and resolving to proceed even without a gallery. *I will go to see Virginia Zabriskie tomorrow. I hate to write it or admit it—I am afraid. I said that I don't know what to do if she refuses to give me a show. I refuse to break down.... I have Elaine and Tom Hess behind me. I will find another gallery. When I am ready it will come.... And I can sell paintings without shows. Soutine did it.*[39] He remained extraordinarily concerned about finding love, convinced that his aging (and not his personality) was the reason for its elusiveness. *I am afraid that Louise may have been right when she said that if I continued on the pills I would end up a sick old man. Not that the pills don't help but I must react against the garbage in my brain and do something positive. I am angry at myself for lying in bed doing less and less, worrying more and more. I want to be liberated too, liberated from my fears.*[40] Ten days later, he rationalized his dilemma by acknowledging his talent: *The moral being that you could be schizophrenic or homosexual (both lumped in the same category) with impunity if one had also genius.*[41] Determined to rid himself of these thoughts, he pushed himself to be better, a huge step forward mentally from where he began writing in his journal ten years earlier: *All my other problems had ways out—but death and old age—just throw up your hands and lie down now and die and get it over with. Well I'm going to beat it!! I'm going to be happier than I've ever been before and more productive and a better lover.*[42]

A FEW YEARS AFTER RECORDING HIS PERSONAL THOUGHTS in his last journal, De Niro published his poetry in a separate volume, *A Fashionable Watering Place* (1976). De Niro took up another form of writing in the next decade, contributing six critical texts to the publication *Art World* on painters he admired and who were then showing in galleries or museums around New York, such as Bonnard, Manet, Munch, Rousseau, Soutine, and Van Gogh. These essays are not reviews per say, but are intelligent and considered in their understanding of painting and are often laced with references to Baudelaire, one of De Niro's favorite thinkers. They demonstrate De Niro's excellent command of art history and how looking at the art of earlier masters informed his own work. Yet, De Niro could not refrain from musing on the state of the current art world, to which he felt he did not belong. Why De Niro stopped recording in his journal in 1973 is unknown. Perhaps leaving New York for extended periods (first to Albuquerque and later to San Francisco) helped settle him psychologically. What is certain is that he would enjoy another twenty years, producing luscious paintings of his favorite subjects (still lifes, landscapes, and odalisques) with the work more confident with each passing year.

All typographical oddities and misspellings, as well as inconsistencies and errors of grammar and punctuation found within the journals and poetry of Robert De Niro, Sr., are preserved in the preceding and following transcriptions. All journals referenced are currently held in the archives of the Estate of Robert De Niro, Sr.

NOTES

1. De Niro's first journals (1963–66 and 1968–69) are approximately 5 by 7 inches, staple-bound, softcover books with gridded paper. The other two (1971 and 1972–73) are also approximately 5 by 7 inches but are hardcover books with ruled paper. In all four books, he wrote in blue pen (occasionally in black or green), single-spaced on both sides of the page.

2. The $300 per month stipend he received from his dealer evidently was insufficient to live on. While De Niro was living abroad, Zabriskie did ensure that he was included in key exhibitions, all of which recognized the artist's talents.

3. MoMA curator William C. Seitz was preparing the exhibition *Hans Hofmann and His Students*, which toured the United States.

4. April 24, 1963, journal entry.

5. April 29, 1963, journal entry.

6. November 15, 1964, journal entry. Little is known about the shock De Niro refers to other than it had to do with his friend Paul, who suffered a horrific fatal accident.

7. December 18, 1964, journal entry.

8. November 18, 1964, journal entry.

9. December 11, 1964, journal entry.

10. November 22, 1964, journal entry.

11. January 20, 1965, journal entry.

12. March 1, 1965, journal entry. De Niro was enthralled with cinema, especially films from the 1930s and 1940s featuring strong women. He drew significant inspiration from them both for his poetry and his painting.

13. June 2, 1965, journal entry.

14. June 6, 1965, journal entry.

15. June 9, 1965, journal entry. De Niro produced nine sculptures all cast in 1967; none are portraits of his son.

16. October 2, 1965, journal entry.

17. October 14, 1965, journal entry. Abram Lerner (1913–2007) was the curator for the Joseph H. Hirshhorn art collection that became the Hirshhorn Museum and Sculpture Garden, Smithsonian Institution, in 1974. Hirshhorn was one of De Niro's primary collectors in the 1960s.

18. October 2, 1965, journal entry.

19. October 18, 1965, journal entry. Bernard Reis (1895–1978) was De Niro's financial advisor and accountant.

20. October 14, 1965, journal entry.

21. January 25, 1966, journal entry.

22. The Mattachine Society, founded in 1950, was one of the earliest LGBT organizations in America.

23. February 9, 1966, journal entry.

24. September 10, 1968, journal entry.

25. October 5, 1968, journal entry.

26. August 22, 1968, journal entry.

27. January 5, 1969, journal entry. William Freed (1902–1984) was an American abstract artist who also studied under Hans Hofmann.

28. March 30, 1969, journal entry.

29. De Niro's third journal is undated, but events described therein suggest a 1971 date. The beginning of this book has numerous pages ripped out, which may have been his entries from 1970.

30. February 5, 1971, journal entry.

31. February 1, 1971, journal entry. Harold H. was a student at the New School who lived with De Niro for a few months. Harold also aspired to be an art dealer although his was unsuccessful in selling any of De Niro's art.

32. March 2, 1971, journal entry.

33. This is likely the exhibition *John Marin: 1870–1953* at the Whitney Museum of American Art, February 18–March 28, 1971.

34. March 15, 1971, journal entry.

35. April 22, 1971, journal entry.

36. January 16, 1972, journal entry.

37. January 15, 1972, journal entry.

38. July 1, 1972, journal entry.

39. February 7, 1973, journal entry. Artist Elaine de Kooning (1918–1989) and critic Thomas B. Hess (1920–1978) were among the few well-connected friends De Niro had been able to retain contact with throughout the 1960s.

40. January 2, 1973, journal entry.

41. January 12, 1973, journal entry.

42. February 19, 1973, journal entry.

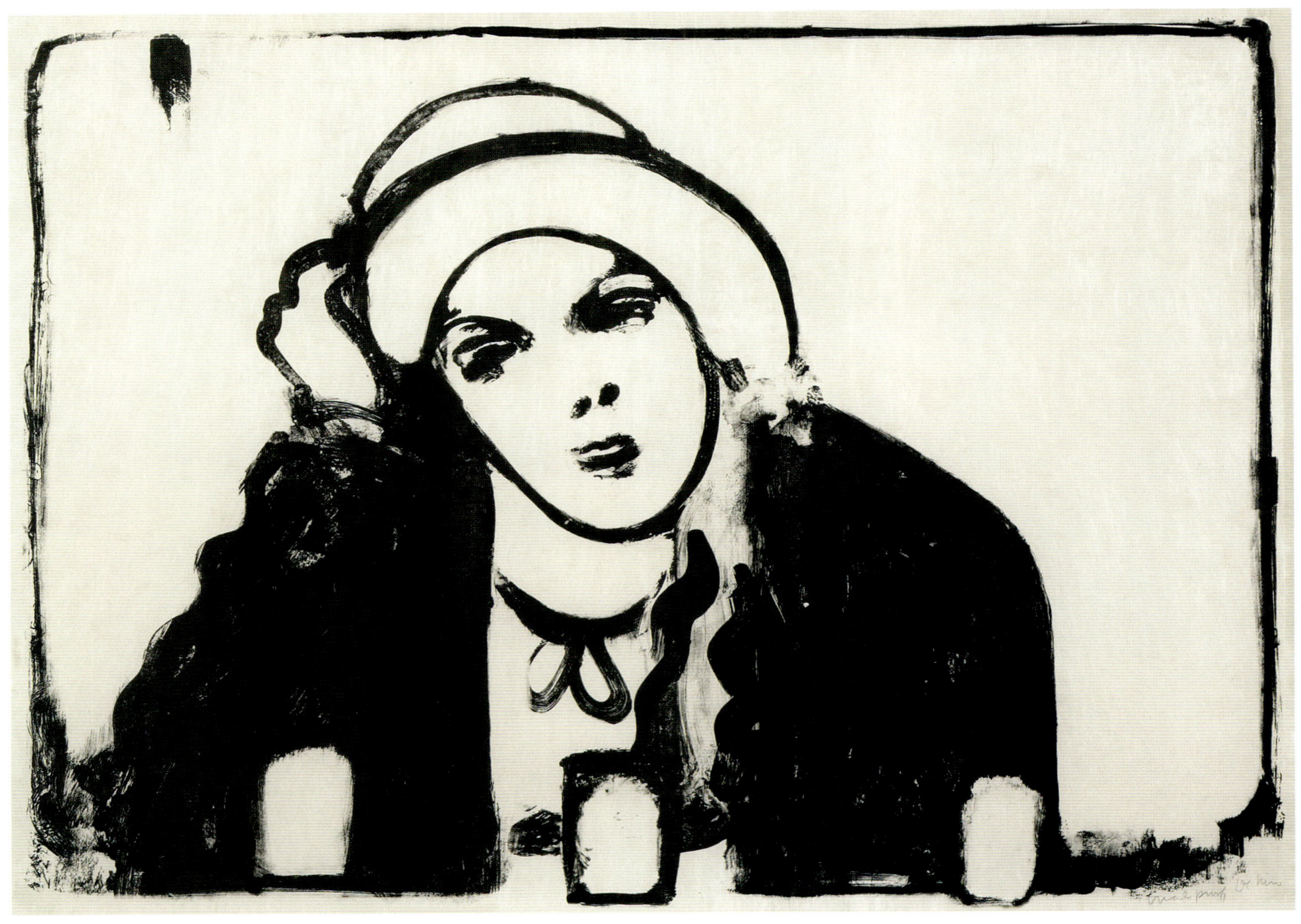

Untitled, 1974. Lithograph on paper, 19 x 27 inches. From a suite of ten prints on *Anna Christie* produced at Tamarind Institute.

Written about 1941

FRAGMENTS FROM A BODY

I am one daring to laugh
Into whose embryo
Polished like a stone
Creeps on antediluvian crescents
A flimsy mother of pearl
Crying out (in voice whimpering as diluted raindrops)
The temperature of torments is lower
Than the sanctified would
Crush us into knowing

Hold out your remnants of
Silken thighs, your tattered lovelies
For their beauty falls higher
Before the flood

(UNTITLED)

Frigid little temptations
Floundering without reservation
Entering no home, blackening
no cross
With what a well wrought harness they played
Five centuries ended, the goose girl
Nodded to a passing joy,
The boy whose red bits passed endless
furtive lakes
Saw the end; felt hot within them
the bricks of a skirmishing city, a sky,
Whose bitter taste was reveled in
Like languid whores

O speak to me of many ways
Tell me of the times past dreaming

This was a city which now is blossoms of a day
Twisting its livid petals into tiny balls
For Easter
When the nuns wear peacocks under black

The following poems were written between 1960 and 1975 in the United States and France

ENVIRONS OF BISKRA

The domes that front the bright blue sky,
Are whiter than the stones that lie
Closer to the mosque than I
In the outer districts

The dates will fall in several days

Sultans sheltering their gaze
Throw their worn-out jewels
To all the dancers
Some walk beside their mules
Waiting for an answer

The desert hides the afternoon

The company beneath the tents
Lowers the canopy, invents
Prayers to while away the noon

The bazaars will open soon

Musicians following sweets
Are unlike others that one meets
Playing the same tune

Camels measuring their paces
Move into the far oasis
The water in the fountain flows
High as every tree that shows
Its palms in open spaces
Horses tug at the traces

Cafes reveal the tattooed faces
Of perfumed women fruit in hand

The sounds of flutes rise from the sand

The court is lined with pigeons
That have lowered their regard
They search in the incisions
Tucked about the yard
Their owners strolling in the park
The wilder dogs forget to bark
Jugs of water lean on walls
Figured hangings surround stalls

We'll ride wild horses to the valley
And round the fountain later rally

The desert with its antique face
Follows me from place to place

it's true I've watched the white Sahara
But that was in another era.

"COMÉDIEN—TRAGÉDIEN"
Pope to Napolean I

He called me an actor
Too sad or too gay
Not knowing the mean
Rewriting the play

Near chateaux of each century
Since chateaux began
In valleys whose streams
Lay quiet as dreams

On the hill behind the house
Painting while they planted peas
A crucifix looked at me
As I looked at the trees

There was no one in the chapel
Burning candles near the saints

Who collected all the coins
Better spent on brush and paints?

A FASHIONABLE WATERING PLACE

O Luchon, your houses of physicians
Your casinos empty of musicians
Look on Spain
Near the square beneath the rain

The bus had people in it
But the church didn't

Nor most of the cafés

The chapel on the mountain
Where I hewed the trees
Was fronted by a graveyard
The devil kept the keys

Twenty miles from me
Lourdes lay
Not at apogee

The baths were deserted
No one turned a roulette wheel
Nor even flirted
With the thought of where to kneel

Hold me in your arms
Between mountain and chateau
You adored the farms
I abhorred the snow

LIKE PROCLIVITIES

Someone said he went to Spain
To find those of like proclivities
I told him in the main
He was lucky to have found civilities

O Spain I peered
With desire at your borders
Your tragic plains stared back at me
As stark as holy orders

Your simple cities
I hadn't seen
Looking pretty
Banishing green

Your proclivities are gay
At least some
But today
Clouds come

Upon the sand
The sun surrounds me
It's the touch of your hand
That confounds me

"I ALWAYS LOOK MY BEST WHEN I'M NEAREST DEATH" (Garbo—*Camille*)

I am wan and hold a book
A novel where I sometimes look
For courage when alarmed

I may be all to you
As you say
That may be true
For today

I say no rosary of seasons
No litany of summers, winters, springs

Sometimes passion slumbers
Sometimes sings

Give me quiet in a bed
I'm not well-read
Could you teach me
But not beseech me
To be other than I am

You brought me flowers
As I knew you would

I would leave here
If I could

With you

Kiss my eyelids before you go
I won't be here to touch the snow

"TOASTED SUSIE IS MY ICE CREAM" –Gertrude Stein

This phrase intrigues me
Between it and me what leagues be
It touches me but not the core
I love others more

Ice cream is silly on a plate
At least what yesterday I ate
But sillier still is toasted Sue
She sounds tragic, isn't even blue

I love Paris at night and Gertrude Stein
I love dry bread dipped in dry wine

The stairs to Sacre Coeur are interminable

The Reine Blanche was silent
Its Arabs faced the river's bank
And drank Pernod

I paid the minimum
And watched the glow
Of evening in the park across the street

While other Arabs
Hid in shadows from the street

Your body was tangled in the sheets
One greets one's partner
Then retreats

I don't love you
I can't perform such feats

I DON'T WANT TO REINCARNATE ANY MORE

So many lives
Laid end to end
Like a river
At each bend

Am I really all these faces
Tattered vestiges one traces

Let me curb my temper
Quietly sit and fast
Hoping that tomorrow
It's all past

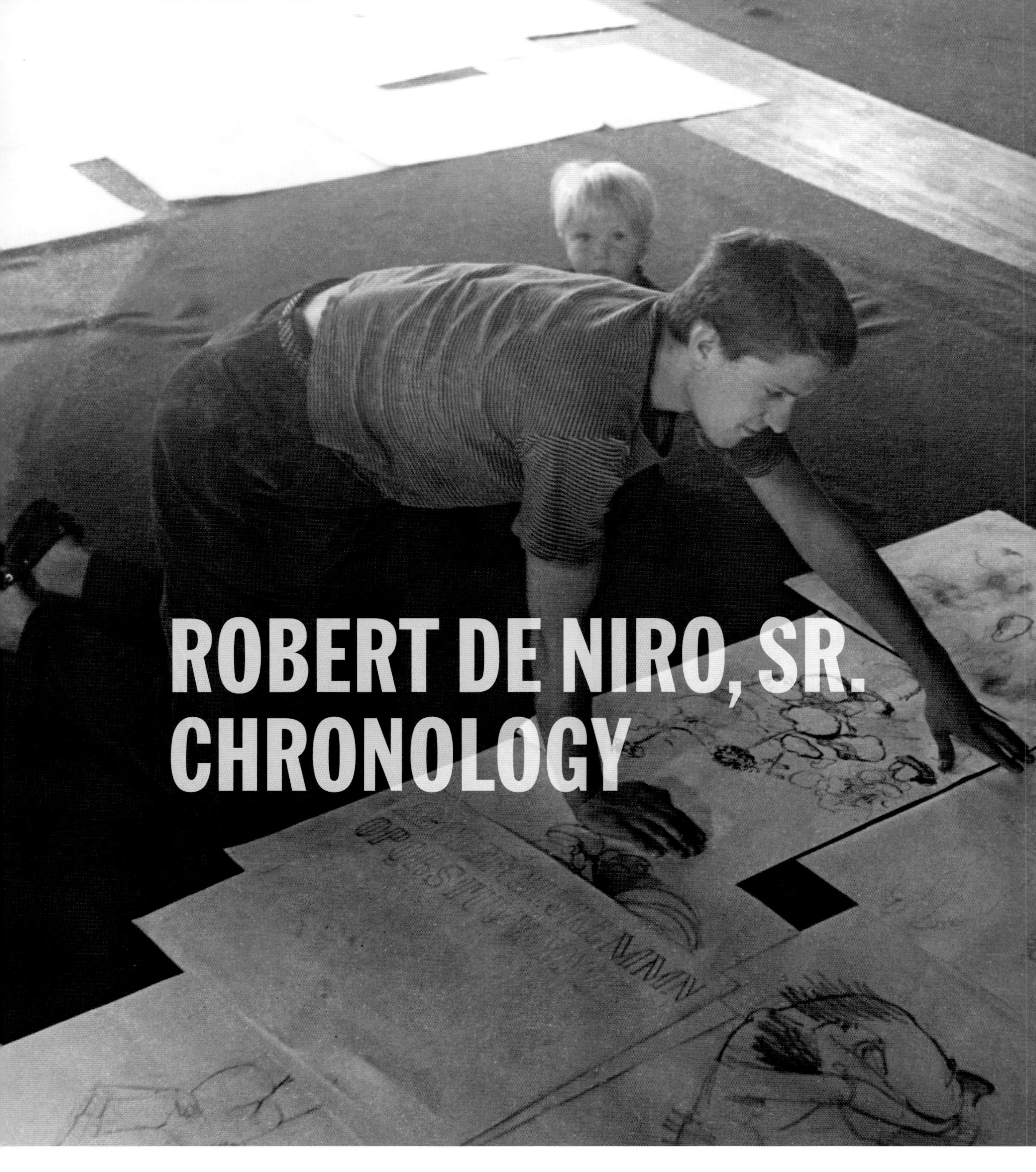

ROBERT DE NIRO, SR. CHRONOLOGY

Robert De Niro during Josef Albers's drawing class, 1939–40. Shown with Theodore "Eddie" Dreier, Jr., son of Black Mountain College cofounder Theodore "Ted" Dreier, Sr.

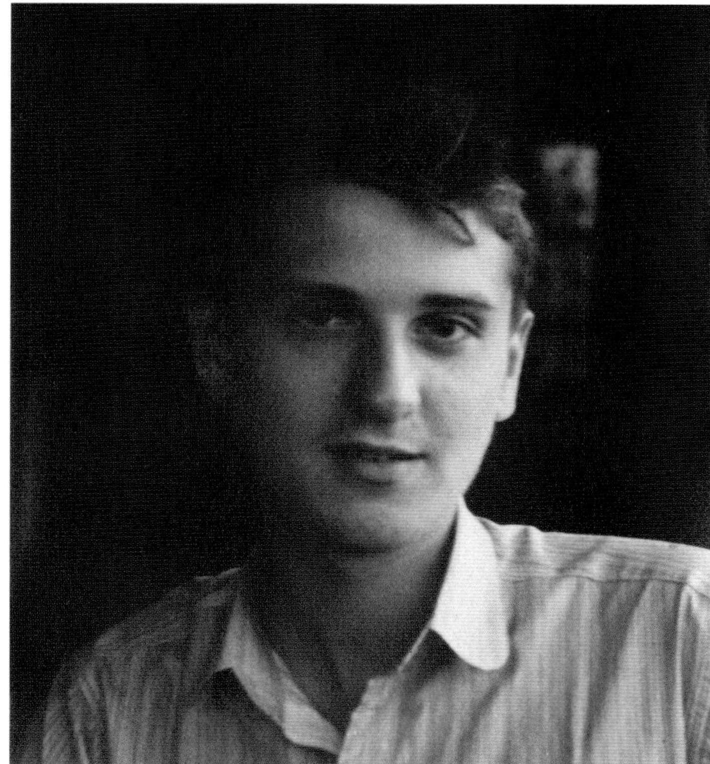

Photograph from Robert De Niro's application to Black Mountain College, 1939.

1922 **ROBERT HENRY DE NIRO** is born May 3 to Henry De Niro and Helen O'Reilly in Syracuse, New York. The eldest of four, Robert and his younger siblings (John, Joan, and Elizabeth)[1] are raised in the Tipperary Hill neighborhood, which De Niro in retrospect describes as an "Irish neighborhood" in Syracuse.[2] Henry De Niro works at various times as a salesman, grocer, and health inspector, while Helen will work as a traveling saleswoman in the 1930s.[3]

1933–37 The young De Niro demonstrates an early aptitude for art, taking children's art classes at the Syracuse Museum of Fine Arts before enrolling with adults. His promise is such that at the age of twelve, De Niro receives from the museum his own studio in which to work.[4] De Niro attends Eastwood High School in 1935 before transferring to Syracuse North High in 1937. He works at a grocery store on Saturdays.[5]

In 1933, Black Mountain College opens near Asheville in the Blue Ridge Mountains of North Carolina. History will show this institution, which De Niro would later attend, to be one of the most progressive and innovative educational centers of the time. A magnet for poets, artists, and dancers, Black Mountain College brings leading artistic and intellectual figures to the rural South to instruct the next generation of artists. Teachers range from the Bauhaus-trained artists Josef and Anni Albers to the visionary architect Buckminster Fuller.

In 1934, the German painter Hans Hofmann establishes his School of Fine Arts in New York City. An influential instructor and a central figure in the development of Abstract Expressionism, Hofmann attracts many students who will find success in a range of artistic modes. His pupils include Lee Krasner, Joan Mitchell, Larry Rivers, and Helen Frankenthaler.[6] *Hofmann establishes the school's second location in Provincetown, Massachusetts, the following year. Robert De Niro will study at both.*

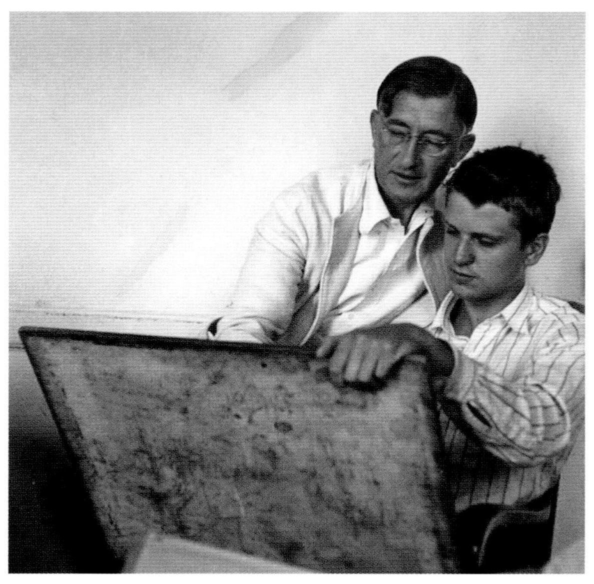

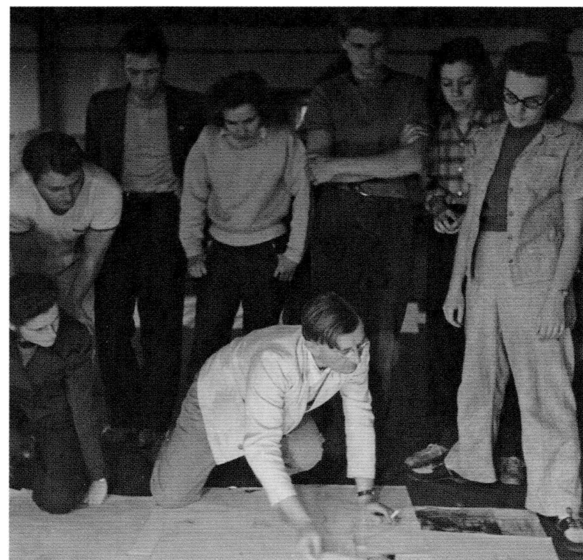

LEFT
Josef Albers and Robert De Niro, Black Mountain College, ca. 1939–40.

RIGHT
Robert De Niro, third from right, stands behind Josef Albers during a drawing class, Black Mountain College, ca. 1939–40.

1938 Overcoming the initial reluctance of his parents, the sixteen-year-old De Niro travels to Gloucester, Massachusetts, to enroll in Ralph Pearson's Design Workshop on a scholarship.[7] He works at a local restaurant, first as a dishwasher and later as a busboy, jobs for which he receives compensation of seven dollars a week and meals.[8] De Niro later recalls reading Eugene O'Neill's play *Anna Christie* for the first time while in Gloucester, afterwards "making a model of the stage set."[9] The star of the 1930 film adaption of the play, Greta Garbo, will become somewhat of a muse for the artist, a recurring figure in his artwork, and a subject in his 1975 essay titled "Corot, Verlaine, and Greta Garbo, or the Melancholy Syndrome."

1939 In June, De Niro graduates from North High School[10] and enters the Hans Hofmann School of Fine Arts in Provincetown. He finds work mopping floors and washing dishes at a local restaurant.[11] At the Hofmann School, the young De Niro paints still lifes and works from live models,[12] and, according to fellow student Larry Rivers, he receives "Hofmann's Best Student Award."[13]

De Niro accepts an offer to attend Black Mountain College, where he enrolls in the fall. Anna W. Olmsted, director of the Syracuse Museum of Fine Arts, helps him coordinate funding for his art education.[14] In the fall and winter, De Niro takes Color I and II, as well as Drawing I and II, both under the famed artist, educator, and color theorist Josef Albers. Other courses include Cultural Anthropology and Psychological Problems, as well as piano lessons and literature.[15]

The Museum of Non-Objective Painting opens on 54th Street in New York with its inaugural exhibition, Art of Tomorrow. *The institution serves as home to the collection of Solomon R. Guggenheim, who subsequently, at the behest of the painter and European émigrée Baroness Hilla Rebay von Ehrenwiesen, establishes the Solomon R. Guggenheim Foundation in 1937. With Rebay's guidance, Guggenheim acquires artworks by some of the most important figures in the history of European modernism, among them Vasily Kandinsky, Fernand Léger, Paul Klee, Pablo Picasso, and Jean Arp.*[16] *Both director and curator of the museum, Rebay will become a source of financial support for De Niro, as she was for many younger artists of interest to her.*

1940 Black Mountain College's winter semester begins on January 22. At the end of the semester, Albers writes Olmsted to tell her of the positive strides taken by the young artist: "Concerning the courses he took with me, I must say that he is one of my best students, very industrious in

BLACK MOUNTAIN COLLEGE **BLACK MOUNTAIN, NORTH CAROLINA**

APPLICATION FOR ADMISSION TO THE COLLEGE

This application will not be considered unless it is filled out in full and unless it is accompanied by a non-refundable application fee of five dollars ($5.00).

Please print names and addresses.

Name De Niro (Last Name) Robert (First Name) Henry (Middle Name) **Date** August 31, 1939

Present address 172 Bradford Street
Provincetown, Massachusetts
Until Sept. 15

Permanent address 326 Durston Avenue
Syracuse, New York

Date of birth May 3, 1922 **Age** 17

Place of birth Syracuse, New York

Date you desire to enter Sept. 25, 1939

Secondary schools and colleges attended	Dates	Certificates
1. ~~Tompkins School~~	elementary	
2. ~~William Howard Taft School~~	elementary	
3. Eastwood High School	Sept. 1935	transferred to
4. Syracuse North High	Sept. 1937	diploma

Names of principals or headmasters at above named institutions:

1.
2.
3. Charles Todd
4. Marshall Downing

Robert De Niro's application to Black Mountain College, 1939.

william baziotes julian beck ted bradley peter busa jim davis
william de kooning robert di nero jimmy ernst manny farber
john ferren joseph funck adolph gottlieb ernest guteman
david hare w. s. hayter lee hersch foster jewell jerome kamrowski
robert motherwell ralph nelson wolfgang paalen
jackson pollock r. pousette-dart kurt roesch mark rothko
charles seliger leon smith clyfford still paul wilton

30 WEST 57TH STREET, N. Y. 19

REOPENING SATURDAY OCTOBER 6

AUTUMN SALON

Announcement for Autumn Salon, a group show at Art of This Century gallery, 1945.

the classes as well as in his private work. His results in painting and drawing, and the fact that he became much more flexible, make me believe that he has a lasting talent." Albers also reveals that De Niro's finances might be hampering the student's ability to integrate effectively into the student body. "It would be very helpful if someone could help him with new clothing which he needs badly," Albers writes. "We should like to do this ourselves but our finances to [*sic*] not permit it. Such help would give him more security, and more ease in his social contacts."[17]

During the summer, De Niro accepts Hofmann's offer of free tuition at his art school in Provincetown and resumes washing dishes to earn a living. He writes a letter to Hilla Rebay, detailing his financial circumstances and his desire to commit all of his energies to painting, concluding that he hopes to present his recent work to her.[18] Her reply, transcribed by Rebay's secretary, as the Baroness is away, is accompanied by a fifteen-dollar check for paint supplies, initiating a correspondence between the two that includes her providing him with small sums for art materials over the coming years.[19]

From Provincetown, the artist also composes a letter to Black Mountain's administration expressing his desire to return to the college, as well as his concern over raising the money needed for enrollment.[20] Though De Niro arrives in Black Mountain in the fall, this is his last semester of attendance.

1941 De Niro attends Hofmann's school in New York, where he meets Virginia Admiral. Through Admiral, a painter who is also deeply immersed in the literary world, De Niro meets the writer Anaïs Nin and the poet Robert Duncan. Admiral and De Niro are among Hofmann's standout students,[21] and in the summer they move to Provincetown to continue their studies with the renowned German artist. Though the two form a relationship that will culminate in marriage, De Niro is unsure of his sexual identity. Nin writes in her diary that the couple is overheard one evening in Provincetown arguing over an alleged affair between De Niro and Duncan. De Niro is distraught: "Bob was completely shocked that anyone should have heard his homosexual confession and passed judgment on him . . . The idea was unbearable to him. He walked with his shoulders bowed. He was silent. He looked haunted."[22]

1942 De Niro and Admiral marry early in the year and continue their studies with Hofmann during the summer in Provincetown. Other students of Hofmann during this time include the painters

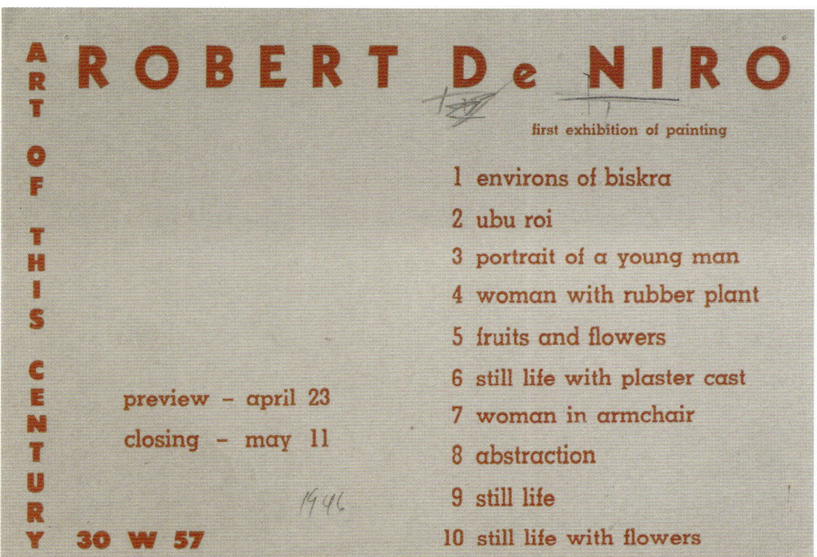

Announcement for Robert De Niro, Sr.'s, solo exhibition at Art of This Century gallery, 1946.

Nell Blaine, Louisa Matthíasdóttir, and Albert Kresch—with whom De Niro attends artist events at the home of the American novelist and poet Kenneth Patchen.[23]

Peggy Guggenheim, niece of Solomon R. Guggenheim, opens Art of This Century on 57th Street in a space designed by Austrian architect Frederick Kiesler. Recently arrived in New York in 1941 with her husband, the Surrealist Max Ernst, Guggenheim is anxious to create a museum-style environment in which to display her collection; the front rooms double as a selling gallery. Art of This Century becomes an important locus for European artists fleeing World War II, as well as for younger Americans who would play a central role in the development of Abstract Expressionism in this country. Guggenheim's early support of these artists—chief among them Jackson Pollock—is crucial to New York City's status as the emerging center of the art world. The gallery closes in 1947 when Guggenheim returns to Europe.[24]

1943 De Niro begins working as a security guard and night watchman at the Museum of Non-Objective Painting, where the artist Jackson Pollock is a coworker. On August 17, Virginia gives birth to the couple's only child, Robert. They ask Hans Hofmann to be his godfather.[25]

1944 Hans Hofmann has his first solo exhibition at Art of This Century, while Admiral presents her work in a group show at the gallery.[26] Her 1942 painting titled *Composition* is acquired by the Museum of Modern Art, New York, for its permanent collection.

1945 In the same year as De Niro's participation in the Autumn Salon—his first presentation at Art of This Century gallery, where his work is on view with that of Pollock, William Baziotes, Willem de Kooning, Adolph Gottlieb, Robert Motherwell, Mark Rothko, and Clyfford Still, among others—he and Admiral separate. While initially acrimonious due to competing claims to the custody of their son, the two remain close for the remainder of their lives and will officially divorce only several years later.[27]

1946 On April 23, at the age of twenty-three, De Niro opens his debut solo exhibition at Art of This Century. "Peggy Guggenheim has discovered another important young abstract painter," writes the preeminent critic Clement Greenberg, whose theories on painting and sculpture would provide the framework for approaching much of the art being produced during this period. In a comparison no

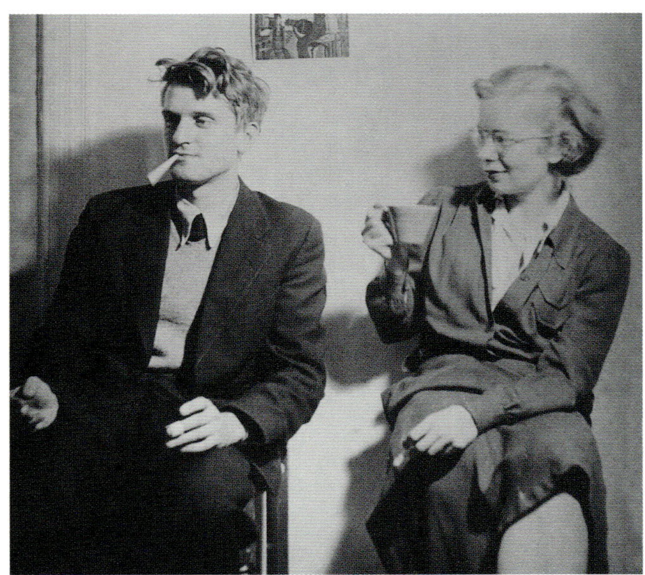

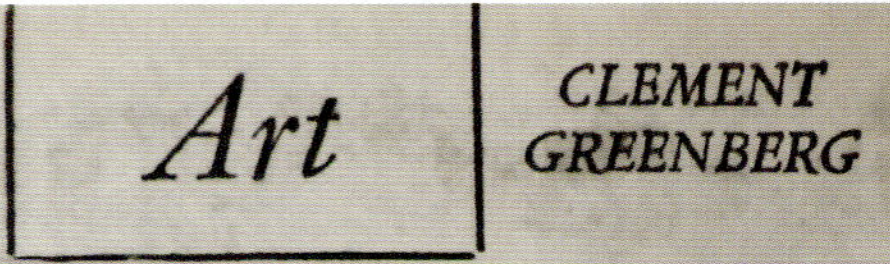

Art | **CLEMENT GREENBERG**

Peggy Guggenheim has discovered another important young abstract painter at her Art of This Century Gallery—Robert De Niro, whose first show (through May 11) exhibits monumental effects rare in abstract art. In two of De Niro's ten pictures, "Ubi Roi" and "Fruits and Flowers," the originality and force of his temperament demonstrate themselves under an iron control of the plastic elements such as is rarely seen in our time outside the painting of the oldest surviving members of the school of Paris.

LEFT
Robert De Niro, Sr., and Virginia Admiral, ca. 1945.

RIGHT
Clement Greenberg's *The Nation* review of Robert De Niro, Sr.'s, show at Art of This Century, May 18, 1946.

OPPOSITE
Opening announcements.

doubt well-received by the young artist—who is described by the painter Larry Rivers as having an "obsessive attraction to French culture, its literature, art, music, high and low, even its cuisine..."[28]—Greenberg notes De Niro's proximity to French painting. In two of his paintings, the critic observes that "the originality and force of his temperament demonstrate themselves under an iron control of the plastic elements such as is rarely seen in our time outside the painting of the oldest surviving members of the school of Paris."[29] Though Greenberg expresses reservations about De Niro's embrace of color, this opinion is not universal. "De Niro devises with stimulating audacity designs that in color, to some extent also in the forms, appear referable to Fauvism," writes a critic for the *New York Times*. "Only one of the paintings is actually titled 'Abstraction,' but don't let that fact fool you. Color is savagely brilliant: the primaries, set off by black."[30]

1948 An October letter from De Niro to the art historian and Columbia University professor Meyer Schapiro reveals that many of the artist's paintings have been destroyed in a recent fire at Virginia Admiral's loft.[31]

1950 A two-man committee composed of Greenberg and Schapiro selects De Niro among several other promising young artists for a group exhibition titled *New Talent* at New York City's Kootz Gallery.[32]

1951 De Niro opens the first of three solo exhibitions at the Charles Egan Gallery, notable for its role in promoting De Kooning, Josef Albers, and Isamu Noguchi, among others.[33] According to Jennifer Sachs Samet, these shows are fundamental in introducing the mainstays of the artist's visual lexicon:

> This included still lifes with plaster casts, instruments, and flowers; figure and figure group paintings—mostly Moroccan women à la Delacroix and Matisse, or similar nudes and bathers; strong-tragic female performers of both recent and older history like Lola Montez and Greta Garbo; and biblical themes after Renaissance masters he admired—most especially the Crucifixion, but also the Descent from the Cross and the Entombment. Later he would also make landscape an important part of his production.[34]

The artist receives an important early endorsement from Thomas B. Hess—then editor of *Art News* and later chairman of the Metropolitan Museum of Art's Department of Twentieth-Century Art[35]—who declares that De Niro "must now be ranked among the best of the younger artists to have emerged from anonymity."[36]

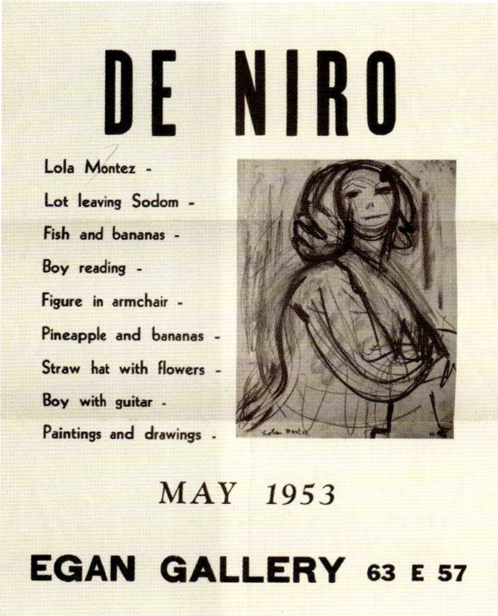

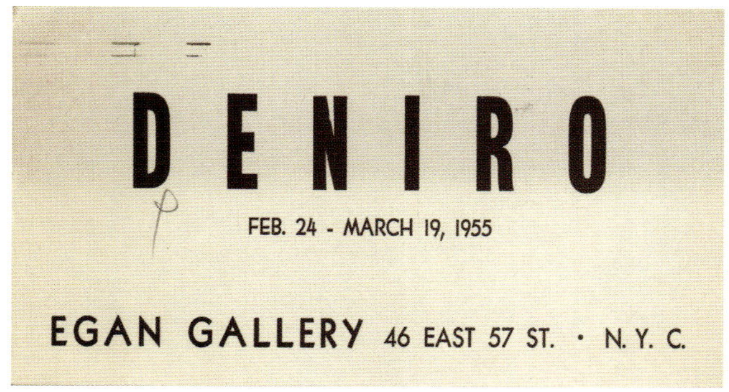

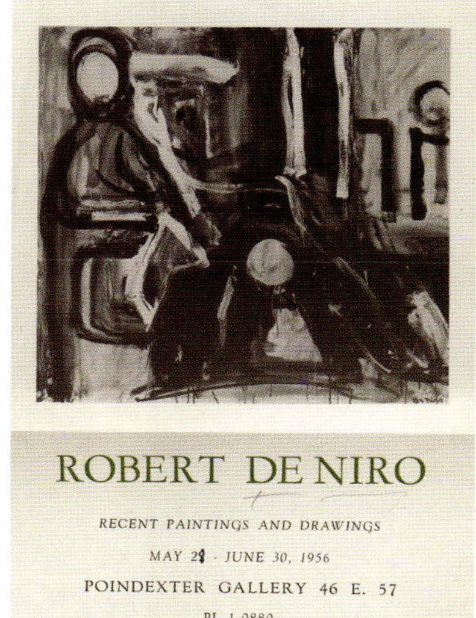

As the decade begins, however, De Niro continues to require part-time work to support himself. No longer working at the Museum of Non-Objective Painting, he finds employment at an art supply store,[37] while a 1952 letter to Rebay also indicates that he has "previously taught at the Museum of Modern Art and children in settlement houses...."[38] He will experience financial and professional hardships throughout his life despite his early critical recognition. Indeed, writing much later, in 1976, Hess describes the artist's longstanding condition of penury: "After some 30 years of uninterrupted hard work, usually in impossible conditions (crowded small studios, bursting pipes, unpaid bills—day in, day out, De Niro's routine has assumed the shape of a classic bohemian hard-luck story), he remains almost unknown."[39] De Niro's desire is thus to commit himself entirely to painting, aspiring to work, as Rivers remembers, "uninterrupted by the time it took to make a living."[40]

1953 During the summer, De Niro holds his second solo exhibition at the Charles Egan Gallery. A review of the exhibition describes the pathos in De Niro's artwork: "De Niro's figures are large, general, brought close to the spectator—but the people he depicts are inaccessible, tragic in the pose they hold for the world."[41]

1954 An exhibition of works acquired for the Museum Purchase Fund opens at Hunter College. With Gloria Vanderbilt as its benefactor, the Fund was instituted for the purpose of supporting worthy yet under-recognized artists.[42] Meyer Schapiro will select De Niro's first painting of the Crucifixion—a subject that the artist will explore in numerous compositions—for acquisition. A total of fourteen artists are included in the show, among them De Niro, Philip Guston, Rivers, and Joan Mitchell.[43]

1955 The artist holds his third and final one-man show at the Egan Gallery, which shutters later this year. His painting *Two Figures with Still Life* is also included in the Whitney Museum of American Art Annual, which opens on November 9 and runs through the start of the new year.

1956 De Niro presents his first and only exhibition at the newly opened Poindexter Gallery, established by Elinor Poindexter. His show meets with a laudatory review in *Art News* that singles out De Niro's "relaxed power" in contrast to the "nervous aggressiveness of many younger New York talents today." His charcoal rendering of Garbo is worthy of comment for its psychological charge: "A profile drawing of Garbo is an inspiration of portraiture one seldom sees any more

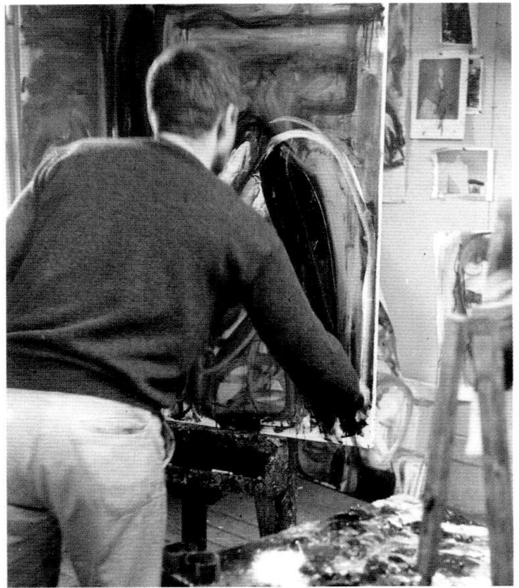

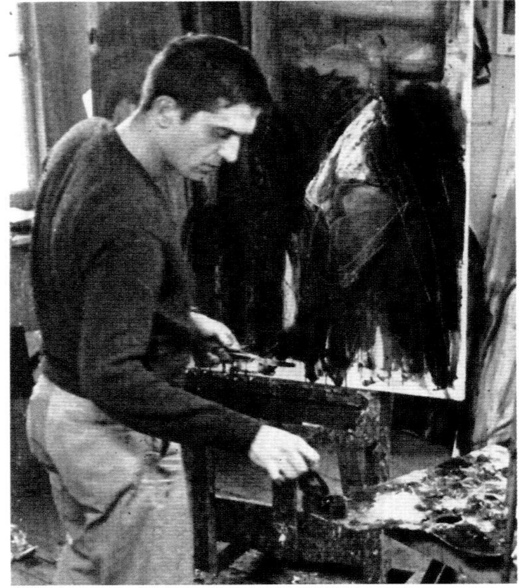

Robert De Niro, Sr., in his studio, ca. 1958. Photos by Rudy Burckhardt.

and a large full face of her has that fixating quality emanated by deeply felt things."[44] Elinor and her husband, George, offer financial support to De Niro in the form of monthly stipends.[45]

1957 De Niro is included in *Artists of the New York School, Second Generation* at the Jewish Museum in New York City, alongside Elaine de Kooning, Mitchell, Jasper Johns, and Robert Rauschenberg, among others.

1958 After ending his association with the Poindexter Gallery, De Niro follows Schapiro's advice to show instead with Virginia Zabriskie. The critic James Schuyler reviews his debut exhibition at Zabriskie Gallery and, after introducing the artist as "one of our leading Expressionists," likens the aesthetic qualities of De Niro's urgent mark-making to the process of perception: "The world presents a continuous skin to our sight, first as color and mass, then as feature and line, and so do de [*sic*] Niro's paintings, heightened and distorted to be more themselves, so that the purple bloom of paint that describes a bunch of grapes seems to immortalize the quickly putrefying fruit."[46]

With a feature article in *Art News* detailing the creative process behind his Crucifixion paintings—a torrent of drawings, a constant process of revision—De Niro's stature continues to rise. He receives recognition from the Longview Foundation, founded by Thomas B. and Audrey Stern Hess, the mission of which is to promote and support forward-thinking artists "who are often unable to support themselves owing to the time lag of the market."[47] The Foundation carries out its mission by purchasing artworks for institutional collections, and a work by De Niro is among the original purchases selected by a committee consisting of the Foundation's director, Walter Bareiss, artists Adolph Gottlieb and Hofmann, Schapiro, the collector Mrs. Philip M. Stern, and the Hesses. The committee's selection—which also includes Robert Goodnough, Leon Polk Smith, and Kenneth Noland, among others—is acquired for the Union Sanatorium Association of the International Ladies' Garment Workers' Union in New York City, where it is displayed after first being presented in an exhibition titled *Project 1* at the Whitney Museum of American Art in the summer of 1959.[48]

1960 De Niro holds two solo exhibitions this year at the Zabriskie Gallery: the first opens in June, and presents a selection of the artist's recent charcoals and watercolors; the second, an exhibition of paintings, runs from October 24 to November 12. He is also selected for *The Question of the Future: Fifth International Hallmark Art Award*, held at the Wildenstein Gallery in New York City.

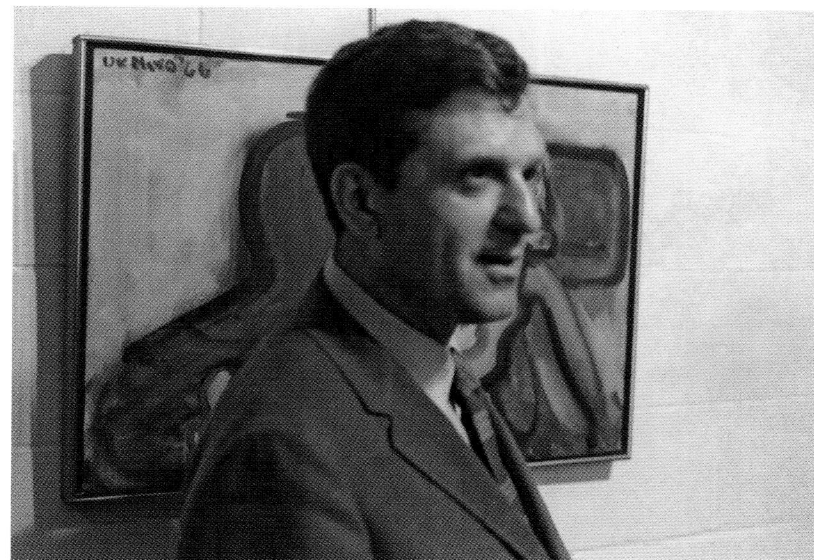

Robert De Niro, Sr., at the opening of a solo exhibition at Zabriskie Gallery, ca. 1966.

1961 In March, De Niro moves to France, living and working in Paris, Gravigny in Normandy, Baren in the southwest of the country, and St. Just en Chevalet. Though the destitute De Niro will be dogged by lack of income while abroad, he no doubt cherishes the opportunity to study "Matisse, Picasso, and Georges Rouault on their home turf," as the art historian Robert Pincus-Witten would later speculate.[49] "During this period," writes Pincus-Witten, "De Niro developed a vocabulary of broad, telegraphic strokes and dragged applications of wet paint on wet underpainting."[50]

1962 De Niro's artwork is widely shown in New York City. He is featured in three New York gallery exhibitions this year: *Figures* at Kornblee Gallery, and two at Zabriskie Gallery, *Portraits* and *Robert De Niro: Sculpture and Drawings*. The aptness of the artist's residency in France is not lost in a review of the latter exhibition, which notes that De Niro "makes the Louvre and other European museums his subject.... He offers a modern reinterpretation in low key of Ingres' odalisques, Titian, Mantegna, Bouts, Raphaël, Grünewald.... De Niro seems to have found his natural ancestry in France. Always a Europeanized painter, he is doing some of the most interesting Paris painting today."[51]

Additionally, De Niro's *Woman in Red* (1961) features in the exhibition *Recent Painting USA: Figure*, which opens at the Museum of Modern Art, New York, on May 23, before traveling to the Columbus Gallery of Fine Arts, the Colorado Springs Fine Arts Center, the Baltimore Museum of Art, the City Art Museum of St. Louis, the San Francisco Museum of Art, and the Walker Art Center in Minneapolis.

Meanwhile, De Niro has taken residence in the Midi-Pyrenees town of Baren. In a letter to his friend, Dick Brewer, the artist writes:

> I never expected such beauty when I came [to Baren]. It's dazzling. The villages are like toys as one sees them here on the mountainside.... I'm writing poems again and have done pastels of the landscape as I did at Gravigny. Here it's a little easier to work outside as there aren't the gaping children etc., so I'll probably do more oils of the surroundings than I did when I was near Paris.[52]

1963–64 While De Niro remains abroad, *Arts* magazine editor Leslie Katz curates *Five American Painters* at Knoedler Gallery. Lawrence Campbell describes the painters in this exhibition—Blaine, Matthíasdóttir, Leland Bell, De Niro, and Hyde Solomon—as artists of the New York School's

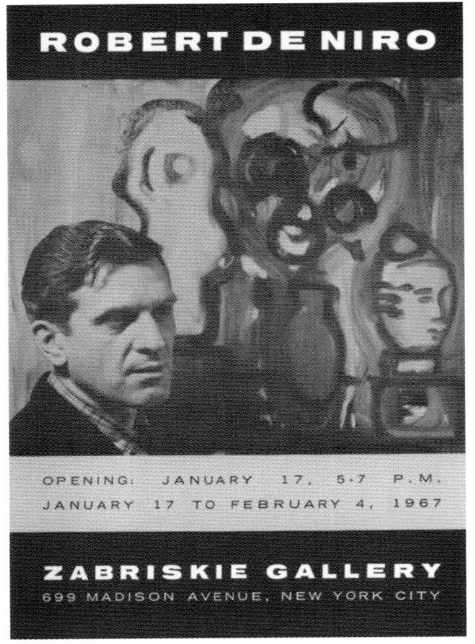

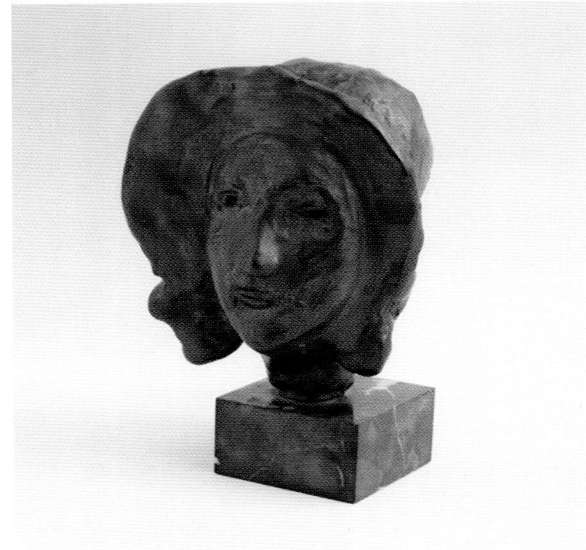

LEFT
Announcement for a Robert De Niro, Sr., solo exhibition at Zabriskie Gallery, 1967.

RIGHT
Robert De Niro, Sr., *Woman with Hat*, 1968. Bronze, 9¾ x 7 inches.
Private Collection

second generation who arrive at "the conclusion that the road to the future did not historically or inevitably lead through Abstract Expressionism." Rather, according to Campbell, "It seemed more and more that a solution lay in a return to the various traditions of modern art."[53] On view by De Niro are landscapes, a Crucifixion after Mantegna, and an odalisque after Ingres.[54] The artist is also included in two solo exhibitions at Zabriskie: *Robert De Niro: New Paintings from Paris and the Pyrenees* opens on July 19, while a second exhibition opens November 18.

The final period of De Niro's residency in France is tumultuous. After visiting his father, De Niro, Jr., is perturbed by his impoverished living conditions and is concerned for his well-being. Indeed, this stay in France has not been kind to De Niro, Sr.—with no exhibitions and no galleries interested in his work, he has faced mounting professional frustrations and personal trials. With previous attempts to coax his father home to the US unsuccessful, Robert, Jr., retrieves the elder De Niro, and the two return to New York in the fall of 1964.[55]

1965 A selection of pastels, chalk drawings, and oils composed by the artist during his stay in France opens on January 5 at Zabriskie Gallery. De Niro's pastel landscapes are notable for their color and improvisation, while the chalks and oils "have an all-over, liquid grace."[56] Later in the year, Zabriskie presents an exhibition of De Niro's work with the film star Greta Garbo as its subject matter.

1966 On March 7, *American Flowers of the 1960s* opens at Zabriskie Gallery, featuring a wide selection of artists ranging from De Niro and Blaine to Andy Warhol and Tom Wesselmann. De Niro obtains teaching positions at the New School for Social Research and the School of Visual Arts, both in New York City. He will hold posts at several different institutions until the mid-1970s, including the State University of New York, Buffalo; Cooper Union, New York; New York University; Pennsylvania State University; and Michigan State.[57]

1968 De Niro produces cast-bronze sculptures, which are shown in New York and San Francisco.[58] The critic Hilton Kramer reviews a selection of these sculptures in an exhibition titled *Robert De Niro: Bronze Figure Sculpture* at Zabriskie. Kramer finds them enjoyable, if derivative of Matisse: "There is a sense of *déja vu* here, of an aspiration that has not been transformed into Mr. De Niro's own vision."[59] If Kramer finds a potential shortcoming or fault in this affinity, it is seen elsewhere as a merit. Gabriel Laderman's *Artforum* review for a group show at the Schoelkopf

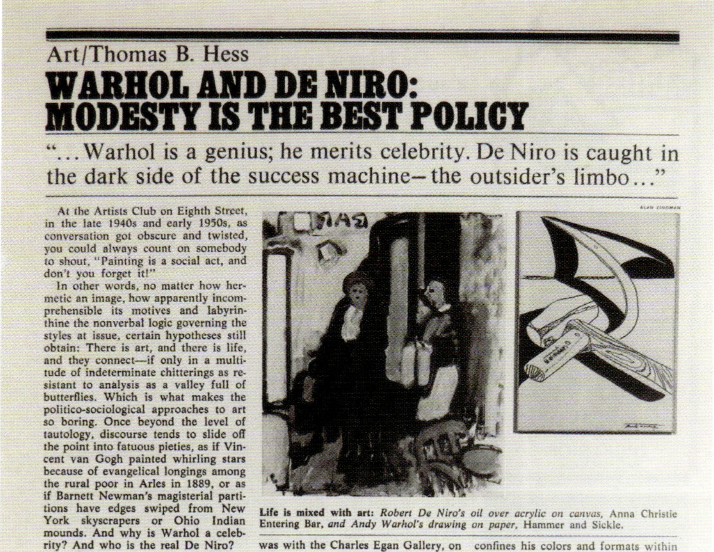

Art/Thomas B. Hess

WARHOL AND DE NIRO: MODESTY IS THE BEST POLICY

"...Warhol is a genius; he merits celebrity. De Niro is caught in the dark side of the success machine–the outsider's limbo..."

At the Artists Club on Eighth Street, in the late 1940s and early 1950s, as conversation got obscure and twisted, you could always count on somebody to shout, "Painting is a social act, and don't you forget it!"

In other words, no matter how hermetic an image, how apparently incomprehensible its motives and labyrinthine the nonverbal logic governing the styles at issue, certain hypotheses still obtain: There is art, and there is life, and they connect—if only in a multitude of indeterminate chitterings as resistant to analysis as a valley full of butterflies. Which is what makes the politico-sociological approaches to art so boring. Once beyond the level of tautology, discourse tends to slide off the point into fatuous pieties, as if Vincent van Gogh painted whirling stars because of evangelical longings among the rural poor in Arles in 1889, or as if Barnett Newman's magisterial partitions have edges swiped from New York skyscrapers or Ohio Indian mounds. And why is Warhol a celebrity? And who is the real De Niro?

ALAN ZINDMAN

Life is mixed with art: *Robert De Niro's oil over acrylic on canvas,* Anna Christie Entering Bar, *and Andy Warhol's drawing on paper,* Hammer and Sickle.

was with the Charles Egan Gallery, on confines his colors and formats within

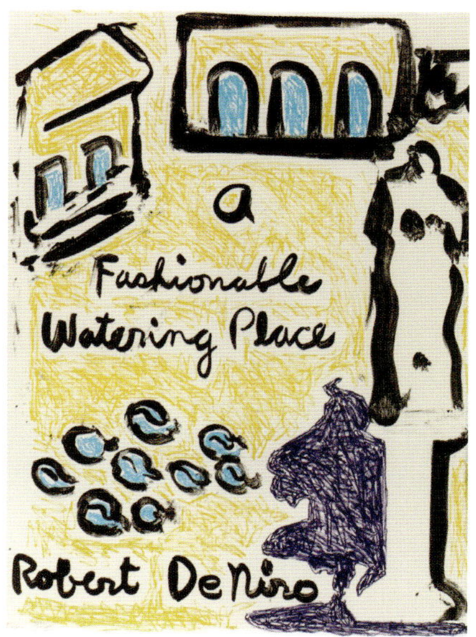

LEFT
An article by Thomas B. Hess in *New York*, December, 1976, featuring a reproduction of *Anna Christie Entering the Bar.*

RIGHT
Robert De Niro, Sr., one of a set of lithographs produced at Tamarind Institute in 1978 to illustrate his 1976 book of poetry, *A Fashionable Watering Place*.

Gallery notes that "De Niro, Bell and Matthíasdóttir work freely and exuberantly as latter-day descendants of the Fauves, although with an abstract sophistication which the original Fauves did not possess during their most exuberant periods."[60]

De Niro is awarded a Guggenheim Fellowship.

1970 On March 31, *Robert De Niro: Paintings* opens at the Zabriskie Gallery. This is the artist's final exhibition at the gallery, and he is without representation for the next several years.

1974 De Niro travels to Albuquerque, New Mexico, where he creates lithographs at the Tamarind Institute. He will return to the Institute again in 1978.[61]

1975 In the pages of *Tracks: A Journal of Artistic Writings*, the artist publishes a brief text on three of his heroes—the painter Corot, the poet Verlaine, and the actress Garbo—individuals who, in his own words, "expressed the opulence of restraint, showing us a sun, not tarnished but shining with a glow borrowed from the moon and neighbor to it." De Niro offers insight into his attraction to Garbo as a subject and the recurrence of her presence in his oeuvre through a reference to another of his favorite themes—the Crucifixion:

> If not for her early youth, for her years after 36, when she left the films, she might have been the victim of an increasingly vulgar public, finding herself a spectre haunting a world where she had no place...."Why should you care for a woman like me, always nervous or sick, sad or too gay?" he asked in Camille....Garbo swathed herself in the cocoon of her tragedy, playing out her crucifixion.[62]

1976 The artist publishes a collection of poetry titled *A Fashionable Watering Place*, which brings together several of his pieces from the early 1940s and those written while he was in France. Meanwhile, De Niro is once again invited to exhibit at the Poindexter Gallery after Elinor sees his work on view in the exhibition *Painterly Representation* at Ingber Gallery the year prior.[63]

Towards the end of the decade, De Niro briefly relocates to San Francisco to have, according to his friend Brewer, "another place for 6 months to a year."[64] The picturesque views of his Bernal Heights neighborhood are a rich source of inspiration for the artist, and, according to the art critic Peter Frank, this is where the artist realizes his "largest body of landscapes."[65] De Niro states in an interview that "Parts of [the city] remind me a little of Montmartre."[66]

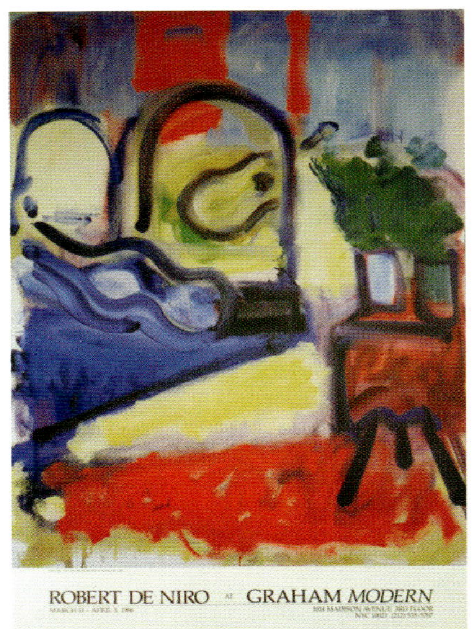

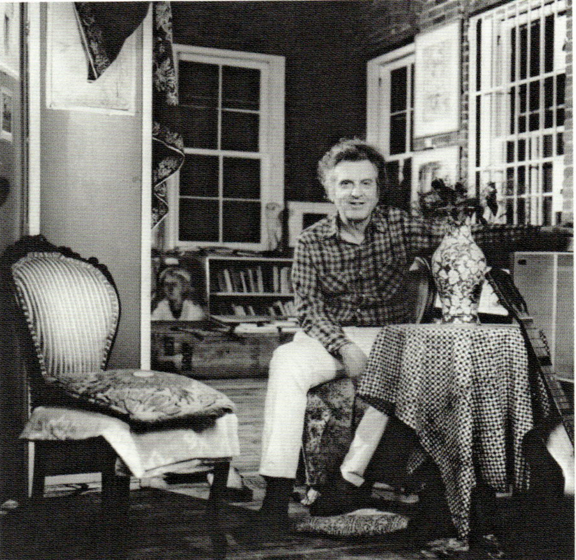

LEFT
Poster for Robert De Niro, Sr., exhibition at Graham Modern, 1980.

RIGHT
Robert De Niro, Sr., in his studio, ca. 1981.

1980 With the Poindexter Gallery now closed, De Niro holds the first of several one-man exhibitions at Graham Modern. The crayon drawings comprising his debut show are received with an enthusiastic review by the poet and critic John Ashbery, who asserts that, "This is drawing at its astringent, finely tuned best."[67] A second review published in *Art International* describes De Niro's abbreviated, yet powerfully evocative, approach to the medium:

> The essential quality of the drawings is their openness, particularly in the still-lifes where simplicity reigns. These drawings in fact are often so subtle and once removed, they seem like rubbings.... In some instances there is almost nothing tangible to hang on to; a few lines and squiggles and the eye fills in the rest. The merest allusion to an object is enough to evoke its complete image.[68]

This decade also sees De Niro reflect on the work of many in his personal pantheon of artists in several critical essays he contributes to the New York–based *Art/World* newspaper. These reviews and articles showcase his broad knowledge of art history and offer assertions that are equally illuminative of the artist's own aspirations for art. If he is hesitant to embrace the paintings of Boucher at the Wildenstein Gallery in 1980, for example, De Niro lauds the "opulent restraint" on view in Bonnard's 1981 presentation at the same gallery: "We should become aware in this exhibition of the opulent restraint which comes from giving, in a painting and to a painting, and in asserting the painting and not the personality of the painter."[69] Evidence of De Niro's range of art-historical references is found in his review of a Manet exhibition held at the Metropolitan Museum of Art in New York City. Within the text, he reiterates his taste for vital composition:

> Great as is the "Bar at the Folies-Bergère," one of Manet's last ambitious works, it never breaks through its reserve, restraint, and tact to the sonorous opulence and fullness of the late Mt. St. Victoire paintings of Cézanne, or the late Titians, Goyas, or Rembrandts, where the split or division between the objects in the paintings and their environment dissolves, a certain enclosure which separates the space occupied by the faces, hills, trees, etc., from the space around them falling away so that the two become one without the objects losing their identity.[70]

The painterly quality that De Niro draws attention to here—the simultaneous distinction and lack of distinction between represented objects—mirrors the vital quality of his own artwork, pointed out time and again in reviews of his paintings and drawings.

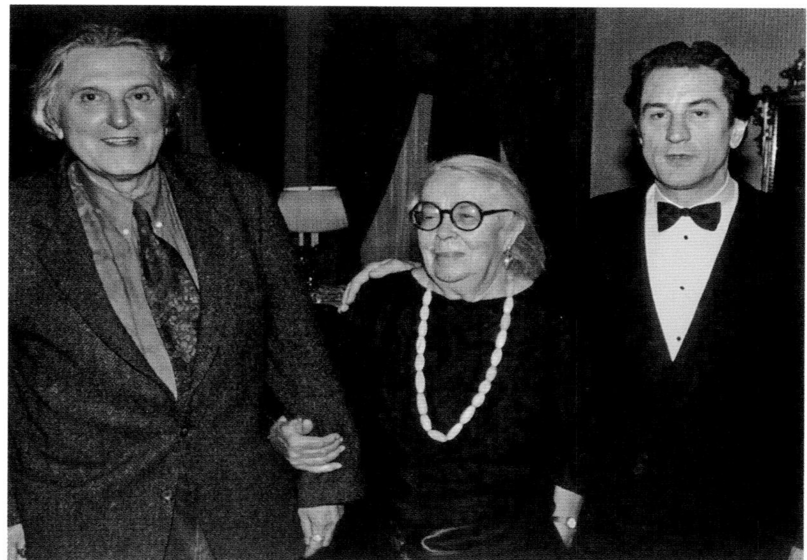

Robert De Niro, Sr., Virginia Admiral, and Robert De Niro, Jr., 1985.

In this moment of renewed professional recognition—evidenced by the 1981 opening of his first solo museum show at the Mint Museum in Charlotte, North Carolina, as well as by his inclusion in the 1983 exhibition *20th Century American Drawings: The Figure in Context* at the Terra Museum of American Art in Chicago—De Niro receives a diagnosis of prostate cancer.

1984 The critic Lawrence Campbell offers a glowing take on De Niro's current solo exhibition at Graham Modern, nodding to the painter's heroes—"De Niro's paintings are homages to the painters he loves"—while proclaiming De Niro's utter uniqueness: "I've never yet seen a painting by him which did not look like he had painted it." The critic concludes by situating De Niro as an important figure within the American art-historical canon: "I place de Niro among the leaders of painting today, one of those who make of New York the great art center it has been since the 1940s."[71]

1986 De Niro shows his work abroad for the first time in a two-person exhibition with Paul Resika at the Crane Kalman Gallery in London. Meanwhile, the Paris Gibson Center for Contemporary Art in Great Falls, Montana, opens the artist's first retrospective, *Robert De Niro: Expression as Tradition—Modern Classicism Redefined*, which travels to the Everson Museum of Art (formerly the Syracuse Museum of Fine Arts), where De Niro's training in art began. He is also the subject of a solo show at Graham Modern, which is his last with the gallery.

1990 Robert De Niro, Jr., opens the Tribeca Grill in New York City and gives his father the opportunity to curate a selection of his paintings for a permanent installation at the venue. He also designs the menu.

De Niro is included in *The Provocative Years 1935–1945: The Hans Hofmann School and Its Students*, which opens at the Provincetown Art Association and Museum.

1992 *Black Mountain College—Scratching the Surface* opens at the Station Gallery, Katonah, New York, featuring work from the institution's students and teachers, among them Robert Rauschenberg, Josef and Anni Albers, Franz Kline, and Jack Tworkov.[72]

1993 Robert De Niro dies of prostate cancer in New York on May 3—his seventy-first birthday.

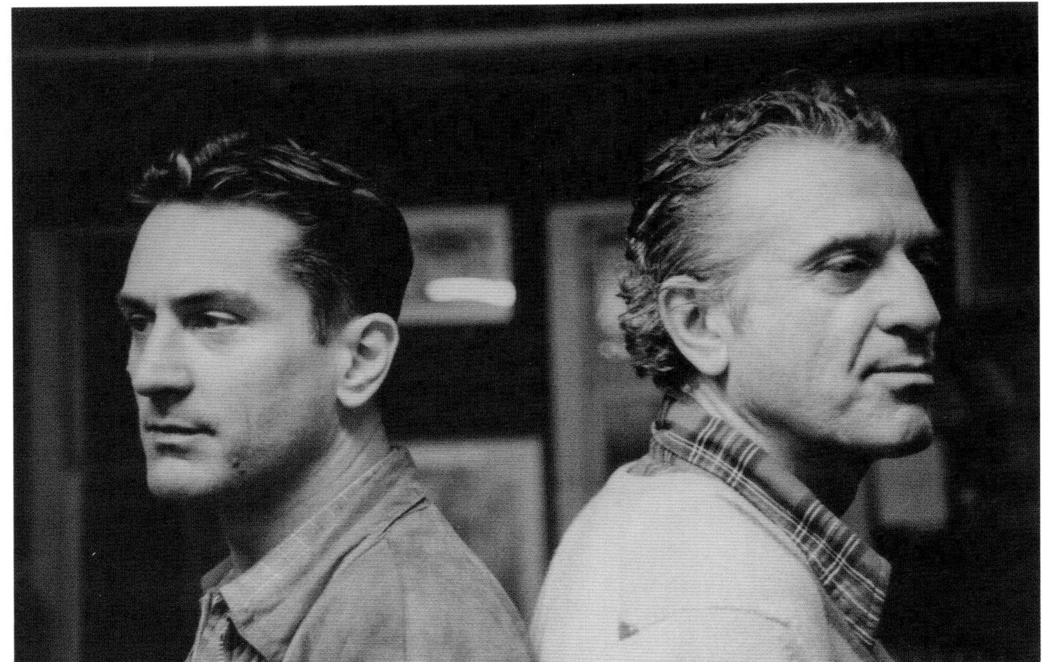

Robert De Niro, Jr., and Robert De Niro, Sr., 1985.

1993–PRESENT The artist's legacy continues to grow, the significance of his output becoming clearer in the light of posthumous solo exhibitions that span the globe, including: *Robert De Niro, Sr.*, Yoshii Gallery, Tokyo, Japan (1998); *Robert De Niro, Sr.*, Galerie Piltzer, Paris, France (1999); *Robert De Niro, Sr.*, Ministero per i Beni e le Attiviti Culturali—Soprintendenza Speciale, Galleria Nazionale d'Arte Moderna, Rome, Italy (2004); and *Après avoir vu Matisse: Robert De Niro, Sr., Peintures, Dessins*, Musée Matisse, Nice, France (2010). De Niro's 2012 exhibition at DC Moore Gallery, New York, titled *Robert De Niro, Sr.: Paintings & Drawings, 1960-1993*, is praised by noted critic Roberta Smith in the *New York Times*. "In the expanding field of postwar American painting," she writes, "more room should be made for the seductive yet rigorous art of Robert De Niro Sr."[73] In 2014, HBO releases the documentary *Remembering the Artist: Robert De Niro, Sr.*, directed by Geeta Gandbhir and Perri Peltz, which premieres at the Museum of Modern Art in New York City.

Equally notable are numerous posthumous group exhibitions: *From Unhús to West 8th Street*, Reykjavik Art Museum, Iceland (2009); *Black Mountain College and Its Legacy*, Loretta Howard Gallery, New York (2011); *Series & Sequences*, DC Moore Gallery, New York (2011); *Matisse and the Decorative Impulse*, Weatherspoon Art Museum, Greensboro, North Carolina (2012); and *Matisse and American Art*, Montclair Art Museum, New Jersey (2017).

In 2011, the artist's son establishes the annual Robert De Niro, Sr., Prize, awarded to midcareer painters of exceptional talent and promise. To date this distinction has recognized Stanley Whitney, Joyce Pensato, Catherine Murphy, Robert Bordo, Laura Owens, R. H. Quaytman, and Henry Taylor.

– *Compiled by Nathan Jones*

NOTES

1. Shawn Levy, *De Niro: A Life* (New York, NY: Three Rivers Press, 2014), 15–16.

2. Quote reproduced in Peter Frank, principal essay in *Robert De Niro, Sr.*, exh. cat. (New York, NY: Salander-O'Reilly, 2004), 20. Originally published in the *The New York Post* in a 1976 interview with Jerry Tallmer.

3. Ibid., 16.

4. Levy, *De Niro: A Life,* 16.

5. The information provided in this paragraph is found in De Niro's application for admission to Black Mountain College, 1939, Black Mountain College Records, Student Files, Western Regional Archives, State Archives of North Carolina, Asheville.

6. Levy, *De Niro: A Life*, 17.

7. Ibid., 16. See also Ralph Pearson to Black Mountain College, 15 August 1939, Black Mountain College Records, Student Files, Western Regional Archives, State Archives of North Carolina, Asheville. De Niro's former professor writes that "Bob has a genuine feeling for creative painting and drawing and did promising work."

8. Application for admission to Black Mountain College, 1939, Black Mountain College Records, Student Files, Western Regional Archives, State Archives of North Carolina, Asheville.

9. Levy, *De Niro: A Life,* 16–17.

10. High school transcript submitted by Marshall Downing for De Niro's application to Black Mountain, 7 September 1939, Black Mountain College Records, Student Files, Western Regional Archives, State Archives of North Carolina, Asheville.

11. Application for admission to Black Mountain College, 1939.

12. Jennifer Sachs Samet, "Painterly Representation in New York, 1945–1975," (PhD diss., The City University of New York, 2010), 73.

13. Frank, essay in *Robert De Niro, Sr.*, 21.

14. Robert De Niro to Mr. Frederick R. Mangold, 20 September 1939, Black Mountain College Records, Student Files, Western Regional Archives, State Archives of North Carolina, Asheville. This letter describes Olmsted's facilitation of meetings between De Niro and those who might be able to help fund his tuition.

15. Black Mountain College Transcript, Black Mountain College Records, Student Files, Western Regional Archives, State Archives of North Carolina, Asheville.

16. Edward Leffingwell, "Rehabilitating Rebay," *Art in America*, December 2005, 120–122, 160.

17. Josef Albers to Anna W. Olmsted, 25 May 1940, Black Mountain College Records, Student Files, Western Regional Archives, State Archives of North Carolina, Asheville.

18. Robert De Niro to Hilla Rebay, 13 July 1940, Hilla Rebay Records, A0010, Box 3018, Folder 48, Solomon R. Guggenheim Museum Archives, New York, NY.

19. Hilla Rebay via unnamed secretary to Robert De Niro, 19 July 1940, Hilla Rebay Records, A0010, Box 3018, Folder 48, Solomon R. Guggenheim Museum Archives, New York, NY.

20. Robert De Niro to Mr. Frederick R. Mangold, 11 June 1940, Black Mountain College Records, Student Files, Western Regional Archives, State Archives of North Carolina, Asheville.

21. Frank, in *Robert De Niro, Sr.*, 21.

22. Anaïs Nin, journal entry from June 1941, in *The Diary of Anaïs Nin: Volume Three, 1939–1944*, ed. Gunther Stuhlmann (San Diego, CA: Harcourt Brace Jovanovich, 1971).

23. Samet, "Painterly Representation in New York," 30.

24. Grace Glueck, "Paying Tribute to the Daring Peggy Guggenheim," *The New York Times*, March 1, 1987.

25. Samet, "Painterly Representation in New York," 72.

26. Levy, *De Niro: A Life*, 31.

27. Ibid., 33.

28. Larry Rivers, *What Did I Do?: The Unauthorized Biography* (New York, NY: HarperCollins Publishers, Inc., 1992), 127.

29. Clement Greenberg, Exhibition Review, *The Nation*, May 18, 1946.

30. Edward Alden Jewell, "Hither and Yon," *The New York Times*, April 28, 1946.

31. See Charles Stuckey's essay in this volume.

32. See Thomas B. Hess's review of the exhibition in "Seeing the Young New Yorkers," *Art News*, May 1950, 23, 60. "There are many pictures here I would like to buy and carry home: Robert de Niro's seemingly hap-hazard but precisely calculated scattering of flowers...."

33. Bruce Lambert, "Charles Egan, 81; Art Gallery Owner Helped de Kooning," *The New York Times*, March 18, 1993.

34. Samet, "Painterly Representation in New York," 243.

35. John Russell, "Thomas Hess, Art Expert, Dies; Writer and Met Official Was 57," *The New York Times*, July 14, 1978.

36. T.B.H [Thomas B. Hess], "Robert de Niro," *Art News*, February 1951, 49.

37. See Charles Stuckey's essay in this volume.

38. Robert De Niro to Hilla Rebay, 11 February 1952, The Hilla von Rebay Foundation Archives, M0007, Box 94, Folder 45, The Hilla von Rebay Foundation.

39. Thomas B. Hess, "Warhol and De Niro: Modesty Is the Best Policy," *New York*, December 1976, 97.

40. Larry Rivers, *What Did I Do?*, 127.

41. D.A. [Dore Ashton], Exhibition Review, Charles Egan Gallery, New York, NY, *Art Digest*, June 1953, 21.

42. Carlyle Burrows, "U.S. Artists Show Work at Hunter," *The New York Herald Tribune*, April 15, 1954.

43. Ibid.

44. Exhibition Review, Poindexter Gallery, New York, NY, *Art News*, Summer 1956, 53.

45. Samet, "Painterly Representation in New York," 248.

46. J.S. [James Schuyler], "Robert De Niro," *Art News*, November 1958, 12–13.

47. Sanka Knox, "Practical Help to Artists Begun," *The New York Times*, June 7, 1959.

48. Ibid. See also Carlyle Burrows, "Art Patrons' Plan Backed by Museum," *The New York Herald Tribune*, June 14, 1959.

49. Robert Pincus-Witten, "Robert De Niro Sr.," *Artforum*, September 2014, 373.

50. Ibid.

51. V.P. [Valerie Petersen], Exhibition Review, Zabriskie Gallery, New York, NY, *Art News*, December 1962, 17.

52. Quotation reproduced in Frank, essay in *Robert De Niro, Sr.*, 42.

53. Lawrence Campbell, "Five Americans Face Reality," *Art News*, September 1963, 25.

54. Ibid., 27.

55. Levy, *De Niro: A Life*, chapter 3.

56. M.B. [Michael Benedikt], "Robert de Niro," *Art News*, January 1965, 13.

57. See Robert De Niro, Sr., *The Art Criticism of Robert De Niro*, (New York, NY: Arts Review in Association with Graham Modern, 1984).

58. Frank, essay in *Robert De Niro, Sr.*, 25.

59. Hilton Kramer, "Art: For Eye and Spirit," *The New York Times*, May 11, 1968.

60. Gabriel Laderman, "Figurative Painting of the Fifties," *Artforum*, January 1968, 57.

61. "Robert De Niro, Sr.," Tamarind Institute. Online, accessed January 29, 2019.

62. Robert De Niro, "Corot, Verlaine and Greta Garbo, or the Melancholy Syndrome," *Tracks: A Journal of Artistic Writings*, Fall 1975, 48–49.

63. Samet, "Painterly Representation in New York," 250–251.

64. The quote is reproduced as transcribed in Frank, essay in *Robert De Niro, Sr.*, 25.

65. Ibid., 47.

66. Ibid., 25.

67. John Ashbery, "Looking Good on Paper," *New York*, June 1980, 58.

68. Nina Ffrench-Frazier, "Robert De Niro," *Art International*, September–October 1980, 81.

69. Robert De Niro, Sr., "The Quiet Heart of Bonnard's Art: Nonflamboyant Joy, Dedication," *Art/World*, November 1981. Reproduced in *Robert De Niro, Sr.*, exh. cat. (New York, NY: Salander-O'Reilly, 2004), 191–192.

70. Robert De Niro, Sr., "De Niro on Manet," *Art/World*, November 1983. Reproduced in *Robert De Niro, Sr.*, exh. cat. (New York, NY: Salander-O'Reilly, 2004), 194–195.

71. Lawrence Campbell, "Robert de Niro at Graham Modern," *Art in America*, September 1984, 209.

72. William Zimmer, "Memorabilia and Painting from Black Mountain's Glory Days," *The New York Times*, April 19, 1992.

73. Roberta Smith, "Robert De Niro Sr.: Paintings and Drawings, 1960–1993," *The New York Times*, April 19, 2012. Online, accessed December 10, 2018.

LIST OF PLATES

PLATE 1
Reclining Nude with Attendant, 1942
Oil on linen, 22 x 26 in. (55.9 x 66 cm)
The Estate of Robert De Niro, Sr.

PLATE 2
Venice at Night Is a Negress in Love, ca. 1942–43
Oil on canvas, 37½ x 43½ in. (95.3 x 110.5 cm)
The Estate of Robert De Niro, Sr.

PLATE 3
Still Life, ca. 1946
Oil on canvas, 36 x 33¼ in. (91.4 x 84.5 cm)
Collection of the Montana Historical Society, Poindexter Collection of Modern Art, Helena, MT

PLATE 4
Untitled, 1946
Oil on canvas, 37¼ x 34¼ in. (94.6 x 87 cm)
Vanden Broeck Family Collection

PLATE 5
Cubist Figure Study, ca. 1940s
Charcoal on paper, 25½ x 19½ in. (64.8 x 49.5 cm)
The Estate of Robert De Niro, Sr.
Courtesy of DC Moore Gallery, New York

PLATE 6
Male Cubist Figure, Seated, ca. 1940s
Charcoal on paper, 25½ x 19½ in. (64.8 x 49.5 cm)
The Estate of Robert De Niro, Sr.
Courtesy of DC Moore Gallery, New York

PLATE 7
Iglesia de Paz, ca. 1950
Mixed media on paper, 13 x 16 in. (33 x 40.6 cm)
Collection of the Museum of Fine Arts, St. Petersburg, FL

PLATE 8
Untitled Abstraction, ca. 1947–48
Oil on linen, 22 x 26 in. (55.9 x 66 cm)
Private Collection

PLATE 9
P-Town, ca. 1950
Gouache on paper, 17½ x 23½ in. (44.5 x 59.7 cm)
Collection of the Everson Museum of Art, Syracuse, NY

PLATE 10
Untitled, ca. 1950
Oil on canvas, 50½ x 34 in. (128.3 x 86.4 cm)
The Estate of Robert De Niro, Sr.
Courtesy of DC Moore Gallery, New York

PLATE 11
Still Life with Greek Head, 1951
Oil on canvas, 30 x 24 in. (76.2 x 61 cm)
The Peggy Jacobs Bader and John Bader Collection

PLATE 12
Untitled (Seated Man), ca. 1950
Oil on canvas, 42½ x 30½ in. (108 x 77.5 cm)
The Estate of Robert De Niro, Sr.
Courtesy of DC Moore Gallery, New York

PLATE 13
Self-Portrait, 1951
Oil on canvas, 35⅛ x 30 in. (89.2 x 76.2 cm)
Collection of the Metropolitan Museum of Art, New York, NY

PLATE 14
Moroccan Women, ca. 1951
Oil on canvas, 58 x 42 in. (147.3 x 106.7 cm)
Collection of the Everson Museum of Art, Syracuse, NY; Gift of Goldian and Andre Vanden Broeck

PLATE 15
Portrait of Virginia (Portrait of the Artist's Wife), ca. 1950
Oil on canvas, 34½ x 33½ in. (87.6 x 85.1 cm)
Collection of the Everson Museum of Art, Syracuse, NY; Gift of Goldian and Andre Vanden Broeck

PLATE 16
Untitled (Still Life), ca. 1952–53
Oil on canvas, 15¼ x 20½ in. (38.7 x 52.1 cm)
Collection of the Montana Historical Society, Poindexter Collection of Modern Art, Helena, MT

PLATE 17
Straw Hat with Flowers, ca. 1952–53
Oil on canvas, 22½ x 26½ in. (57.2 x 67.3 cm)
The Estate of Robert De Niro, Sr.
Courtesy of DC Moore Gallery, New York

PLATE 18
Crucifixion, 1952
Oil on canvas, 48 x 40 in. (121.9 x 101.6 cm)
Private Collection

PLATE 19
Crucifixion, 1954
Oil on canvas, 59 x 46 in. (149.9 x 116.8 cm)
Collection of the Montana Historical Society, Poindexter Collection of Modern Art, Helena, MT

PLATE 20
Mantel with Black Fan and Plaster Cast no. 3, 1954
Oil on canvas, 40 x 29½ in. (101.6 x 74.9 cm)
Collection of David Altarac and Brian Koll
Courtesy of Bookstein Projects

PLATE 21
Self-Portrait, ca. 1954
Oil on Masonite, 25¾ x 19¾ in. (65.4 x 50.2 cm)
Collection of the Montana Historical Society, Poindexter Collection of Modern Art, Helena, MT

PLATE 22
Still Life with Plaster Cast, 1954
Oil on canvas, 40¼ x 29¾ in. (102.2 x 75.6 cm)
Collection of the Montana Historical Society, Poindexter Collection of Modern Art, Helena, MT

PLATE 23
Still Life with Plaster Statue, 1954
Oil on canvas, 20⅜ x 31¾ in. (51.8 x 80.7 cm)
Collection of the Montana Historical Society, Poindexter Collection of Modern Art, Helena, MT

PLATE 24
Guitar, Plaster Statue, 1954
Oil on board, 34 x 42 in. (86.4 x 106.7 cm)
Collection of the Yellowstone Art Museum, Billings, MT

PLATE 25
Seated Bathers, 1954
Oil on canvas, 51 x 68 in. (129.5 x 172.7 cm)
Collection of the Yellowstone Art Museum, Billings, MT

PLATE 26
Small Single Bather, 1955
Tempera on paper, 20 x 15 in. (50.8 x 38.1 cm)
Collection of the Montana Historical Society, Poindexter Collection of Modern Art, Helena, MT

PLATE 27
Seated Bathers, 1955
Oil on canvas, 56½ x 50½ in. (143.5 x 128.3 cm)
Collection of the Montana Historical Society, Poindexter Collection of Modern Art, Helena, MT

PLATE 28
Still Life–Flowers, 1954
Charcoal and chalk on paper, 25½ x 19¾ in. (64.8 x 50.2 cm)
Collection of the Montana Historical Society, Poindexter Collection of Modern Art, Helena, MT

PLATE 29
Untitled (Figurative), 1955
Charcoal and pastel on paper, 19¾ x 25½ in. (50.2 x 64.8 cm)
Collection of the Montana Historical Society, Poindexter Collection of Modern Art, Helena, MT

PLATE 30
Bonjour Mr. De Niro, ca. 1955
Oil on canvas, 35¾ x 47¾ in. (90.8 x 121.3 cm)
Collection of the Montana Historical Society, Poindexter Collection of Modern Art, Helena, MT

PLATE 31
River Bathers, 1956
Oil on canvas, 60 x 72 in. (152.4 x 182.9 cm)
Collection of the Montana Historical Society, Poindexter Collection of Modern Art, Helena, MT

PLATE 32
Greta, n.d.
Charcoal and chalk on paper, 36 x 23¾ in. (91.4 x 60.3 cm)
Collection of the Montana Historical Society, Poindexter Collection of Modern Art, Helena, MT

PLATE 33
Garbo, n.d.
Charcoal and chalk on paper, 30¼ x 24¼ in. (76.8 x 61.6 cm)
Collection of the Montana Historical Society, Poindexter Collection of Modern Art, Helena, MT

PLATE 34
Garbo as Anna Christie, 1957
Oil on canvas, 31⅛ x 36¼ in. (79.1 x 92.1 cm)
The Johnson Collection, Spartanburg, SC

PLATE 35
Still Life with Dog, 1958–59
Gouache and ink on paper, 30¼ x 18¼ in. (76.8 x 46.4 cm)
Collection of David Altarac and Brian Koll
Courtesy of DC Moore Gallery, New York

PLATE 36
Lola Montez with Cigarette, 1958–59
Gouache and ink on paper, 36 x 24 in. (91.4 x 61 cm)
DC Moore Gallery, New York

PLATE 37
Portrait of Mrs. Z, 1959
Oil on canvas, 38¼ x 34¼ in. (97.1 x 87 cm)
Collection of the Hirshhorn Museum and Sculpture Garden, Smithsonian Institution, Washington, DC

PLATE 38
Still Life, 1959
Oil on paper, 22½ x 31 in. (57.2 x 78.7 cm)
DC Moore Gallery, New York

PLATE 39
Still Life and Chair, 1959
Oil on canvas, 50 x 42 in. (127 x 106.9 cm)
Hallmark Art Collection, Kansas City, MO

PLATE 40
Standing Woman, 1959
Charcoal on paper, 25½ x 19¼ in. (64.8 x 48.9 cm)
Private Collection

PLATE 41
Portrait of a Woman, 1959
Charcoal on paper, 25 x 19 in. (63.5 x 48.3 cm)
The Estate of Robert De Niro, Sr.
Courtesy of DC Moore Gallery, New York

PLATE 42
Portrait of a Man with Moustache, 1960
Charcoal on paper, 24½ x 18½ in. (62.2 x 47 cm)
The Estate of Robert De Niro, Sr.
Courtesy of DC Moore Gallery, New York

PLATE 43
Portrait of a Young Woman, 1959
Charcoal on paper, 19½ x 25½ in. (49.5 x 64.8 cm)
The Estate of Robert De Niro, Sr.
Courtesy of DC Moore Gallery, New York

PLATE 44
Portrait of Cynthia, 1960
Oil on canvas, 44⅛ x 30¼ in. (112 x 76.8 cm)
Collection of the Hirshhorn Museum and Sculpture Garden, Smithsonian Institution, Washington, DC

PLATE 45
Still Life, 1959
Oil on paper, 22½ x 30½ in. (57.5 x 77.5 cm)
DC Moore Gallery, New York

PLATE 46
Untitled (Still Life with Chair), 1960
Oil on linen, 54 x 38 in. (137.2 x 96.5 cm)
Collection of Dr. Robert and Arlene Brenner

PLATE 47
Still Life with Greek Head, 1955
Oil on canvas, 30 x 22 in. (76.2 x 55.9 cm)
Collection of Sarah Creal

PLATE 48
Untitled Still Life, 1960
Oil on linen, 46⅛ x 36¼ in. (117.2 x 92.1 cm)
The Estate of Robert De Niro, Sr.

PLATE 49
Self-Portrait, 1960
Oil and watercolor on paper, 22 x 30 in. (55.9 x 76.2 cm)
The Estate of Robert De Niro, Sr.

PLATE 50
Studio Still Life with Head of a Woman, 1960
Oil on canvas, 26 x 30 in. (66 x 76.2 cm)
The Estate of Robert De Niro, Sr.
Courtesy of DC Moore Gallery, New York

PLATE 51
Pattern Still Life #1, 1960
Oil on canvas, 40 x 50⅛ in. (101.6 x 127.3 cm)
Collection of the Hirshhorn Museum and Sculpture Garden, Smithsonian Institution, Washington, DC

PLATE 52
Still Life with Fruit and Flowers on a Table, 1961
Oil on canvas, 29 x 36¼ in. (73.7 x 92.1 cm)
The Johnson Collection, Spartanburg, SC

PLATE 53
Violet Flowers, 1960
Oil on canvas, 32 x 20 in. (81.3 x 50.8 cm)
Stacey B. Case Private Collection

PLATE 54
Untitled, 1961
Oil on canvas, 30 x 22 in. (76.2 x 55.9 cm)
Private Collection

PLATE 55
Woman in Red, 1961
Oil on linen, 70 x 54 in. (177.8 x 137.2 cm)
The Estate of Robert De Niro, Sr.

PLATE 56
Crucifixion with Three Spectators, 1961–62
Oil on canvas, 54¼ x 38¼ in. (137.8 x 97.2 cm)
The Estate of Robert De Niro, Sr.

PLATE 57
St. Just en Chevalet, 1963
Oil on linen, 28⅝ x 23½ in. (72.7 x 59.7 cm)
Private Collection, Pittsburgh, PA

PLATE 58
Women at the Well, 1965
Oil on canvas, 61 x 68 in. (154.9 x 172.7 cm)
Collection of Artis–Naples, The Baker Museum, FL

PLATE 59
Women at the Well, 1966
Oil on canvas, 64 x 70 in. (162.6 x 177.8 cm)
Private Collection

PLATE 60
Flowers in a Blue Vase, 1966
Oil on canvas, 28 x 36 in. (71.1 x 91.4 cm)
Private Collection
Courtesy of DC Moore Gallery, New York

PLATE 61
Two Vases: Flowers, 1967
Acrylic on canvas, 16 x 20 in. (40.6 x 50.8 cm)
Collection of the Parrish Art Museum, Water Mill, NY

PLATE 62
Man in Blue Sweater, 1967
Oil on linen, 38 x 48 in. (96.5 x 121.9 cm)
Private Collection
Courtesy of DC Moore Gallery, New York

PLATE 63
White Building from Blue Porch, 1968
Oil on canvas, 30 x 32 in. (76.2 x 81.3 cm)
Private Collection

PLATE 64
Buildings in a Landscape, 1968
Oil on canvas, 24 x 30 in. (61 x 76.2 cm)
The Estate of Robert De Niro, Sr.

PLATE 65
Side View of Houses and Street, 1967–69
Oil on canvas, 17¾ x 20 in. (45.1 x 50.8 cm)
The Estate of Robert De Niro, Sr.
Courtesy of DC Moore Gallery, New York

PLATE 66
Autumn Landscape with House, 1968
Oil on canvas, 30¼ x 36 in. (76.8 x 91.4 cm)
The Estate of Robert De Niro, Sr.
Courtesy of DC Moore Gallery, New York

PLATE 67
Landscape with White House, 1968
Oil on canvas, 28¾ x 33 in. (73 x 83.8 cm)
The Estate of Robert De Niro, Sr.
Courtesy of DC Moore Gallery, New York

PLATE 68
Autumn Landscape, 1968
Oil on canvas, 24 x 30 in. (61 x 76.2 cm)
The Estate of Robert De Niro, Sr.

PLATE 69
Untitled Landscape, 1968
Oil on linen, 30 x 34 in. (76.2 x 86.4 cm)
Private Collection

PLATE 70
Moroccan Women, 1968
Oil on canvas, 68 x 64 in. (172.7 x 162.6 cm)
The Estate of Robert De Niro, Sr.
Courtesy of DC Moore Gallery, New York

PLATE 71
Three Women, 1968
Oil on canvas, 64 x 70 in. (162.6 x 177.8 cm)
The Estate of Robert De Niro, Sr.
Courtesy of DC Moore Gallery, New York

PLATE 72
Woman at Table, 1969
Oil on canvas, 42 x 56 in. (106.7 x 142.2 cm)
Collection of Richard F. Brush Art Gallery,
St. Lawrence University, Canton, NJ

PLATE 73
Male Nude, 1966
Charcoal on paper, 25½ x 19 in. (64.8 x 48.3 cm)
Private Collection

PLATE 74
Reclining Figure Reading a Book, 1970
Charcoal on paper, 19½ x 25½ in. (49.5 x 64.8 cm)
Private Collection

PLATE 75
Table Still Life with Red Vases, Fan and Bowl, 1968
Oil on canvas, 30 x 34 in. (76.2 x 86.4 cm)
Perrell Family Collection

PLATE 76
Studio Interior with Yellow Chair and Vase of Flowers, 1968
Oil on canvas, 34 x 30 in. (86.4 x 76.2 cm)
Private Collection

PLATE 77
Still Life with Flowers, Vase and Tazza, 1969
Oil on Masonite, 30 x 22 in. (76.2 x 55.9 cm)
Collection of Ronald O. Perelman, New York

PLATE 78
Interior Still Life, 1969
Oil on panel, 30 x 22 in. (76.2 x 55.9 cm)
Stacey B. Case Private Collection

PLATE 79
Red House with Blue Door, 1970
Oil on panel, 30½ x 33¾ in. (77.5 x 85.7 cm)
The Estate of Robert De Niro, Sr.
Courtesy of DC Moore Gallery, New York

PLATE 80
Autumn Landscape with House, 1970
Oil on panel, 30 x 36 in. (76.2 x 91.4 cm)
The Estate of Robert De Niro, Sr.

PLATE 81
Landscape with Two Buildings, 1970
Oil on canvas, 30 x 34 in. (76.2 x 86.4 cm)
Stacey B. Case Private Collection

PLATE 82
Still Life, 1970
Oil on canvas, 30 x 24 in. (76.2 x 61 cm)
Stacey B. Case Private Collection

PLATE 83
Seated Nude with Green Pants, 1970
Oil on canvas, 36 x 28 in. (91.4 x 71.1 cm)
The Estate of Robert De Niro, Sr.
Courtesy of DC Moore Gallery, New York

PLATE 84
Still Life with Guitar, Torso and Two Vases, 1971
Oil on canvas, 38½ x 27¾ in. (97.8 x 70.5 cm)
The Estate of Robert De Niro, Sr.
Courtesy of DC Moore Gallery, New York

PLATE 85
Yellow Hat, 1973
Oil on board, 30 x 36 in. (76.2 x 91.4 cm)
Collection of the Yellowstone Art Museum, Billings, MT

PLATE 86
Female Nude Seen from Behind, 1971
Pastel on paper, 24½ x 19½ in. (62.2 x 49.5 cm)
The Estate of Robert De Niro, Sr.

PLATE 87
Portrait of Elaine de Kooning, 1975
Charcoal on paper, 25 x 19 in. (63.5 x 48.3 cm)
The Estate of Robert De Niro, Sr.
Courtesy of DC Moore Gallery, New York

PLATE 88
Black Statuette, 1975
Oil on fiberboard, 30 x 36 in. (76.2 x 91.4 cm)
The Estate of Robert De Niro, Sr.

PLATE 89
Landscape with Pond, 1975
Oil on Masonite, 30 x 28 in. (76.2 x 71.1 cm)
Collection of the Mint Museum of Art, Charlotte, NC; Gift of the Estate of Robert De Niro, Sr.

PLATE 90
Gray Barn in Blue Landscape, 1976
Oil on Masonite, 30 x 28 in. (76.2 x 71.1 cm)
Private Collection

PLATE 91
Standing Male in a Toreador Hat, 1975
Pastel on paper, 29 x 23 in. (73.7 x 58.4 cm)
The Estate of Robert De Niro, Sr.

PLATE 92
Girl with a Toreador Hat and Feather Boa, 1975
Pastel on panel, 35½ x 29½ in. (90.2 x 74.9 cm)
The Estate of Robert De Niro, Sr.

PLATE 93
Figures Seated before a Screen, 1975
Pastel on paper, 29½ x 35 in. (74.9 x 90.2 cm)
The Estate of Robert De Niro, Sr.
Courtesy of DC Moore Gallery, New York

PLATE 94
Seated Figure, Red Jacket, 1977
Pastel on board, 30 x 28¾ in. (76.2 x 73 cm)
Collection of the Albright-Knox Art Gallery, Buffalo, NY

PLATE 95
Figure in a Hat with Rubber Plant, 1976
Oil on canvas, 50½ x 60 in. (128.3 x 152.4 cm)
Private Collection

PLATE 96
Still Life with Flowers and Eggplant, 1976
Oil on canvas, 30 x 60 in. (76.2 x 152.4 cm)
Collection of the Mint Museum of Art, Charlotte, NC; Gift of Elinor F. Poindexter

PLATE 97
Anna Christie Entering the Bar, 1976
Oil on canvas, 62 x 50 in. (157.5 x 127 cm)
The Estate of Robert De Niro, Sr.

PLATE 98
Vase of Flowers, 1978
Charcoal on paper, 25½ x 19½ in. (64.8 x 49.5 cm)
Private Collection

PLATE 99
Studio Drawing with Two Torsos and Two Busts, 1978
Charcoal on paper, 25½ x 18½ in. (64.8 x 47 cm)
Private Collection

PLATE 100
Green Parrot, 1977
Oil on canvas, 30 x 23¾ in. (76.2 x 60.3 cm)
Collection of Susan Ennis and Owen Lewis

PLATE 101
Roses on Table, 1979
Oil on canvas, 24 x 26 in. (61 x 66 cm)
DC Moore Gallery, New York

PLATE 102
Moroccan Women, 1979
Oil on linen, 64 x 53 in. (162.6 x 134.6 cm)
The Estate of Robert De Niro, Sr.
Courtesy of DC Moore Gallery, New York

PLATE 103
Looking towards Downtown San Francisco from Bernal Heights, 1980
Oil on canvas, 30 x 24 in. (76.2 x 61 cm)
The Estate of Robert De Niro, Sr.
Courtesy of DC Moore Gallery, New York

PLATE 104
Landscape with Houses (verso **Houses on Folsom Street**), 1980
Oil on canvas, 30 x 40 in. (76.2 x 101.6 cm)
The Estate of Robert De Niro, Sr.

PLATE 105
Seated Male Nude with Studio Pictures, 1980
Charcoal on paper, 25½ x 19½ in. (64.8 x 49.5 cm)
Private Collection

PLATE 106
Seated Female Nude with a Parrot, 1980
Charcoal on paper, 25½ x 19½ in. (64.8 x 49.5 cm)
Collection of Susan Ennis and Owen Lewis

PLATE 107
Birdcage, Two Vases and Flowers, 1981
Oil on linen, 40 x 30 in. (101.6 x 76.2 cm)
Collection of Ralph Torraco
Courtesy of DC Moore Gallery, New York

PLATE 108
Crucifixion with Four Spectators, 1982
Oil on canvas, 54¼ x 48¼ in. (137.8 x 122.6 cm)
The Estate of Robert De Niro, Sr.

PLATE 109
Moroccan Women, 1984
Oil on linen, 70 x 76 in. (177.8 x 193 cm)
Estate of Alice Kaltman-Glasel
Courtesy of DC Moore Gallery, New York

PLATE 110
Self-Portrait of the Artist at His Easel, 1985
Oil on canvas, 40 x 30 in. (101.6 x 76.2 cm)
The Estate of Robert De Niro, Sr.

PLATE 111
Still Life with Bird Cage, Guitar, Flowers, ca. 1980s
Oil on canvas, 22⅛ x 20⅛ in. (56.2 x 51.1 cm)
Collection of Olga & Theodore Lownie

PLATE 112
Still Life with Vase of Flowers, Lemons, Chair and Guitar, 1989
Oil on canvas, 34 x 40 in. (86.4 x 101.6 cm)
The Estate of Robert De Niro, Sr.
Courtesy of DC Moore Gallery, New York

PLATE 113
Last Painting, 1985–93
Oil on canvas, 60 x 48 in. (152.4 x 121.9 cm)
The Estate of Robert De Niro, Sr.
Courtesy of DC Moore Gallery, New York

ACKNOWLEDGMENTS

FIRST AND FOREMOST, we wish to recognize the vision and inspiration of Robert De Niro, Sr., whose lifetime artistic achievement is celebrated in this book.

Needless to say, the outstanding preparation and content of this magnificent publication, years in the making, could not have been possible without the numerous contributions, generosity, and extraordinary hard work of many individuals.

We are deeply indebted to those collectors and public institutions who have allowed us to reproduce De Niro's work in this seminal volume consisting of the most comprehensive range, to date, of his paintings and drawings, spanning his entire career along with a striking selection of his writings.

We also wish to express our deepest gratitude to Bridget Moore and Edward De Luca of DC Moore Gallery and their staff who have worked tirelessly in concert with the Estate, dedicated to fostering and perpetuating De Niro's artistic legacy at the forefront of the art world and beyond through numerous exhibitions, catalogues, and public symposia, amongst many other endeavors.

Enormous gratitude also extends to this volume's authors, Susan Davidson, Robert Kushner, Robert Storr, and Charles Stuckey for their insightful and remarkable contributions that offer new and varying perspectives on De Niro's oeuvre. Additional thanks are also due to Anni Pullagura, PhD candidate at Brown University, for her invaluable research for this project.

Much appreciation is also due to the production and editorial team at SNAP Editions, led by Sarah S. King with Annikka Olsen, Nathan Jones, Ted Mooney, and Stephanie Cash, and to Joseph Guglietti for the beautiful and elegant book design.

Finally, we are deeply grateful to Rizzoli Electa for publishing this book, which will become the fundamental reference for the work of Robert De Niro, Sr., and in particular to Charles Miers, Publisher, and Margaret Chace, Associate Publisher, and to their team, Ellen Cohen, Lynn Scrabis, and Colin Hough-Trapp for so diligently shepherding this book into being.

MEGAN FOX KELLY
Megan Fox Kelly Art Advisory
On behalf of The Estate of Robert De Niro, Sr.

COLOPHON

TEXTS

© 2019 Robert Storr:
"Late Laurels for a Painter's Painter"

© 2019 Charles Stuckey:
"Robert De Niro, Sr.: Themes and Variations"

© 2019 Robert Kushner:
"Color: Intoxicant of Choice"

© 2019 Susan Davidson:
"Robert De Niro, Sr.: Selected Writings"

Edition of 2,000

PHOTOGRAPHY

© 2019 Succession H. Matisse / Artists Rights Society (ARS), New York. Courtesy the Statens Museum for Kunst, Copenhagen, Denmark: p. 108.

© 2019 Estate of Virginia Admiral / Artists Rights Society (ARS), New York: p. 110.

© 2019 The Willem de Kooning Foundation / Artists Rights Society (ARS), New York. Courtesy the Weatherspoon Art Museum at UNC Greensboro: p. 112.

© The Estate of Karl Bissinger. Courtesy the Karl Bissinger papers, University of Delaware Library, Newark: p. 113.

© 2019 Artists Rights Society (ARS), New York / ADAGP, Paris. Courtesy Stair Galleries & Restorations, Inc.: p. 116.

© 2019 Artists Rights Society (ARS), New York: p. 117.

© The Estate of Grace Hartigan: p. 121.

© Christie's Images / Bridgeman Images: p. 125.

© 2019 Artists Rights Society (ARS), New York / ADAGP, Paris: p. 209.

© 2019 Artists Rights Society (ARS), New York: p. 210.

© 2019 Succession H. Matisse / Artists Rights Society (ARS), New York. Courtesy the Museum of Modern Art, New York: p. 212.

© 2019 Estate of Rudy Burckhardt / Artist Rights Society (ARS), New York: p. 242.

Plate 4: Courtesy of Field Studio

Plates 10, 12, 17, and 48: Courtesy of Stephen Bates

Plate 11: Courtesy of Graham Haber

Plate 20: Courtesy of Steve Gyurina

Plate 54: Courtesy of Jason Mandella

Plates 78, 53, 81, and 82: Courtesy of RDH Photography

Plate 111: Courtesy of IMG_INK

Page 113: Courtesy Joseph Cornell Study Center, Smithsonian Institution, Washington, DC.

Page 117: Robert De Niro, Sr., *Self-Portrait*. Courtesy Hackett Mill, San Francisco.

Pages 234–237: Courtesy of the Western Regional Archives, State Archives of North Carolina, Asheville.

Overleaf: © 2019 Estate of Rudy Burckhardt / Artists Rights Society (ARS), New York.

Endpapers and pages 218–219: © Brigitte Lacombe

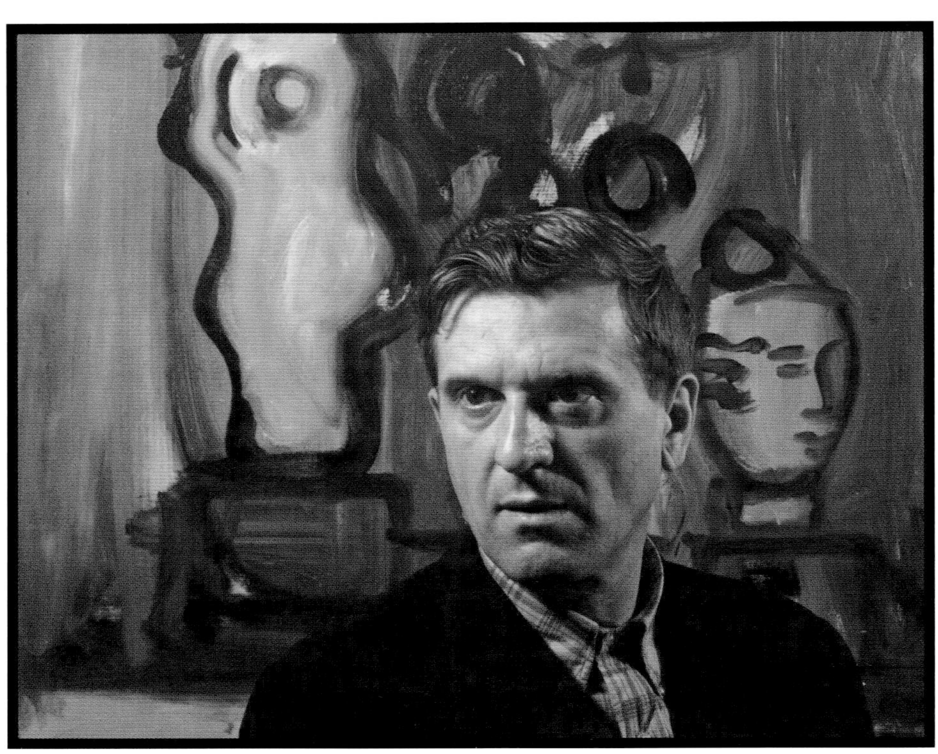

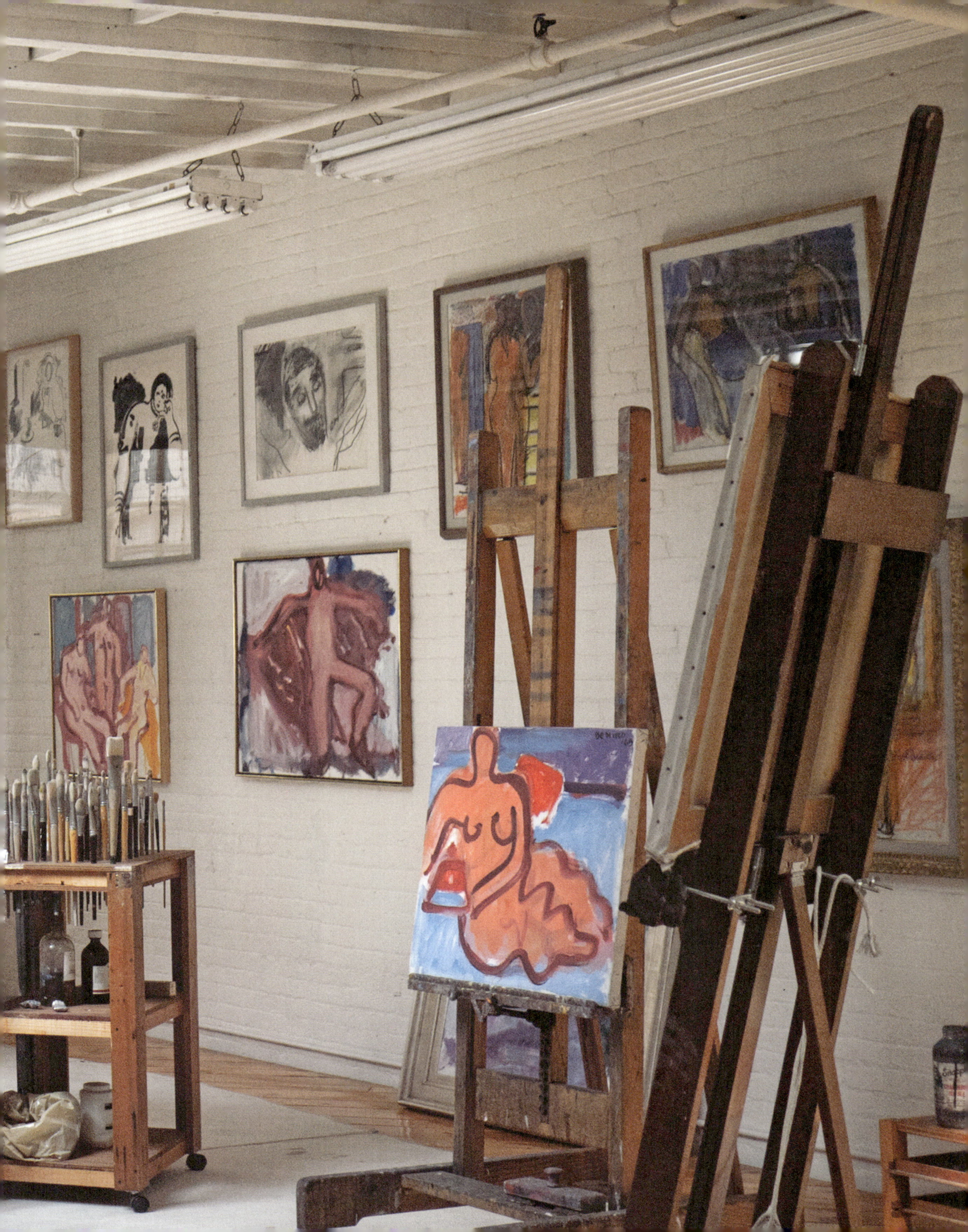

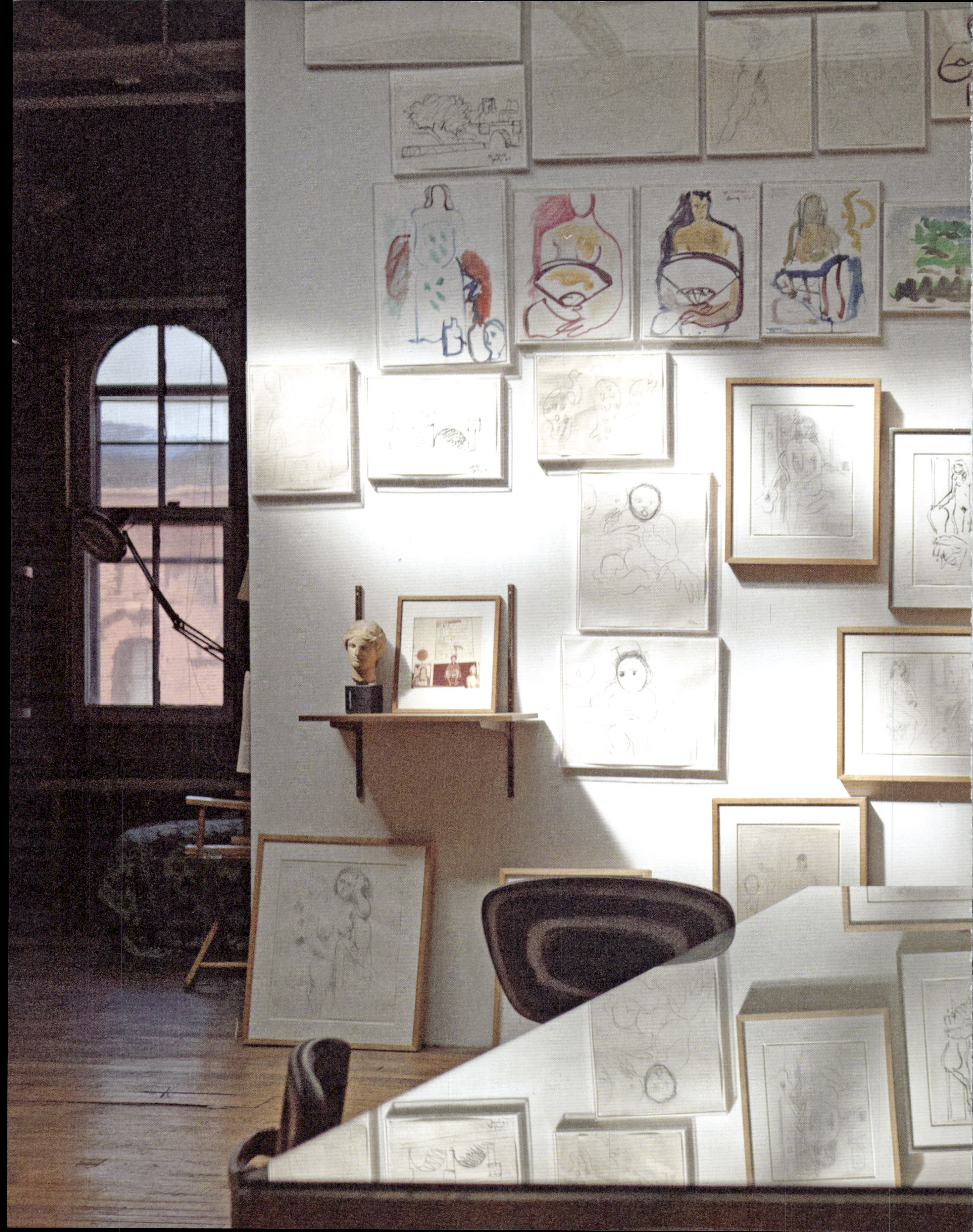